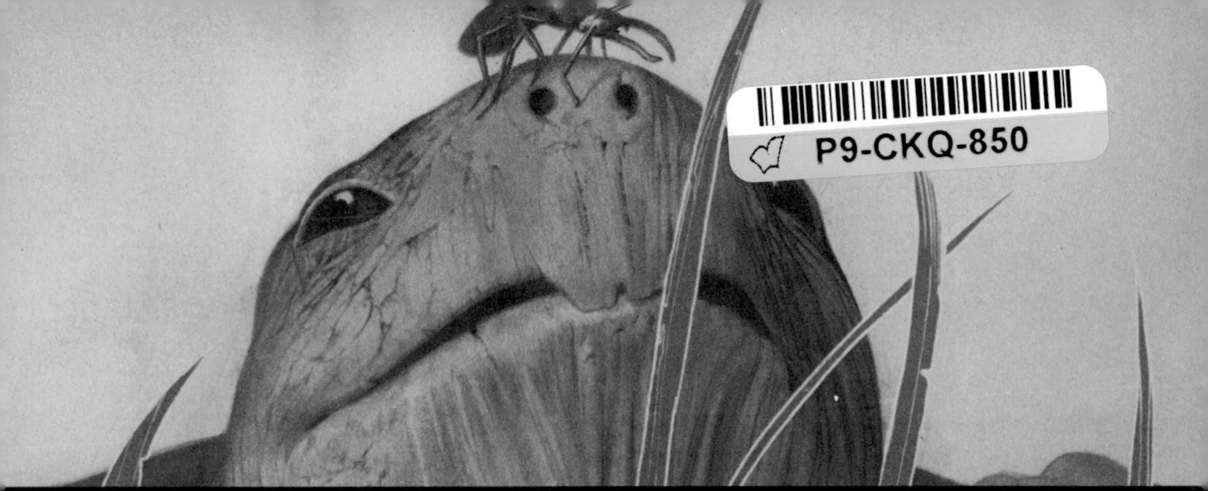

FABLES: INHERIT THE WIND

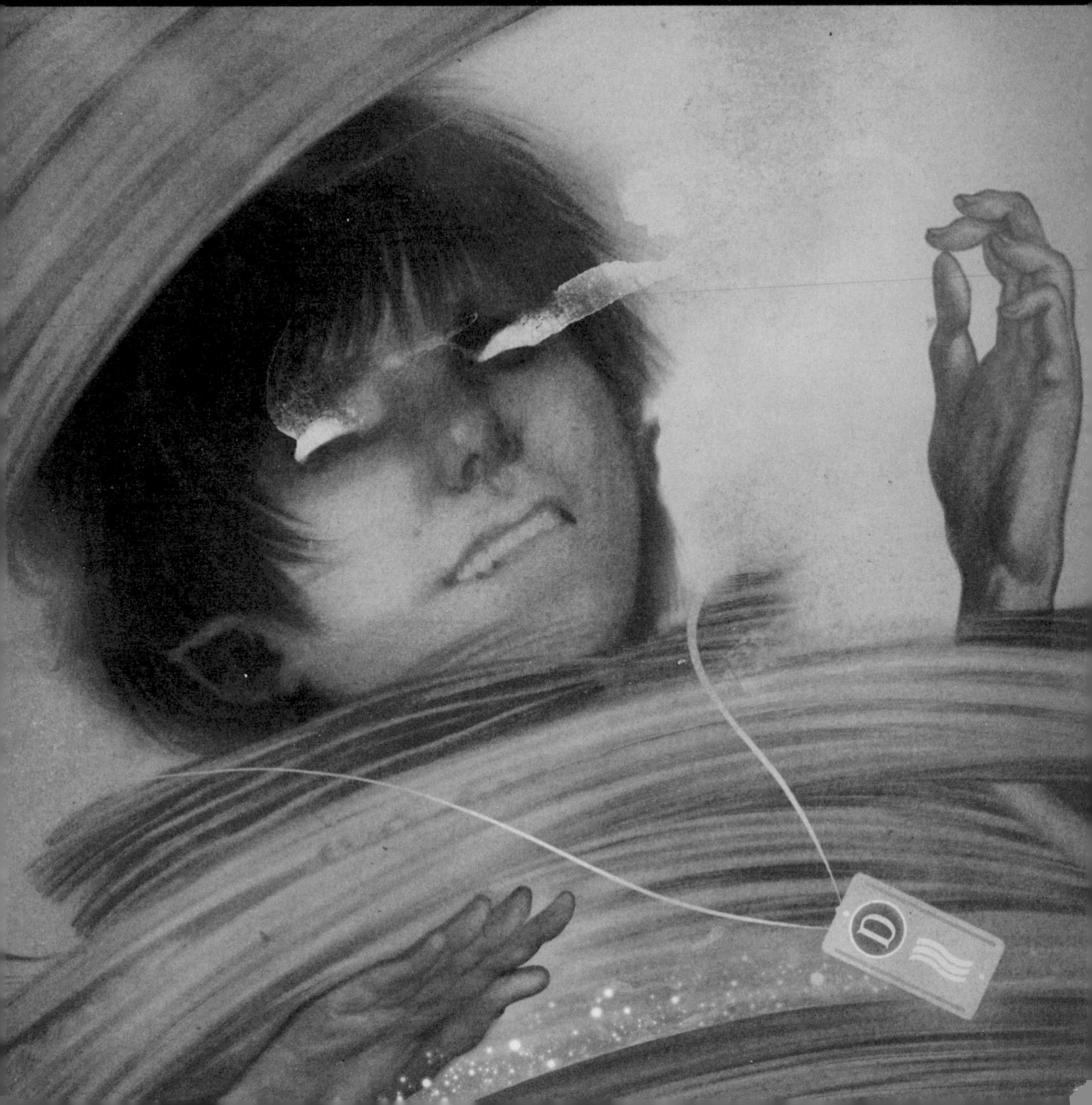

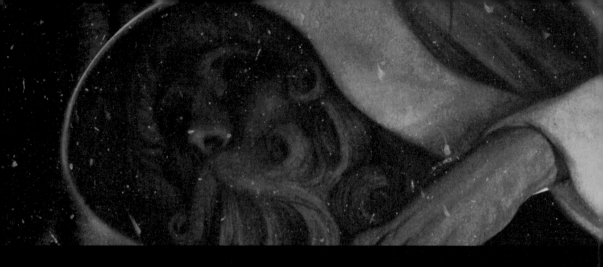

Bill Willingham
Writer

Mark Buckingham
Steve Leialoha
Shawn McManus
Andrew Pepoy
Dan Green
Rick Leonardi
Ron Randall
P. Craig Russell
Zander Cannon
Jim Fern
Ramon Bachs
Adam Hughes
Artists

Lee Loughridge
Lovern Kindzierski
Colorists

Todd Klein
Letterer

Joao Ruas
Cover Art and
Original Series Covers

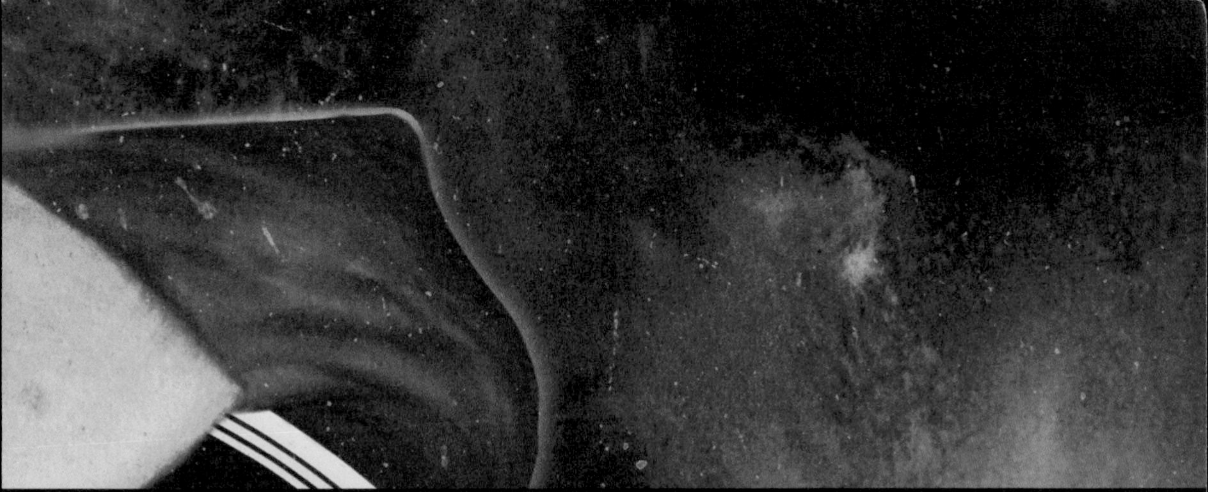

FABLES: INHERIT THE WIND

FABLES CREATED BY BILL WILLINGHAM

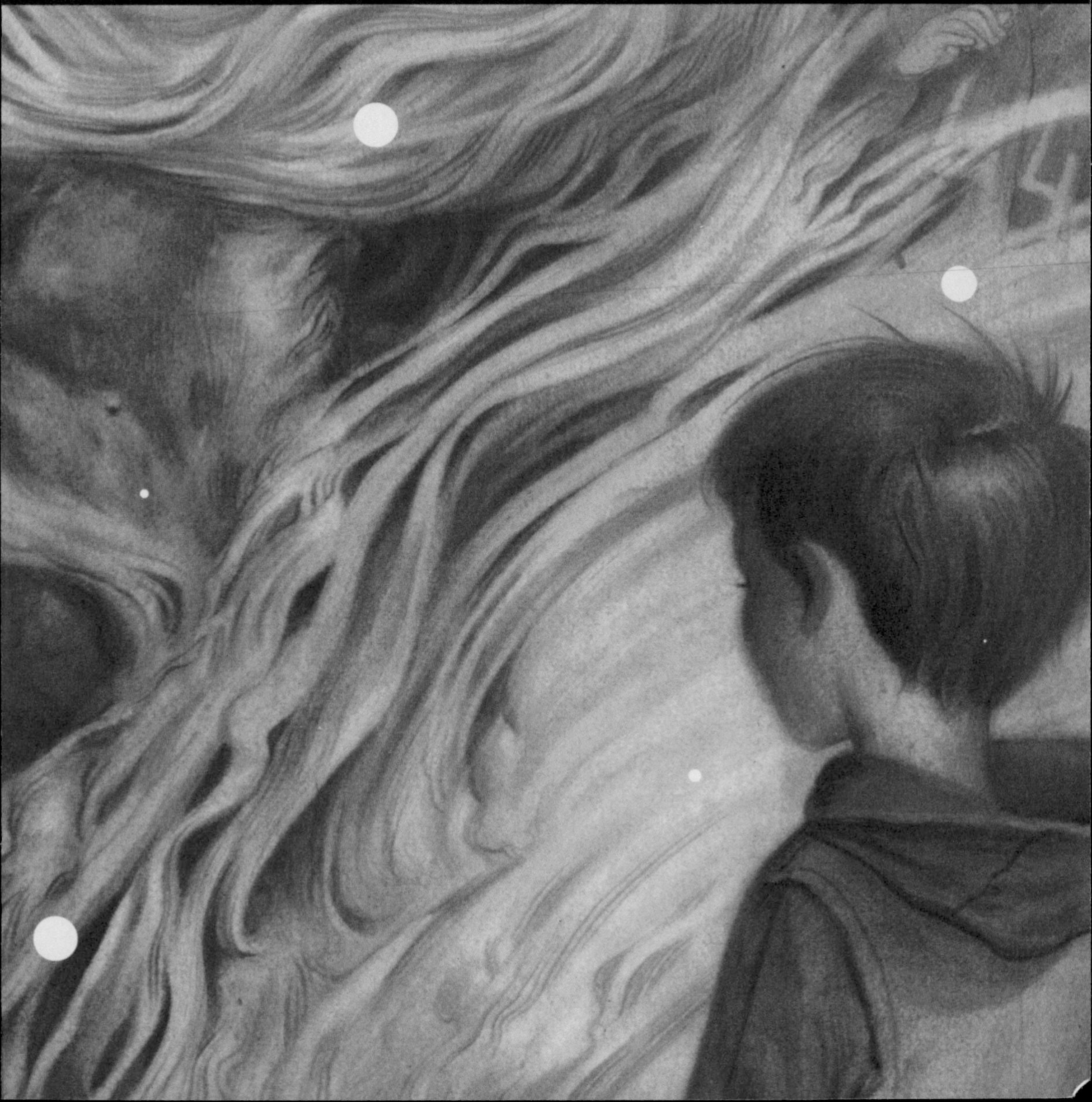

SHELLY BOND
Editor – Original Series

GREGORY LOCKARD
Assistant Editor – Original Series

SCOTT NYBAKKEN
Editor

ROBBIN BROSTERMAN
Design Director – Books

KAREN BERGER
Senior VP – Executive Editor, Vertigo

BOB HARRAS
VP – Editor-in-Chief

DIANE NELSON
President

DAN DIDIO and **JIM LEE**
Co-Publishers

GEOFF JOHNS
Chief Creative Officer

JOHN ROOD
Executive VP – Sales, Marketing and Business Development

AMY GENKINS
Senior VP – Business and Legal Affairs

NAIRI GARDINER
Senior VP – Finance

JEFF BOISON
VP – Publishing Operations

MARK CHIARELLO
VP – Art Direction and Design

JOHN CUNNINGHAM
VP – Marketing

TERRI CUNNINGHAM
VP – Talent Relations and Services

ALISON GILL
Senior VP – Manufacturing and Operations

HANK KANALZ
Senior VP – Digital

JAY KOGAN
VP – Business and Legal Affairs, Publishing

JACK MAHAN
VP – Business Affairs, Talent

NICK NAPOLITANO
VP – Manufacturing Administration

SUE POHJA
VP – Book Sales

COURTNEY SIMMONS
Senior VP – Publicity

BOB WAYNE
Senior VP – Sales

This volume of storms and frosty calamities is dedicated to Stephanie Cooke, with affection.
— Bill Willingham

To my wonderful wife Irma, for all her love and exceptional tolerance as I juggled drawing this arc with our moving countries; and to Elena, for being equally tolerant with me as well as being the very best of friends to us both.
— Mark Buckingham

Logo design by Brainchild Studios/NYC

FABLES: INHERIT THE WIND

Published by DC Comics. Cover and compilation Copyright © 2012 Bill Willingham and DC Comics. All Rights Reserved.

Originally published in single magazine form as FABLES 108-113. Copyright © 2011, 2012 Bill Willingham and DC Comics.
All Rights Reserved. All characters, their distinctive likenesses and related elements featured in this publication are trademarks of Bill Willingham. VERTIGO is a trademark of DC Comics. The stories, characters and incidents featured in this publication are entirely fictional. DC Comics does not read or accept unsolicited submissions of ideas, stories or artwork.

DC Comics, 1700 Broadway, New York, NY 10019
A Warner Bros. Entertainment Company.
Printed in the USA. First Printing.
ISBN: 978-1-4012-3516-1

SUSTAINABLE FORESTRY INITIATIVE   Certified Sourcing
www.sfiprogram.org
SFI-01042
APPLIES TO TEXT STOCK ONLY

Table of Contents

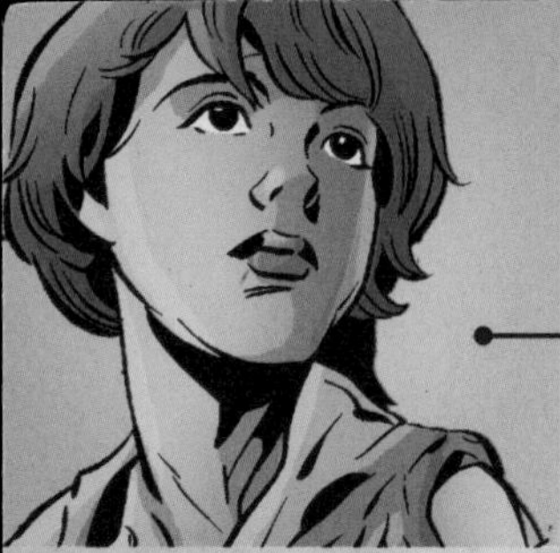

WHO'S WHO IN FABLETOWN

ROSE RED

Leader-in-exile of the Farm — home of the non-human Fables — and sister to Snow White.

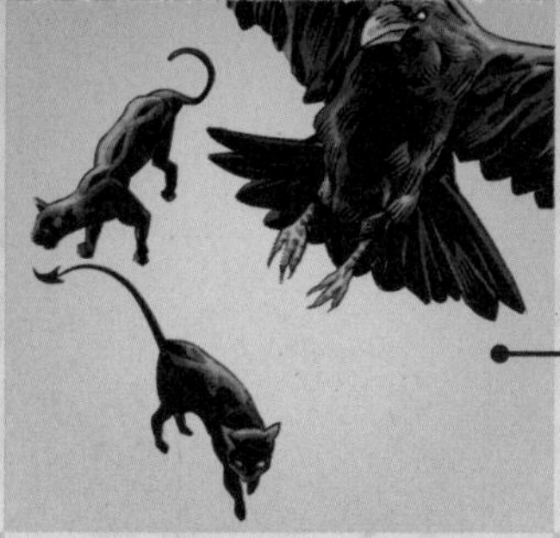

BAGHEERA, CLAR AND MADDY

Three of the Farm-dwelling Fables, each with a surprising story to tell.

BIGBY

The celebrated Big Bad Wolf and former sheriff of Fabletown.

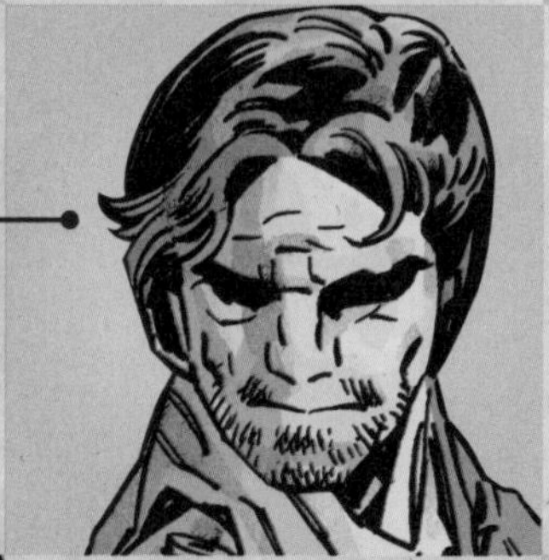

SNOW WHITE

Fabletown's former deputy mayor, wife of Bigby, and mother to their seven cubs.

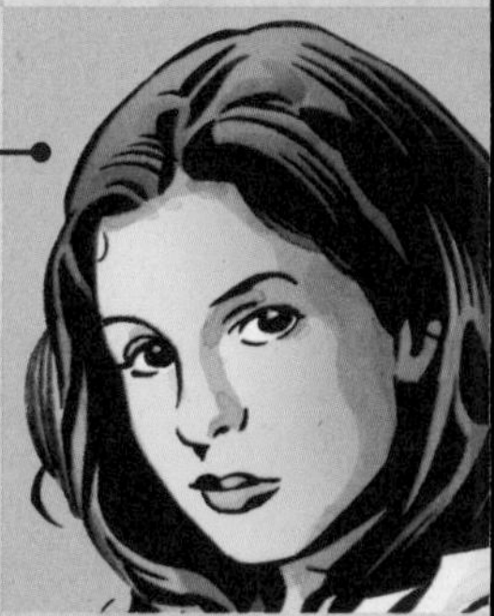

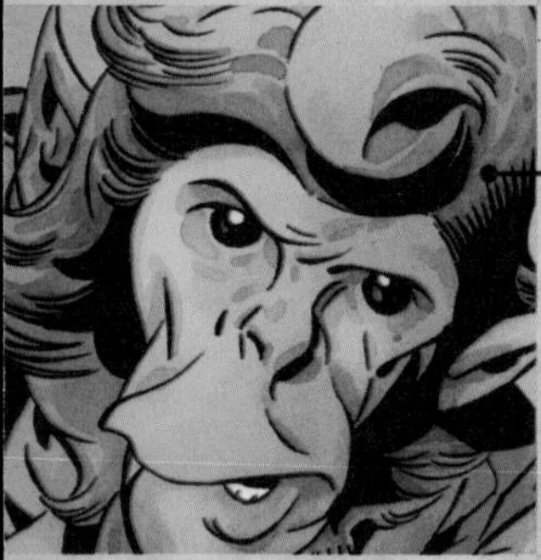

BUFKIN

A former member of Oz's Flying Monkey Air Corps, he has appointed himself the leader of a rebellion against the land's newly crowned emperor, Roquat the Red.

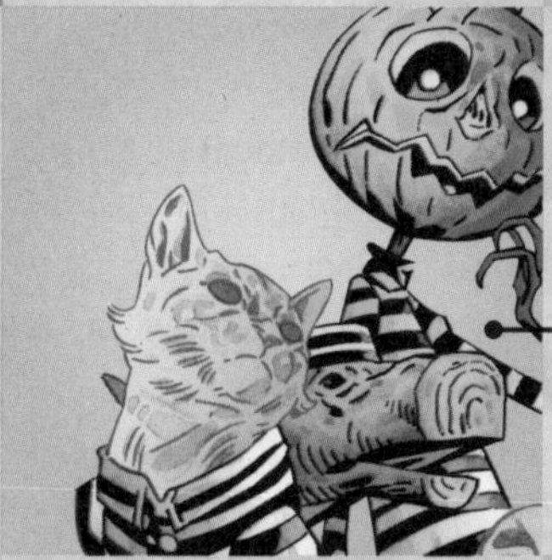

BUNGLE, SAWHORSE AND JACK PUMPKINHE

Three fugitives on the run fro Roquat the Red — formerly known as the Nome King.

OZMA

The misleadingly youthful-looking leader of Fabletown's wizards and witches.

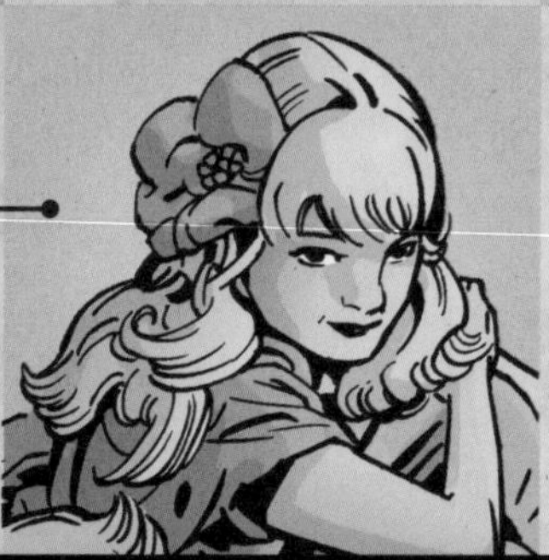

BELLFLOWER

Once known as Frau Totenkinder, she led Fabletown's witches through their greatest trials, including an epic confrontation with Mister Dark.

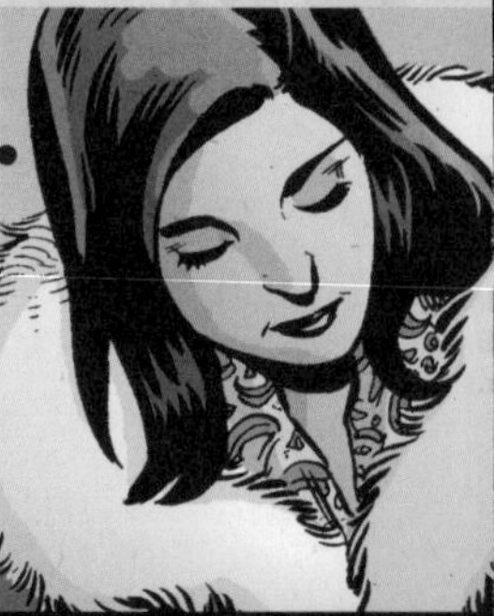

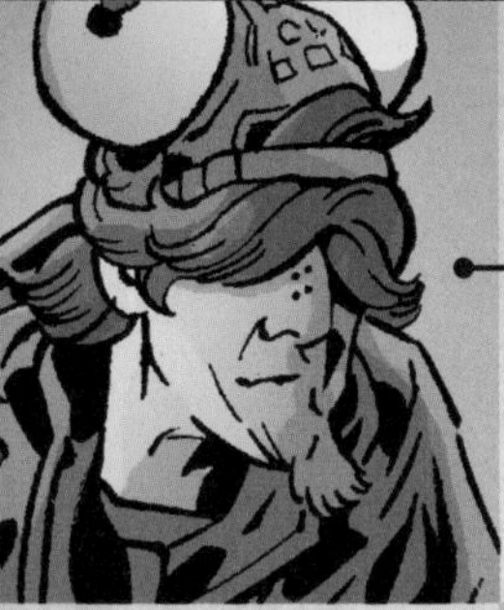

FLYCATCHER

The former Frog Prince and ruler of the Kingdom of Haven in the liberated Homelands.

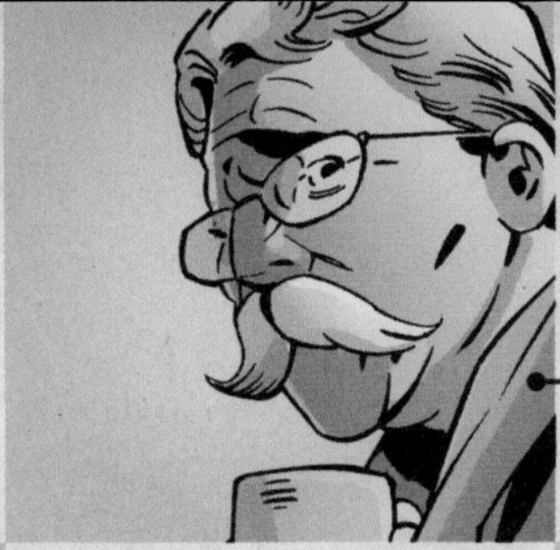

KING COLE

The once and future mayor of Fabletown.

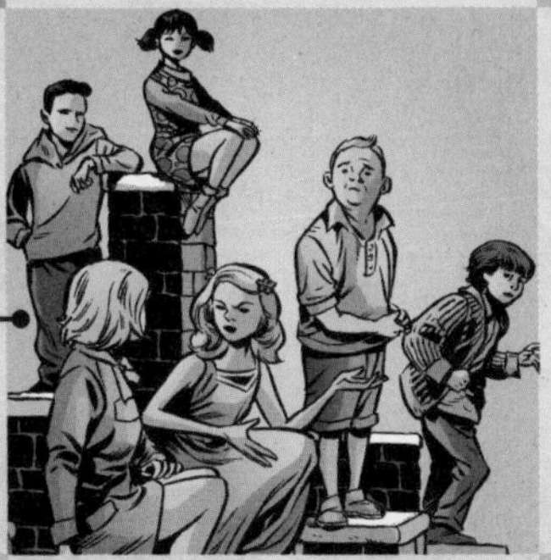

THE CUBS

Bigby and Snow's children, seen and unseen.

THE ZEPHYRS

Loyal retainers of the North Wind.

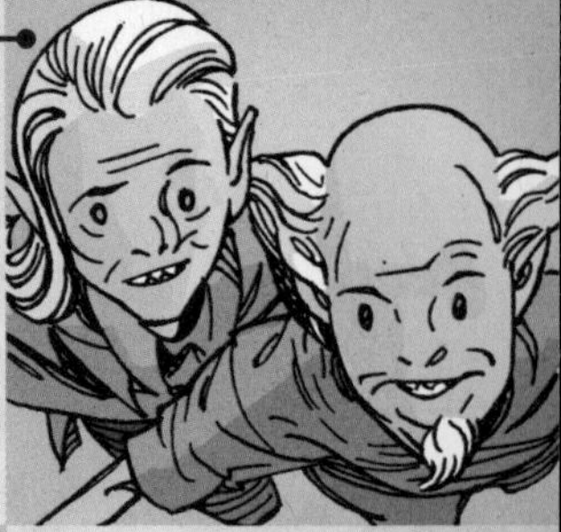

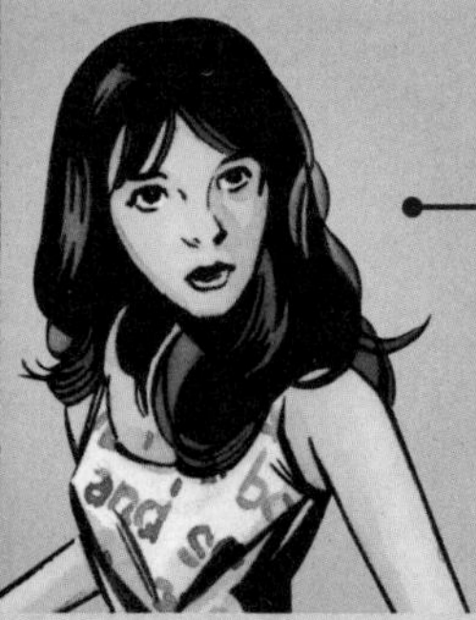

LILY MARTAGON

A wee Barleycorn Bride with a taste for adventure.

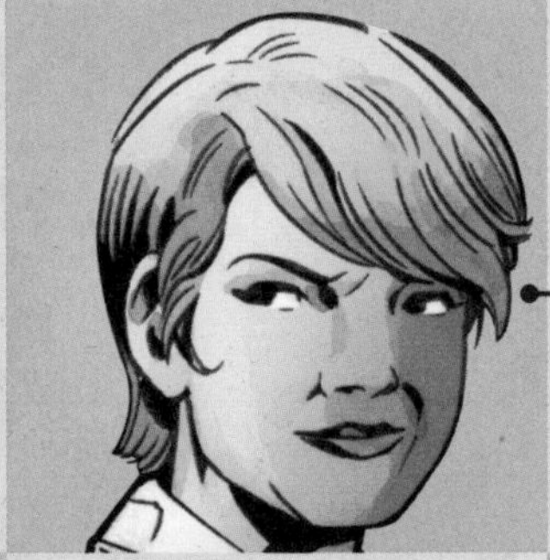

MISS SPRATT

Jack Spratt's newly lean widow, bent on taking revenge for her recently deceased patron, Mister Dark.

DUNSTER HAPP

A former commander of the Imperial Warlock Corps' élite Boxing League and Bellflower's new husband.

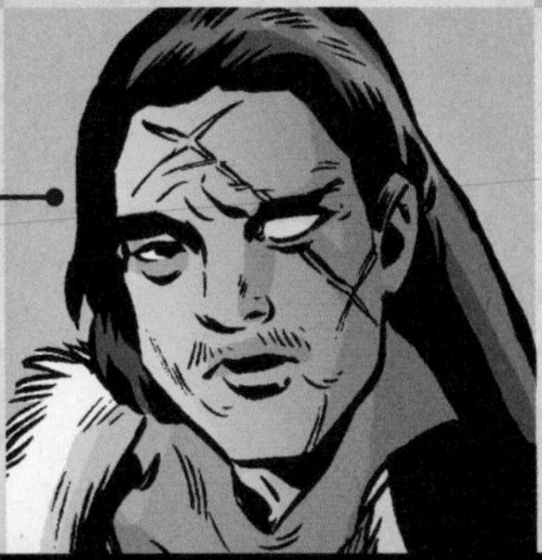

THE STORY SO FAR

With their backs against the wall and their stronghold in the Mundane World destroyed, the surviving Free Fables gathered in the Kingdom of Haven and prepared to make their last stand against Mister Dark. Few dared to hope for victory, having seen their carefully laid offensives and their most powerful sorceress all vanquished by this seemingly unstoppable foe. In the end, however, the Fables' last-ditch defenses went untested, as Mister Dark was destroyed single-handedly by the North Wind — at the cost of his own life. Now, as the rebuilding begins, some difficult choices have to be made — and some unpleasant truths must be faced.

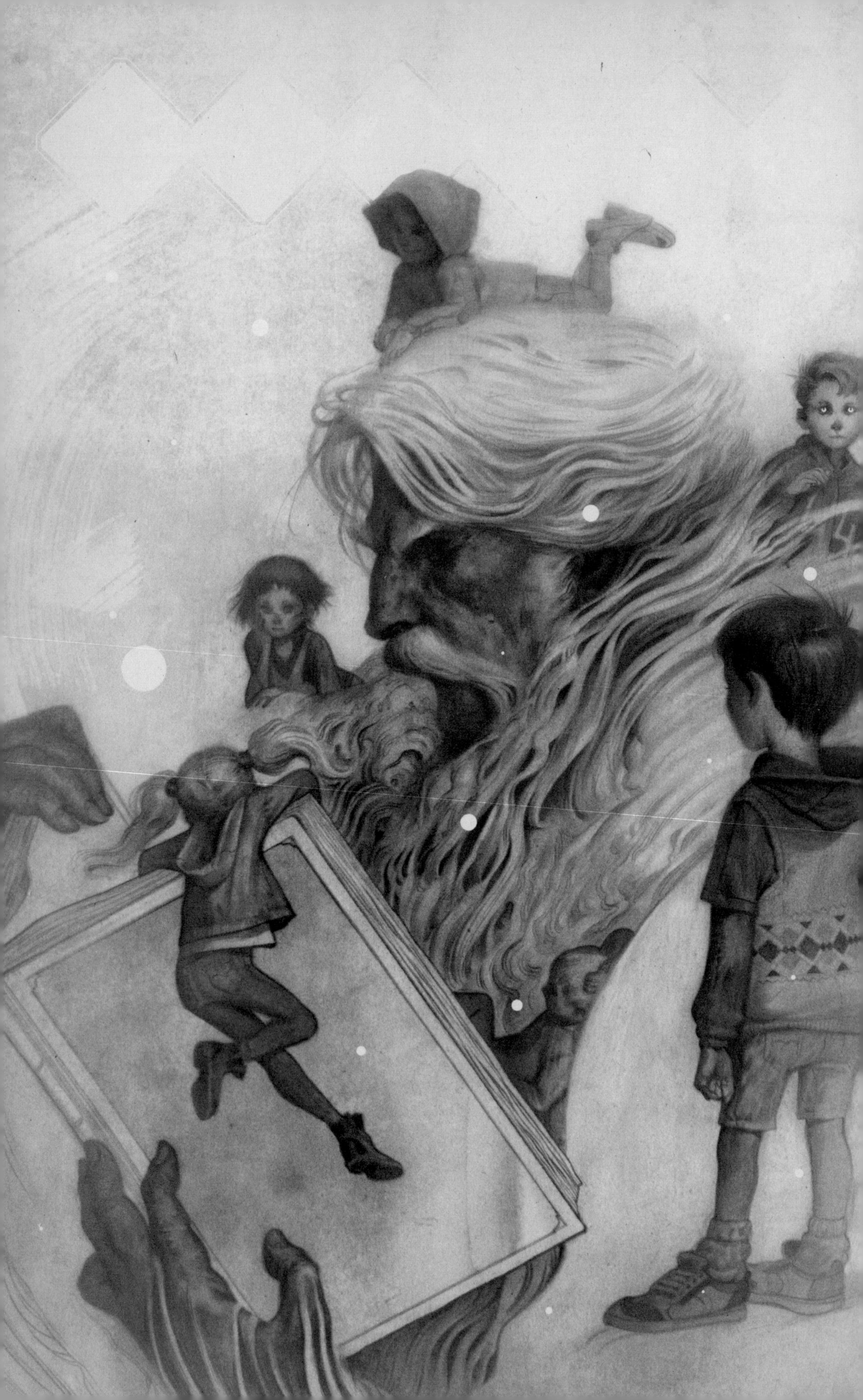

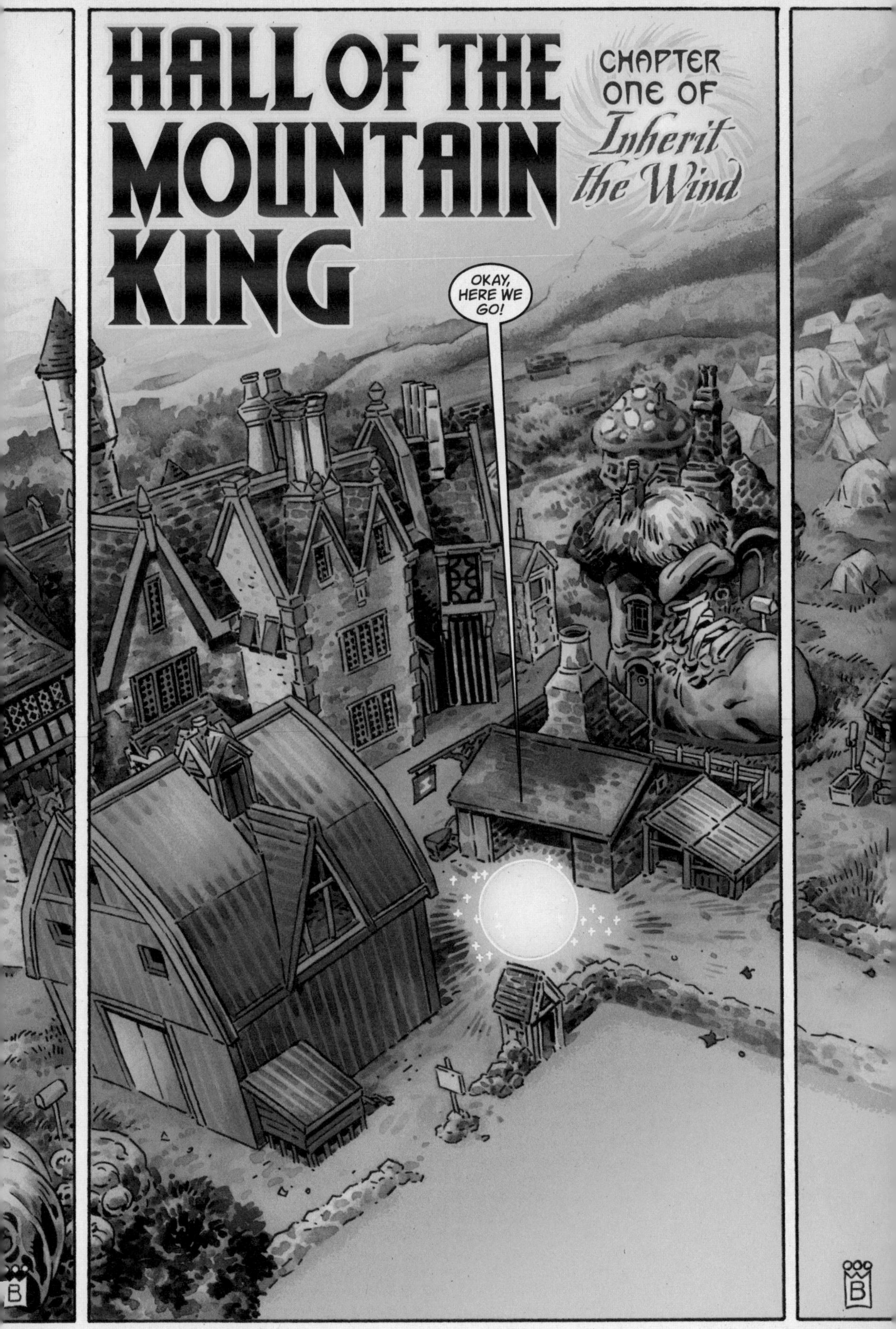
HALL OF THE MOUNTAIN KING
CHAPTER ONE OF *Inherit the Wind*
OKAY, HERE WE GO!

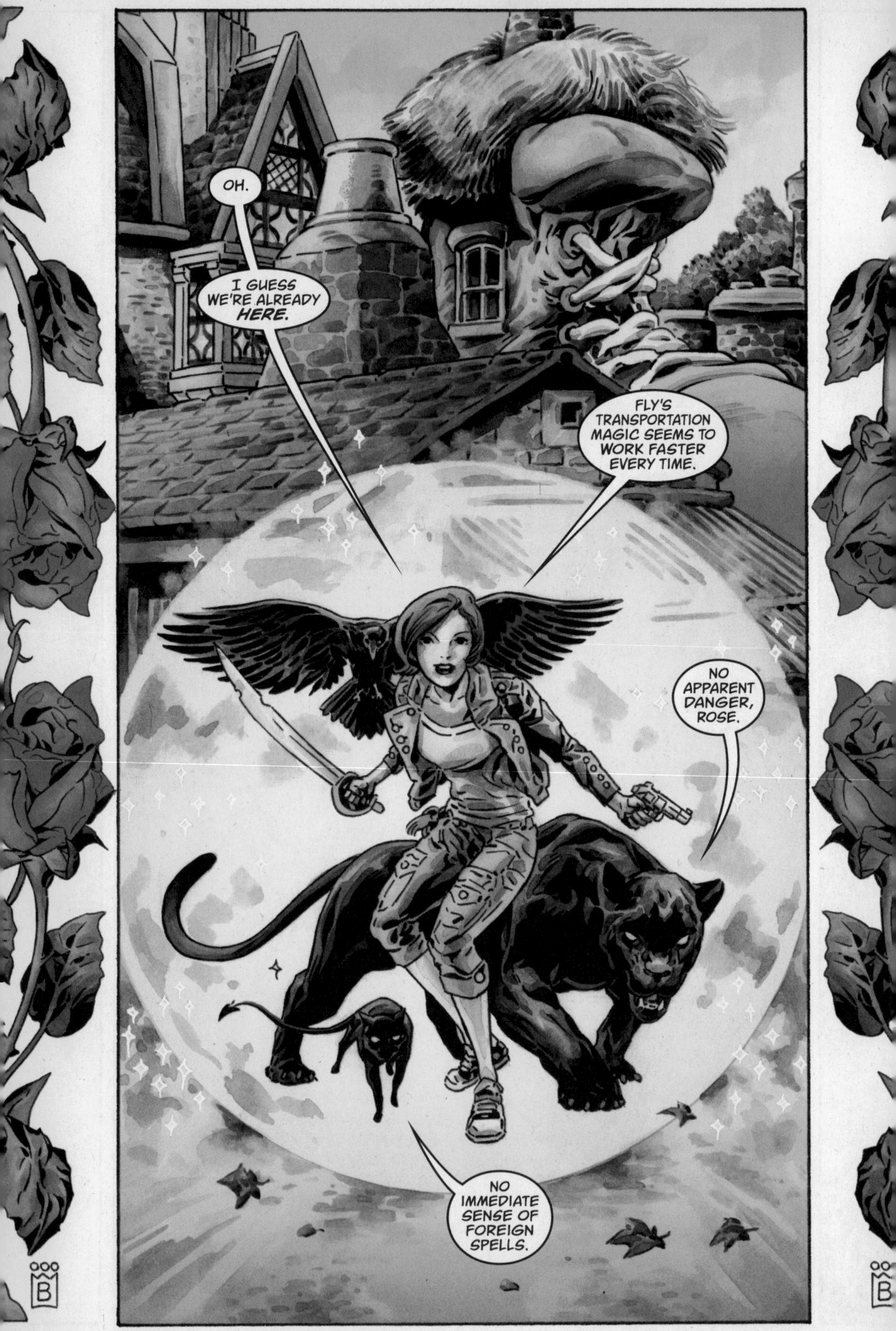
OH.
I GUESS WE'RE ALREADY HERE.
FLY'S TRANSPORTATION MAGIC SEEMS TO WORK FASTER EVERY TIME.
NO APPARENT DANGER, ROSE.
NO IMMEDIATE SENSE OF FOREIGN SPELLS.

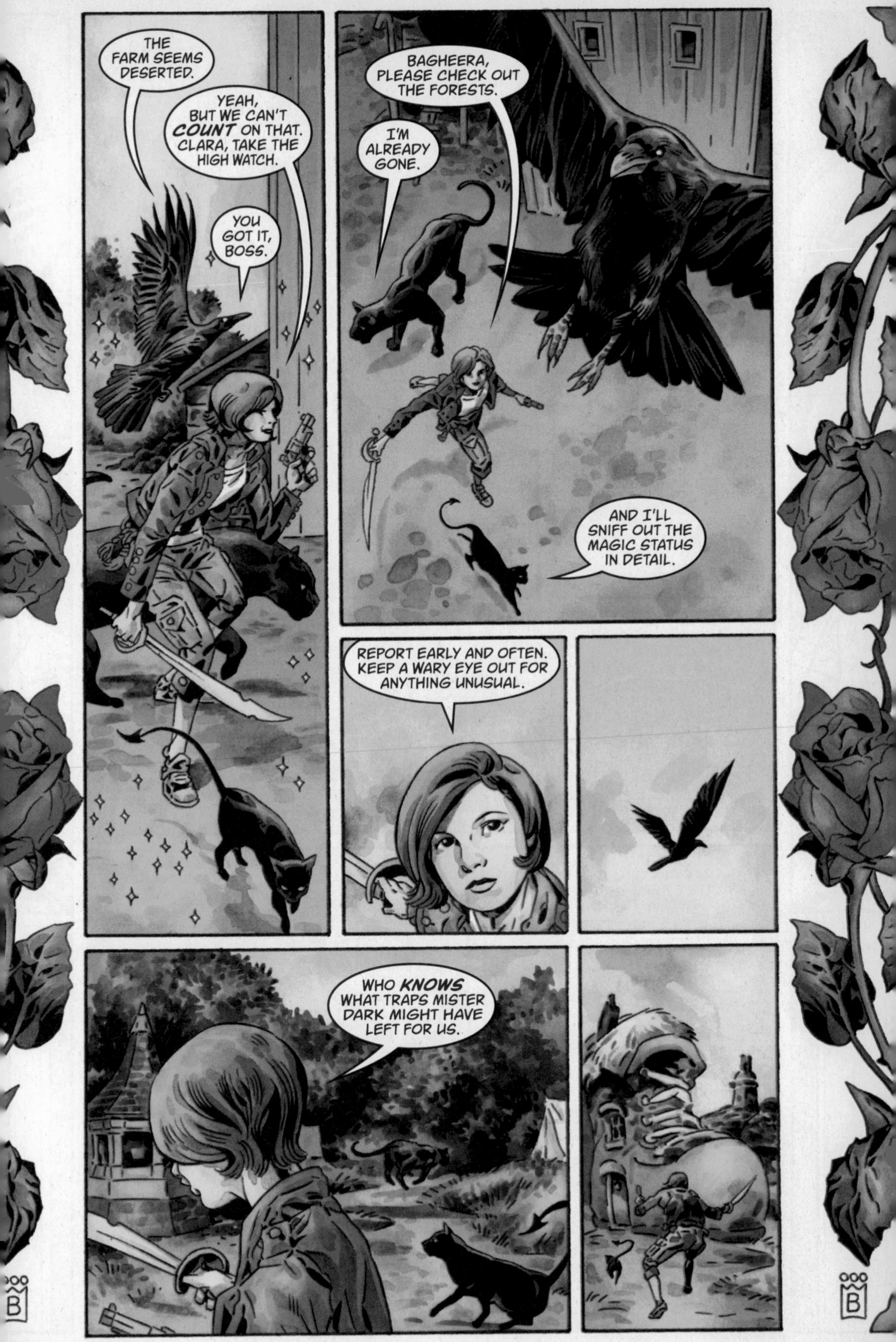
THE FARM SEEMS DESERTED.
YEAH, BUT WE CAN'T COUNT ON THAT. CLARA, TAKE THE HIGH WATCH.
YOU GOT IT, BOSS.
BAGHEERA, PLEASE CHECK OUT THE FORESTS.
I'M ALREADY GONE.
AND I'LL SNIFF OUT THE MAGIC STATUS IN DETAIL.
REPORT EARLY AND OFTEN. KEEP A WARY EYE OUT FOR ANYTHING UNUSUAL.
WHO KNOWS WHAT TRAPS MISTER DARK MIGHT HAVE LEFT FOR US.

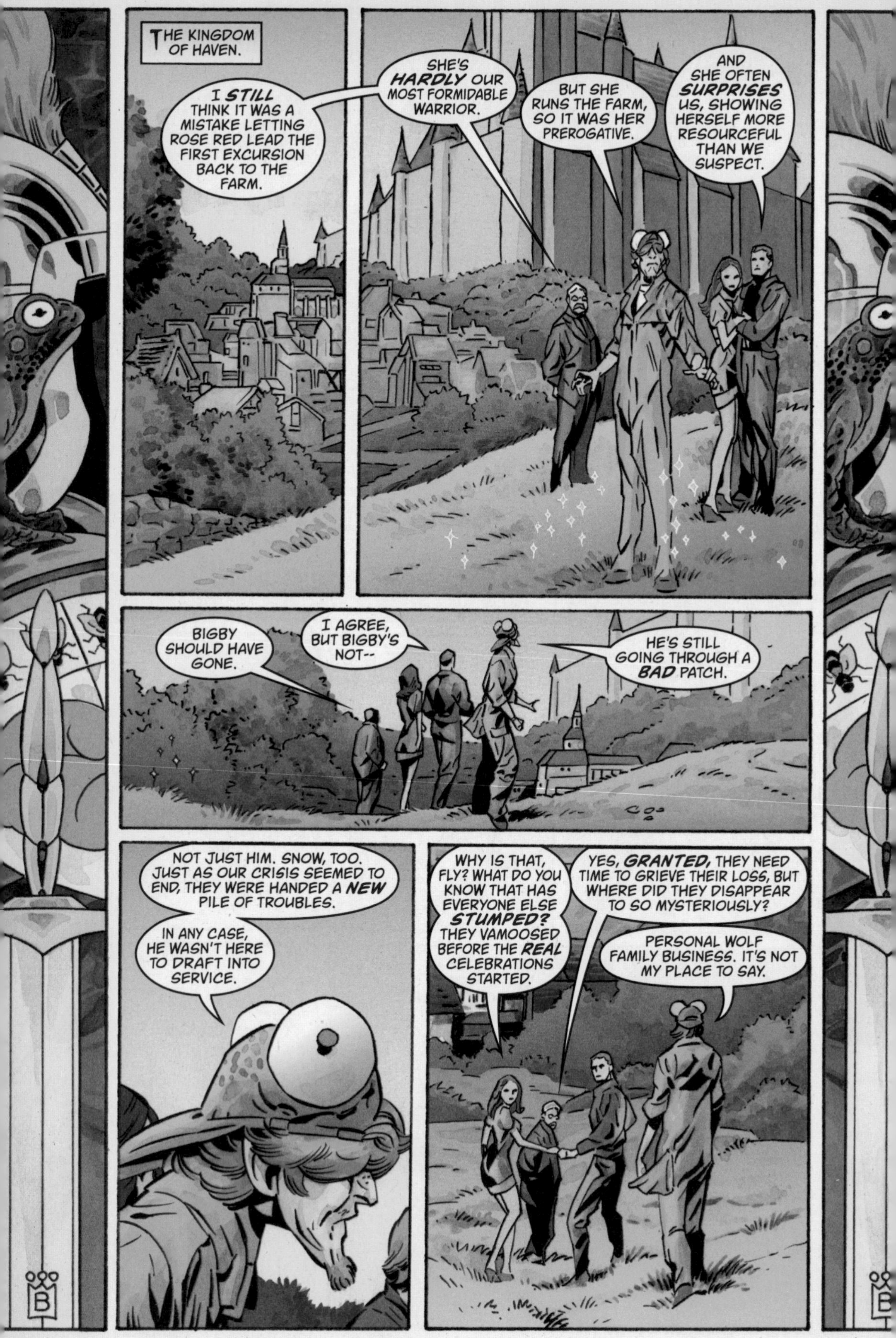
THE KINGDOM OF HAVEN.
I STILL THINK IT WAS A MISTAKE LETTING ROSE RED LEAD THE FIRST EXCURSION BACK TO THE FARM.
SHE'S HARDLY OUR MOST FORMIDABLE WARRIOR.
BUT SHE RUNS THE FARM, SO IT WAS HER PREROGATIVE.
AND SHE OFTEN SURPRISES US, SHOWING HERSELF MORE RESOURCEFUL THAN WE SUSPECT.
BIGBY SHOULD HAVE GONE.
I AGREE, BUT BIGBY'S NOT--
HE'S STILL GOING THROUGH A BAD PATCH.
NOT JUST HIM. SNOW, TOO. JUST AS OUR CRISIS SEEMED TO END, THEY WERE HANDED A NEW PILE OF TROUBLES.
IN ANY CASE, HE WASN'T HERE TO DRAFT INTO SERVICE.
WHY IS THAT, FLY? WHAT DO YOU KNOW THAT HAS EVERYONE ELSE STUMPED? THEY VAMOOSED BEFORE THE REAL CELEBRATIONS STARTED.
YES, GRANTED, THEY NEED TIME TO GRIEVE THEIR LOSS, BUT WHERE DID THEY DISAPPEAR TO SO MYSTERIOUSLY?
PERSONAL WOLF FAMILY BUSINESS. IT'S NOT MY PLACE TO SAY.

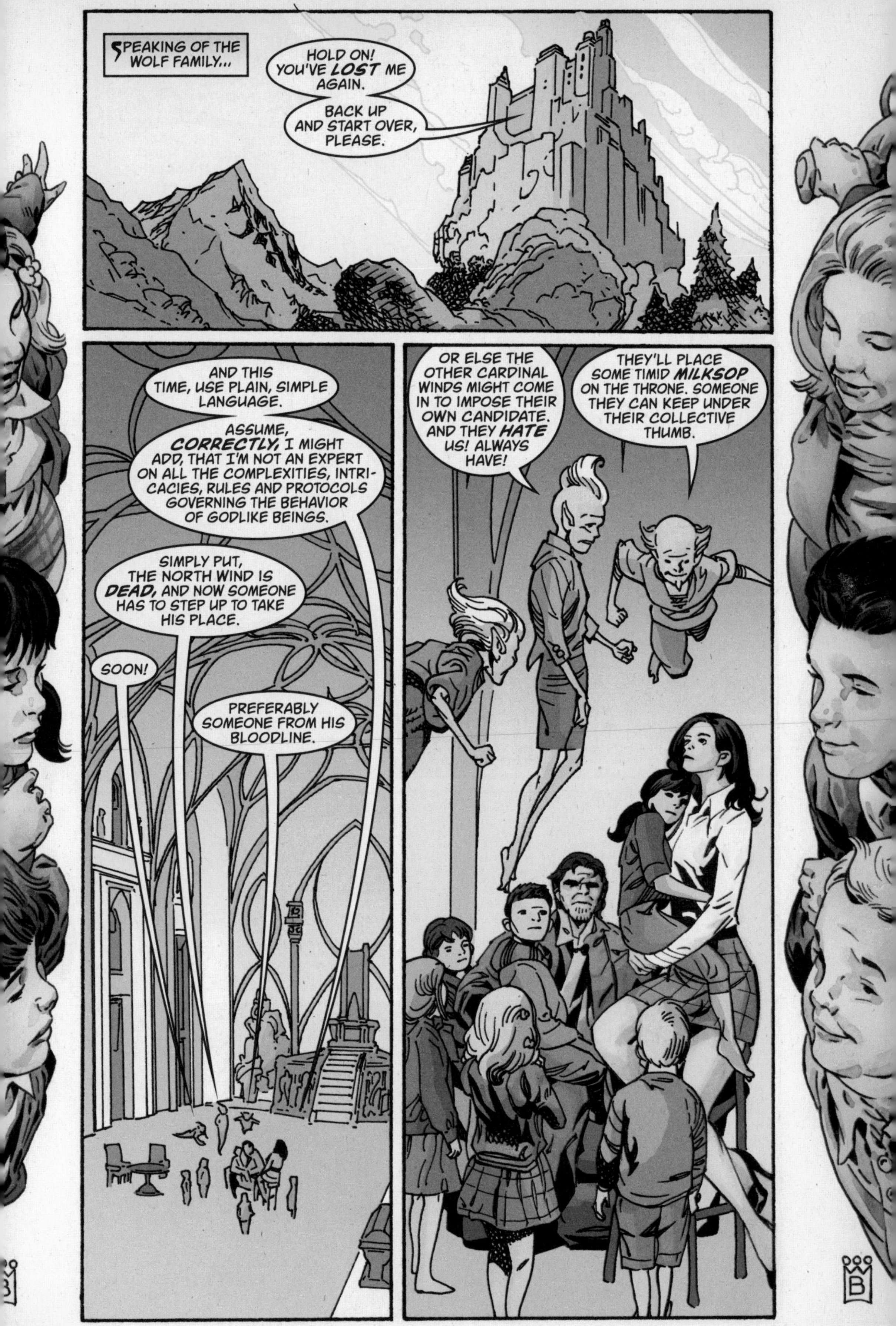
SPEAKING OF THE WOLF FAMILY...
HOLD ON! YOU'VE LOST ME AGAIN.
BACK UP AND START OVER, PLEASE.
AND THIS TIME, USE PLAIN, SIMPLE LANGUAGE.
ASSUME, CORRECTLY, I MIGHT ADD, THAT I'M NOT AN EXPERT ON ALL THE COMPLEXITIES, INTRICACIES, RULES AND PROTOCOLS GOVERNING THE BEHAVIOR OF GODLIKE BEINGS.
SIMPLY PUT, THE NORTH WIND IS DEAD, AND NOW SOMEONE HAS TO STEP UP TO TAKE HIS PLACE.
SOON!
PREFERABLY SOMEONE FROM HIS BLOODLINE.
OR ELSE THE OTHER CARDINAL WINDS MIGHT COME IN TO IMPOSE THEIR OWN CANDIDATE. AND THEY HATE US! ALWAYS HAVE!
THEY'LL PLACE SOME TIMID MILKSOP ON THE THRONE. SOMEONE THEY CAN KEEP UNDER THEIR COLLECTIVE THUMB.

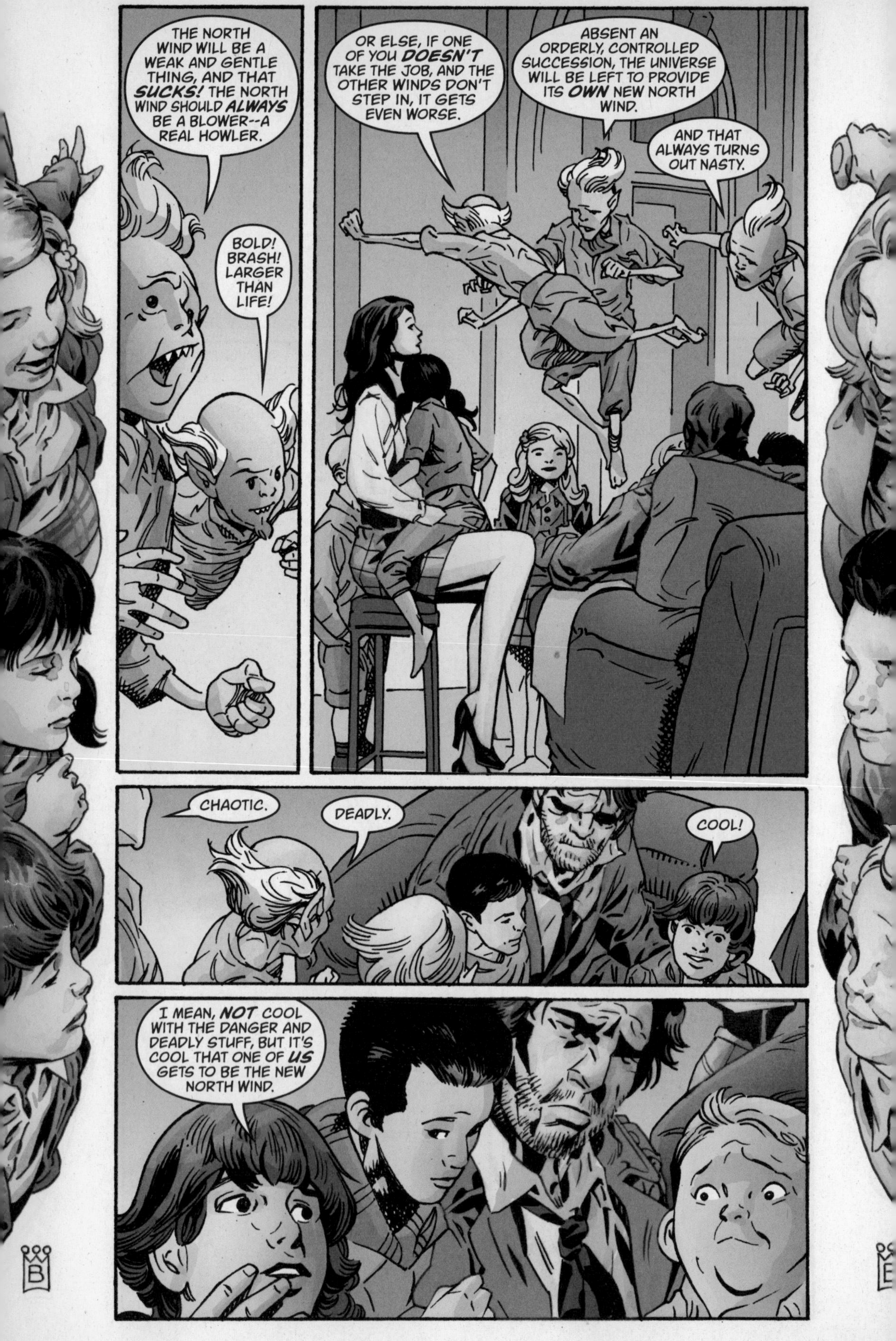
THE NORTH WIND WILL BE A WEAK AND GENTLE THING, AND THAT SUCKS! THE NORTH WIND SHOULD ALWAYS BE A BLOWER--A REAL HOWLER.
BOLD! BRASH! LARGER THAN LIFE!
OR ELSE, IF ONE OF YOU DOESN'T TAKE THE JOB, AND THE OTHER WINDS DON'T STEP IN, IT GETS EVEN WORSE.
ABSENT AN ORDERLY, CONTROLLED SUCCESSION, THE UNIVERSE WILL BE LEFT TO PROVIDE ITS OWN NEW NORTH WIND.
AND THAT ALWAYS TURNS OUT NASTY.
CHAOTIC.
DEADLY.
COOL!
I MEAN, NOT COOL WITH THE DANGER AND DEADLY STUFF, BUT IT'S COOL THAT ONE OF US GETS TO BE THE NEW NORTH WIND.

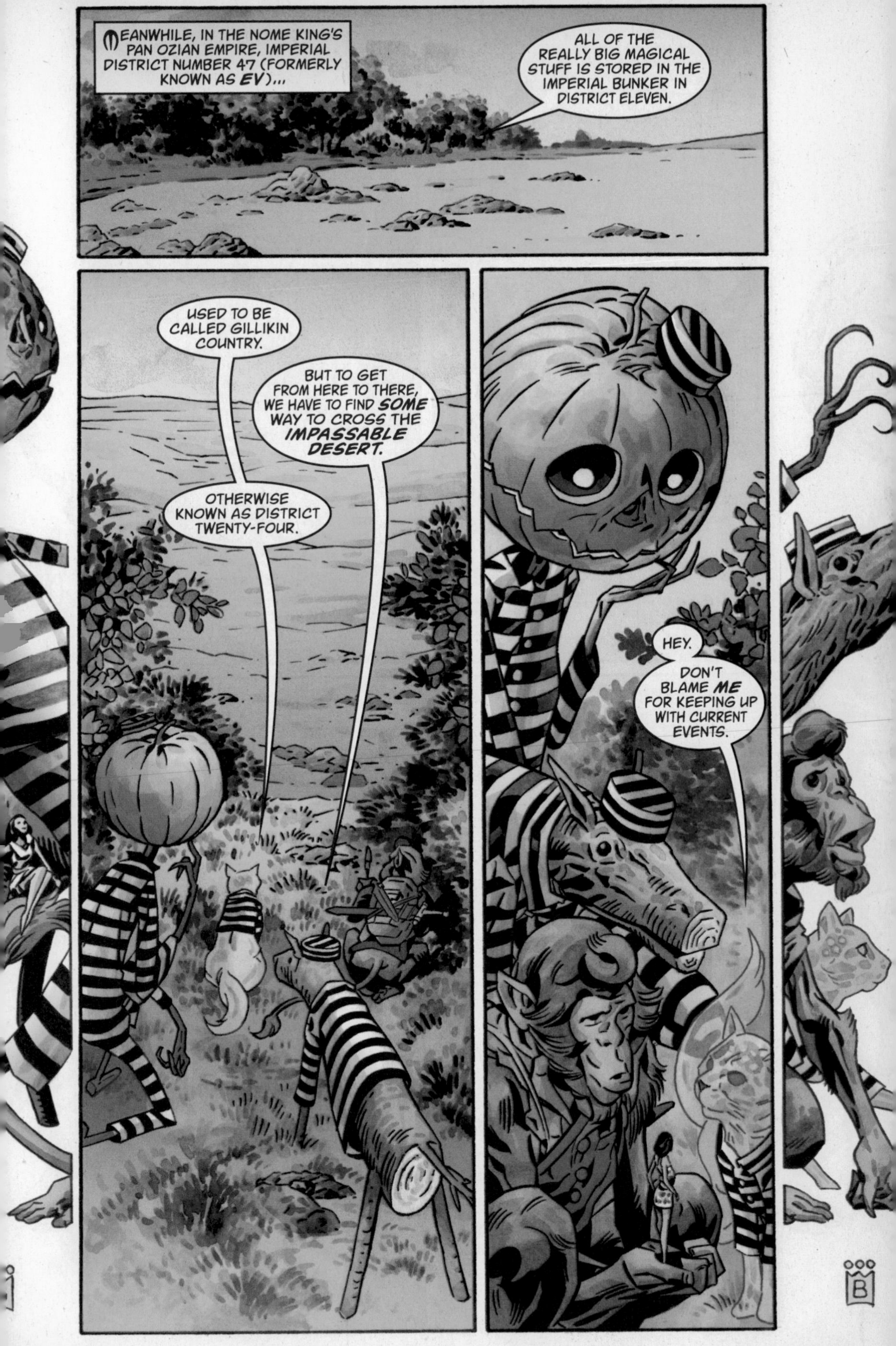
MEANWHILE, IN THE NOME KING'S PAN OZIAN EMPIRE, IMPERIAL DISTRICT NUMBER 47 (FORMERLY KNOWN AS EV)...
ALL OF THE REALLY BIG MAGICAL STUFF IS STORED IN THE IMPERIAL BUNKER IN DISTRICT ELEVEN.
USED TO BE CALLED GILLIKIN COUNTRY.
OTHERWISE KNOWN AS DISTRICT TWENTY-FOUR.
BUT TO GET FROM HERE TO THERE, WE HAVE TO FIND SOME WAY TO CROSS THE IMPASSABLE DESERT.
HEY.
DON'T BLAME ME FOR KEEPING UP WITH CURRENT EVENTS.

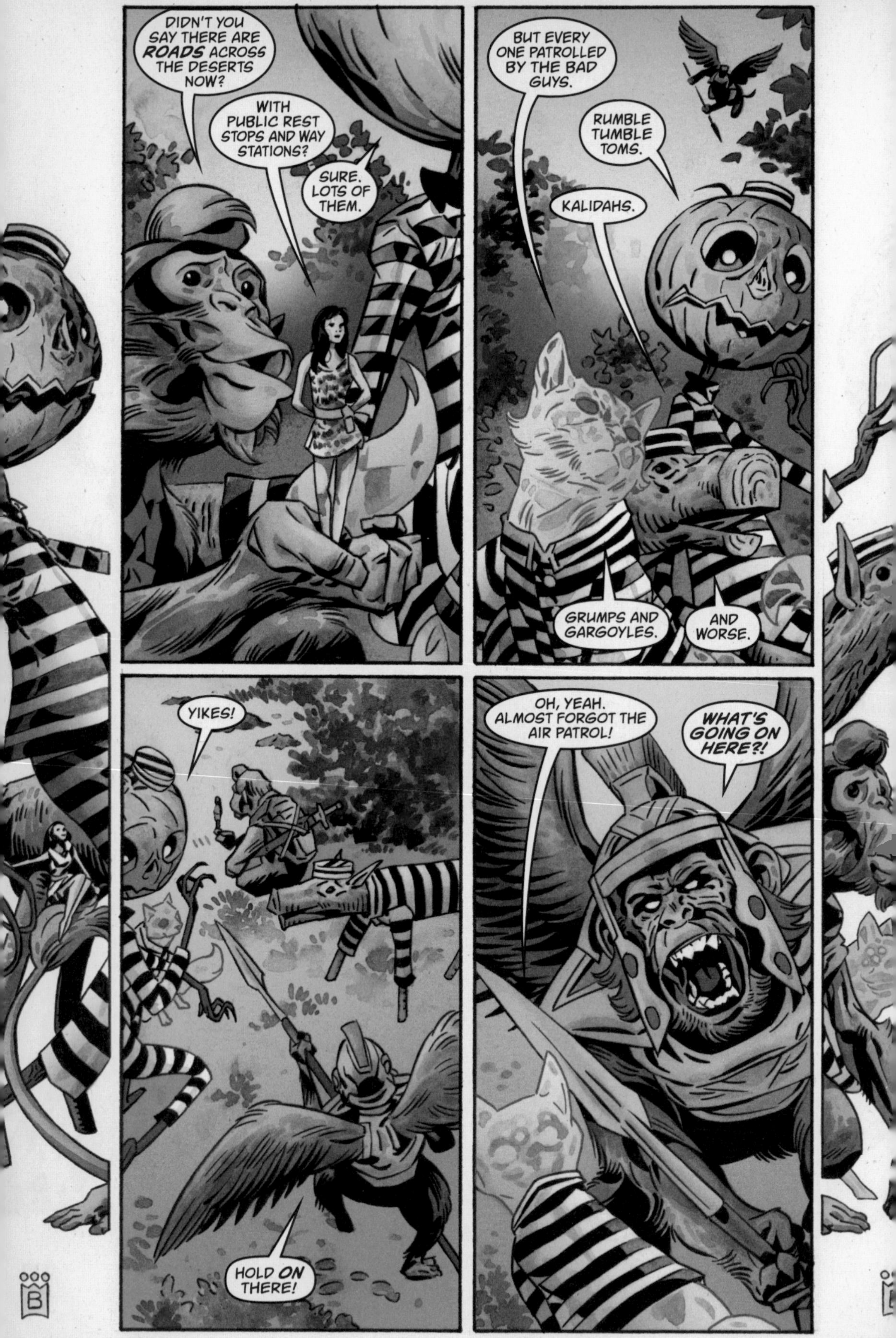
DIDN'T YOU SAY THERE ARE ROADS ACROSS THE DESERTS NOW?
WITH PUBLIC REST STOPS AND WAY STATIONS?
SURE. LOTS OF THEM.
BUT EVERY ONE PATROLLED BY THE BAD GUYS.
RUMBLE TUMBLE TOMS.
KALIDAHS.
GRUMPS AND GARGOYLES.
AND WORSE.
YIKES!
HOLD ON THERE!
OH, YEAH. ALMOST FORGOT THE AIR PATROL!
WHAT'S GOING ON HERE?!

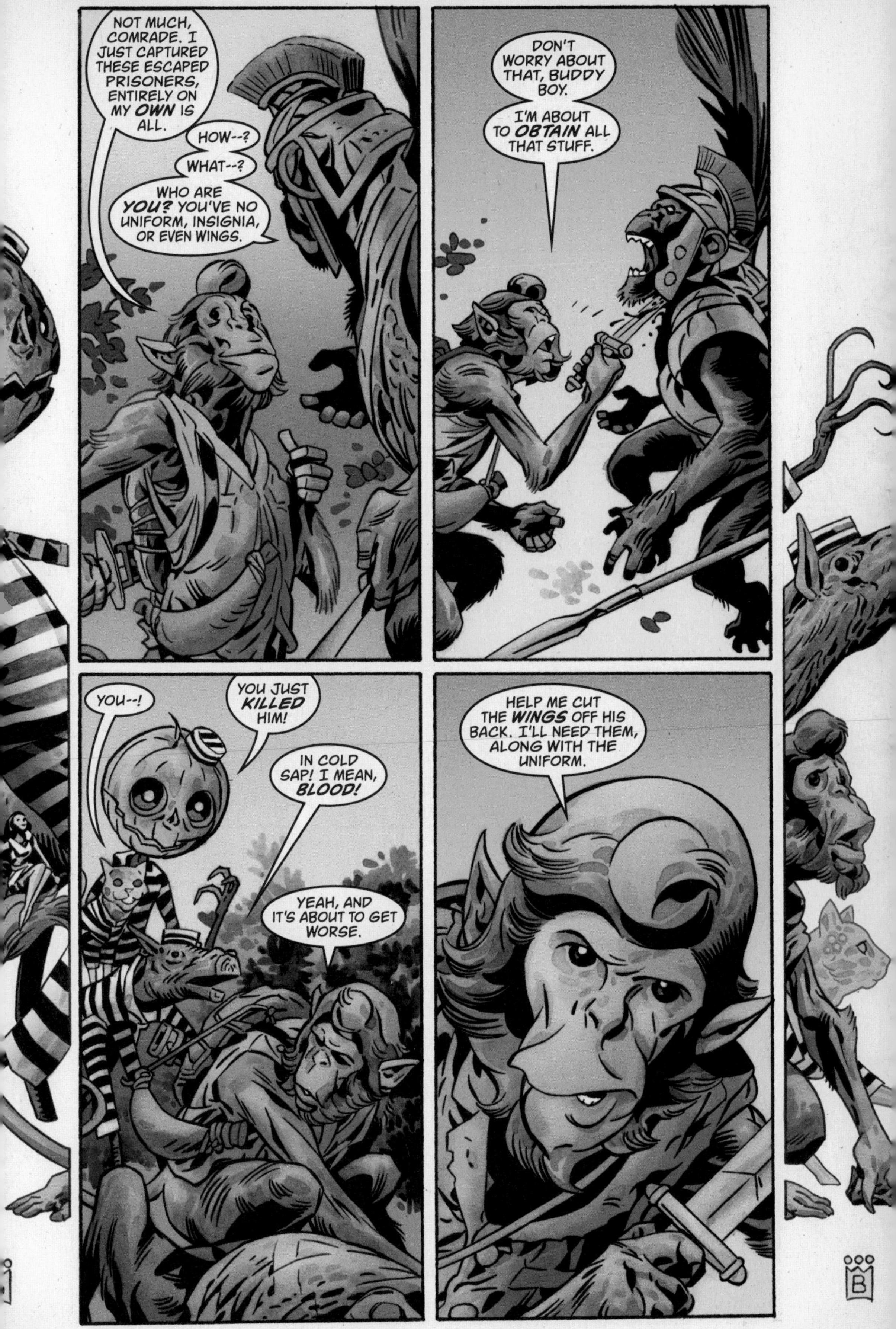
NOT MUCH, COMRADE. I JUST CAPTURED THESE ESCAPED PRISONERS, ENTIRELY ON MY OWN IS ALL.
HOW--?
WHAT--?
WHO ARE YOU? YOU'VE NO UNIFORM, INSIGNIA, OR EVEN WINGS.
DON'T WORRY ABOUT THAT, BUDDY BOY.
I'M ABOUT TO OBTAIN ALL THAT STUFF.
YOU--!
YOU JUST KILLED HIM!
IN COLD SAP! I MEAN, BLOOD!
YEAH, AND IT'S ABOUT TO GET WORSE.
HELP ME CUT THE WINGS OFF HIS BACK. I'LL NEED THEM, ALONG WITH THE UNIFORM.

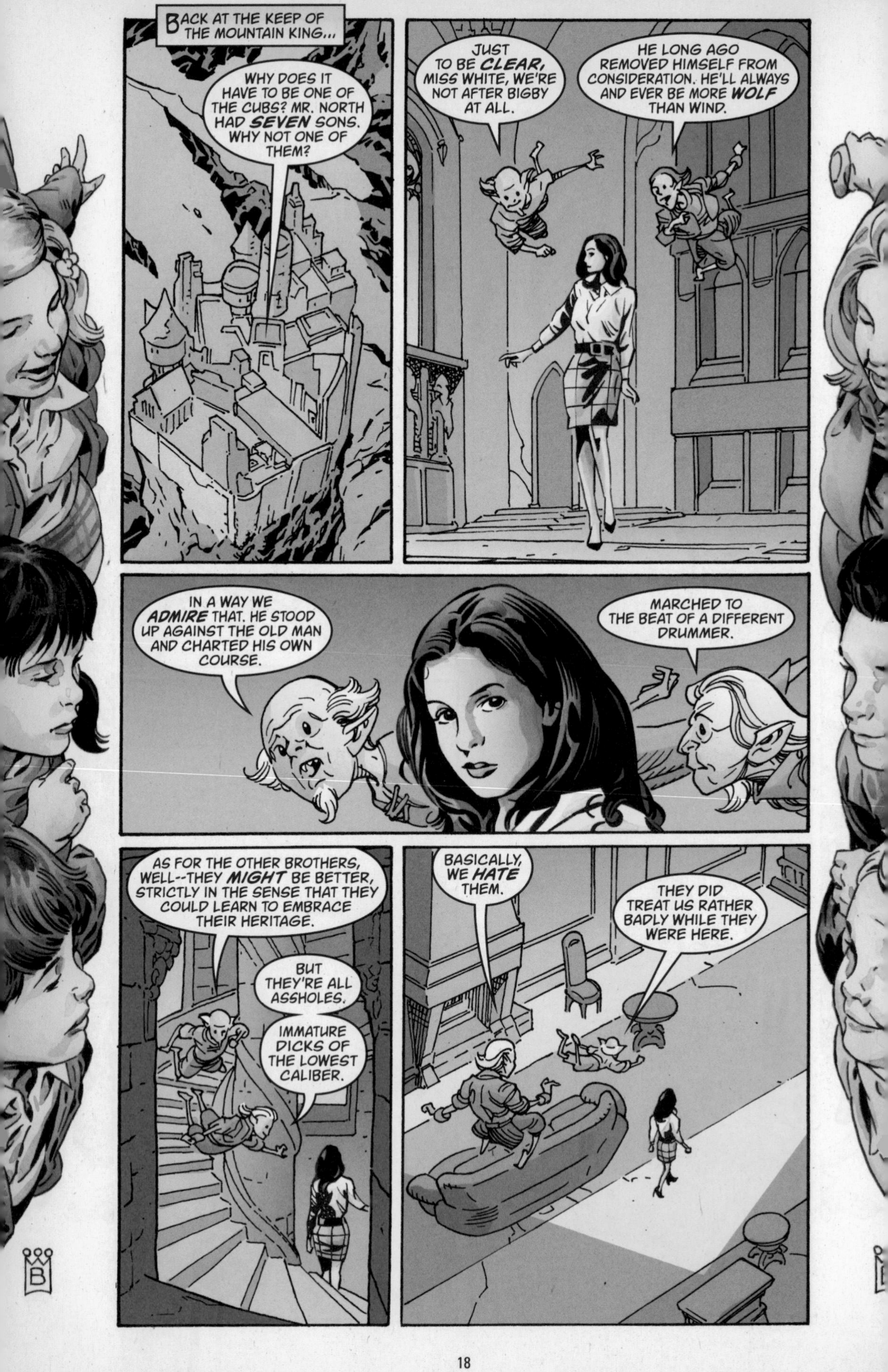

BACK AT THE KEEP OF THE MOUNTAIN KING...
WHY DOES IT HAVE TO BE ONE OF THE CUBS? MR. NORTH HAD SEVEN SONS. WHY NOT ONE OF THEM?
JUST TO BE CLEAR, MISS WHITE, WE'RE NOT AFTER BIGBY AT ALL.
HE LONG AGO REMOVED HIMSELF FROM CONSIDERATION. HE'LL ALWAYS AND EVER BE MORE WOLF THAN WIND.
IN A WAY WE ADMIRE THAT. HE STOOD UP AGAINST THE OLD MAN AND CHARTED HIS OWN COURSE.
MARCHED TO THE BEAT OF A DIFFERENT DRUMMER.
AS FOR THE OTHER BROTHERS, WELL--THEY MIGHT BE BETTER, STRICTLY IN THE SENSE THAT THEY COULD LEARN TO EMBRACE THEIR HERITAGE.
BUT THEY'RE ALL ASSHOLES.
IMMATURE DICKS OF THE LOWEST CALIBER.
BASICALLY, WE HATE THEM.
THEY DID TREAT US RATHER BADLY WHILE THEY WERE HERE.

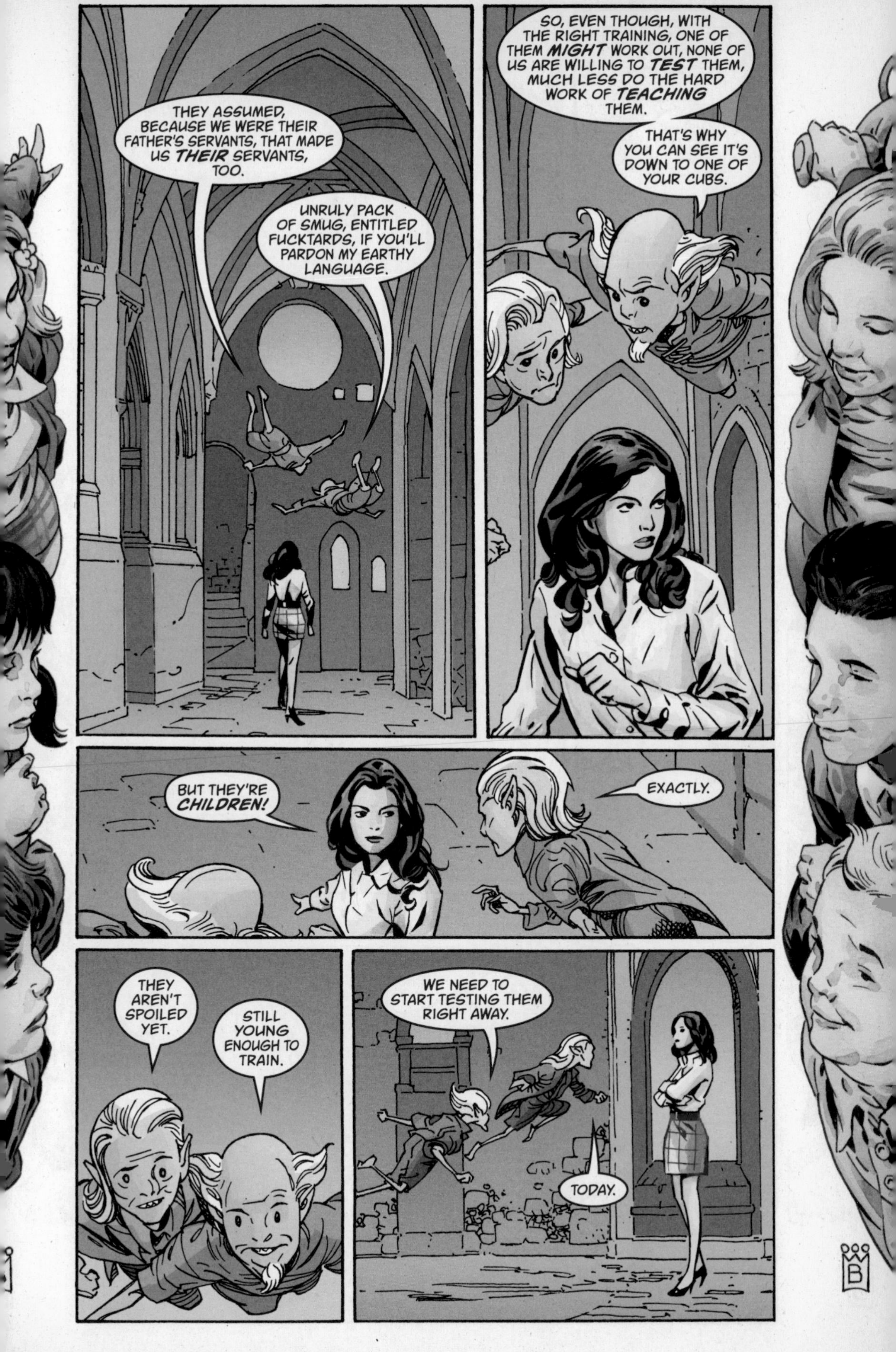
THEY ASSUMED, BECAUSE WE WERE THEIR FATHER'S SERVANTS, THAT MADE US THEIR SERVANTS, TOO.
UNRULY PACK OF SMUG, ENTITLED FUCKTARDS, IF YOU'LL PARDON MY EARTHY LANGUAGE.
SO, EVEN THOUGH, WITH THE RIGHT TRAINING, ONE OF THEM MIGHT WORK OUT, NONE OF US ARE WILLING TO TEST THEM, MUCH LESS DO THE HARD WORK OF TEACHING THEM.
THAT'S WHY YOU CAN SEE IT'S DOWN TO ONE OF YOUR CUBS.
BUT THEY'RE CHILDREN!
EXACTLY.
THEY AREN'T SPOILED YET.
STILL YOUNG ENOUGH TO TRAIN.
WE NEED TO START TESTING THEM RIGHT AWAY.
TODAY.

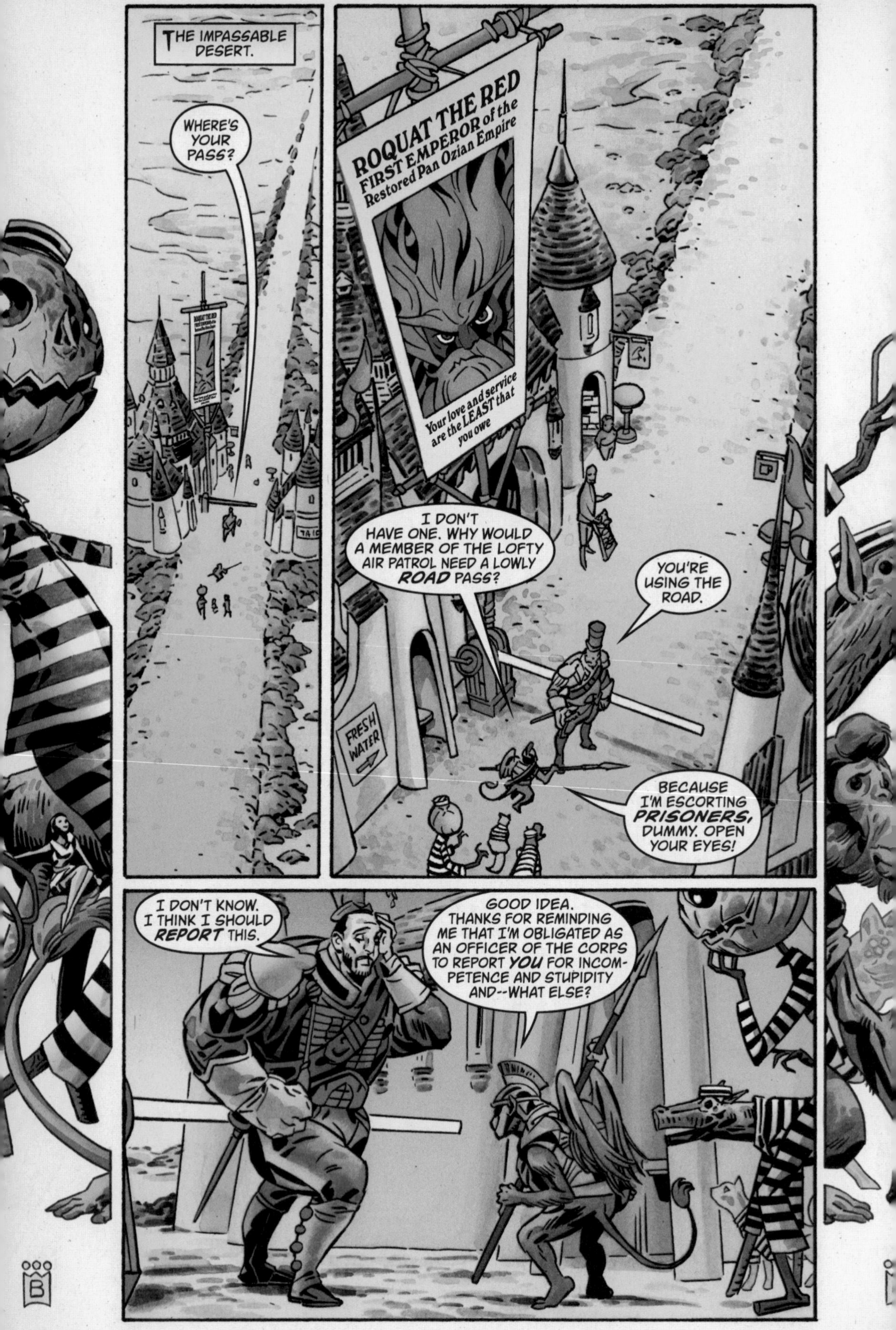
THE IMPASSABLE DESERT.
WHERE'S YOUR PASS?
ROQUAT THE RED
FIRST EMPEROR of the Restored Pan Ozian Empire
Your love and service are the LEAST that you owe
I DON'T HAVE ONE. WHY WOULD A MEMBER OF THE LOFTY AIR PATROL NEED A LOWLY ROAD PASS?
YOU'RE USING THE ROAD.
FRESH WATER
BECAUSE I'M ESCORTING PRISONERS, DUMMY. OPEN YOUR EYES!
I DON'T KNOW. I THINK I SHOULD REPORT THIS.
GOOD IDEA. THANKS FOR REMINDING ME THAT I'M OBLIGATED AS AN OFFICER OF THE CORPS TO REPORT YOU FOR INCOMPETENCE AND STUPIDITY AND--WHAT ELSE?

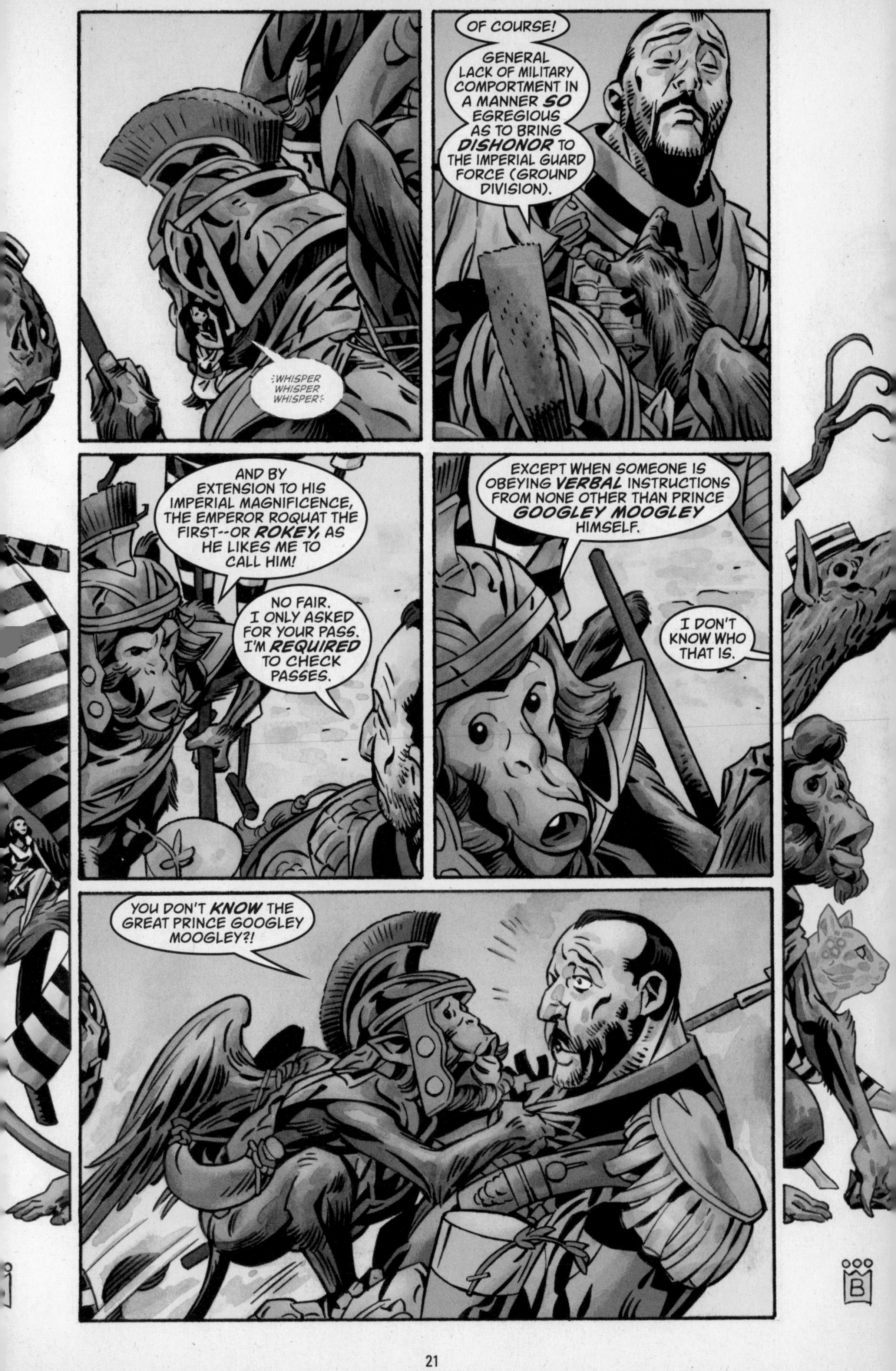
OF COURSE!
GENERAL LACK OF MILITARY COMPORTMENT IN A MANNER SO EGREGIOUS AS TO BRING DISHONOR TO THE IMPERIAL GUARD FORCE (GROUND DIVISION).
WHISPER WHISPER WHISPER
AND BY EXTENSION TO HIS IMPERIAL MAGNIFICENCE, THE EMPEROR ROQUAT THE FIRST--OR ROKEY, AS HE LIKES ME TO CALL HIM!
NO FAIR. I ONLY ASKED FOR YOUR PASS. I'M REQUIRED TO CHECK PASSES.
EXCEPT WHEN SOMEONE IS OBEYING VERBAL INSTRUCTIONS FROM NONE OTHER THAN PRINCE GOOGLEY MOOGLEY HIMSELF.
I DON'T KNOW WHO THAT IS.
YOU DON'T KNOW THE GREAT PRINCE GOOGLEY MOOGLEY?!

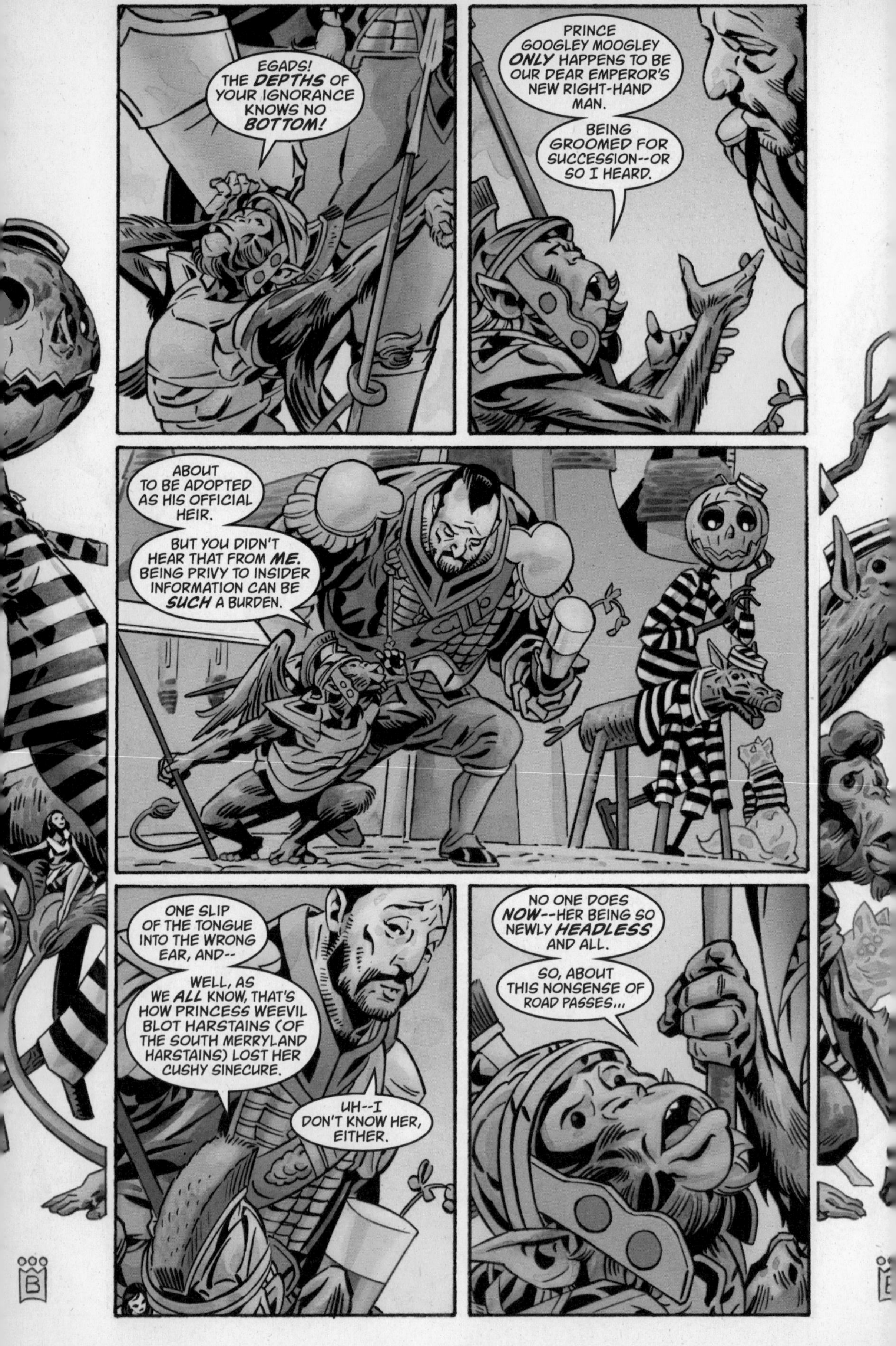
EGADS! THE DEPTHS OF YOUR IGNORANCE KNOWS NO BOTTOM!
PRINCE GOOGLEY MOOGLEY ONLY HAPPENS TO BE OUR DEAR EMPEROR'S NEW RIGHT-HAND MAN.
BEING GROOMED FOR SUCCESSION--OR SO I HEARD.
ABOUT TO BE ADOPTED AS HIS OFFICIAL HEIR.
BUT YOU DIDN'T HEAR THAT FROM ME. BEING PRIVY TO INSIDER INFORMATION CAN BE SUCH A BURDEN.
ONE SLIP OF THE TONGUE INTO THE WRONG EAR, AND--
WELL, AS WE ALL KNOW, THAT'S HOW PRINCESS WEEVIL BLOT HARSTAINS (OF THE SOUTH MERRYLAND HARSTAINS) LOST HER CUSHY SINECURE.
UH--I DON'T KNOW HER, EITHER.
NO ONE DOES NOW--HER BEING SO NEWLY HEADLESS AND ALL.
SO, ABOUT THIS NONSENSE OF ROAD PASSES...

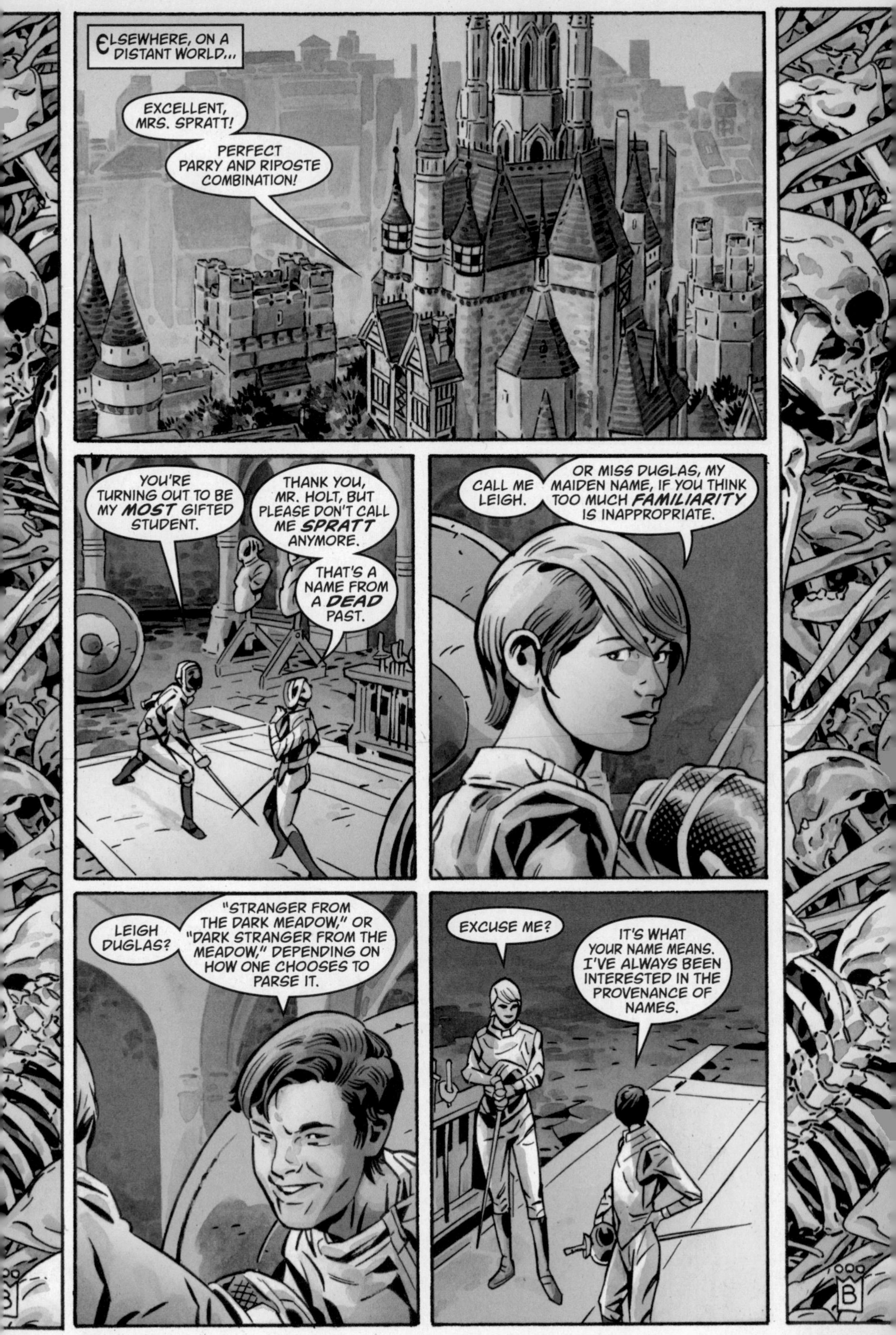
ELSEWHERE, ON A DISTANT WORLD...
EXCELLENT, MRS. SPRATT!
PERFECT PARRY AND RIPOSTE COMBINATION!
YOU'RE TURNING OUT TO BE MY MOST GIFTED STUDENT.
THANK YOU, MR. HOLT, BUT PLEASE DON'T CALL ME SPRATT ANYMORE.
THAT'S A NAME FROM A DEAD PAST.
CALL ME LEIGH.
OR MISS DUGLAS, MY MAIDEN NAME, IF YOU THINK TOO MUCH FAMILIARITY IS INAPPROPRIATE.
LEIGH DUGLAS?
"STRANGER FROM THE DARK MEADOW," OR "DARK STRANGER FROM THE MEADOW," DEPENDING ON HOW ONE CHOOSES TO PARSE IT.
EXCUSE ME?
IT'S WHAT YOUR NAME MEANS. I'VE ALWAYS BEEN INTERESTED IN THE PROVENANCE OF NAMES.

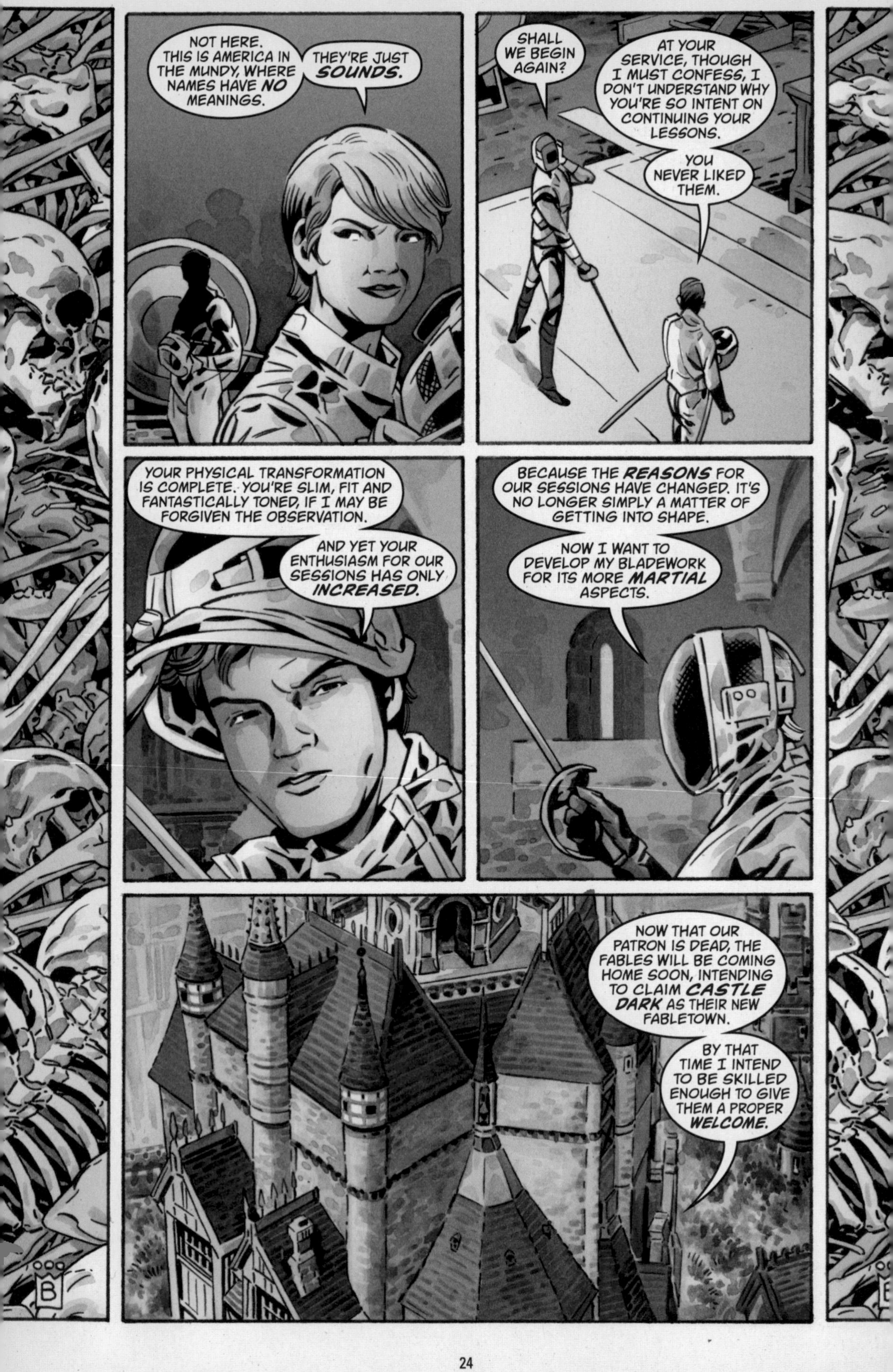
NOT HERE. THIS IS AMERICA IN THE MUNDY, WHERE NAMES HAVE NO MEANINGS.
THEY'RE JUST SOUNDS.
SHALL WE BEGIN AGAIN?
AT YOUR SERVICE, THOUGH I MUST CONFESS, I DON'T UNDERSTAND WHY YOU'RE SO INTENT ON CONTINUING YOUR LESSONS.
YOU NEVER LIKED THEM.
YOUR PHYSICAL TRANSFORMATION IS COMPLETE. YOU'RE SLIM, FIT AND FANTASTICALLY TONED, IF I MAY BE FORGIVEN THE OBSERVATION.
AND YET YOUR ENTHUSIASM FOR OUR SESSIONS HAS ONLY INCREASED.
BECAUSE THE REASONS FOR OUR SESSIONS HAVE CHANGED. IT'S NO LONGER SIMPLY A MATTER OF GETTING INTO SHAPE.
NOW I WANT TO DEVELOP MY BLADEWORK FOR ITS MORE MARTIAL ASPECTS.
NOW THAT OUR PATRON IS DEAD, THE FABLES WILL BE COMING HOME SOON, INTENDING TO CLAIM CASTLE DARK AS THEIR NEW FABLETOWN.
BY THAT TIME I INTEND TO BE SKILLED ENOUGH TO GIVE THEM A PROPER WELCOME.

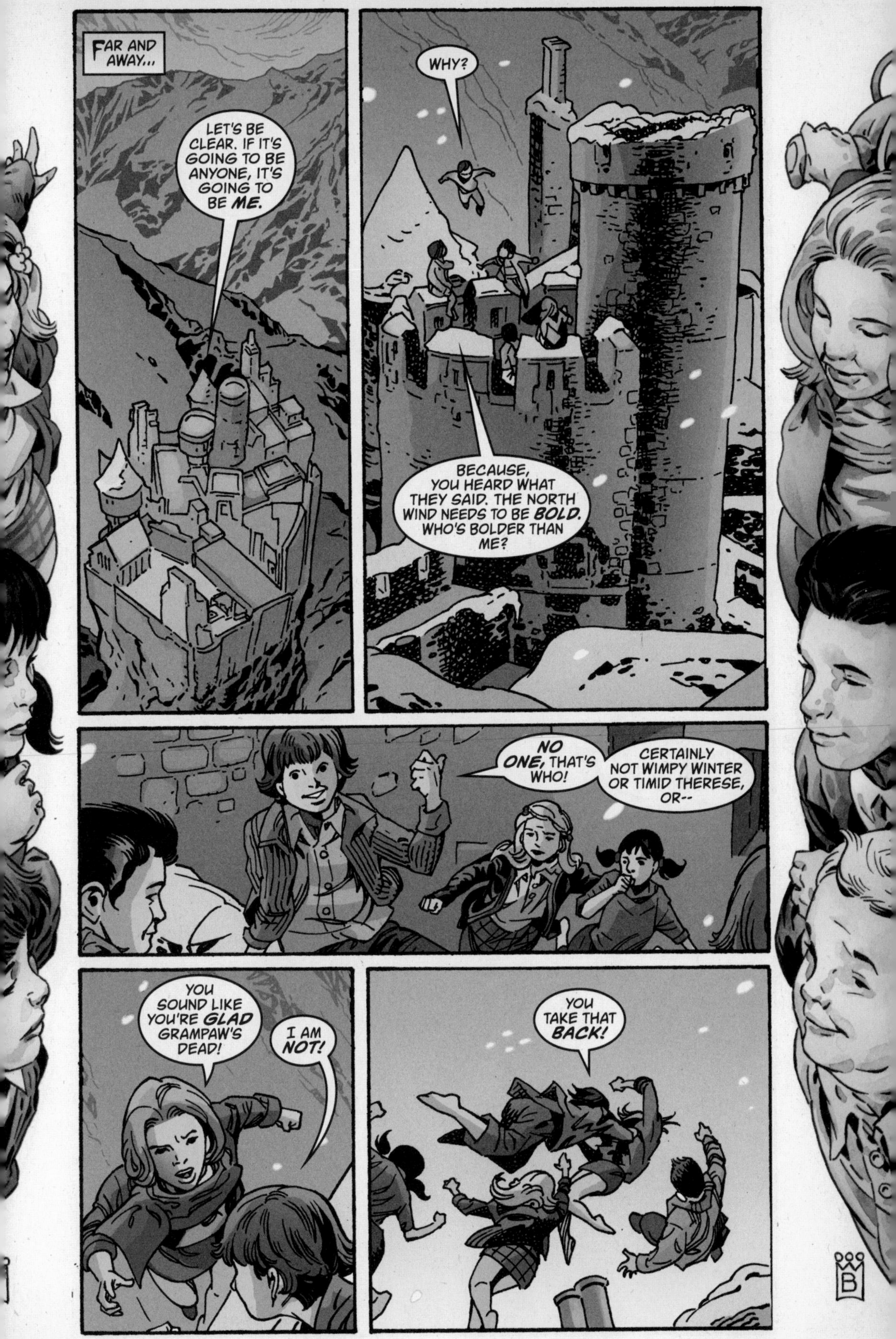
FAR AND AWAY...
LET'S BE CLEAR. IF IT'S GOING TO BE ANYONE, IT'S GOING TO BE ME.
WHY?
BECAUSE, YOU HEARD WHAT THEY SAID. THE NORTH WIND NEEDS TO BE BOLD. WHO'S BOLDER THAN ME?
NO ONE, THAT'S WHO!
CERTAINLY NOT WIMPY WINTER OR TIMID THERESE, OR--
YOU SOUND LIKE YOU'RE GLAD GRAMPAW'S DEAD!
I AM NOT!
YOU TAKE THAT BACK!

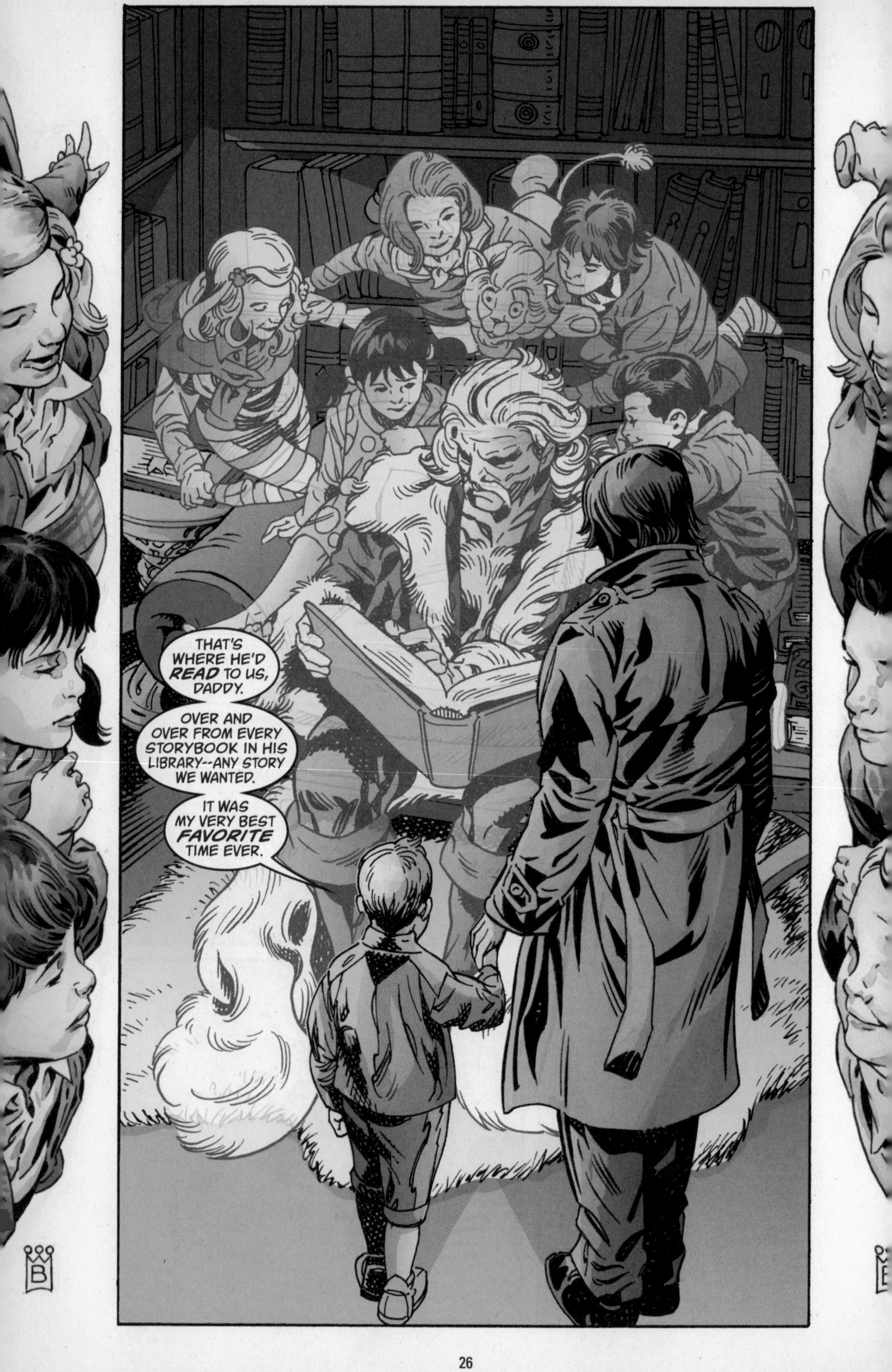
THAT'S WHERE HE'D READ TO US, DADDY.
OVER AND OVER FROM EVERY STORYBOOK IN HIS LIBRARY--ANY STORY WE WANTED.
IT WAS MY VERY BEST FAVORITE TIME EVER.

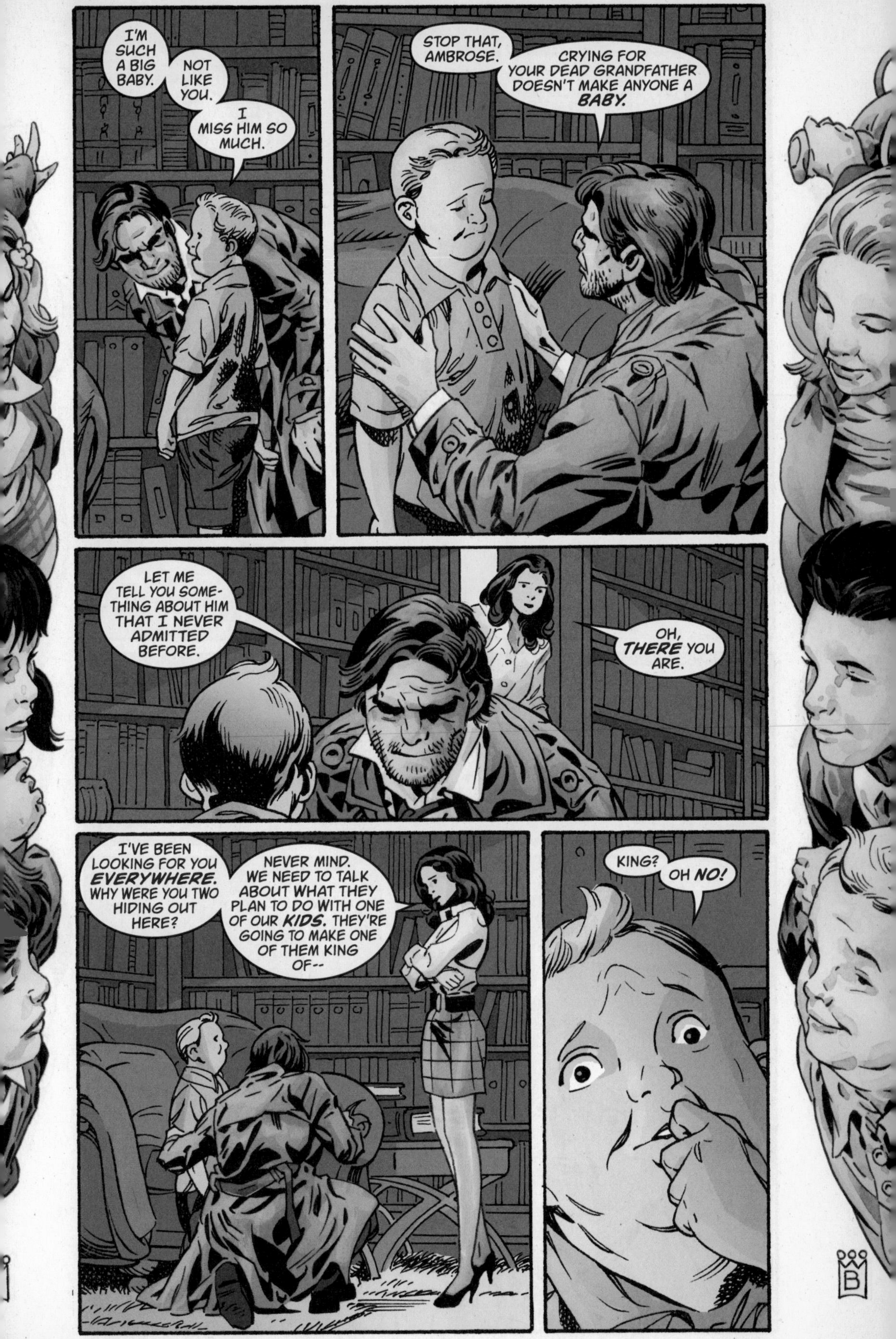
I'M SUCH A BIG BABY.
NOT LIKE YOU.
I MISS HIM SO MUCH.
STOP THAT, AMBROSE.
CRYING FOR YOUR DEAD GRANDFATHER DOESN'T MAKE ANYONE A BABY.
LET ME TELL YOU SOMETHING ABOUT HIM THAT I NEVER ADMITTED BEFORE.
OH, THERE YOU ARE.
I'VE BEEN LOOKING FOR YOU EVERYWHERE. WHY WERE YOU TWO HIDING OUT HERE?
NEVER MIND. WE NEED TO TALK ABOUT WHAT THEY PLAN TO DO WITH ONE OF OUR KIDS. THEY'RE GOING TO MAKE ONE OF THEM KING OF--
KING?
OH NO!

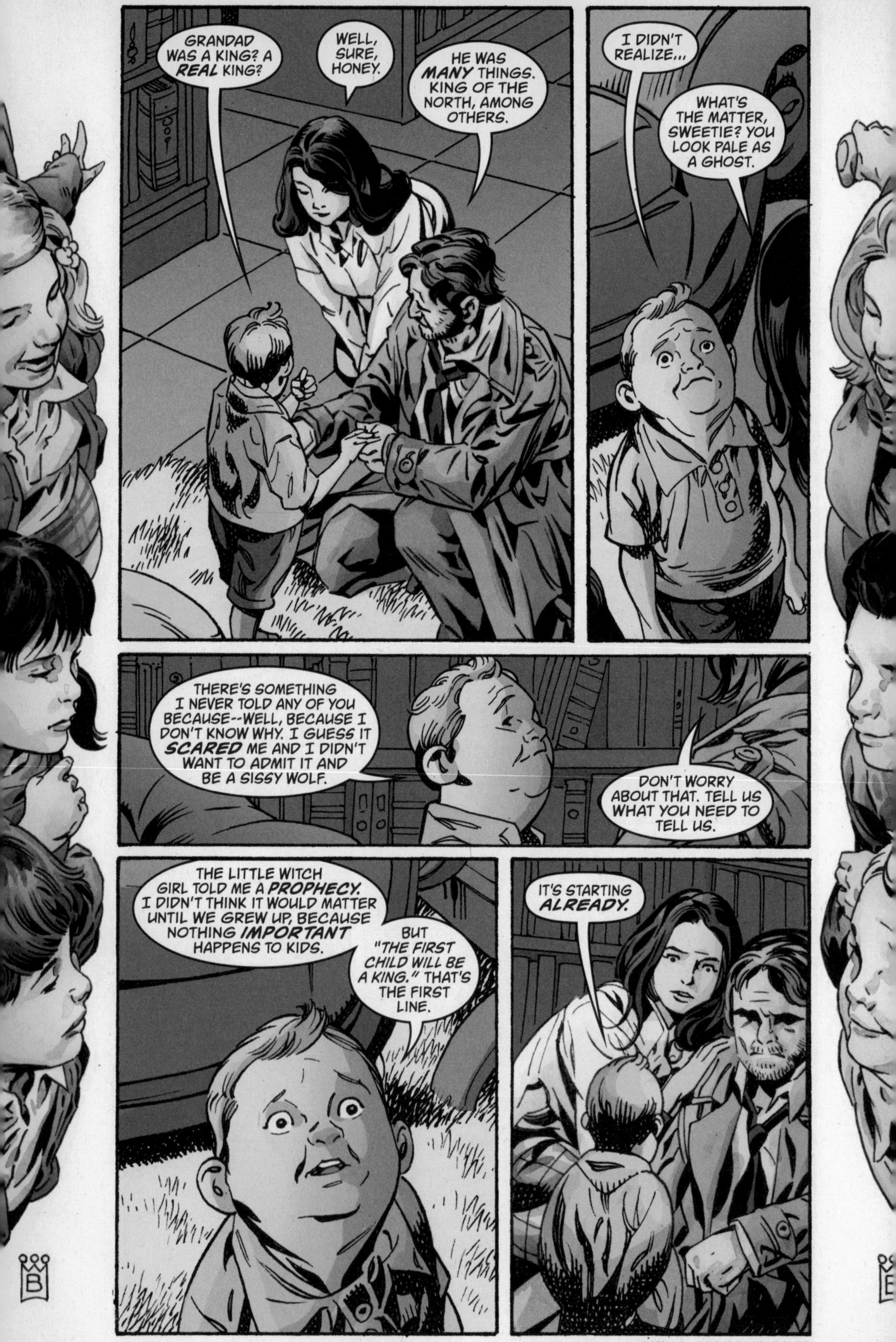
GRANDAD WAS A KING? A REAL KING?
WELL, SURE, HONEY.
HE WAS MANY THINGS. KING OF THE NORTH, AMONG OTHERS.
I DIDN'T REALIZE...
WHAT'S THE MATTER, SWEETIE? YOU LOOK PALE AS A GHOST.
THERE'S SOMETHING I NEVER TOLD ANY OF YOU BECAUSE--WELL, BECAUSE I DON'T KNOW WHY. I GUESS IT SCARED ME AND I DIDN'T WANT TO ADMIT IT AND BE A SISSY WOLF.
DON'T WORRY ABOUT THAT. TELL US WHAT YOU NEED TO TELL US.
THE LITTLE WITCH GIRL TOLD ME A PROPHECY. I DIDN'T THINK IT WOULD MATTER UNTIL WE GREW UP, BECAUSE NOTHING IMPORTANT HAPPENS TO KIDS.
BUT "THE FIRST CHILD WILL BE A KING." THAT'S THE FIRST LINE.
IT'S STARTING ALREADY.

NEXT: TRAINING DAZE

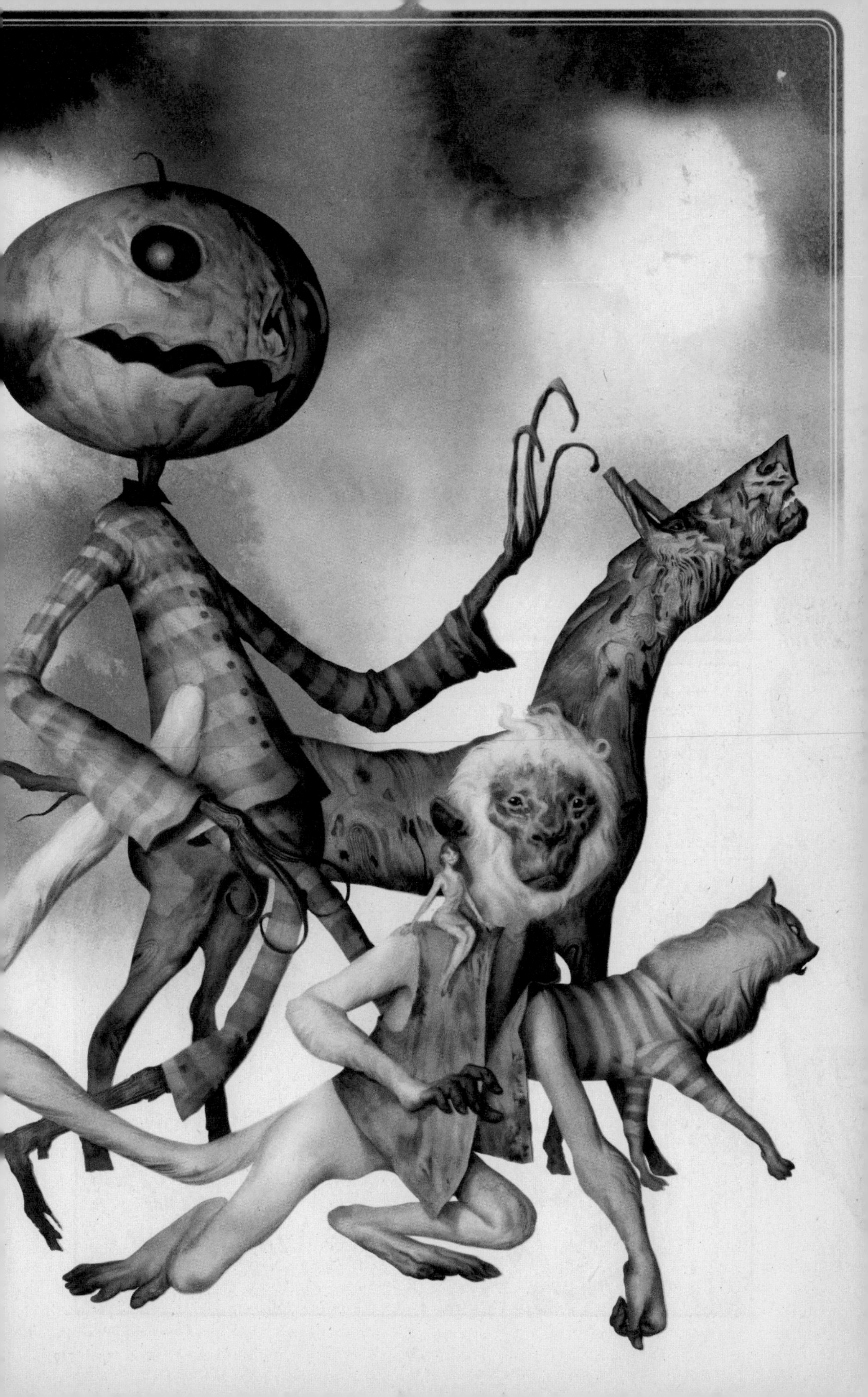

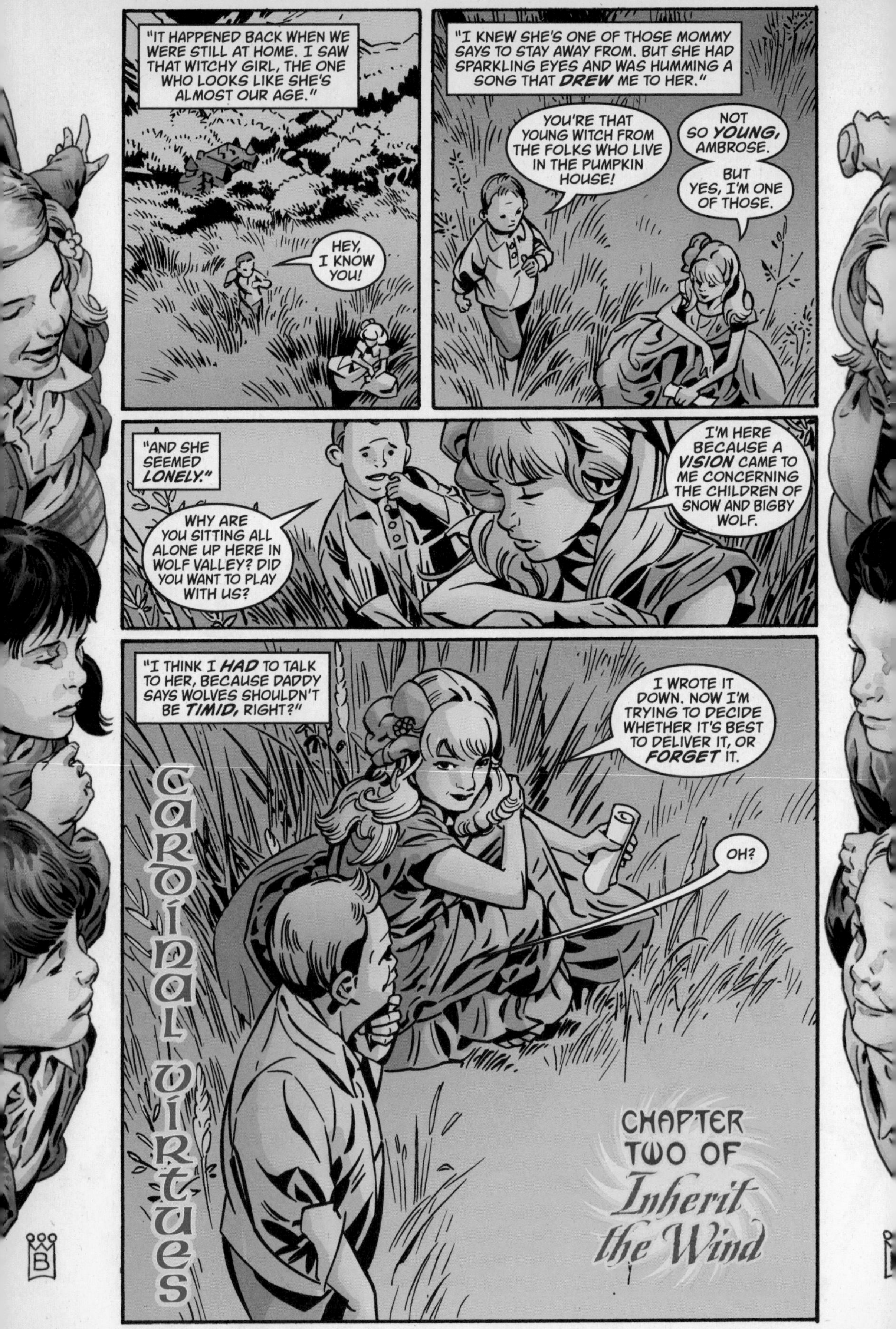
"IT HAPPENED BACK WHEN WE WERE STILL AT HOME. I SAW THAT WITCHY GIRL, THE ONE WHO LOOKS LIKE SHE'S ALMOST OUR AGE."
HEY, I KNOW YOU!
"I KNEW SHE'S ONE OF THOSE MOMMY SAYS TO STAY AWAY FROM. BUT SHE HAD SPARKLING EYES AND WAS HUMMING A SONG THAT DREW ME TO HER."
YOU'RE THAT YOUNG WITCH FROM THE FOLKS WHO LIVE IN THE PUMPKIN HOUSE!
NOT SO YOUNG, AMBROSE.
BUT YES, I'M ONE OF THOSE.
"AND SHE SEEMED LONELY."
WHY ARE YOU SITTING ALL ALONE UP HERE IN WOLF VALLEY? DID YOU WANT TO PLAY WITH US?
I'M HERE BECAUSE A VISION CAME TO ME CONCERNING THE CHILDREN OF SNOW AND BIGBY WOLF.
"I THINK I HAD TO TALK TO HER, BECAUSE DADDY SAYS WOLVES SHOULDN'T BE TIMID, RIGHT?"
I WROTE IT DOWN. NOW I'M TRYING TO DECIDE WHETHER IT'S BEST TO DELIVER IT, OR FORGET IT.
OH?
CARDINAL VIRTUES
CHAPTER TWO OF
Inherit the Wind

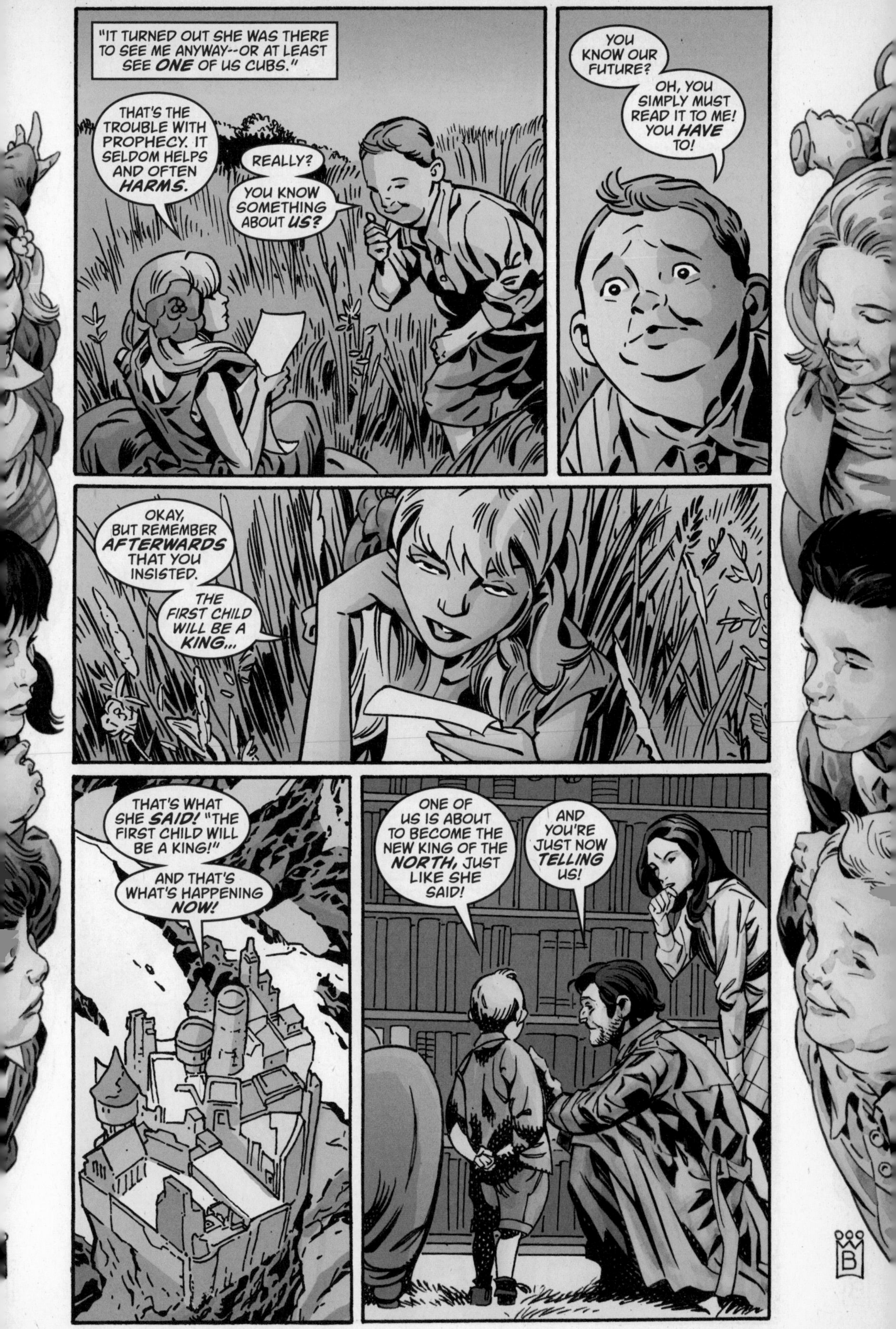
"IT TURNED OUT SHE WAS THERE TO SEE ME ANYWAY--OR AT LEAST SEE ONE OF US CUBS."
THAT'S THE TROUBLE WITH PROPHECY. IT SELDOM HELPS AND OFTEN HARMS.
REALLY?
YOU KNOW SOMETHING ABOUT US?
YOU KNOW OUR FUTURE?
OH, YOU SIMPLY MUST READ IT TO ME! YOU HAVE TO!
OKAY, BUT REMEMBER AFTERWARDS THAT YOU INSISTED.
THE FIRST CHILD WILL BE A KING...
THAT'S WHAT SHE SAID! "THE FIRST CHILD WILL BE A KING!"
AND THAT'S WHAT'S HAPPENING NOW!
ONE OF US IS ABOUT TO BECOME THE NEW KING OF THE NORTH, JUST LIKE SHE SAID!
AND YOU'RE JUST NOW TELLING US!

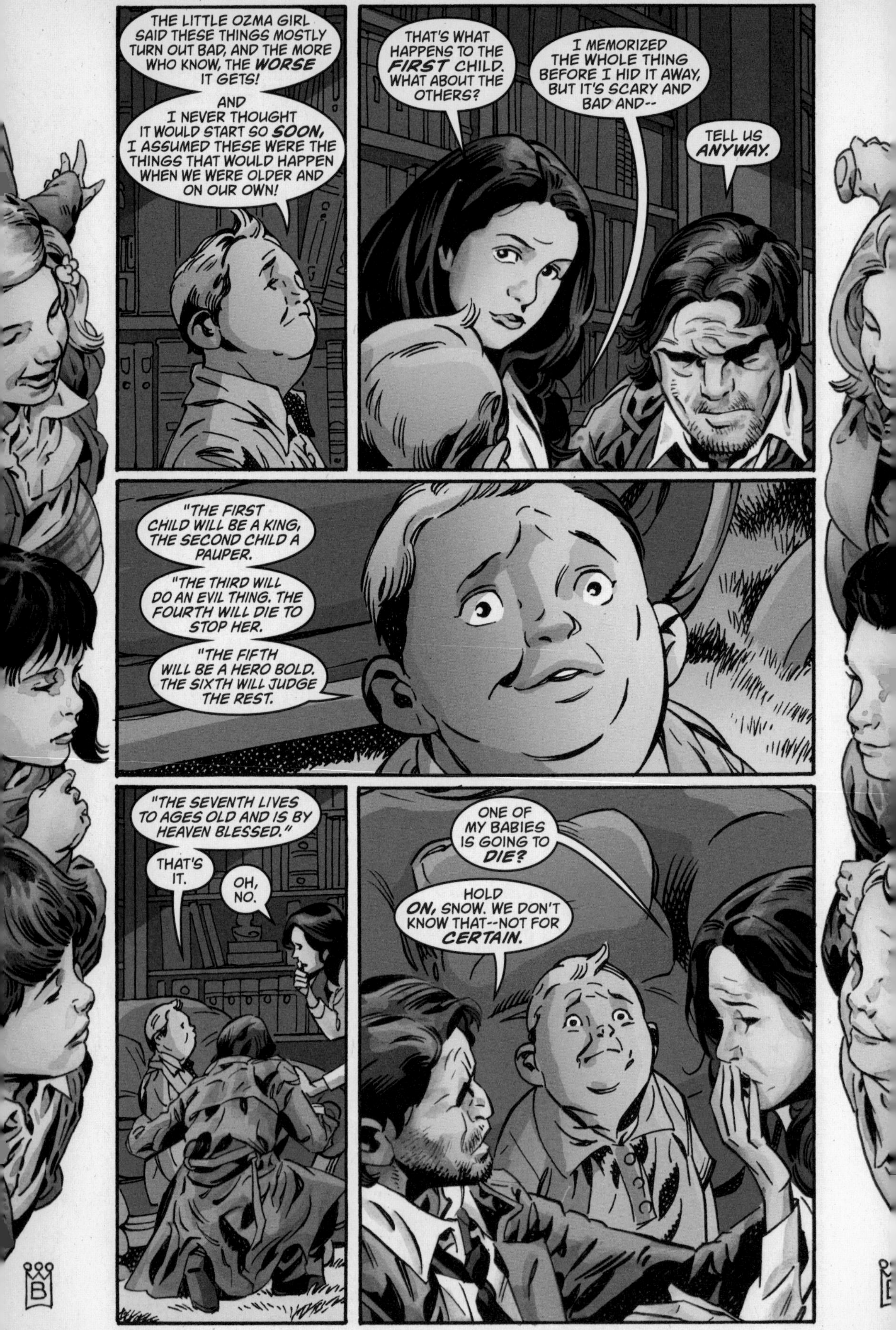
THE LITTLE OZMA GIRL SAID THESE THINGS MOSTLY TURN OUT BAD, AND THE MORE WHO KNOW, THE WORSE IT GETS!
AND I NEVER THOUGHT IT WOULD START SO SOON, I ASSUMED THESE WERE THE THINGS THAT WOULD HAPPEN WHEN WE WERE OLDER AND ON OUR OWN!
THAT'S WHAT HAPPENS TO THE FIRST CHILD. WHAT ABOUT THE OTHERS?
I MEMORIZED THE WHOLE THING BEFORE I HID IT AWAY, BUT IT'S SCARY AND BAD AND--
TELL US ANYWAY.
"THE FIRST CHILD WILL BE A KING, THE SECOND CHILD A PAUPER.
"THE THIRD WILL DO AN EVIL THING. THE FOURTH WILL DIE TO STOP HER.
"THE FIFTH WILL BE A HERO BOLD. THE SIXTH WILL JUDGE THE REST.
"THE SEVENTH LIVES TO AGES OLD AND IS BY HEAVEN BLESSED."
THAT'S IT.
OH, NO.
ONE OF MY BABIES IS GOING TO DIE?
HOLD ON, SNOW. WE DON'T KNOW THAT--NOT FOR CERTAIN.

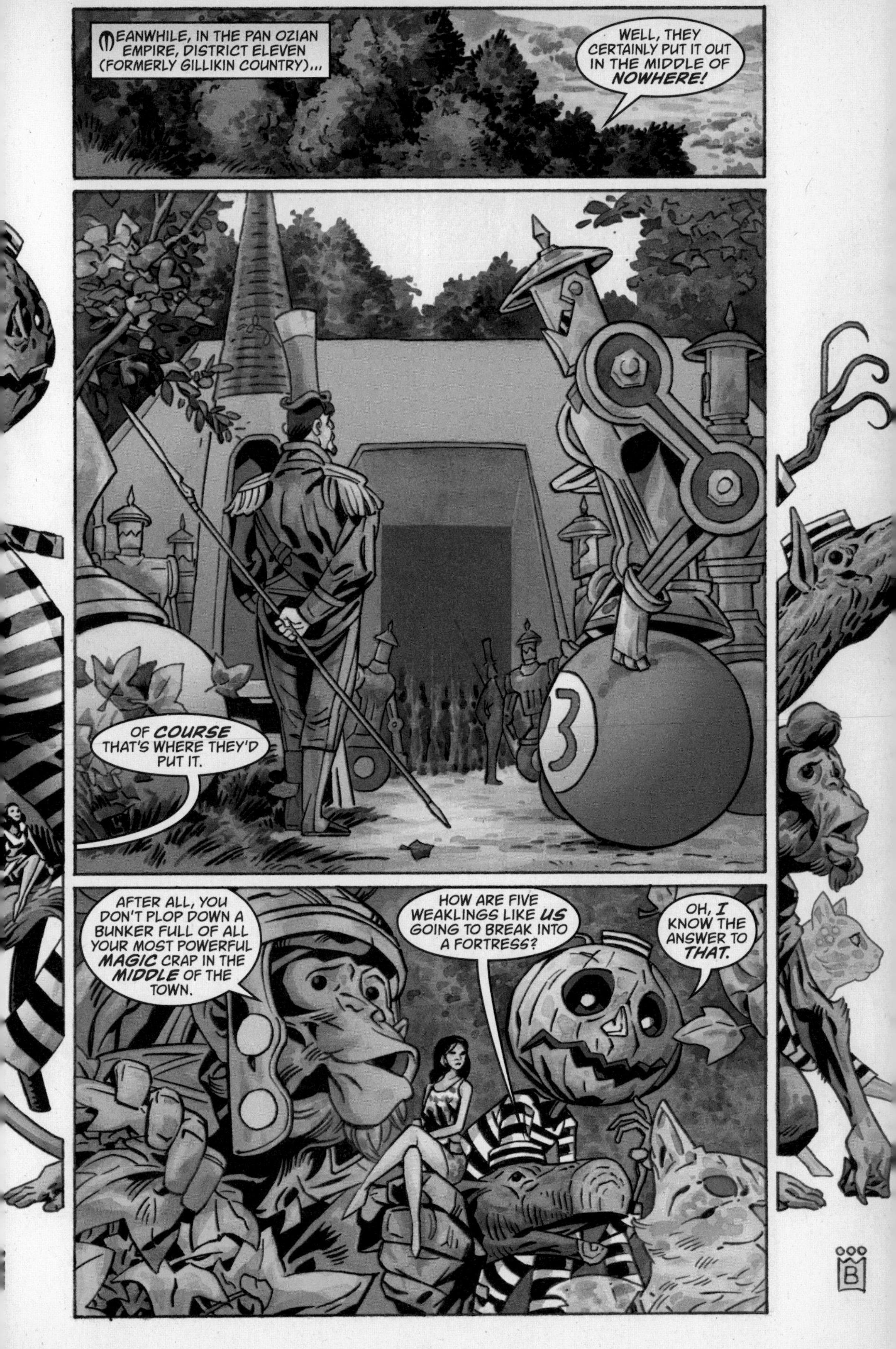
MEANWHILE, IN THE PAN OZIAN EMPIRE, DISTRICT ELEVEN (FORMERLY GILLIKIN COUNTRY)...
WELL, THEY CERTAINLY PUT IT OUT IN THE MIDDLE OF NOWHERE!
OF COURSE THAT'S WHERE THEY'D PUT IT.
AFTER ALL, YOU DON'T PLOP DOWN A BUNKER FULL OF ALL YOUR MOST POWERFUL MAGIC CRAP IN THE MIDDLE OF THE TOWN.
HOW ARE FIVE WEAKLINGS LIKE US GOING TO BREAK INTO A FORTRESS?
OH, I KNOW THE ANSWER TO THAT.

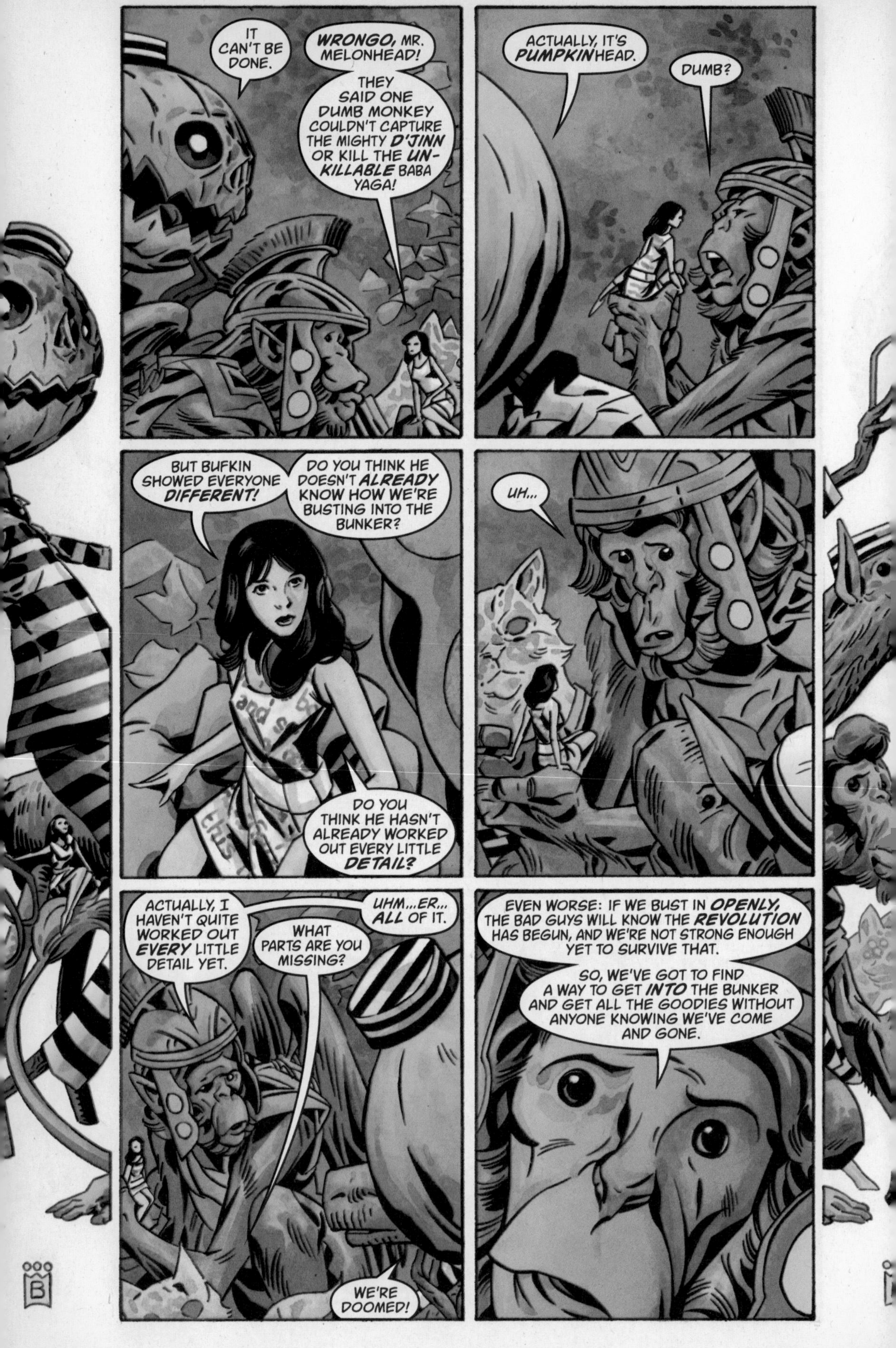
IT CAN'T BE DONE.
WRONGO, MR. MELONHEAD!
THEY SAID ONE DUMB MONKEY COULDN'T CAPTURE THE MIGHTY D'JINN OR KILL THE UN-KILLABLE BABA YAGA!
ACTUALLY, IT'S PUMPKINHEAD.
DUMB?
BUT BUFKIN SHOWED EVERYONE DIFFERENT!
DO YOU THINK HE DOESN'T ALREADY KNOW HOW WE'RE BUSTING INTO THE BUNKER?
DO YOU THINK HE HASN'T ALREADY WORKED OUT EVERY LITTLE DETAIL?
UH...
ACTUALLY, I HAVEN'T QUITE WORKED OUT EVERY LITTLE DETAIL YET.
UHM...ER... ALL OF IT.
WHAT PARTS ARE YOU MISSING?
WE'RE DOOMED!
EVEN WORSE: IF WE BUST IN OPENLY, THE BAD GUYS WILL KNOW THE REVOLUTION HAS BEGUN, AND WE'RE NOT STRONG ENOUGH YET TO SURVIVE THAT.
SO, WE'VE GOT TO FIND A WAY TO GET INTO THE BUNKER AND GET ALL THE GOODIES WITHOUT ANYONE KNOWING WE'VE COME AND GONE.

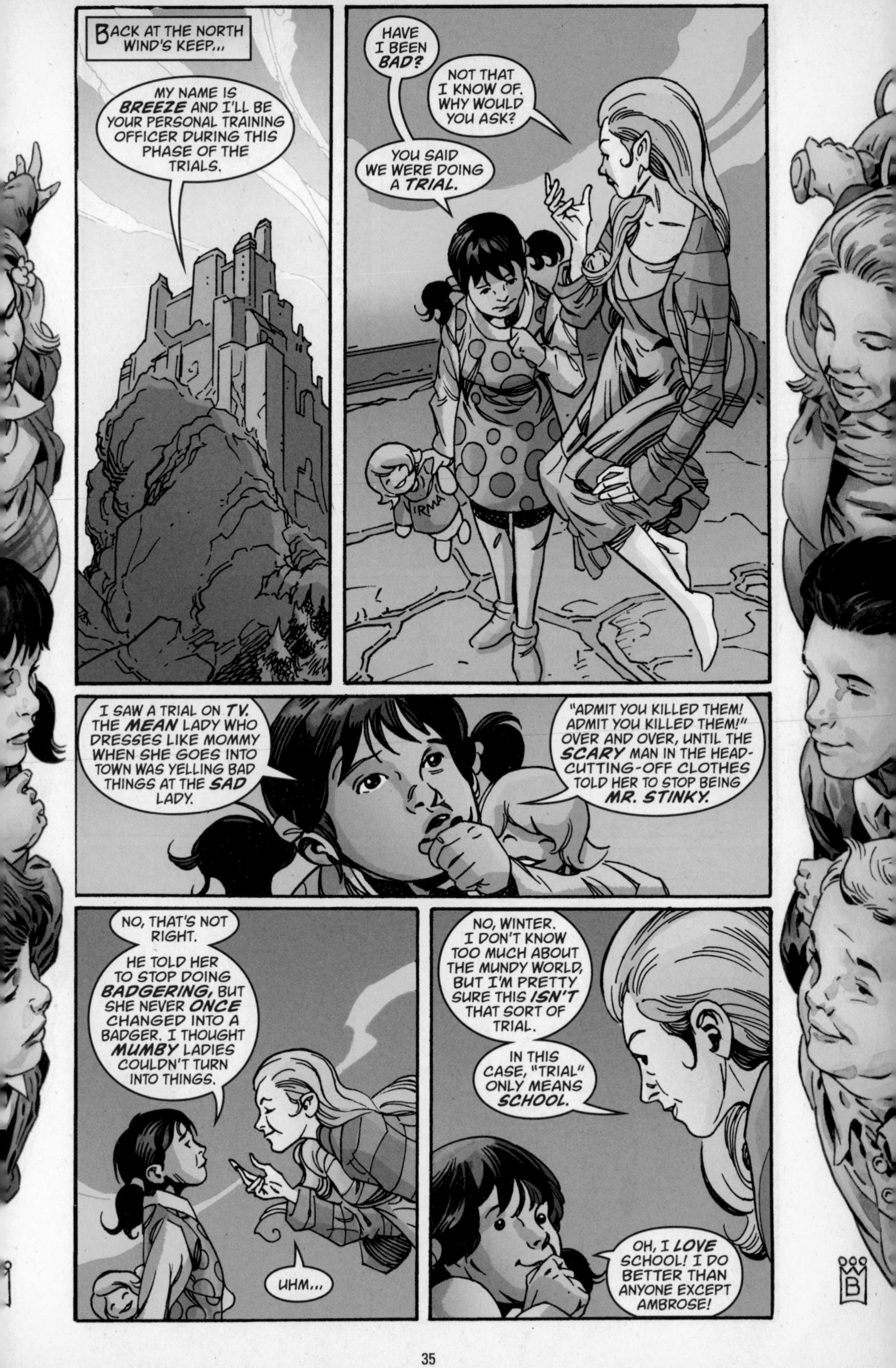
BACK AT THE NORTH WIND'S KEEP...
MY NAME IS BREEZE AND I'LL BE YOUR PERSONAL TRAINING OFFICER DURING THIS PHASE OF THE TRIALS.
HAVE I BEEN BAD?
NOT THAT I KNOW OF. WHY WOULD YOU ASK?
YOU SAID WE WERE DOING A TRIAL.
IRMA
I SAW A TRIAL ON TV. THE MEAN LADY WHO DRESSES LIKE MOMMY WHEN SHE GOES INTO TOWN WAS YELLING BAD THINGS AT THE SAD LADY.
"ADMIT YOU KILLED THEM! ADMIT YOU KILLED THEM!" OVER AND OVER, UNTIL THE SCARY MAN IN THE HEAD-CUTTING-OFF CLOTHES TOLD HER TO STOP BEING MR. STINKY.
NO, THAT'S NOT RIGHT.
HE TOLD HER TO STOP DOING BADGERING, BUT SHE NEVER ONCE CHANGED INTO A BADGER. I THOUGHT MUMBY LADIES COULDN'T TURN INTO THINGS.
UHM...
NO, WINTER. I DON'T KNOW TOO MUCH ABOUT THE MUNDY WORLD, BUT I'M PRETTY SURE THIS ISN'T THAT SORT OF TRIAL.
IN THIS CASE, "TRIAL" ONLY MEANS SCHOOL.
OH, I LOVE SCHOOL! I DO BETTER THAN ANYONE EXCEPT AMBROSE!

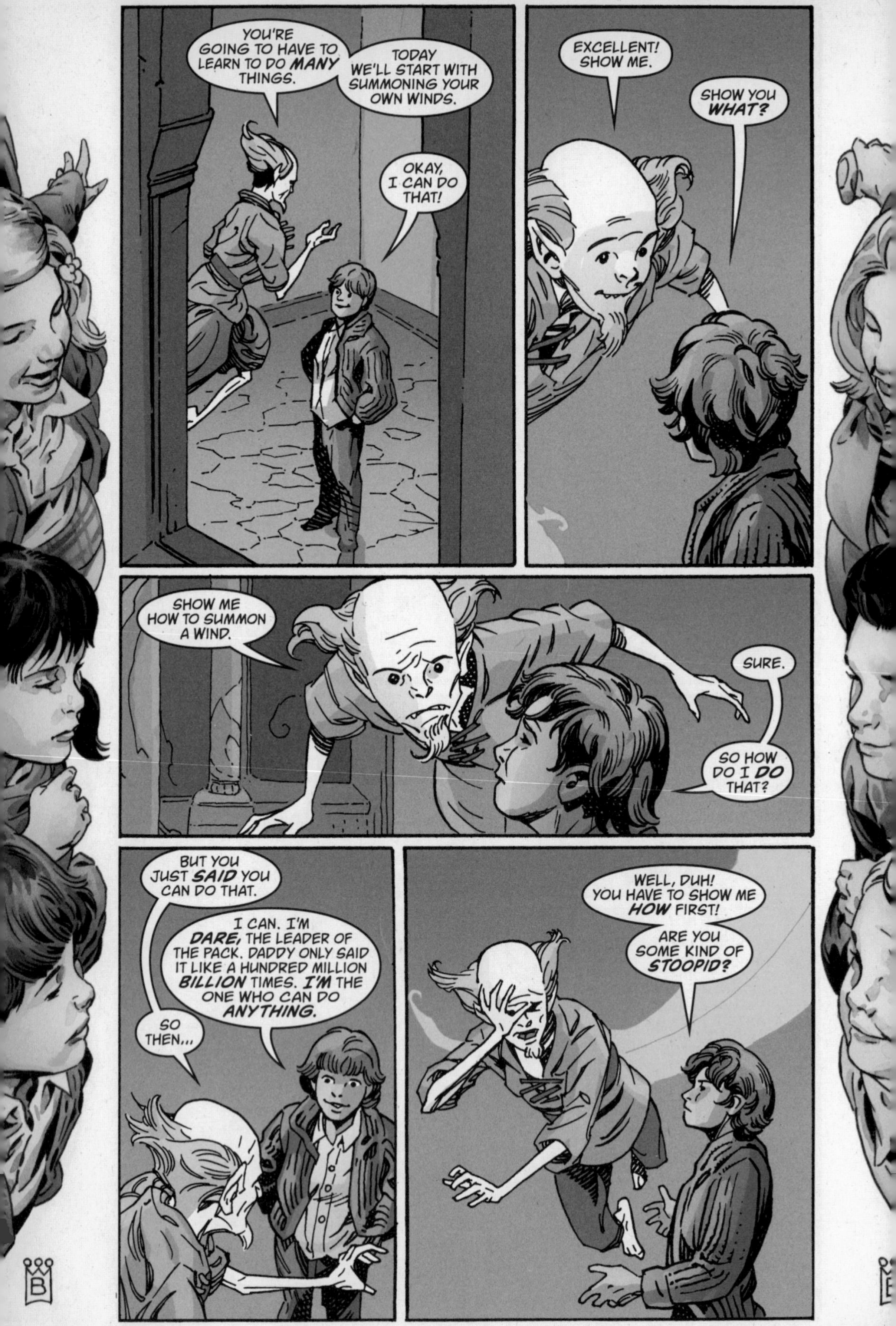
YOU'RE GOING TO HAVE TO LEARN TO DO MANY THINGS.
TODAY WE'LL START WITH SUMMONING YOUR OWN WINDS.
OKAY, I CAN DO THAT!
EXCELLENT! SHOW ME.
SHOW YOU WHAT?
SHOW ME HOW TO SUMMON A WIND.
SURE.
SO HOW DO I DO THAT?
BUT YOU JUST SAID YOU CAN DO THAT.
I CAN. I'M DARE, THE LEADER OF THE PACK. DADDY ONLY SAID IT LIKE A HUNDRED MILLION BILLION TIMES. I'M THE ONE WHO CAN DO ANYTHING.
SO THEN...
WELL, DUH! YOU HAVE TO SHOW ME HOW FIRST!
ARE YOU SOME KIND OF STOOPID?

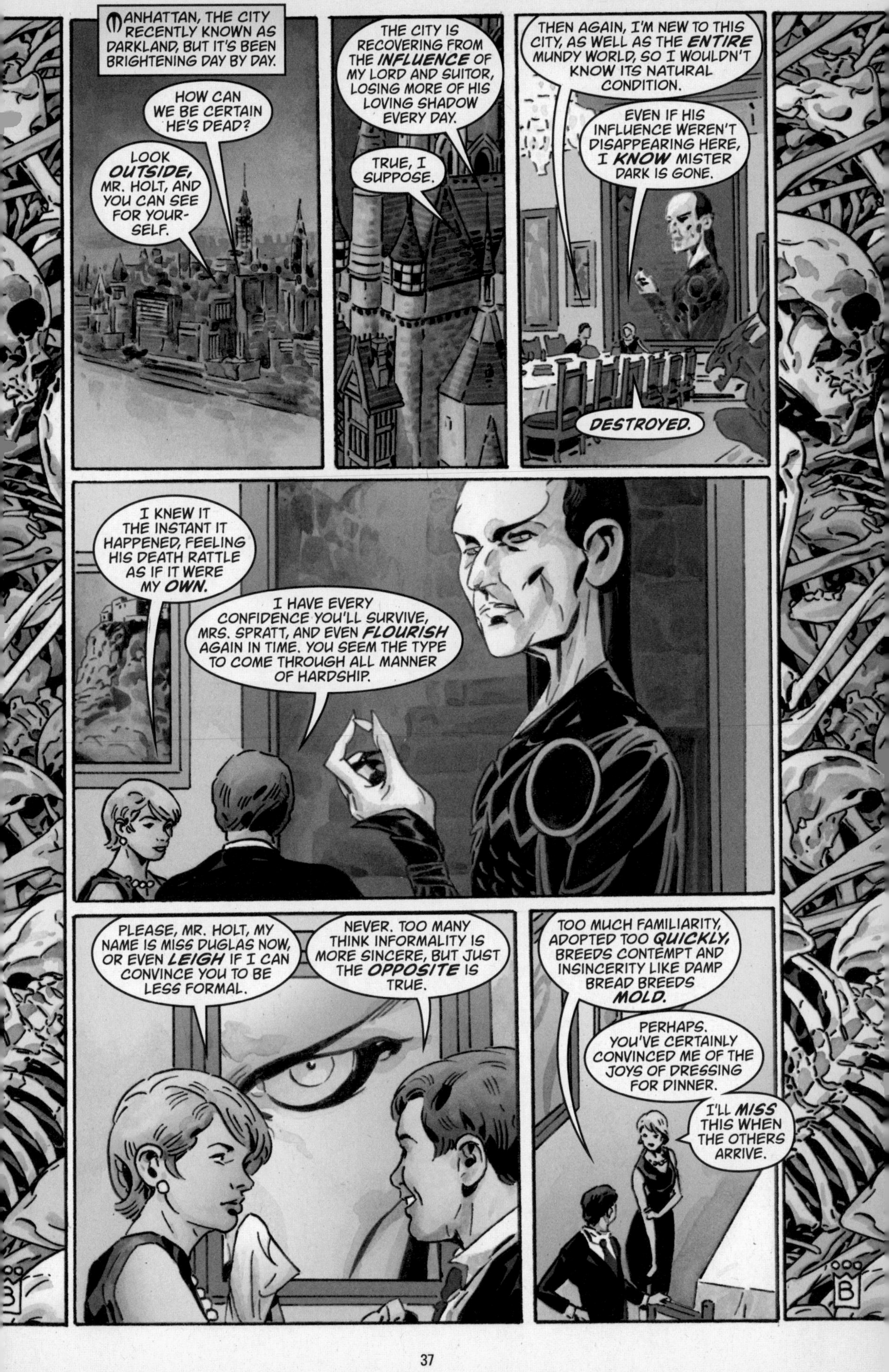
MANHATTAN, THE CITY RECENTLY KNOWN AS DARKLAND, BUT IT'S BEEN BRIGHTENING DAY BY DAY.
HOW CAN WE BE CERTAIN HE'S DEAD?
LOOK OUTSIDE, MR. HOLT, AND YOU CAN SEE FOR YOURSELF.
THE CITY IS RECOVERING FROM THE INFLUENCE OF MY LORD AND SUITOR, LOSING MORE OF HIS LOVING SHADOW EVERY DAY.
TRUE, I SUPPOSE.
THEN AGAIN, I'M NEW TO THIS CITY, AS WELL AS THE ENTIRE MUNDY WORLD, SO I WOULDN'T KNOW ITS NATURAL CONDITION.
EVEN IF HIS INFLUENCE WEREN'T DISAPPEARING HERE, I KNOW MISTER DARK IS GONE.
DESTROYED.
I KNEW IT THE INSTANT IT HAPPENED, FEELING HIS DEATH RATTLE AS IF IT WERE MY OWN.
I HAVE EVERY CONFIDENCE YOU'LL SURVIVE, MRS. SPRATT, AND EVEN FLOURISH AGAIN IN TIME. YOU SEEM THE TYPE TO COME THROUGH ALL MANNER OF HARDSHIP.
PLEASE, MR. HOLT, MY NAME IS MISS DUGLAS NOW, OR EVEN LEIGH IF I CAN CONVINCE YOU TO BE LESS FORMAL.
NEVER. TOO MANY THINK INFORMALITY IS MORE SINCERE, BUT JUST THE OPPOSITE IS TRUE.
TOO MUCH FAMILIARITY, ADOPTED TOO QUICKLY, BREEDS CONTEMPT AND INSINCERITY LIKE DAMP BREAD BREEDS MOLD.
PERHAPS. YOU'VE CERTAINLY CONVINCED ME OF THE JOYS OF DRESSING FOR DINNER.
I'LL MISS THIS WHEN THE OTHERS ARRIVE.

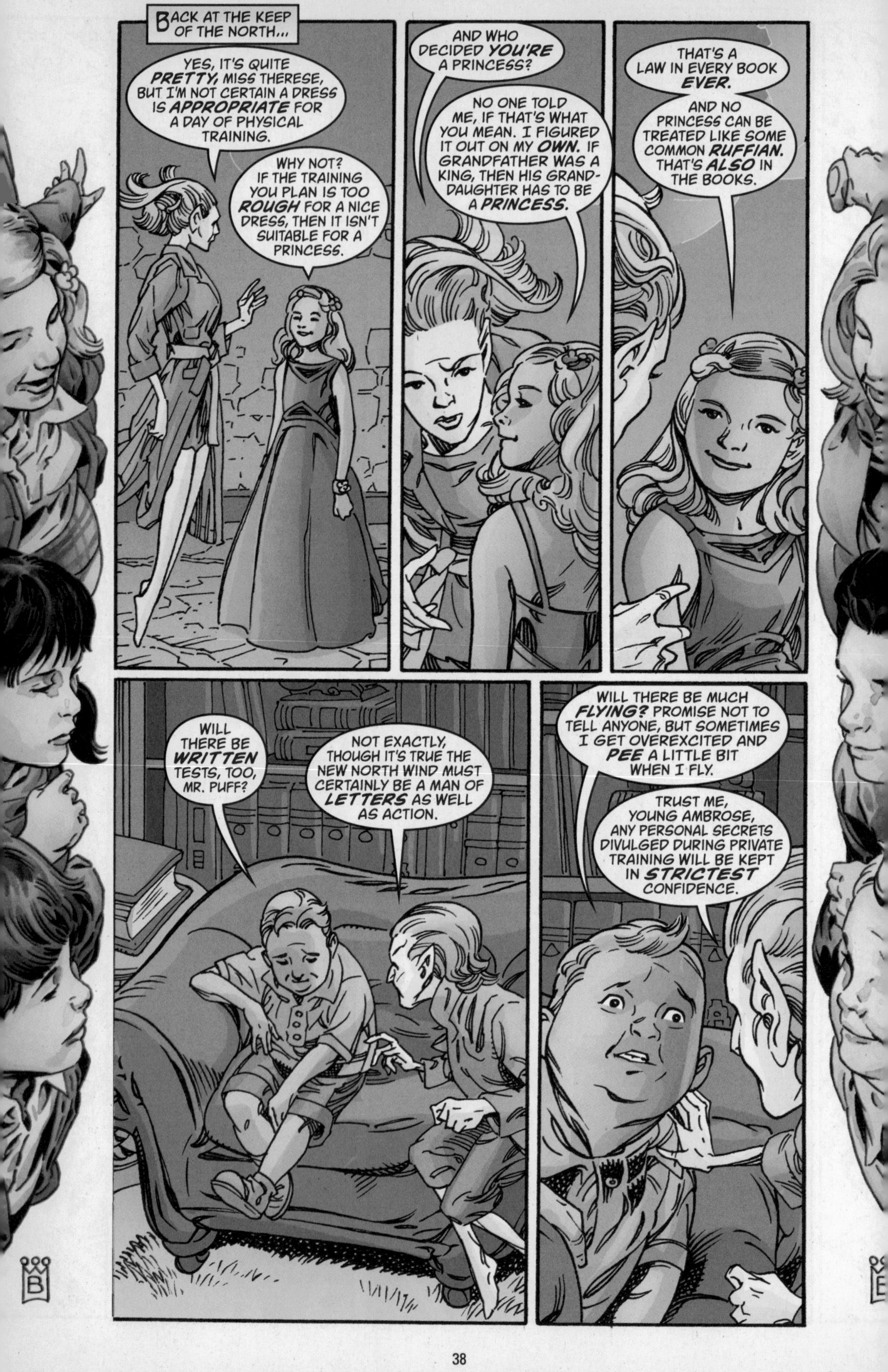

BACK AT THE KEEP OF THE NORTH...
YES, IT'S QUITE PRETTY, MISS THERESE, BUT I'M NOT CERTAIN A DRESS IS APPROPRIATE FOR A DAY OF PHYSICAL TRAINING.
WHY NOT? IF THE TRAINING YOU PLAN IS TOO ROUGH FOR A NICE DRESS, THEN IT ISN'T SUITABLE FOR A PRINCESS.
AND WHO DECIDED YOU'RE A PRINCESS?
NO ONE TOLD ME, IF THAT'S WHAT YOU MEAN. I FIGURED IT OUT ON MY OWN. IF GRANDFATHER WAS A KING, THEN HIS GRAND-DAUGHTER HAS TO BE A PRINCESS.
THAT'S A LAW IN EVERY BOOK EVER.
AND NO PRINCESS CAN BE TREATED LIKE SOME COMMON RUFFIAN. THAT'S ALSO IN THE BOOKS.
WILL THERE BE WRITTEN TESTS, TOO, MR. PUFF?
NOT EXACTLY, THOUGH IT'S TRUE THE NEW NORTH WIND MUST CERTAINLY BE A MAN OF LETTERS AS WELL AS ACTION.
WILL THERE BE MUCH FLYING? PROMISE NOT TO TELL ANYONE, BUT SOMETIMES I GET OVEREXCITED AND PEE A LITTLE BIT WHEN I FLY.
TRUST ME, YOUNG AMBROSE, ANY PERSONAL SECRETS DIVULGED DURING PRIVATE TRAINING WILL BE KEPT IN STRICTEST CONFIDENCE.

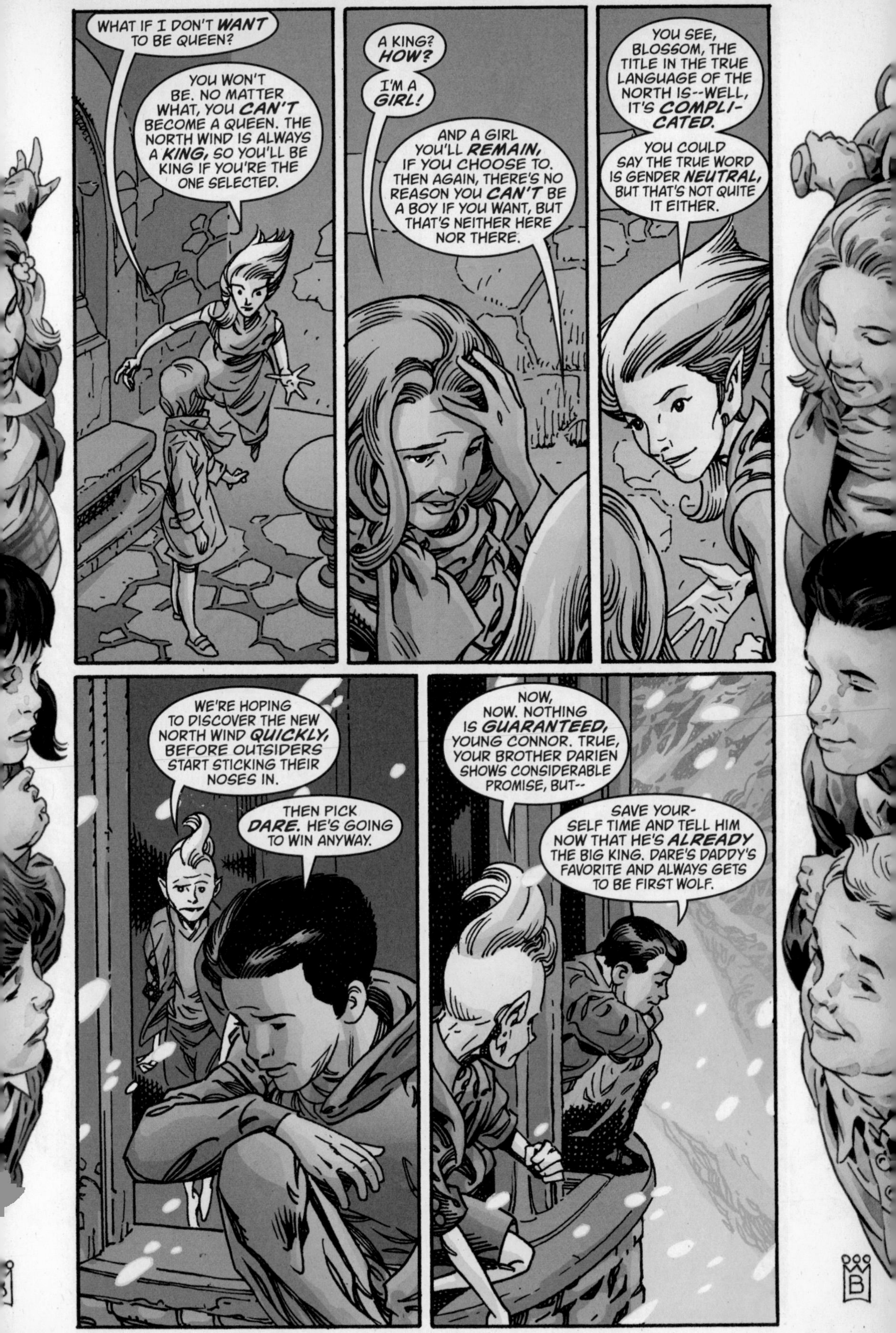
WHAT IF I DON'T WANT TO BE QUEEN?
YOU WON'T BE. NO MATTER WHAT, YOU CAN'T BECOME A QUEEN. THE NORTH WIND IS ALWAYS A KING, SO YOU'LL BE KING IF YOU'RE THE ONE SELECTED.
A KING? HOW?
I'M A GIRL!
AND A GIRL YOU'LL REMAIN, IF YOU CHOOSE TO. THEN AGAIN, THERE'S NO REASON YOU CAN'T BE A BOY IF YOU WANT, BUT THAT'S NEITHER HERE NOR THERE.
YOU SEE, BLOSSOM, THE TITLE IN THE TRUE LANGUAGE OF THE NORTH IS--WELL, IT'S COMPLICATED.
YOU COULD SAY THE TRUE WORD IS GENDER NEUTRAL, BUT THAT'S NOT QUITE IT EITHER.
WE'RE HOPING TO DISCOVER THE NEW NORTH WIND QUICKLY, BEFORE OUTSIDERS START STICKING THEIR NOSES IN.
THEN PICK DARE. HE'S GOING TO WIN ANYWAY.
NOW, NOW. NOTHING IS GUARANTEED, YOUNG CONNOR. TRUE, YOUR BROTHER DARIEN SHOWS CONSIDERABLE PROMISE, BUT--
SAVE YOURSELF TIME AND TELL HIM NOW THAT HE'S ALREADY THE BIG KING. DARE'S DADDY'S FAVORITE AND ALWAYS GETS TO BE FIRST WOLF.

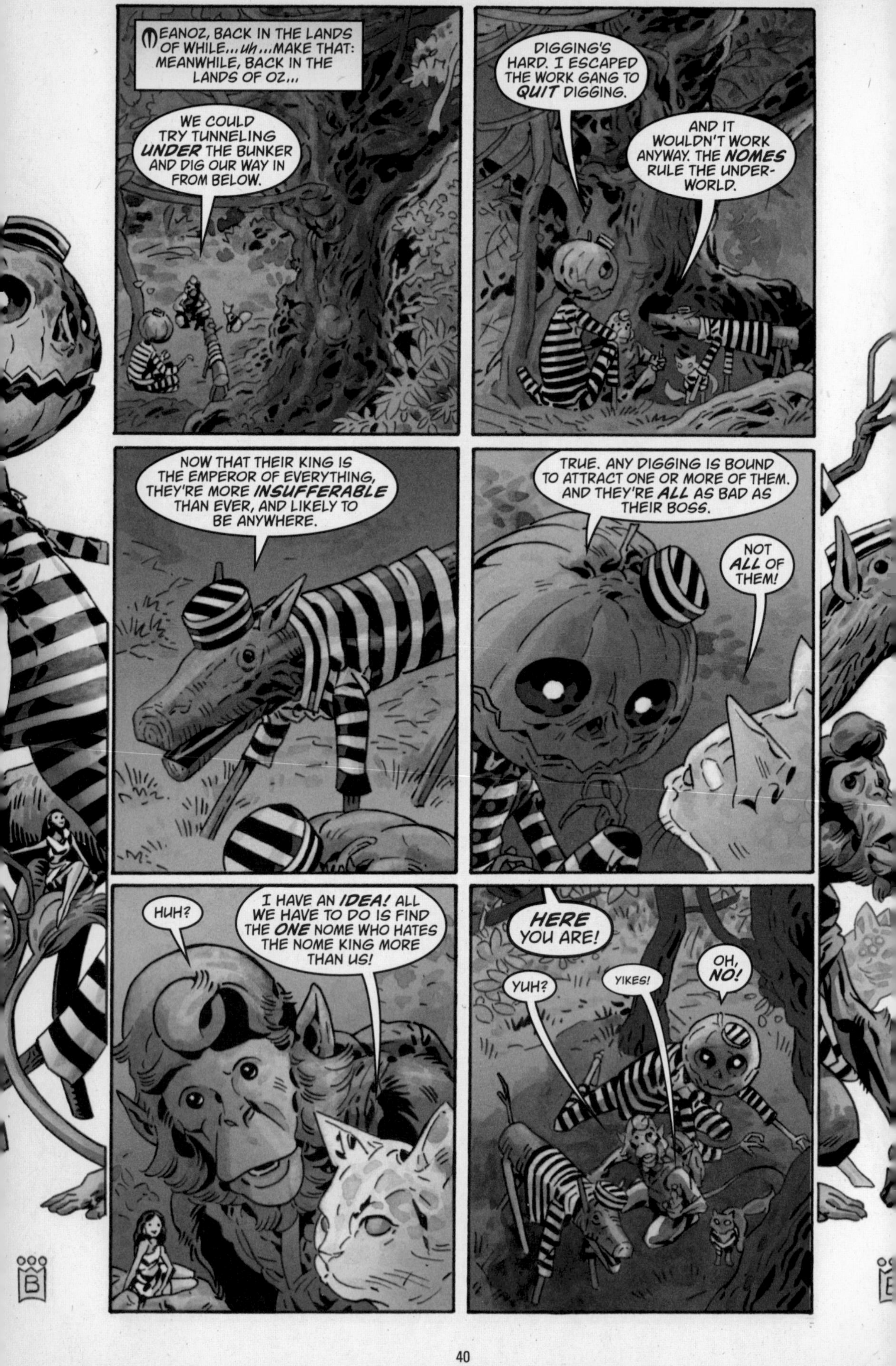
MEANOZ, BACK IN THE LANDS OF WHILE... uh ...MAKE THAT: MEANWHILE, BACK IN THE LANDS OF OZ...
WE COULD TRY TUNNELING UNDER THE BUNKER AND DIG OUR WAY IN FROM BELOW.
DIGGING'S HARD. I ESCAPED THE WORK GANG TO QUIT DIGGING.
AND IT WOULDN'T WORK ANYWAY. THE NOMES RULE THE UNDER-WORLD.
NOW THAT THEIR KING IS THE EMPEROR OF EVERYTHING, THEY'RE MORE INSUFFERABLE THAN EVER, AND LIKELY TO BE ANYWHERE.
TRUE. ANY DIGGING IS BOUND TO ATTRACT ONE OR MORE OF THEM. AND THEY'RE ALL AS BAD AS THEIR BOSS.
NOT ALL OF THEM!
HUH?
I HAVE AN IDEA! ALL WE HAVE TO DO IS FIND THE ONE NOME WHO HATES THE NOME KING MORE THAN US!
HERE YOU ARE!
YUH?
YIKES!
OH, NO!

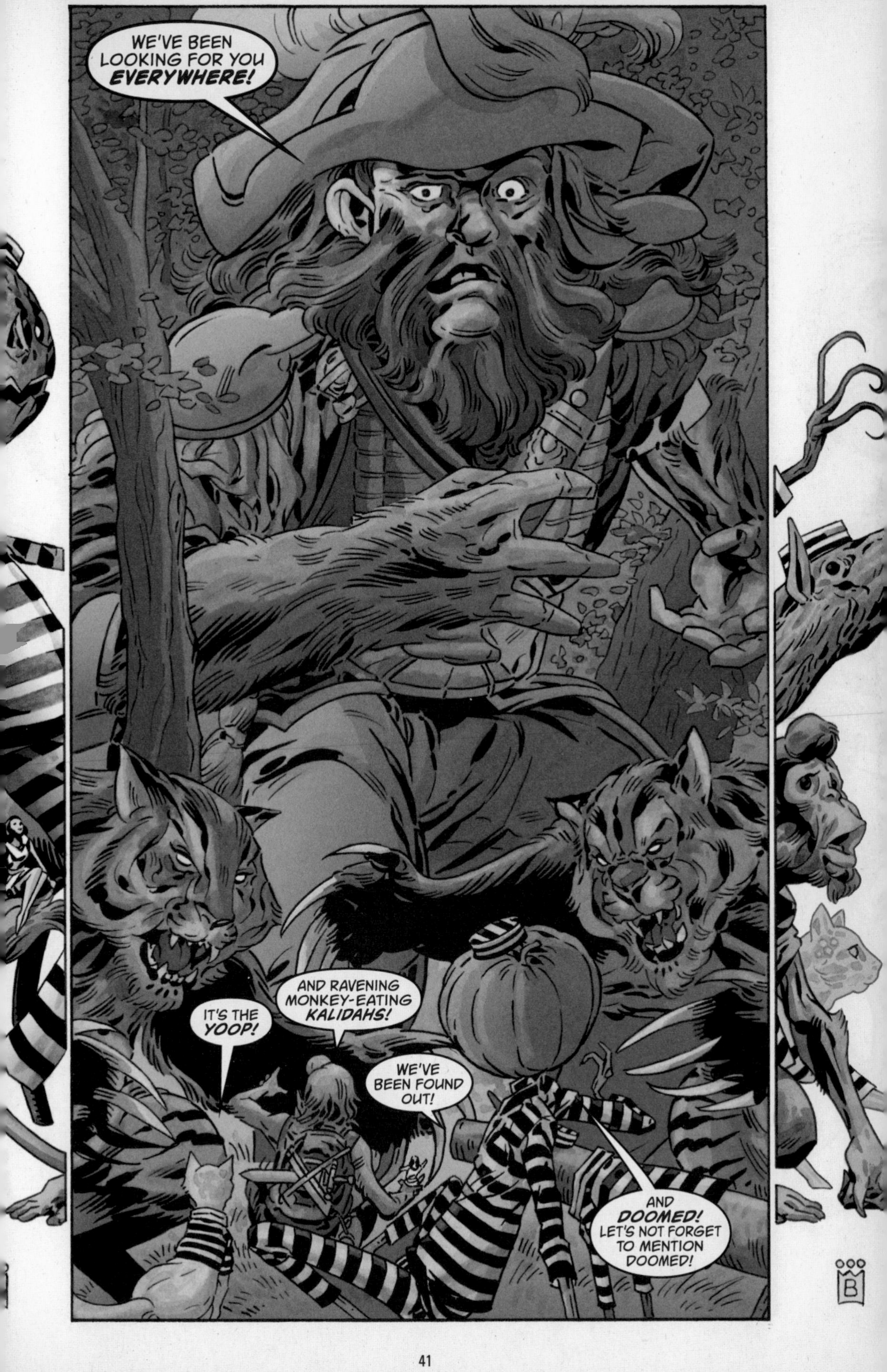
WE'VE BEEN LOOKING FOR YOU *EVERYWHERE!*
IT'S THE *YOOP!*
AND RAVENING MONKEY-EATING *KALIDAHS!*
WE'VE BEEN FOUND OUT!
AND *DOOMED!* LET'S NOT FORGET TO MENTION DOOMED!

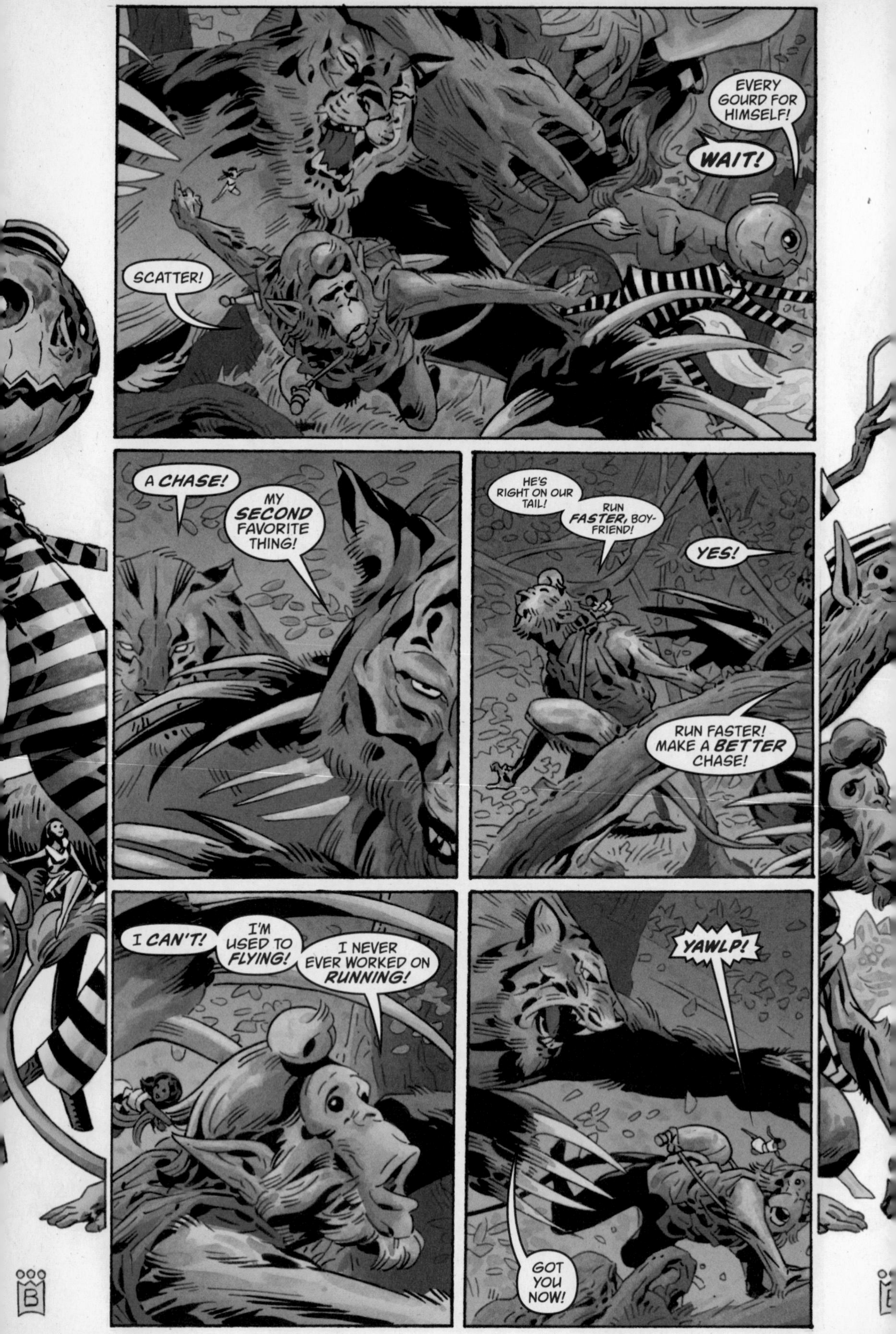
EVERY GOURD FOR HIMSELF!
WAIT!
SCATTER!
A CHASE!
MY SECOND FAVORITE THING!
HE'S RIGHT ON OUR TAIL!
RUN FASTER, BOY-FRIEND!
YES!
RUN FASTER! MAKE A BETTER CHASE!
I CAN'T!
I'M USED TO FLYING!
I NEVER EVER WORKED ON RUNNING!
YAWLP!
GOT YOU NOW!

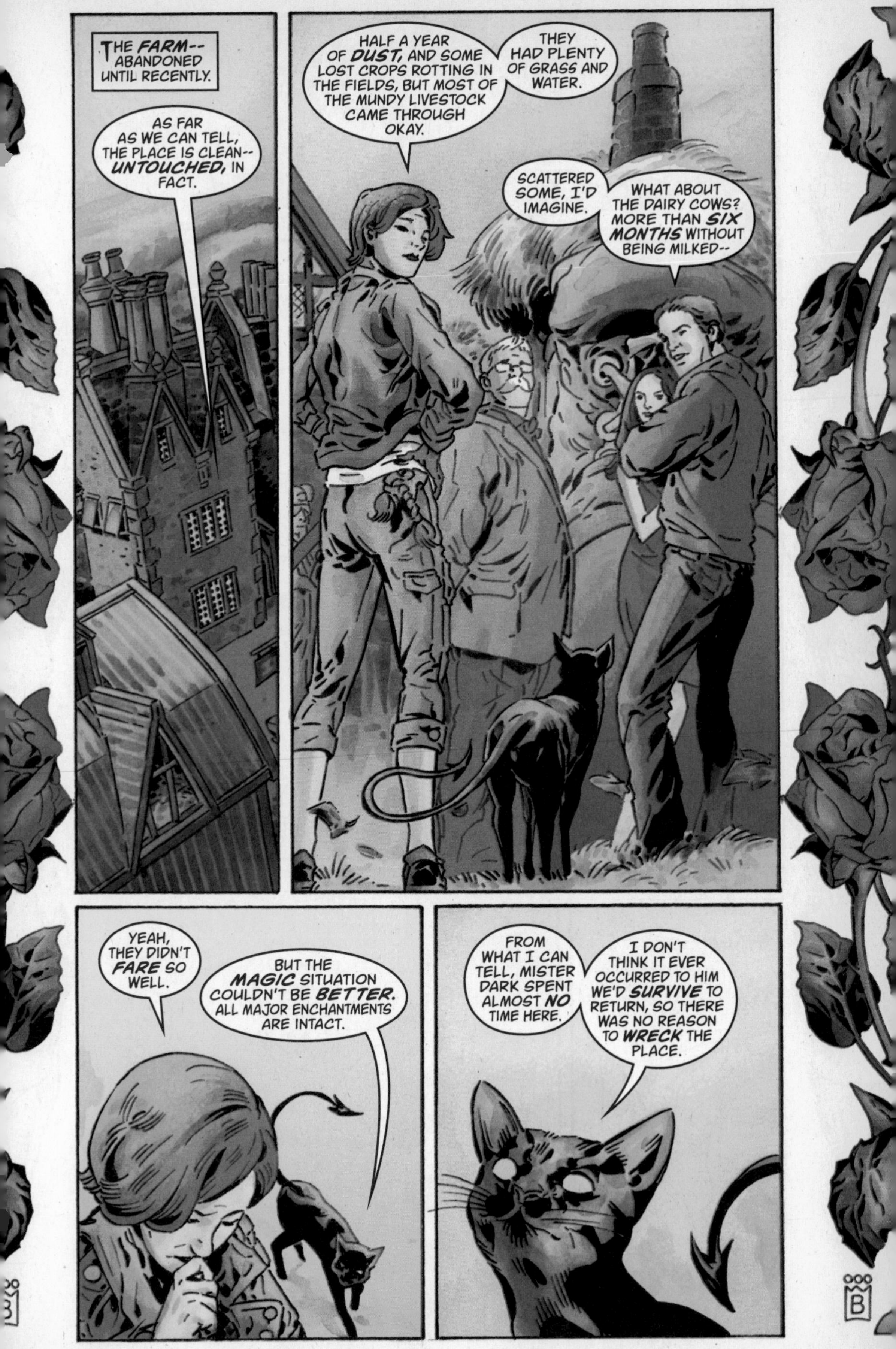

THE FARM-- ABANDONED UNTIL RECENTLY.
AS FAR AS WE CAN TELL, THE PLACE IS CLEAN-- UNTOUCHED, IN FACT.
HALF A YEAR OF DUST, AND SOME LOST CROPS ROTTING IN THE FIELDS, BUT MOST OF THE MUNDY LIVESTOCK CAME THROUGH OKAY.
THEY HAD PLENTY OF GRASS AND WATER.
SCATTERED SOME, I'D IMAGINE.
WHAT ABOUT THE DAIRY COWS? MORE THAN SIX MONTHS WITHOUT BEING MILKED--
YEAH, THEY DIDN'T FARE SO WELL.
BUT THE MAGIC SITUATION COULDN'T BE BETTER. ALL MAJOR ENCHANTMENTS ARE INTACT.
FROM WHAT I CAN TELL, MISTER DARK SPENT ALMOST NO TIME HERE.
I DON'T THINK IT EVER OCCURRED TO HIM WE'D SURVIVE TO RETURN, SO THERE WAS NO REASON TO WRECK THE PLACE.

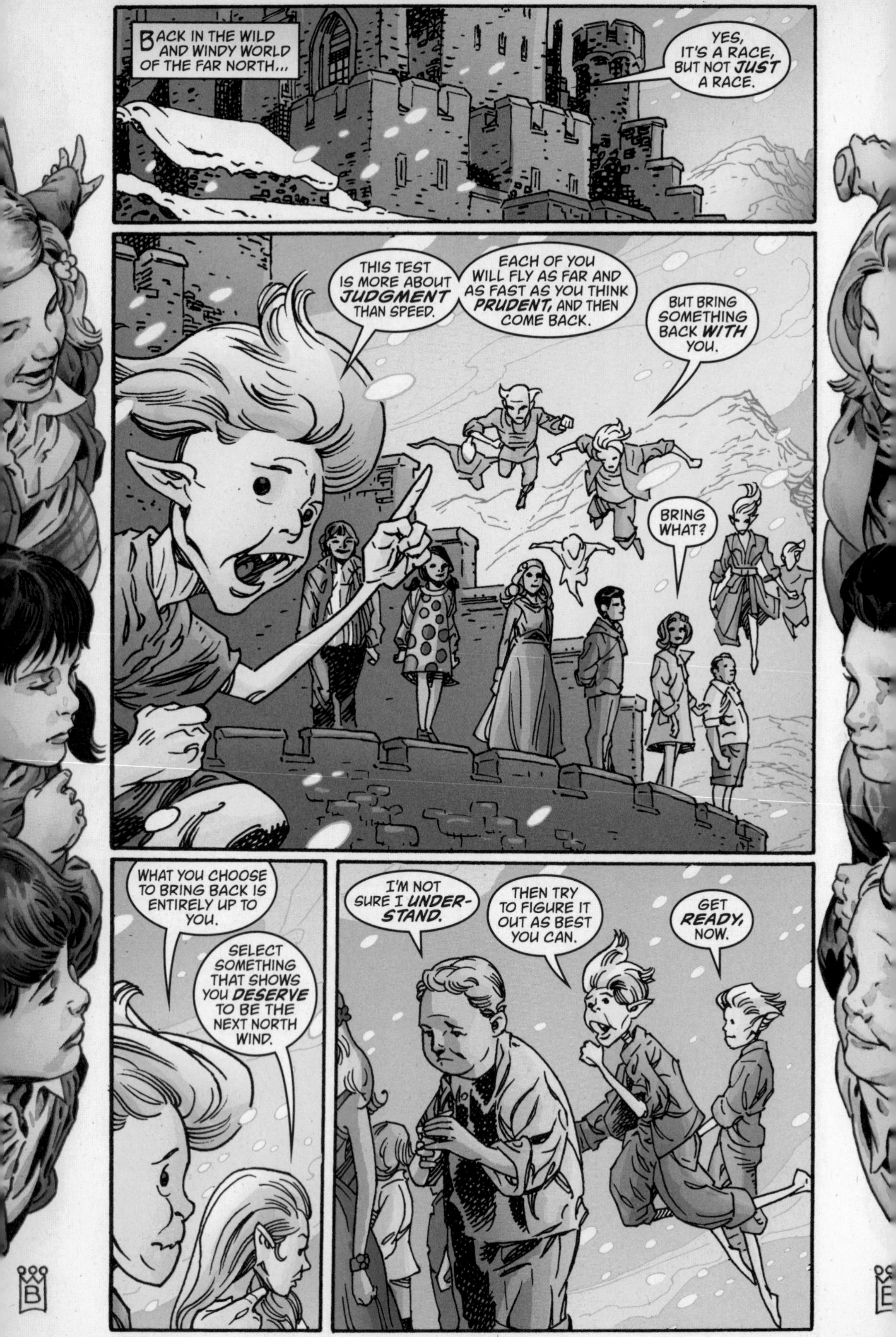

BACK IN THE WILD AND WINDY WORLD OF THE FAR NORTH...
YES, IT'S A RACE, BUT NOT JUST A RACE.
THIS TEST IS MORE ABOUT JUDGMENT THAN SPEED.
EACH OF YOU WILL FLY AS FAR AND AS FAST AS YOU THINK PRUDENT, AND THEN COME BACK.
BUT BRING SOMETHING BACK WITH YOU.
BRING WHAT?
WHAT YOU CHOOSE TO BRING BACK IS ENTIRELY UP TO YOU.
SELECT SOMETHING THAT SHOWS YOU DESERVE TO BE THE NEXT NORTH WIND.
I'M NOT SURE I UNDER-STAND.
THEN TRY TO FIGURE IT OUT AS BEST YOU CAN.
GET READY, NOW.

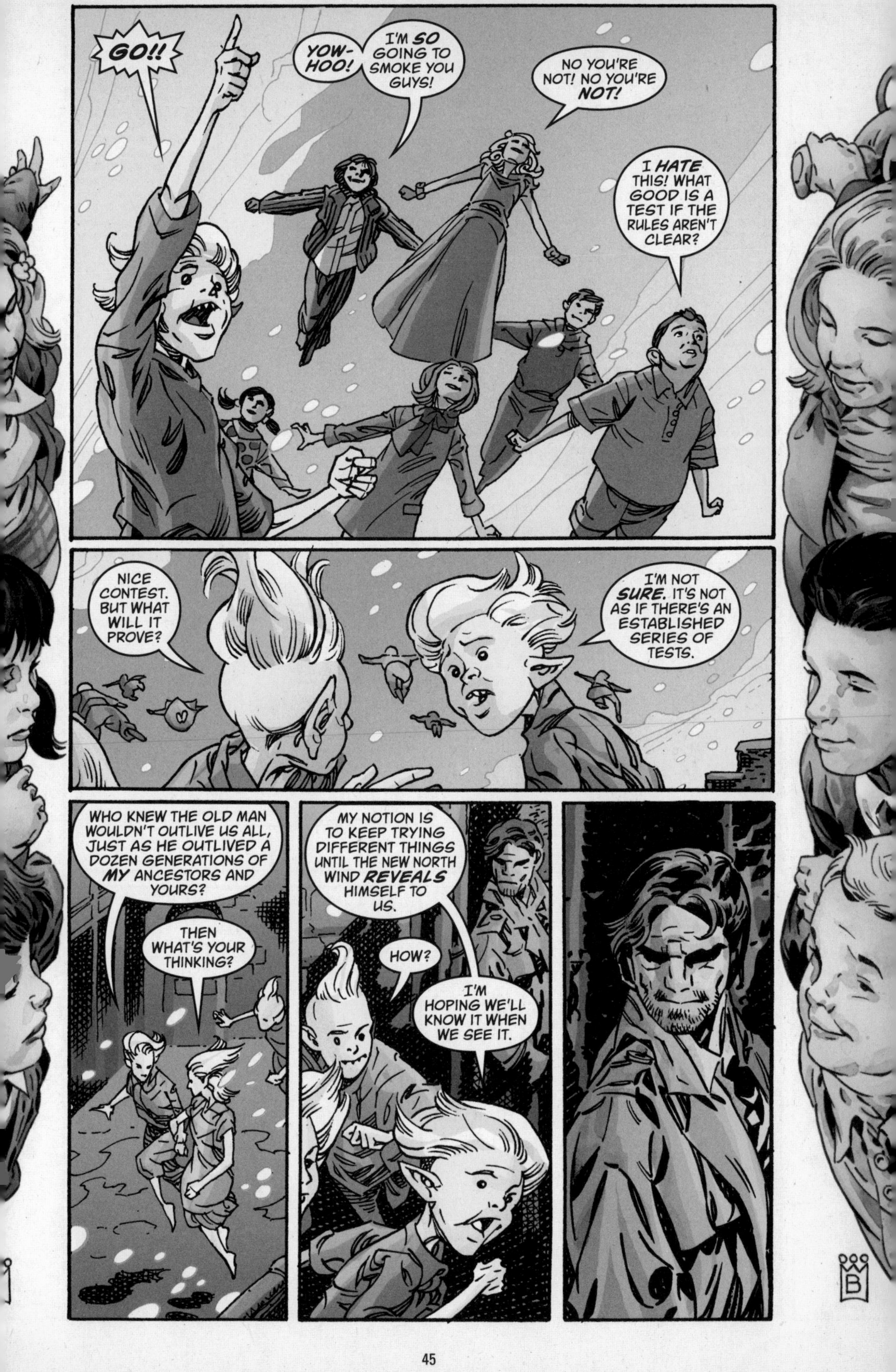
GO!!
YOW-HOO!
I'M SO GOING TO SMOKE YOU GUYS!
NO YOU'RE NOT! NO YOU'RE NOT!
I HATE THIS! WHAT GOOD IS A TEST IF THE RULES AREN'T CLEAR?
NICE CONTEST. BUT WHAT WILL IT PROVE?
I'M NOT SURE. IT'S NOT AS IF THERE'S AN ESTABLISHED SERIES OF TESTS.
WHO KNEW THE OLD MAN WOULDN'T OUTLIVE US ALL, JUST AS HE OUTLIVED A DOZEN GENERATIONS OF MY ANCESTORS AND YOURS?
THEN WHAT'S YOUR THINKING?
MY NOTION IS TO KEEP TRYING DIFFERENT THINGS UNTIL THE NEW NORTH WIND REVEALS HIMSELF TO US.
HOW?
I'M HOPING WE'LL KNOW IT WHEN WE SEE IT.

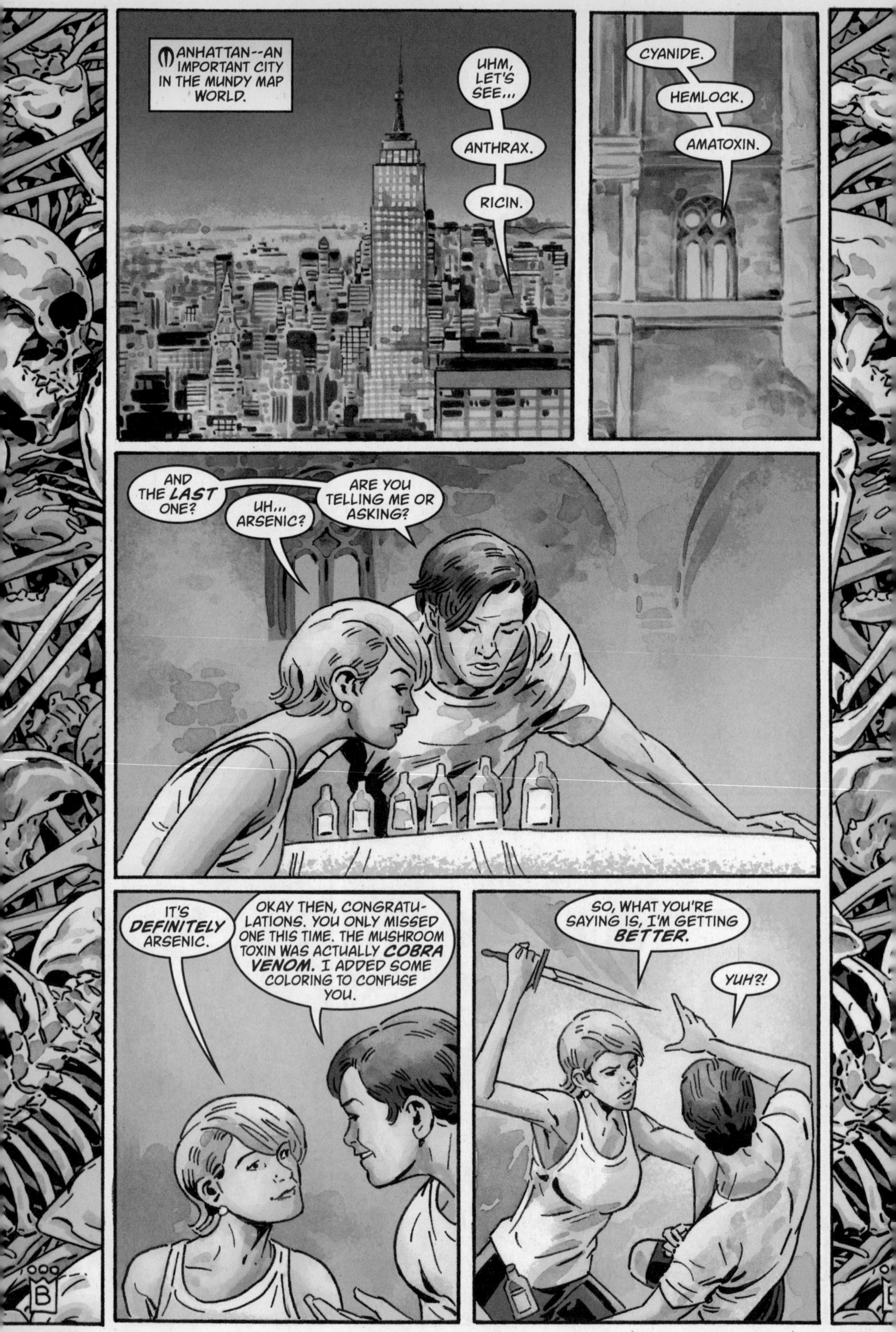
MANHATTAN--AN IMPORTANT CITY IN THE MUNDY MAP WORLD.
UHM, LET'S SEE...
ANTHRAX.
RICIN.
CYANIDE.
HEMLOCK.
AMATOXIN.
AND THE LAST ONE?
UH... ARSENIC?
ARE YOU TELLING ME OR ASKING?
IT'S DEFINITELY ARSENIC.
OKAY THEN, CONGRATU-LATIONS. YOU ONLY MISSED ONE THIS TIME. THE MUSHROOM TOXIN WAS ACTUALLY COBRA VENOM. I ADDED SOME COLORING TO CONFUSE YOU.
SO, WHAT YOU'RE SAYING IS, I'M GETTING BETTER.
YUH?!

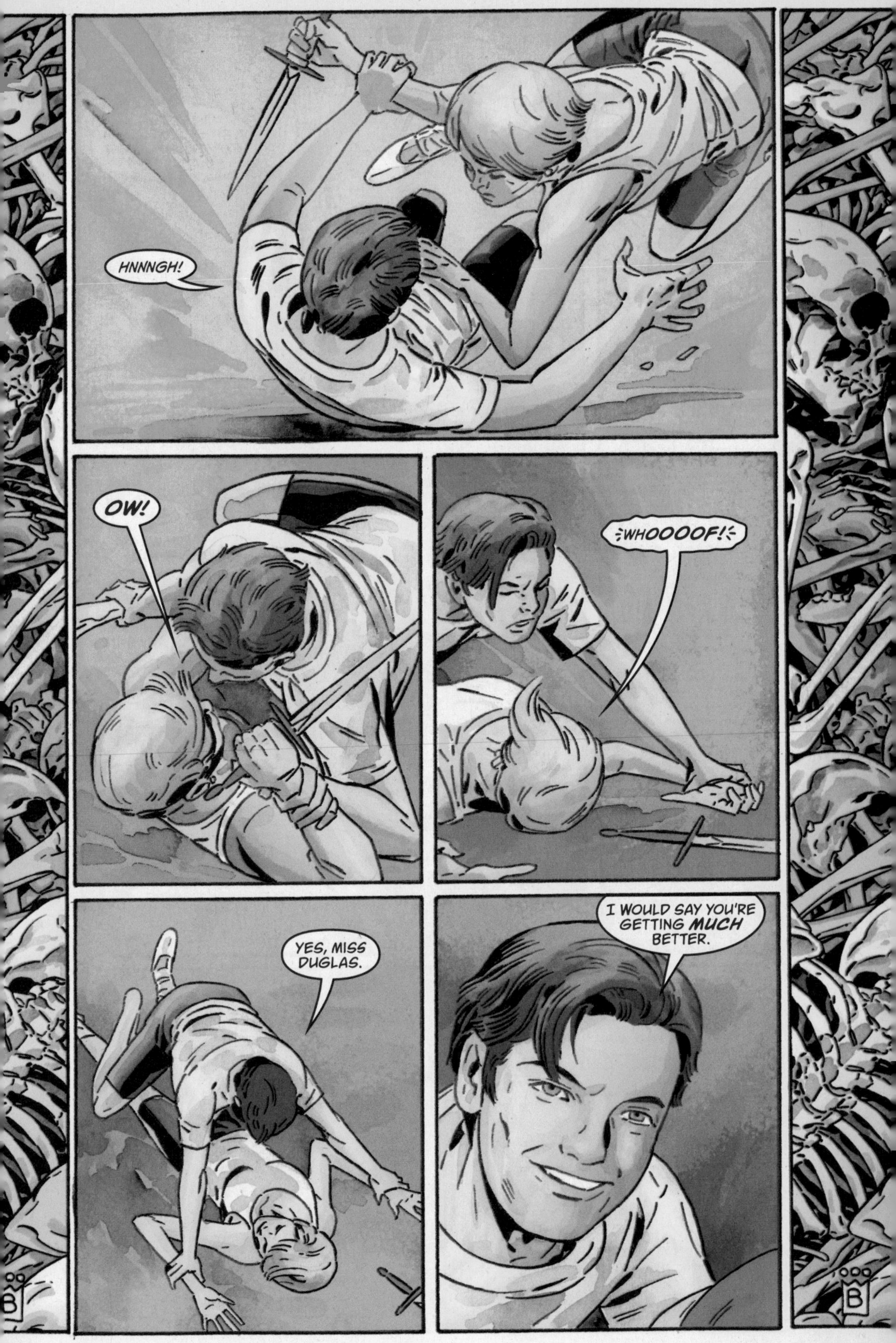
HNNNGH!
OW!
WHOOOOF!
YES, MISS DUGLAS.
I WOULD SAY YOU'RE GETTING **MUCH** BETTER.

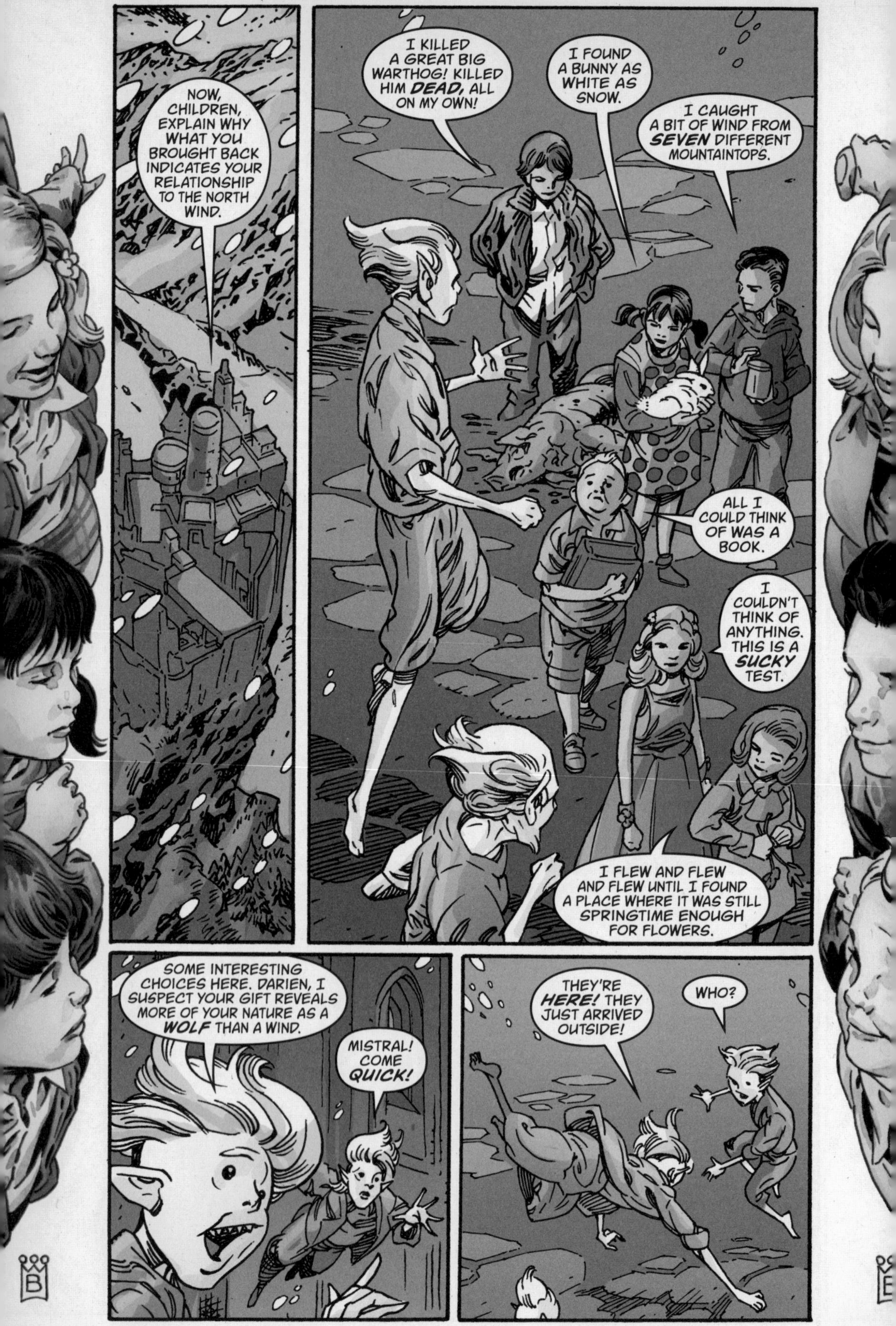
NOW, CHILDREN, EXPLAIN WHY WHAT YOU BROUGHT BACK INDICATES YOUR RELATIONSHIP TO THE NORTH WIND.
I KILLED A GREAT BIG WARTHOG! KILLED HIM DEAD, ALL ON MY OWN!
I FOUND A BUNNY AS WHITE AS SNOW.
I CAUGHT A BIT OF WIND FROM SEVEN DIFFERENT MOUNTAINTOPS.
ALL I COULD THINK OF WAS A BOOK.
I COULDN'T THINK OF ANYTHING. THIS IS A SUCKY TEST.
I FLEW AND FLEW AND FLEW UNTIL I FOUND A PLACE WHERE IT WAS STILL SPRINGTIME ENOUGH FOR FLOWERS.
SOME INTERESTING CHOICES HERE. DARIEN, I SUSPECT YOUR GIFT REVEALS MORE OF YOUR NATURE AS A WOLF THAN A WIND.
MISTRAL! COME QUICK!
THEY'RE HERE! THEY JUST ARRIVED OUTSIDE!
WHO?

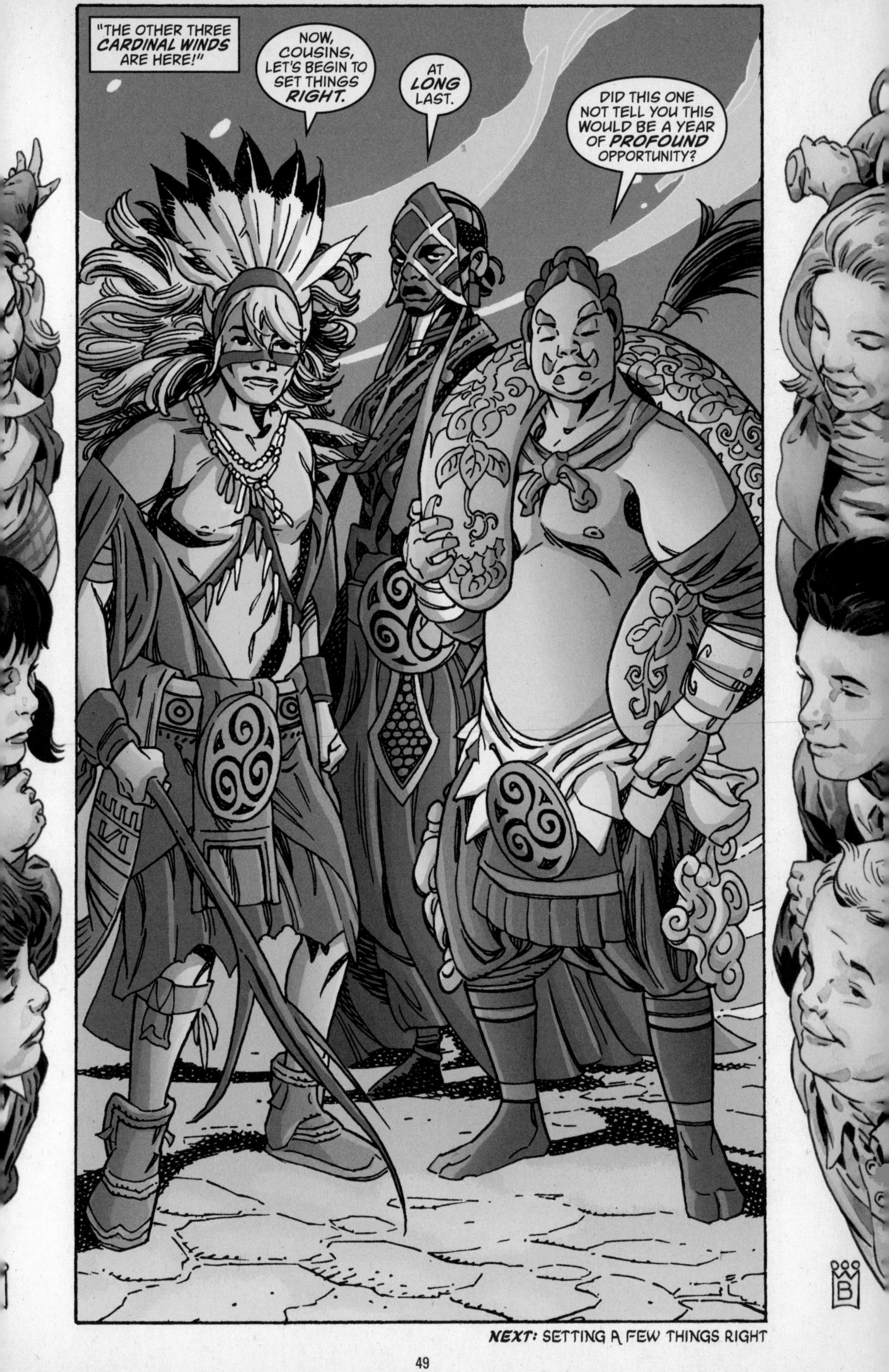
"THE OTHER THREE CARDINAL WINDS ARE HERE!"
NOW, COUSINS, LET'S BEGIN TO SET THINGS RIGHT.
AT LONG LAST.
DID THIS ONE NOT TELL YOU THIS WOULD BE A YEAR OF PROFOUND OPPORTUNITY?

NEXT: SETTING A FEW THINGS RIGHT

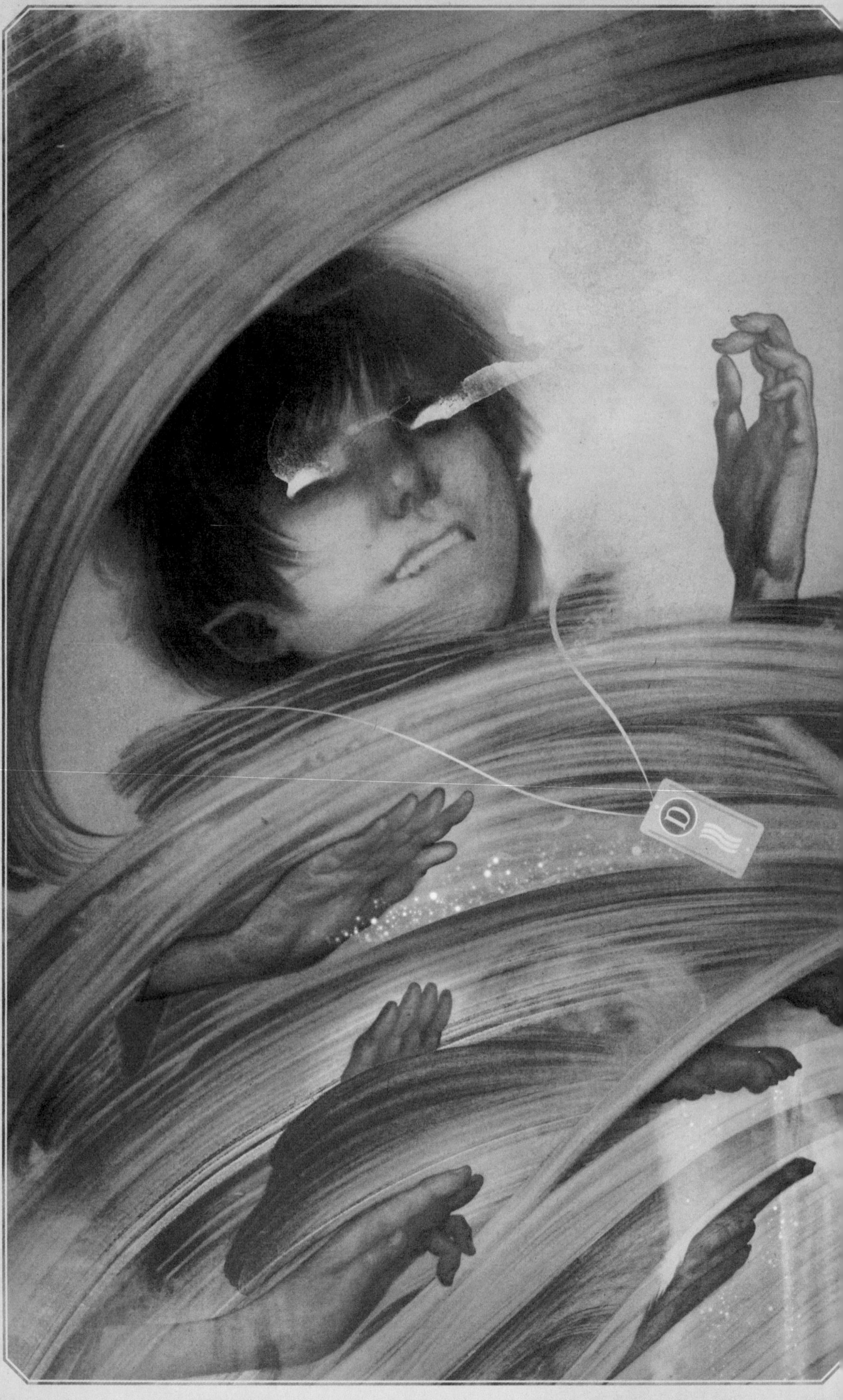

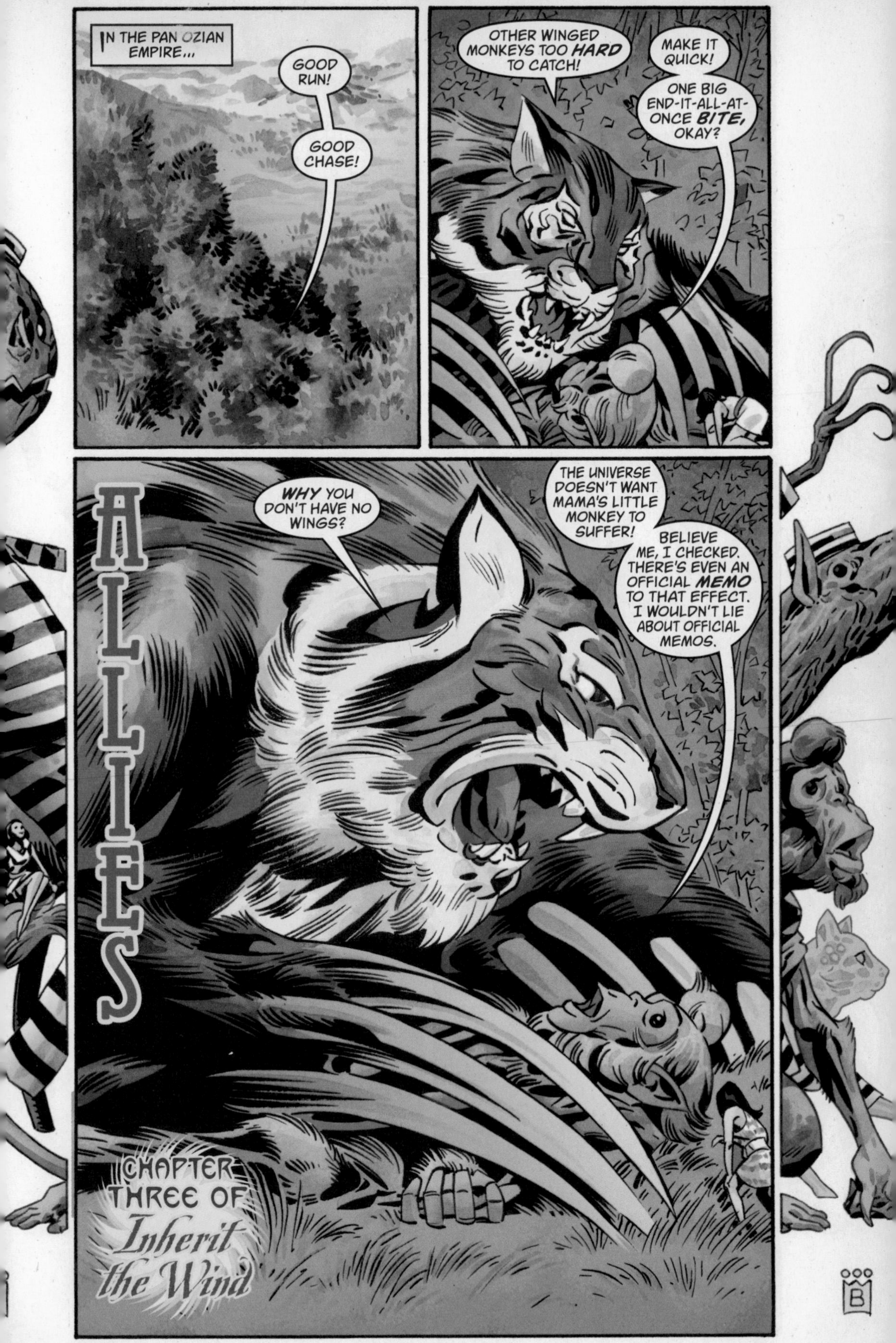
IN THE PAN OZIAN EMPIRE...
GOOD RUN!
GOOD CHASE!
OTHER WINGED MONKEYS TOO HARD TO CATCH!
MAKE IT QUICK!
ONE BIG END-IT-ALL-AT-ONCE BITE, OKAY?
WHY YOU DON'T HAVE NO WINGS?
THE UNIVERSE DOESN'T WANT MAMA'S LITTLE MONKEY TO SUFFER!
BELIEVE ME, I CHECKED. THERE'S EVEN AN OFFICIAL MEMO TO THAT EFFECT. I WOULDN'T LIE ABOUT OFFICIAL MEMOS.
ALLIES
CHAPTER THREE OF
Inherit the Wind

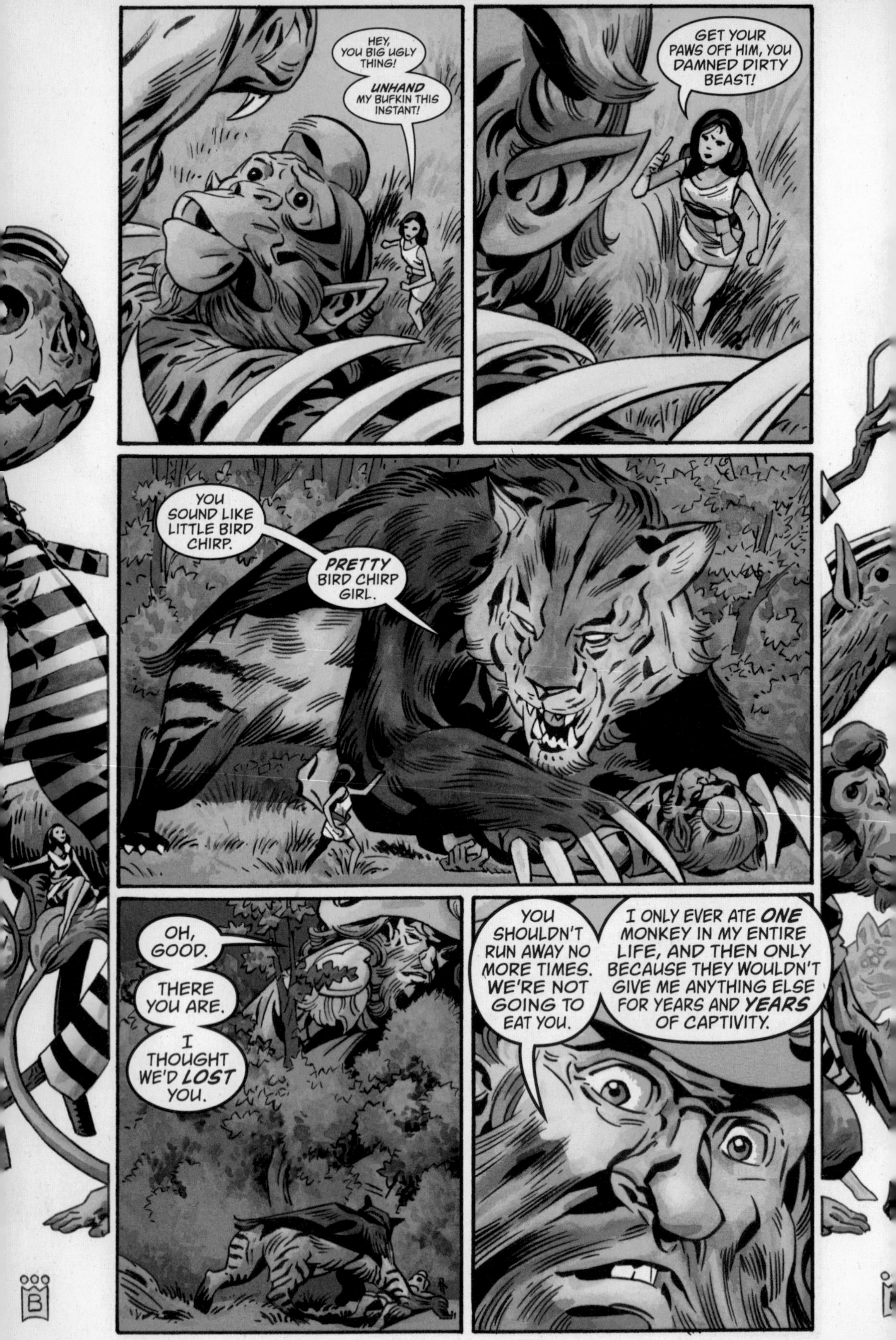
HEY, YOU BIG UGLY THING!
UNHAND MY BUFKIN THIS INSTANT!
GET YOUR PAWS OFF HIM, YOU DAMNED DIRTY BEAST!
YOU SOUND LIKE LITTLE BIRD CHIRP.
PRETTY BIRD CHIRP GIRL.
OH, GOOD.
THERE YOU ARE.
I THOUGHT WE'D LOST YOU.
YOU SHOULDN'T RUN AWAY NO MORE TIMES. WE'RE NOT GOING TO EAT YOU.
I ONLY EVER ATE ONE MONKEY IN MY ENTIRE LIFE, AND THEN ONLY BECAUSE THEY WOULDN'T GIVE ME ANYTHING ELSE FOR YEARS AND YEARS OF CAPTIVITY.

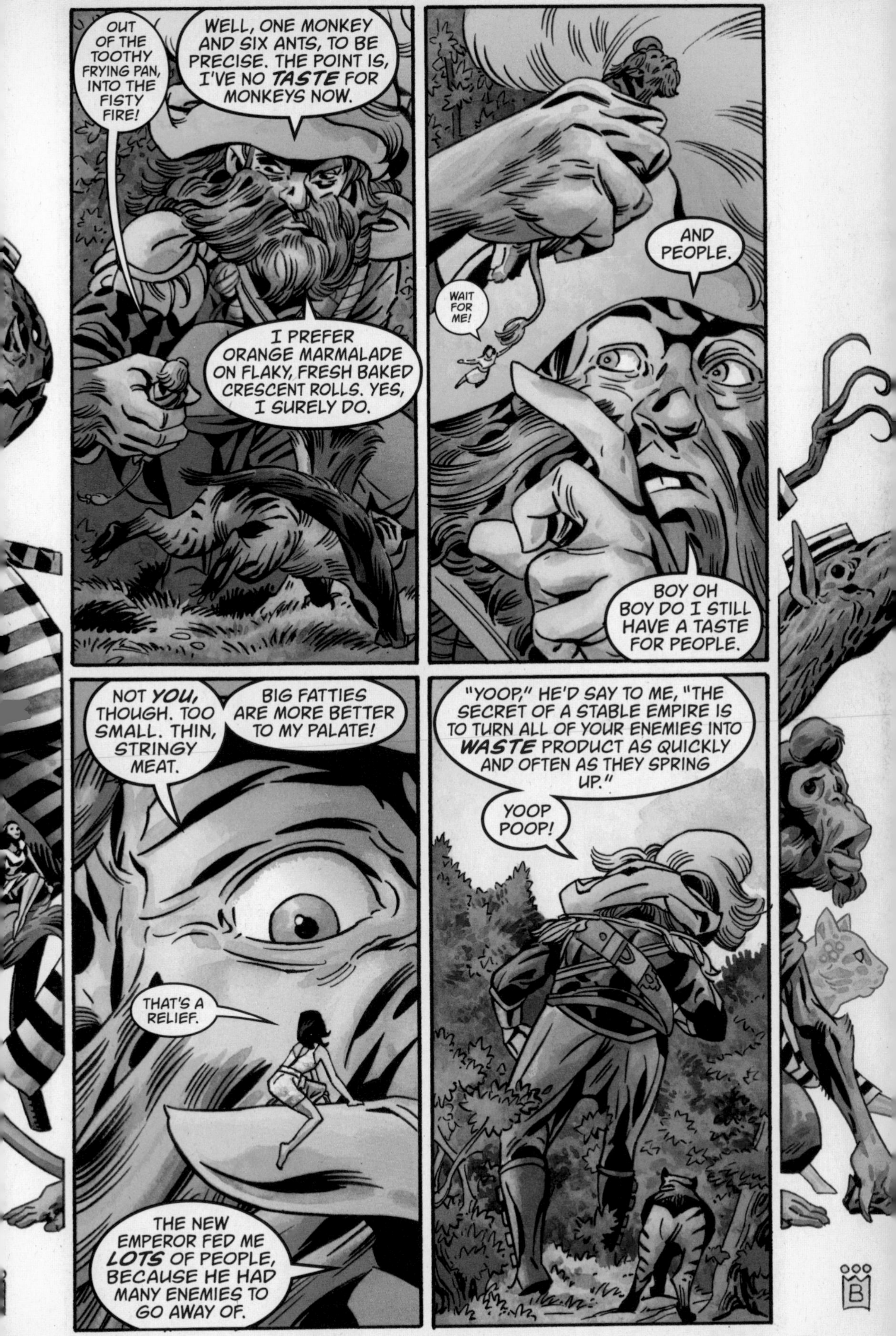
OUT OF THE TOOTHY FRYING PAN, INTO THE FISTY FIRE!
WELL, ONE MONKEY AND SIX ANTS, TO BE PRECISE. THE POINT IS, I'VE NO TASTE FOR MONKEYS NOW.
I PREFER ORANGE MARMALADE ON FLAKY, FRESH BAKED CRESCENT ROLLS. YES, I SURELY DO.
AND PEOPLE.
WAIT FOR ME!
BOY OH BOY DO I STILL HAVE A TASTE FOR PEOPLE.
NOT YOU, THOUGH. TOO SMALL. THIN, STRINGY MEAT.
BIG FATTIES ARE MORE BETTER TO MY PALATE!
THAT'S A RELIEF.
THE NEW EMPEROR FED ME LOTS OF PEOPLE, BECAUSE HE HAD MANY ENEMIES TO GO AWAY OF.
"YOOP," HE'D SAY TO ME, "THE SECRET OF A STABLE EMPIRE IS TO TURN ALL OF YOUR ENEMIES INTO WASTE PRODUCT AS QUICKLY AND OFTEN AS THEY SPRING UP."
YOOP POOP!

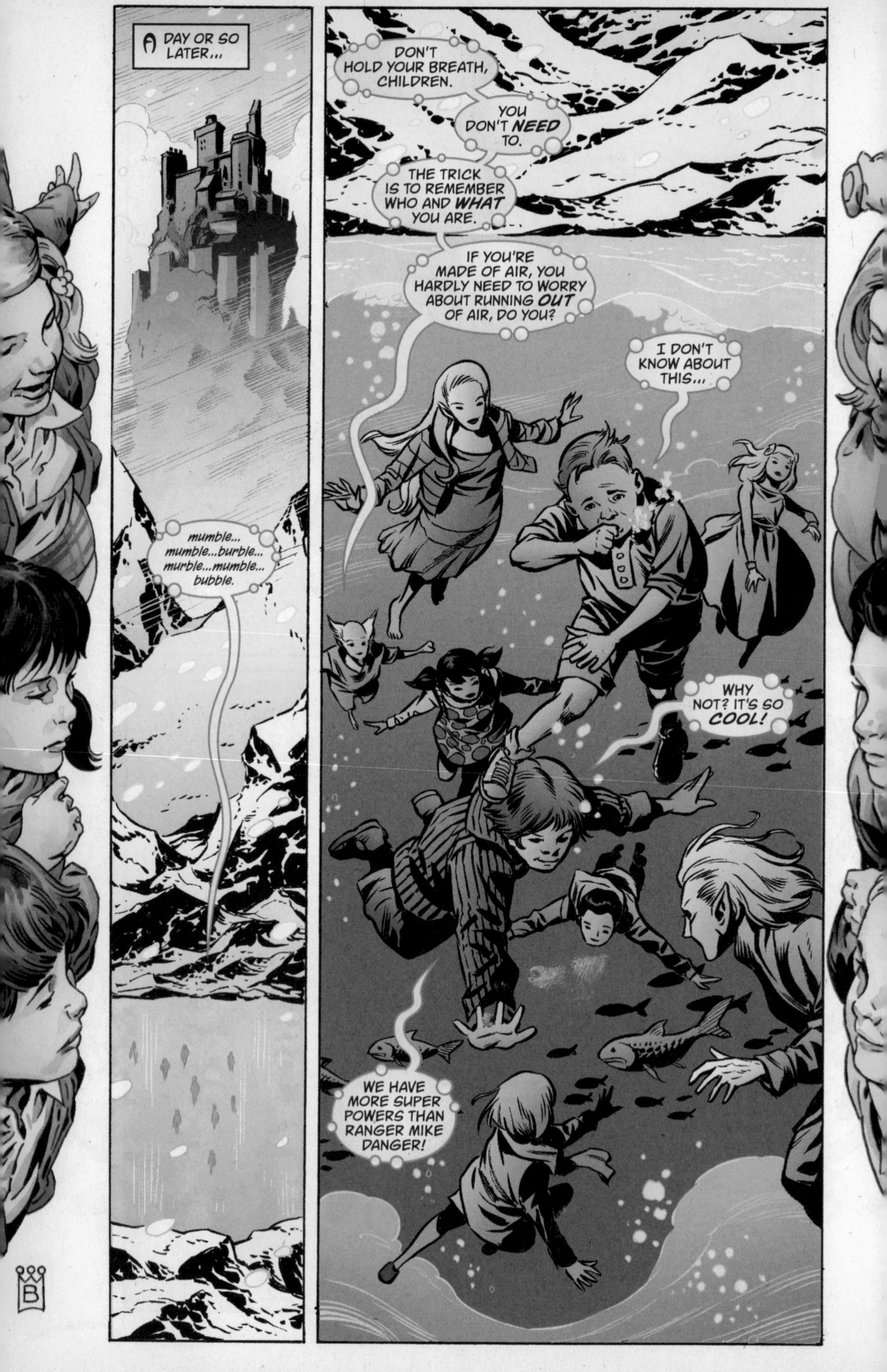
A DAY OR SO LATER...
mumble... mumble...burble... murble...mumble... bubble.
DON'T HOLD YOUR BREATH, CHILDREN.
YOU DON'T NEED TO.
THE TRICK IS TO REMEMBER WHO AND WHAT YOU ARE.
IF YOU'RE MADE OF AIR, YOU HARDLY NEED TO WORRY ABOUT RUNNING OUT OF AIR, DO YOU?
I DON'T KNOW ABOUT THIS...
WHY NOT? IT'S SO COOL!
WE HAVE MORE SUPER POWERS THAN RANGER MIKE DANGER!

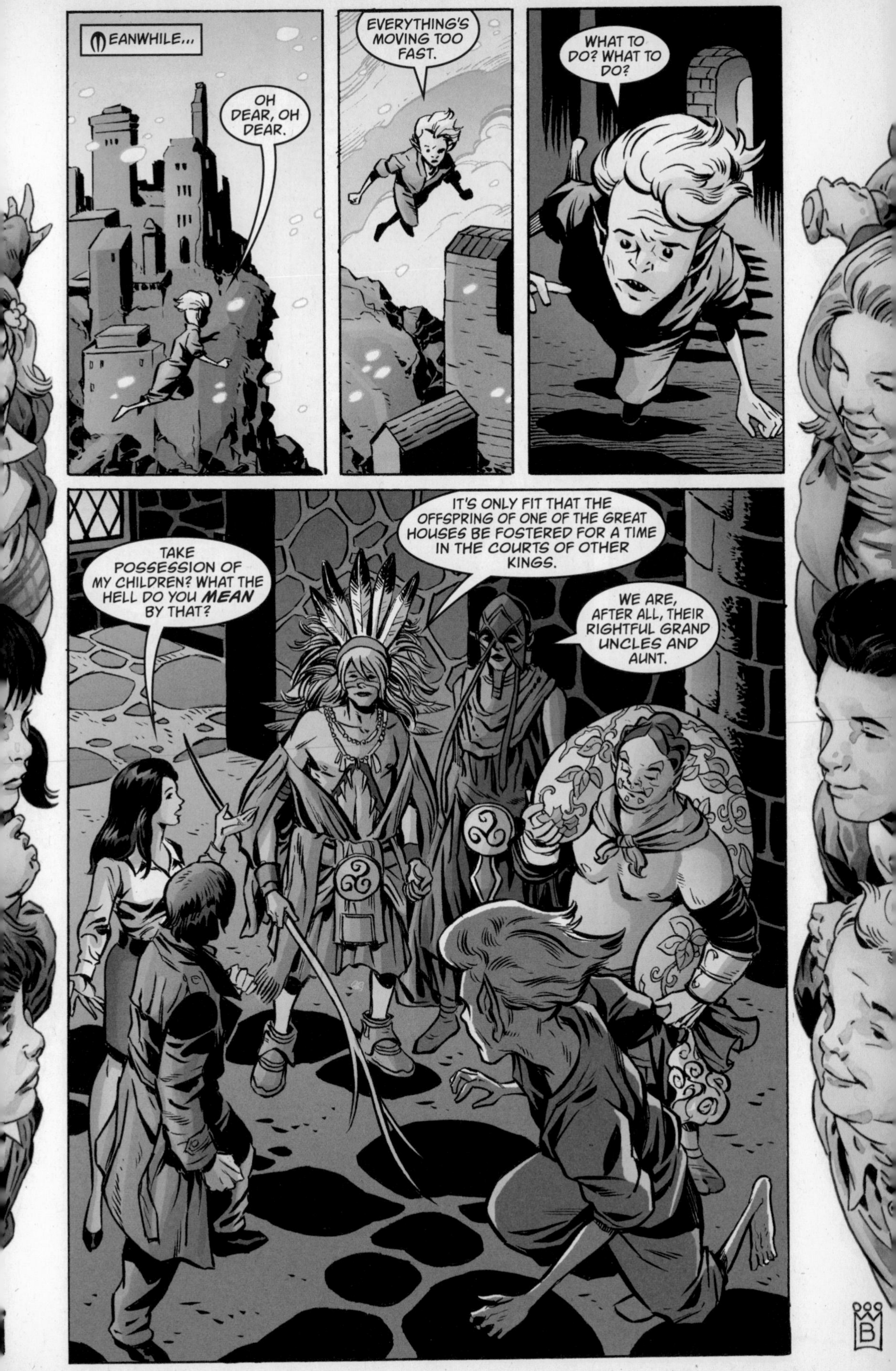
MEANWHILE...
OH DEAR, OH DEAR.
EVERYTHING'S MOVING TOO FAST.
WHAT TO DO? WHAT TO DO?
TAKE POSSESSION OF MY CHILDREN? WHAT THE HELL DO YOU MEAN BY THAT?
IT'S ONLY FIT THAT THE OFFSPRING OF ONE OF THE GREAT HOUSES BE FOSTERED FOR A TIME IN THE COURTS OF OTHER KINGS.
WE ARE, AFTER ALL, THEIR RIGHTFUL GRAND UNCLES AND AUNT.

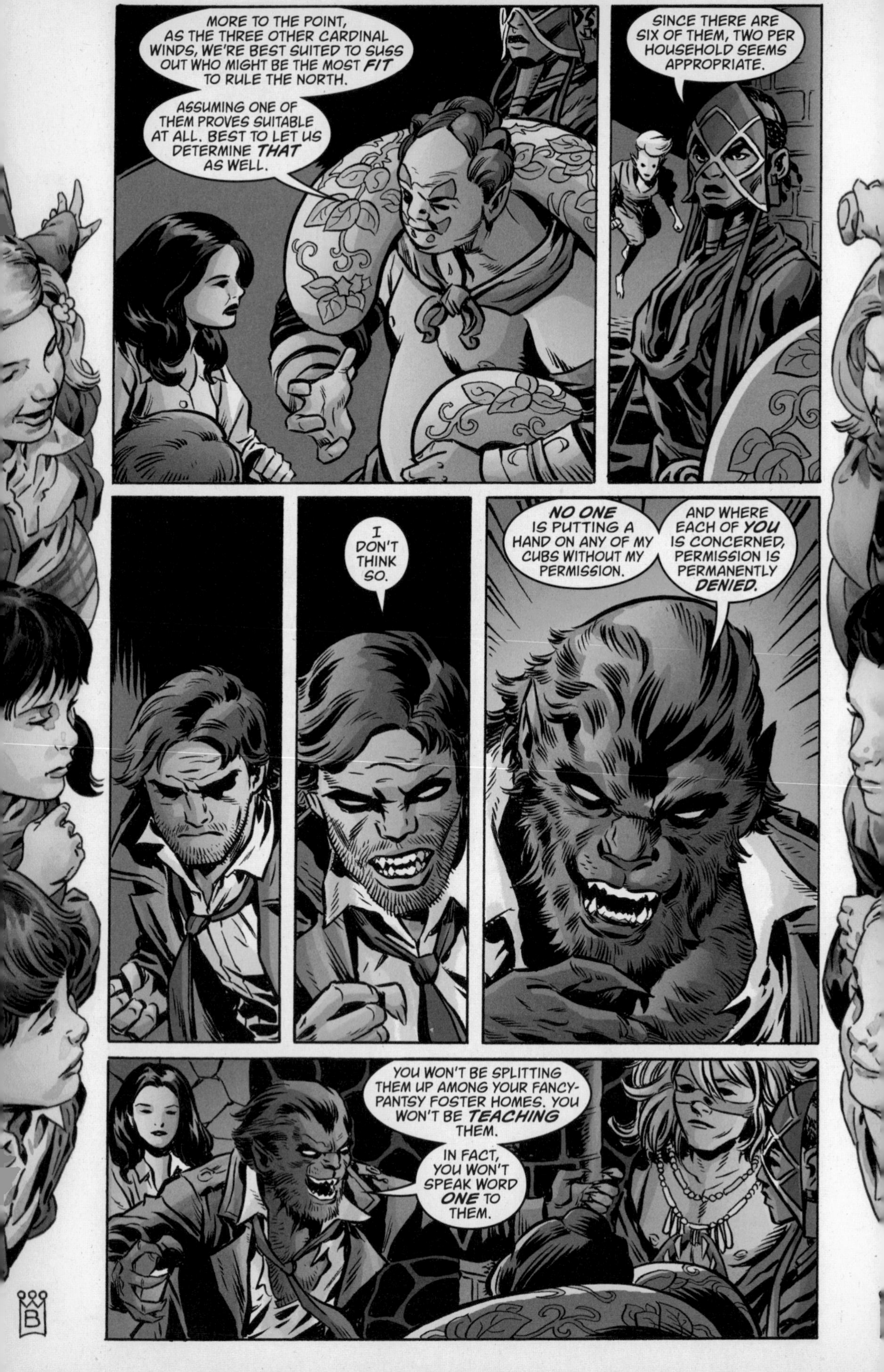
MORE TO THE POINT, AS THE THREE OTHER CARDINAL WINDS, WE'RE BEST SUITED TO SUSS OUT WHO MIGHT BE THE MOST *FIT* TO RULE THE NORTH.
ASSUMING ONE OF THEM PROVES SUITABLE AT ALL. BEST TO LET US DETERMINE *THAT* AS WELL.
SINCE THERE ARE SIX OF THEM, TWO PER HOUSEHOLD SEEMS APPROPRIATE.
I DON'T THINK SO.
NO ONE IS PUTTING A HAND ON ANY OF MY CUBS WITHOUT MY PERMISSION.
AND WHERE EACH OF *YOU* IS CONCERNED, PERMISSION IS PERMANENTLY *DENIED.*
YOU WON'T BE SPLITTING THEM UP AMONG YOUR FANCY-PANTSY FOSTER HOMES. YOU WON'T BE *TEACHING* THEM.
IN FACT, YOU WON'T SPEAK WORD *ONE* TO THEM.

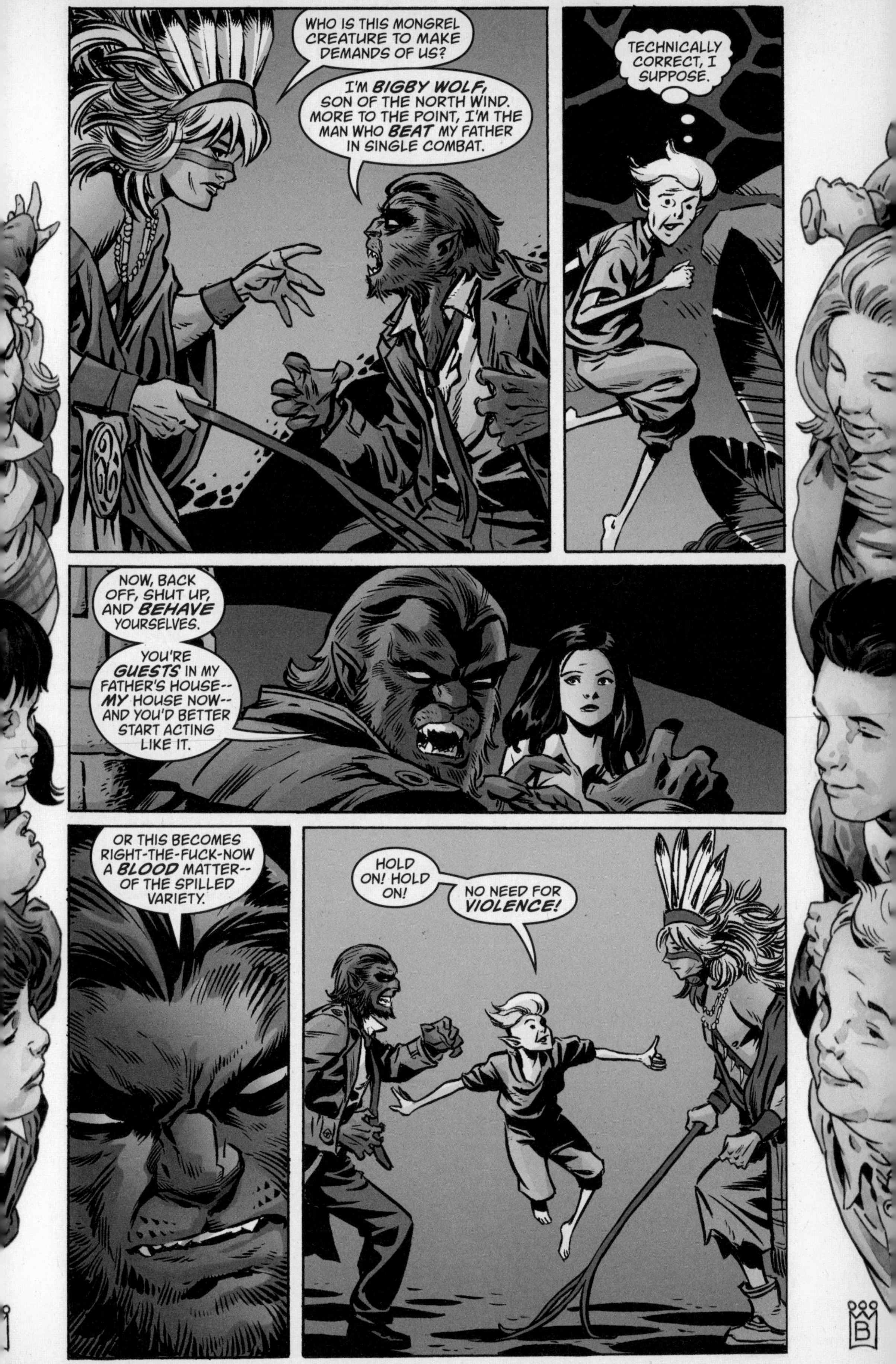
WHO IS THIS MONGREL CREATURE TO MAKE DEMANDS OF US?
I'M BIGBY WOLF, SON OF THE NORTH WIND. MORE TO THE POINT, I'M THE MAN WHO BEAT MY FATHER IN SINGLE COMBAT.
TECHNICALLY CORRECT, I SUPPOSE.
NOW, BACK OFF, SHUT UP, AND BEHAVE YOURSELVES.
YOU'RE GUESTS IN MY FATHER'S HOUSE-- MY HOUSE NOW-- AND YOU'D BETTER START ACTING LIKE IT.
OR THIS BECOMES RIGHT-THE-FUCK-NOW A BLOOD MATTER-- OF THE SPILLED VARIETY.
HOLD ON! HOLD ON!
NO NEED FOR VIOLENCE!

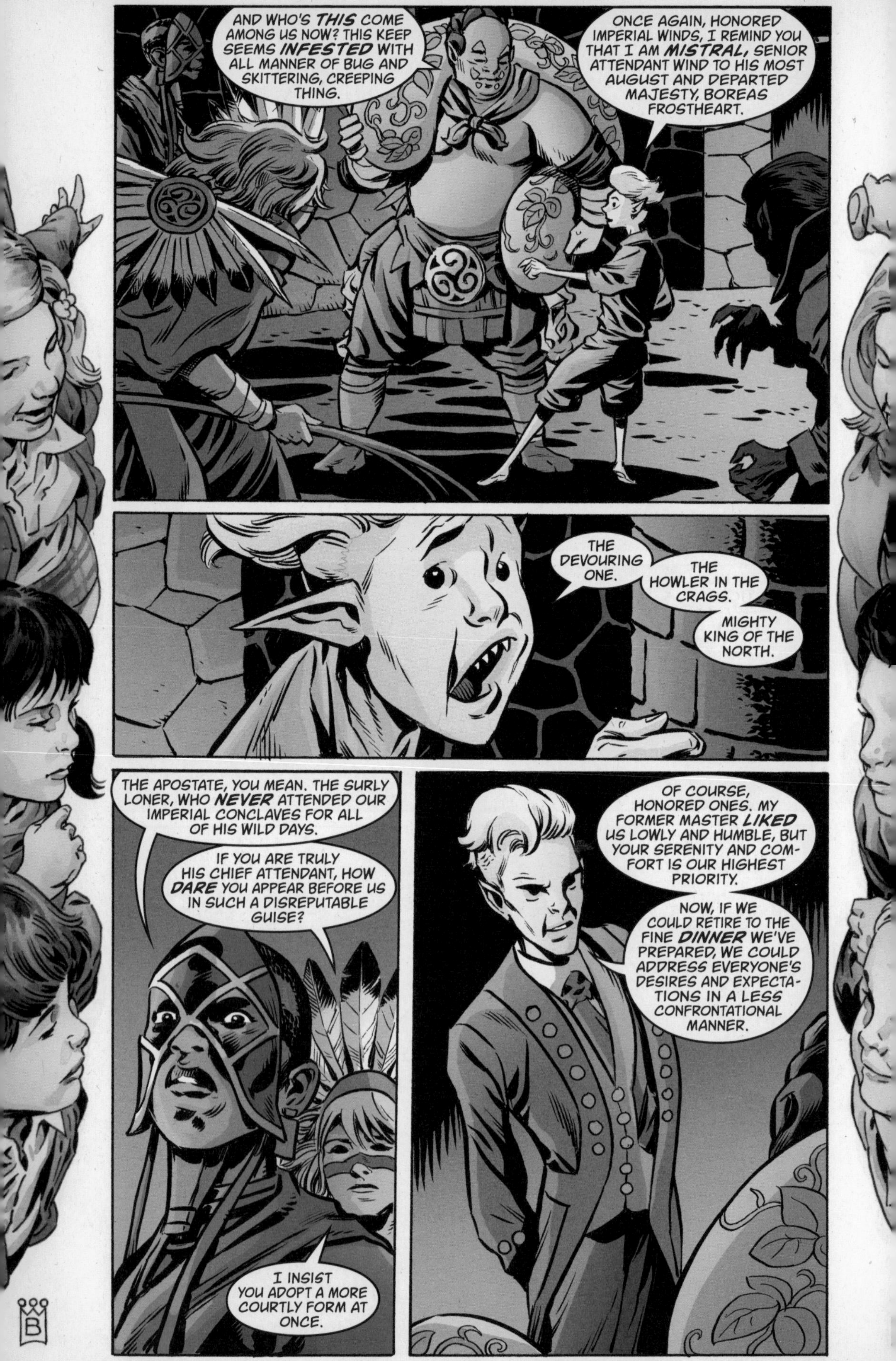
AND WHO'S THIS COME AMONG US NOW? THIS KEEP SEEMS INFESTED WITH ALL MANNER OF BUG AND SKITTERING, CREEPING THING.
ONCE AGAIN, HONORED IMPERIAL WINDS, I REMIND YOU THAT I AM MISTRAL, SENIOR ATTENDANT WIND TO HIS MOST AUGUST AND DEPARTED MAJESTY, BOREAS FROSTHEART.
THE DEVOURING ONE.
THE HOWLER IN THE CRAGS.
MIGHTY KING OF THE NORTH.
THE APOSTATE, YOU MEAN. THE SURLY LONER, WHO NEVER ATTENDED OUR IMPERIAL CONCLAVES FOR ALL OF HIS WILD DAYS.
IF YOU ARE TRULY HIS CHIEF ATTENDANT, HOW DARE YOU APPEAR BEFORE US IN SUCH A DISREPUTABLE GUISE?
I INSIST YOU ADOPT A MORE COURTLY FORM AT ONCE.
OF COURSE, HONORED ONES. MY FORMER MASTER LIKED US LOWLY AND HUMBLE, BUT YOUR SERENITY AND COMFORT IS OUR HIGHEST PRIORITY.
NOW, IF WE COULD RETIRE TO THE FINE DINNER WE'VE PREPARED, WE COULD ADDRESS EVERYONE'S DESIRES AND EXPECTATIONS IN A LESS CONFRONTATIONAL MANNER.

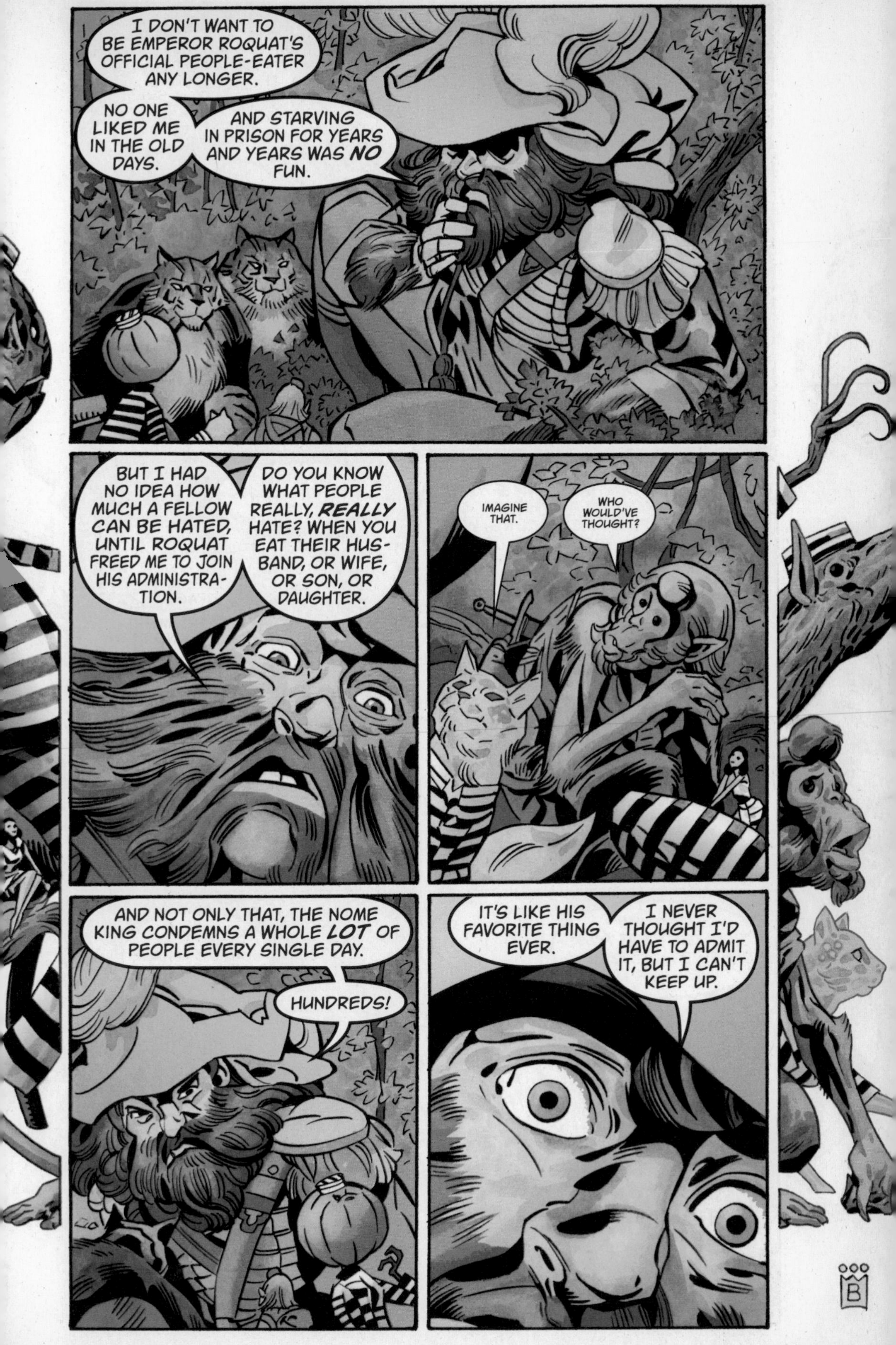
I DON'T WANT TO BE EMPEROR ROQUAT'S OFFICIAL PEOPLE-EATER ANY LONGER.
NO ONE LIKED ME IN THE OLD DAYS.
AND STARVING IN PRISON FOR YEARS AND YEARS WAS NO FUN.
BUT I HAD NO IDEA HOW MUCH A FELLOW CAN BE HATED, UNTIL ROQUAT FREED ME TO JOIN HIS ADMINISTRATION.
DO YOU KNOW WHAT PEOPLE REALLY, REALLY HATE? WHEN YOU EAT THEIR HUSBAND, OR WIFE, OR SON, OR DAUGHTER.
IMAGINE THAT.
WHO WOULD'VE THOUGHT?
AND NOT ONLY THAT, THE NOME KING CONDEMNS A WHOLE LOT OF PEOPLE EVERY SINGLE DAY.
HUNDREDS!
IT'S LIKE HIS FAVORITE THING EVER.
I NEVER THOUGHT I'D HAVE TO ADMIT IT, BUT I CAN'T KEEP UP.

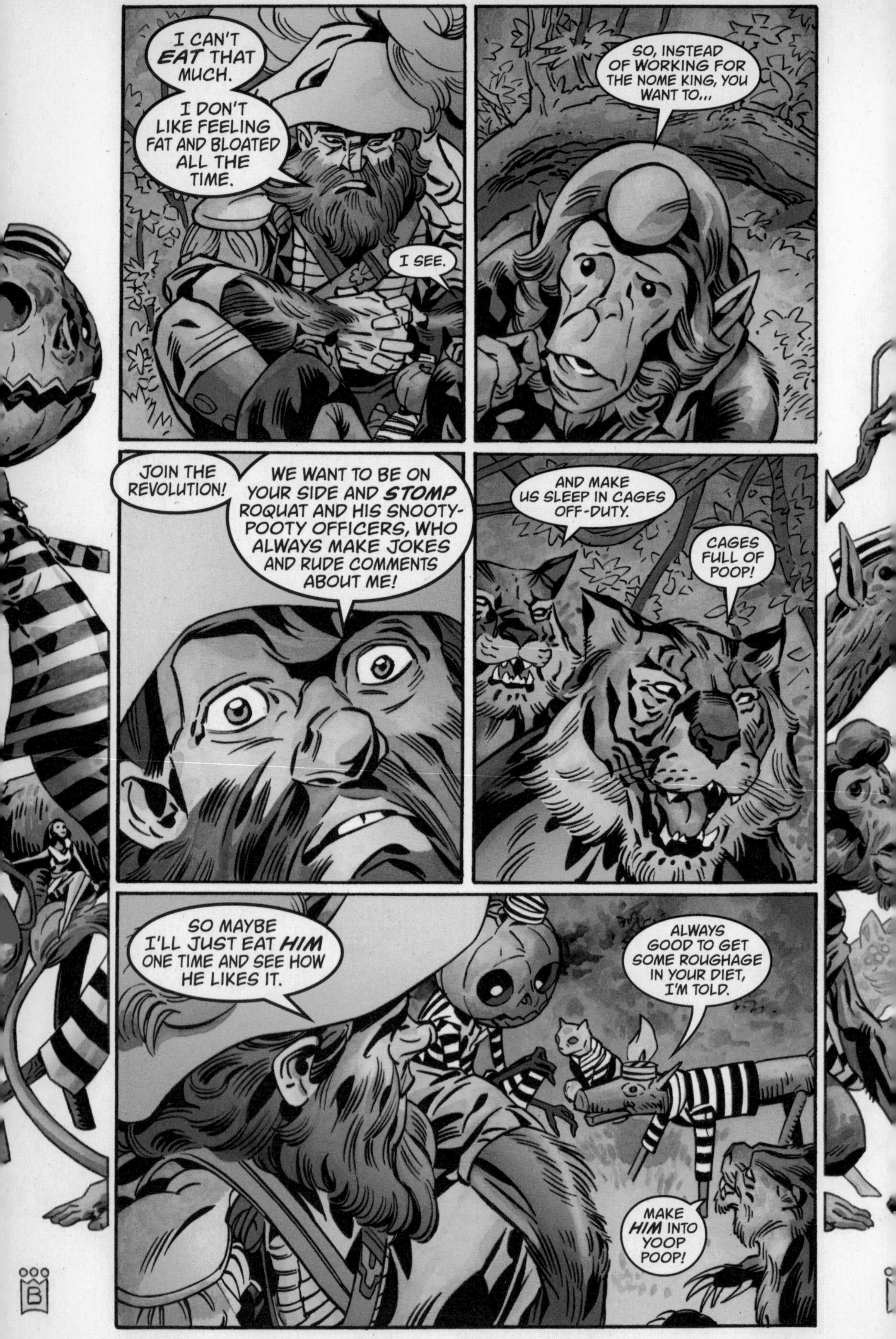

I CAN'T EAT THAT MUCH.
I DON'T LIKE FEELING FAT AND BLOATED ALL THE TIME.
I SEE.
SO, INSTEAD OF WORKING FOR THE NOME KING, YOU WANT TO...
JOIN THE REVOLUTION!
WE WANT TO BE ON YOUR SIDE AND STOMP ROQUAT AND HIS SNOOTY-POOTY OFFICERS, WHO ALWAYS MAKE JOKES AND RUDE COMMENTS ABOUT ME!
AND MAKE US SLEEP IN CAGES OFF-DUTY.
CAGES FULL OF POOP!
SO MAYBE I'LL JUST EAT HIM ONE TIME AND SEE HOW HE LIKES IT.
ALWAYS GOOD TO GET SOME ROUGHAGE IN YOUR DIET, I'M TOLD.
MAKE HIM INTO YOOP POOP!

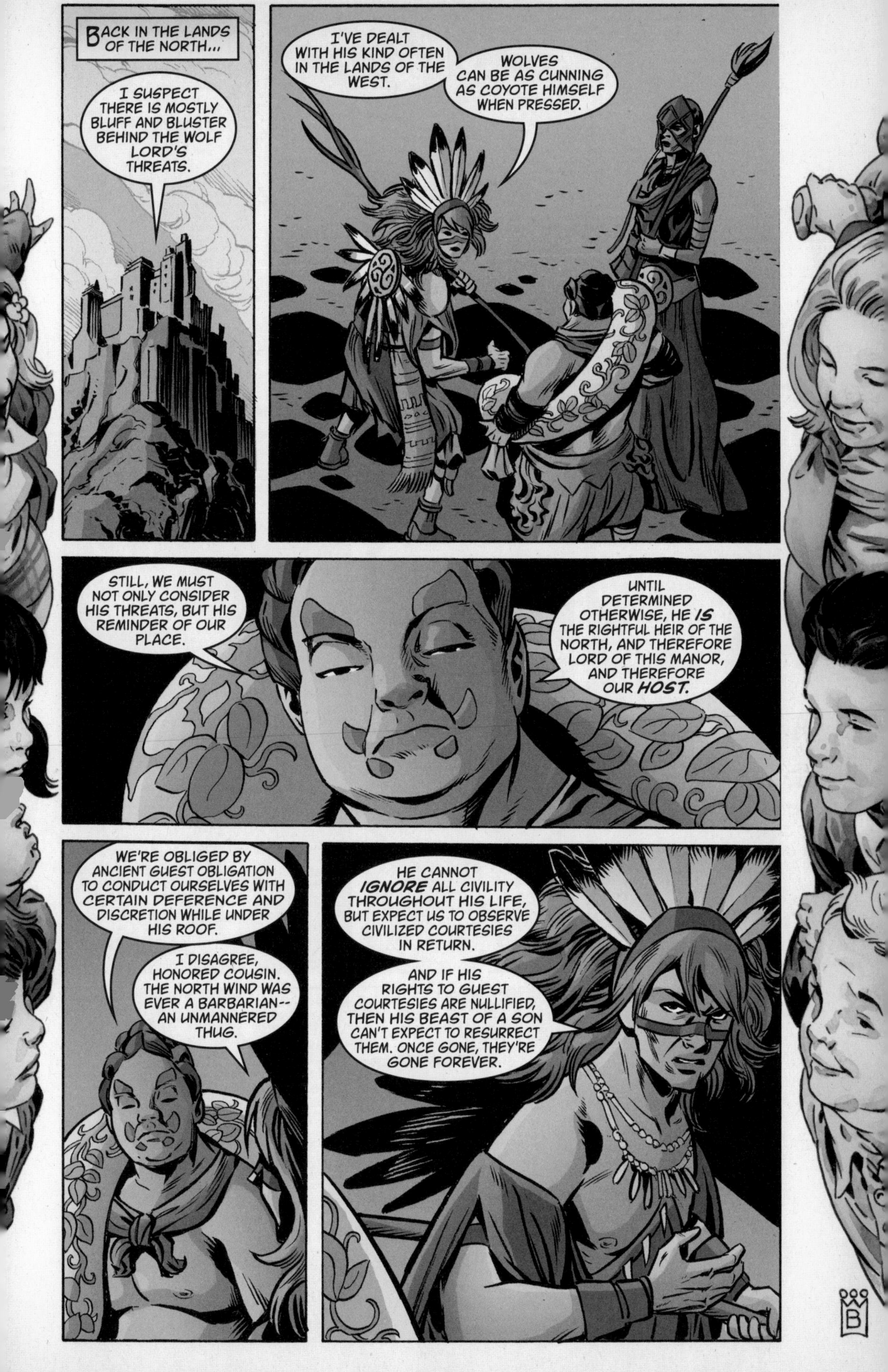
BACK IN THE LANDS OF THE NORTH...
I SUSPECT THERE IS MOSTLY BLUFF AND BLUSTER BEHIND THE WOLF LORD'S THREATS.
I'VE DEALT WITH HIS KIND OFTEN IN THE LANDS OF THE WEST.
WOLVES CAN BE AS CUNNING AS COYOTE HIMSELF WHEN PRESSED.
STILL, WE MUST NOT ONLY CONSIDER HIS THREATS, BUT HIS REMINDER OF OUR PLACE.
UNTIL DETERMINED OTHERWISE, HE IS THE RIGHTFUL HEIR OF THE NORTH, AND THEREFORE LORD OF THIS MANOR, AND THEREFORE OUR HOST.
WE'RE OBLIGED BY ANCIENT GUEST OBLIGATION TO CONDUCT OURSELVES WITH CERTAIN DEFERENCE AND DISCRETION WHILE UNDER HIS ROOF.
I DISAGREE, HONORED COUSIN. THE NORTH WIND WAS EVER A BARBARIAN-- AN UNMANNERED THUG.
HE CANNOT IGNORE ALL CIVILITY THROUGHOUT HIS LIFE, BUT EXPECT US TO OBSERVE CIVILIZED COURTESIES IN RETURN.
AND IF HIS RIGHTS TO GUEST COURTESIES ARE NULLIFIED, THEN HIS BEAST OF A SON CAN'T EXPECT TO RESURRECT THEM. ONCE GONE, THEY'RE GONE FOREVER.

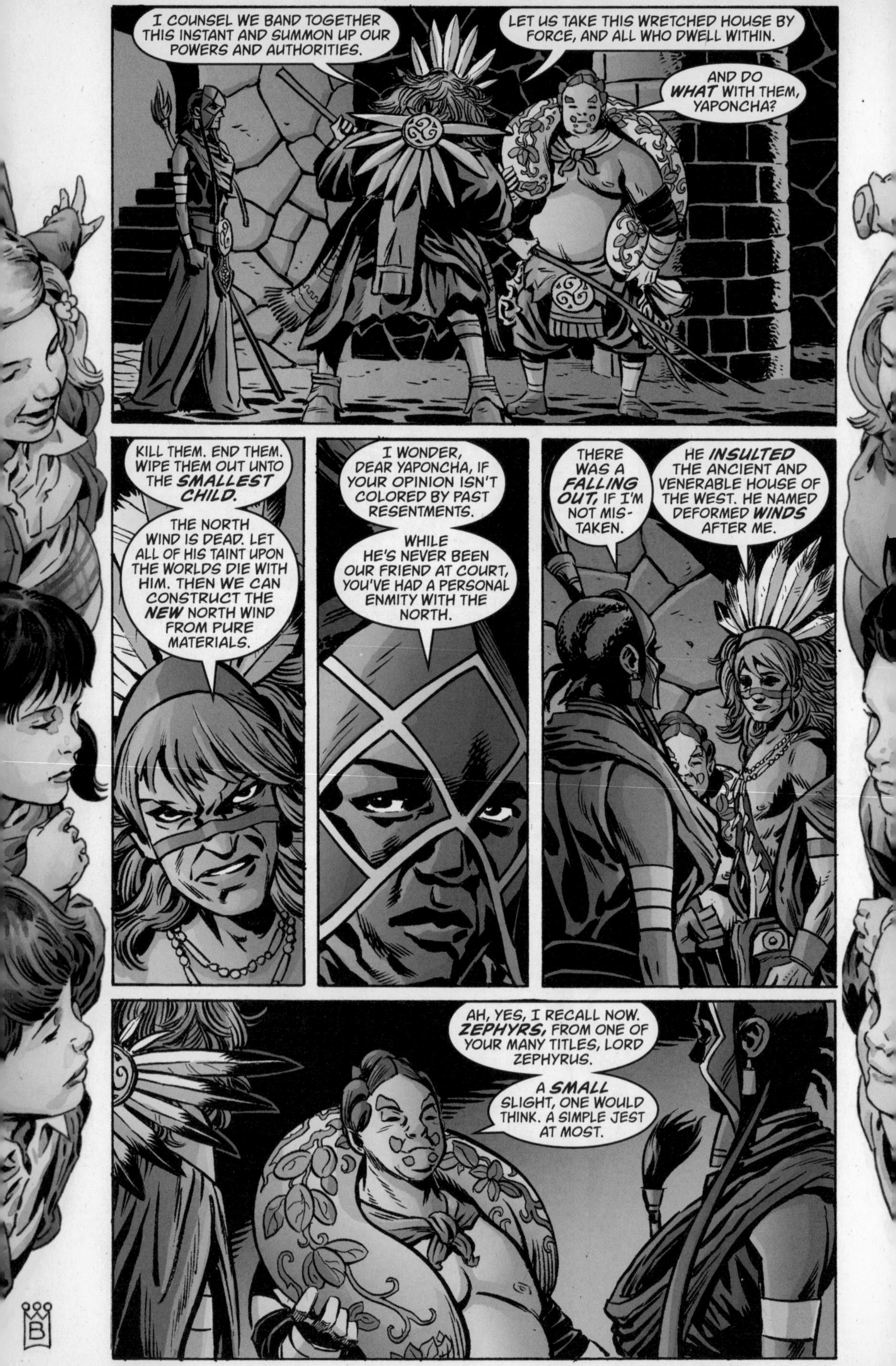

I COUNSEL WE BAND TOGETHER THIS INSTANT AND SUMMON UP OUR POWERS AND AUTHORITIES.
LET US TAKE THIS WRETCHED HOUSE BY FORCE, AND ALL WHO DWELL WITHIN.
AND DO WHAT WITH THEM, YAPONCHA?
KILL THEM. END THEM. WIPE THEM OUT UNTO THE SMALLEST CHILD.
THE NORTH WIND IS DEAD. LET ALL OF HIS TAINT UPON THE WORLDS DIE WITH HIM. THEN WE CAN CONSTRUCT THE NEW NORTH WIND FROM PURE MATERIALS.
I WONDER, DEAR YAPONCHA, IF YOUR OPINION ISN'T COLORED BY PAST RESENTMENTS.
WHILE HE'S NEVER BEEN OUR FRIEND AT COURT, YOU'VE HAD A PERSONAL ENMITY WITH THE NORTH.
THERE WAS A FALLING OUT, IF I'M NOT MIS-TAKEN.
HE INSULTED THE ANCIENT AND VENERABLE HOUSE OF THE WEST. HE NAMED DEFORMED WINDS AFTER ME.
AH, YES, I RECALL NOW. ZEPHYRS, FROM ONE OF YOUR MANY TITLES, LORD ZEPHYRUS.
A SMALL SLIGHT, ONE WOULD THINK. A SIMPLE JEST AT MOST.

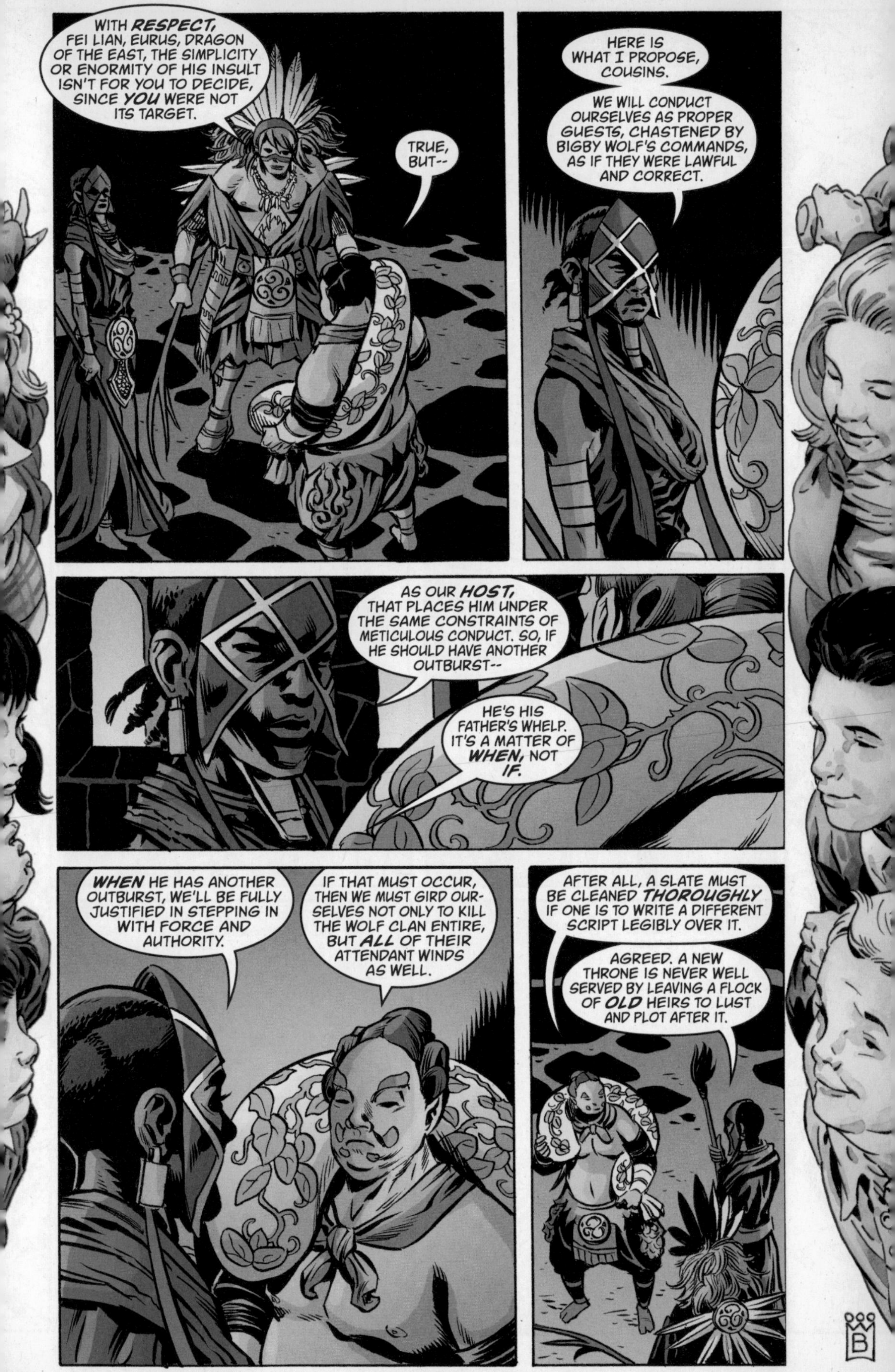
WITH RESPECT, FEI LIAN, EURUS, DRAGON OF THE EAST, THE SIMPLICITY OR ENORMITY OF HIS INSULT ISN'T FOR YOU TO DECIDE, SINCE YOU WERE NOT ITS TARGET.
TRUE, BUT--
HERE IS WHAT I PROPOSE, COUSINS.
WE WILL CONDUCT OURSELVES AS PROPER GUESTS, CHASTENED BY BIGBY WOLF'S COMMANDS, AS IF THEY WERE LAWFUL AND CORRECT.
AS OUR HOST, THAT PLACES HIM UNDER THE SAME CONSTRAINTS OF METICULOUS CONDUCT. SO, IF HE SHOULD HAVE ANOTHER OUTBURST--
HE'S HIS FATHER'S WHELP. IT'S A MATTER OF WHEN, NOT IF.
WHEN HE HAS ANOTHER OUTBURST, WE'LL BE FULLY JUSTIFIED IN STEPPING IN WITH FORCE AND AUTHORITY.
IF THAT MUST OCCUR, THEN WE MUST GIRD OURSELVES NOT ONLY TO KILL THE WOLF CLAN ENTIRE, BUT ALL OF THEIR ATTENDANT WINDS AS WELL.
AFTER ALL, A SLATE MUST BE CLEANED THOROUGHLY IF ONE IS TO WRITE A DIFFERENT SCRIPT LEGIBLY OVER IT.
AGREED. A NEW THRONE IS NEVER WELL SERVED BY LEAVING A FLOCK OF OLD HEIRS TO LUST AND PLOT AFTER IT.

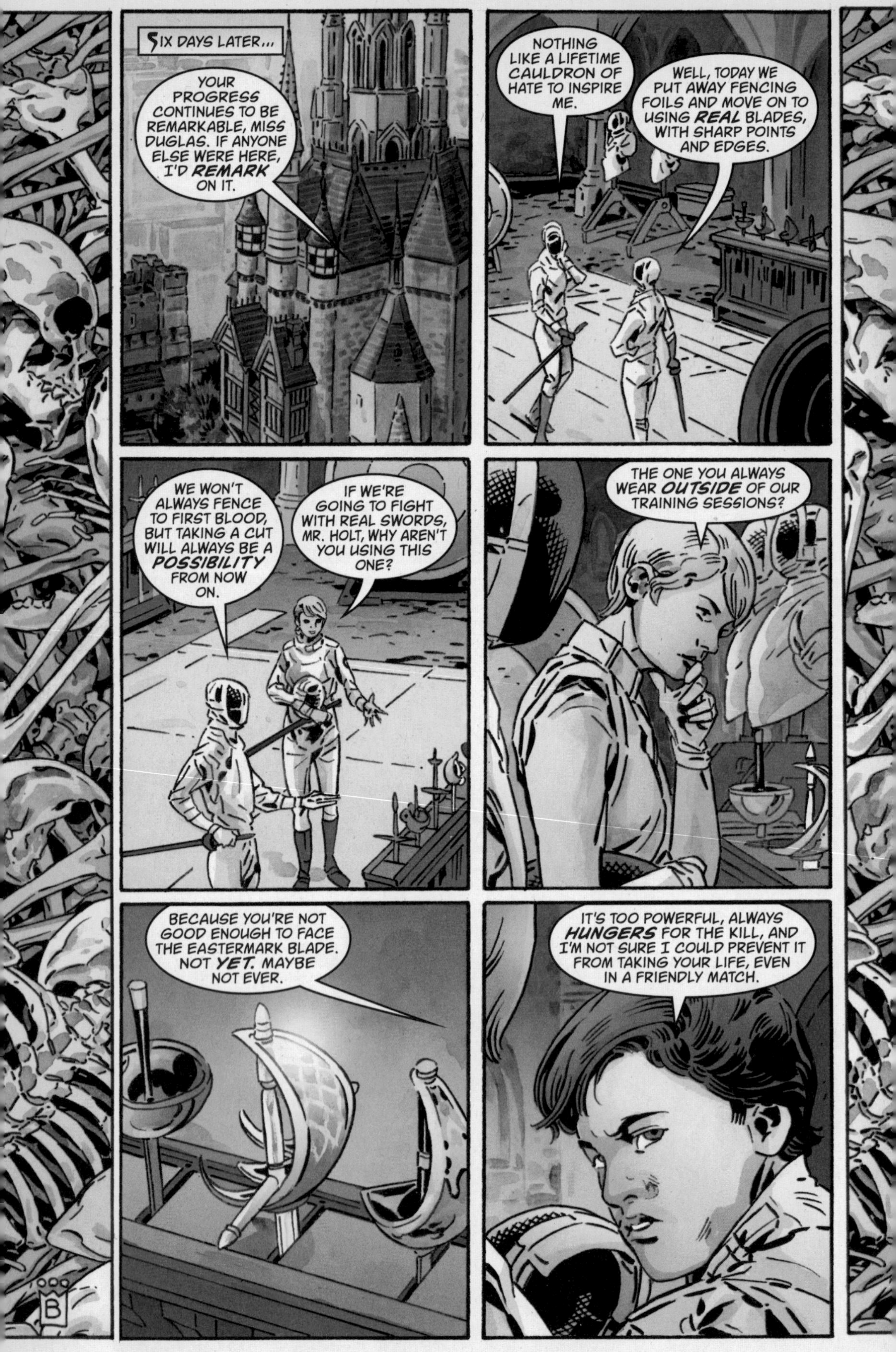
SIX DAYS LATER...
YOUR PROGRESS CONTINUES TO BE REMARKABLE, MISS DUGLAS. IF ANYONE ELSE WERE HERE, I'D REMARK ON IT.
NOTHING LIKE A LIFETIME CAULDRON OF HATE TO INSPIRE ME.
WELL, TODAY WE PUT AWAY FENCING FOILS AND MOVE ON TO USING REAL BLADES, WITH SHARP POINTS AND EDGES.
WE WON'T ALWAYS FENCE TO FIRST BLOOD, BUT TAKING A CUT WILL ALWAYS BE A POSSIBILITY FROM NOW ON.
IF WE'RE GOING TO FIGHT WITH REAL SWORDS, MR. HOLT, WHY AREN'T YOU USING THIS ONE?
THE ONE YOU ALWAYS WEAR OUTSIDE OF OUR TRAINING SESSIONS?
BECAUSE YOU'RE NOT GOOD ENOUGH TO FACE THE EASTERMARK BLADE. NOT YET. MAYBE NOT EVER.
IT'S TOO POWERFUL, ALWAYS HUNGERS FOR THE KILL, AND I'M NOT SURE I COULD PREVENT IT FROM TAKING YOUR LIFE, EVEN IN A FRIENDLY MATCH.

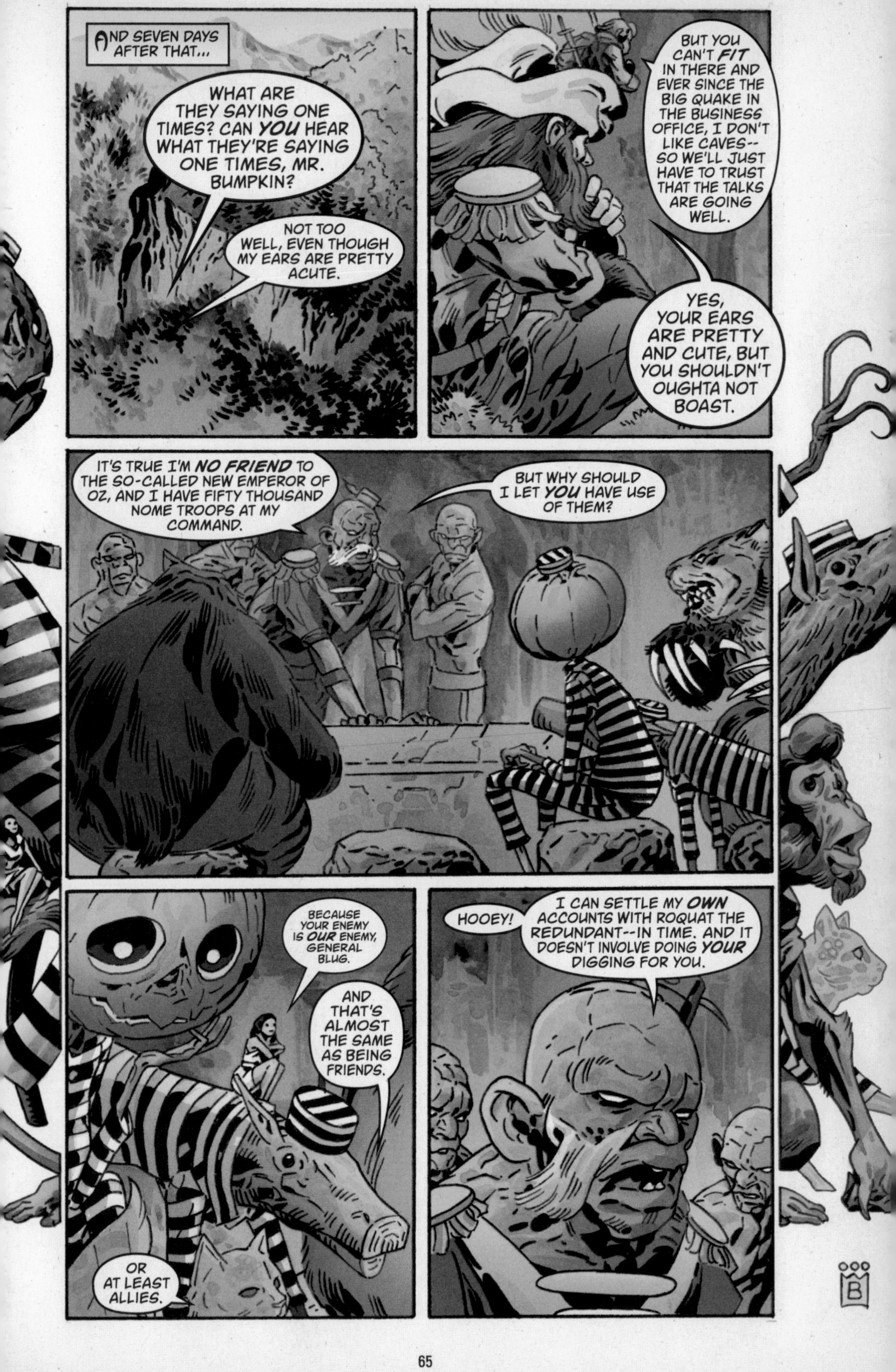
AND SEVEN DAYS AFTER THAT...
WHAT ARE THEY SAYING ONE TIMES? CAN YOU HEAR WHAT THEY'RE SAYING ONE TIMES, MR. BUMPKIN?
NOT TOO WELL, EVEN THOUGH MY EARS ARE PRETTY ACUTE.
BUT YOU CAN'T FIT IN THERE AND EVER SINCE THE BIG QUAKE IN THE BUSINESS OFFICE, I DON'T LIKE CAVES-- SO WE'LL JUST HAVE TO TRUST THAT THE TALKS ARE GOING WELL.
YES, YOUR EARS ARE PRETTY AND CUTE, BUT YOU SHOULDN'T OUGHTA NOT BOAST.
IT'S TRUE I'M NO FRIEND TO THE SO-CALLED NEW EMPEROR OF OZ, AND I HAVE FIFTY THOUSAND NOME TROOPS AT MY COMMAND.
BUT WHY SHOULD I LET YOU HAVE USE OF THEM?
BECAUSE YOUR ENEMY IS OUR ENEMY, GENERAL BLUG.
AND THAT'S ALMOST THE SAME AS BEING FRIENDS.
OR AT LEAST ALLIES.
HOOEY!
I CAN SETTLE MY OWN ACCOUNTS WITH ROQUAT THE REDUNDANT--IN TIME. AND IT DOESN'T INVOLVE DOING YOUR DIGGING FOR YOU.

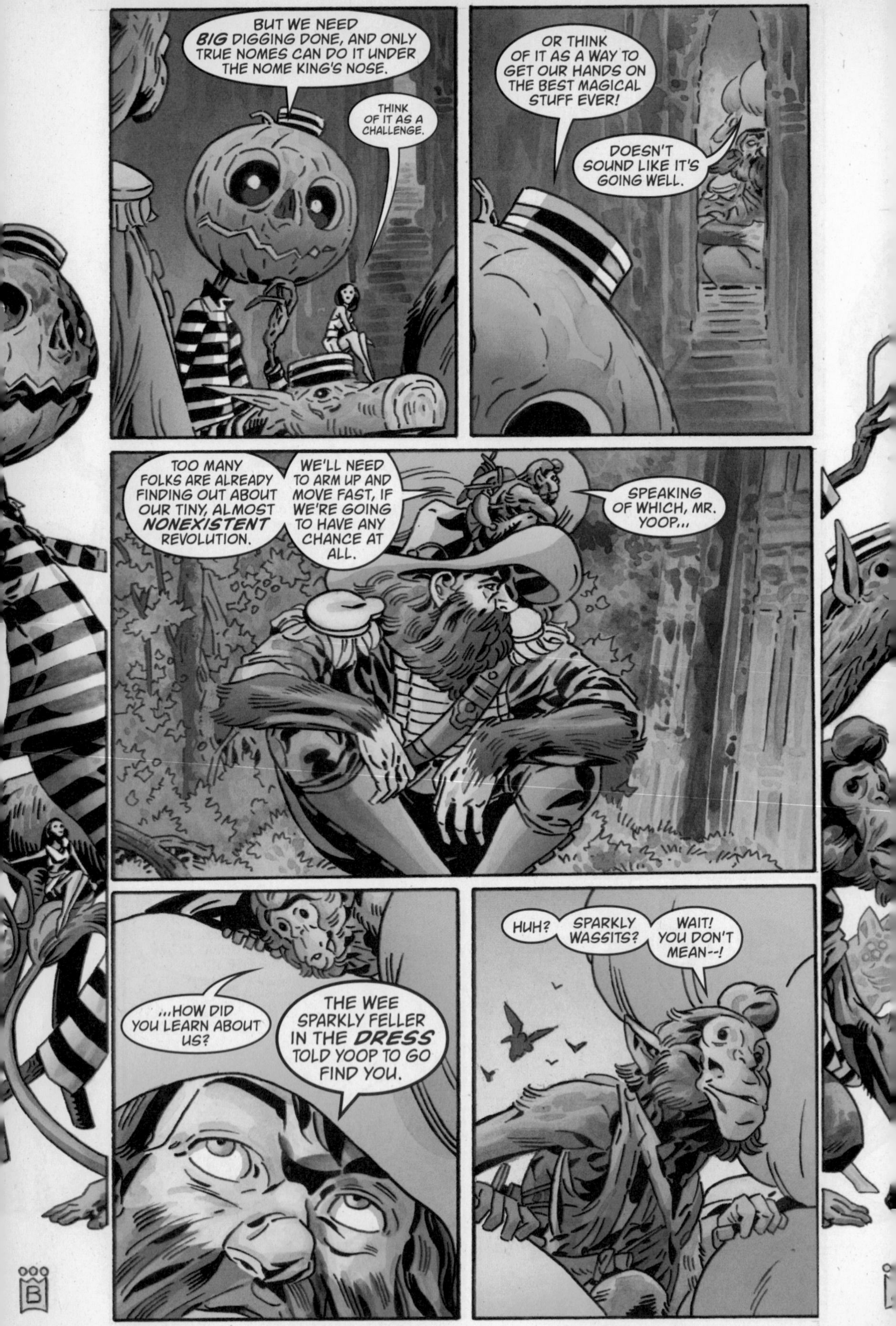

BUT WE NEED BIG DIGGING DONE, AND ONLY TRUE NOMES CAN DO IT UNDER THE NOME KING'S NOSE.
THINK OF IT AS A CHALLENGE.
OR THINK OF IT AS A WAY TO GET OUR HANDS ON THE BEST MAGICAL STUFF EVER!
DOESN'T SOUND LIKE IT'S GOING WELL.
TOO MANY FOLKS ARE ALREADY FINDING OUT ABOUT OUR TINY, ALMOST NONEXISTENT REVOLUTION.
WE'LL NEED TO ARM UP AND MOVE FAST, IF WE'RE GOING TO HAVE ANY CHANCE AT ALL.
SPEAKING OF WHICH, MR. YOOP...
...HOW DID YOU LEARN ABOUT US?
THE WEE SPARKLY FELLER IN THE DRESS TOLD YOOP TO GO FIND YOU.
HUH?
SPARKLY WASSITS?
WAIT! YOU DON'T MEAN--!

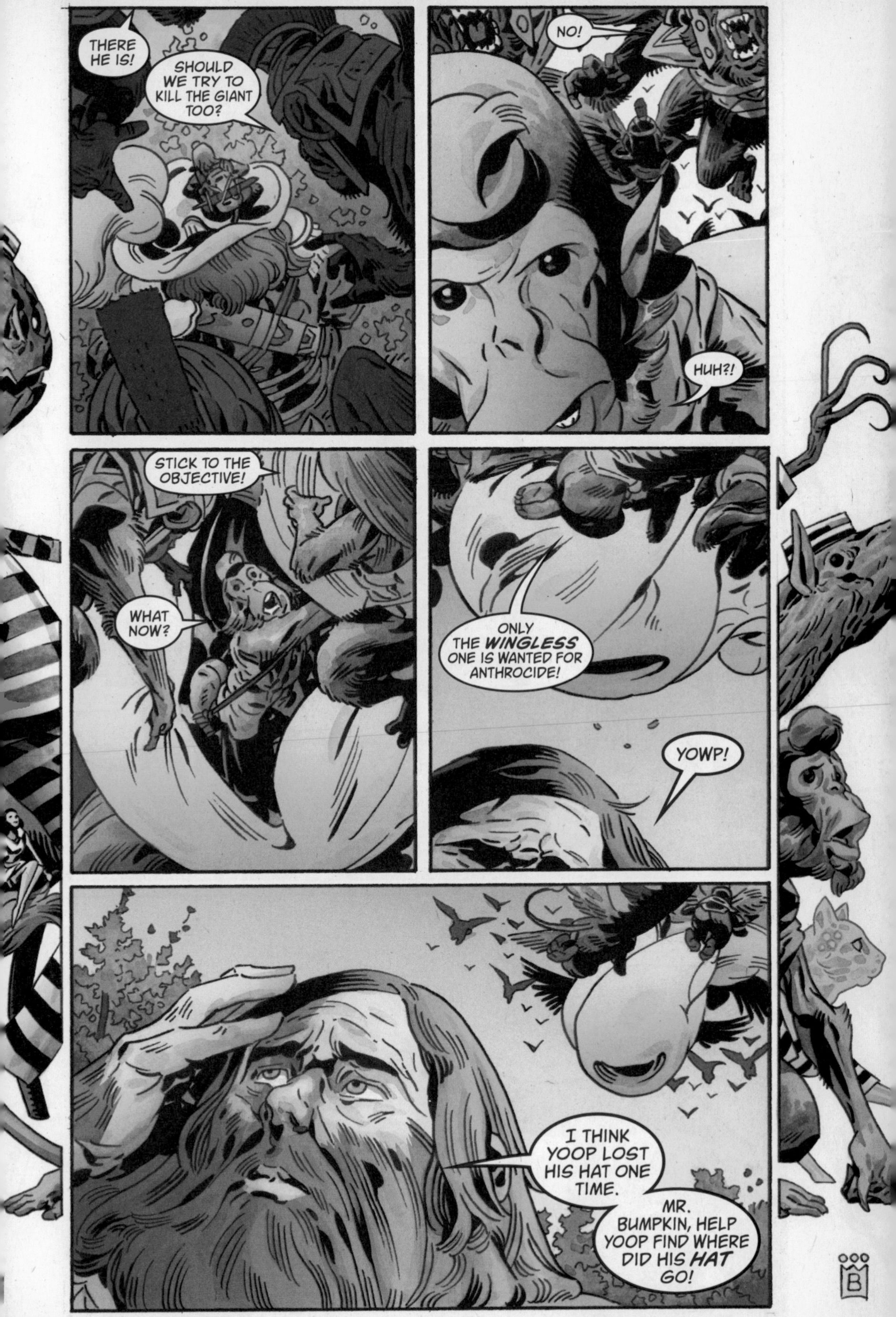
THERE HE IS!
SHOULD WE TRY TO KILL THE GIANT TOO?
NO!
HUH?!
STICK TO THE OBJECTIVE!
WHAT NOW?
ONLY THE WINGLESS ONE IS WANTED FOR ANTHROCIDE!
YOWP!
I THINK YOOP LOST HIS HAT ONE TIME.
MR. BUMPKIN, HELP YOOP FIND WHERE DID HIS HAT GO!

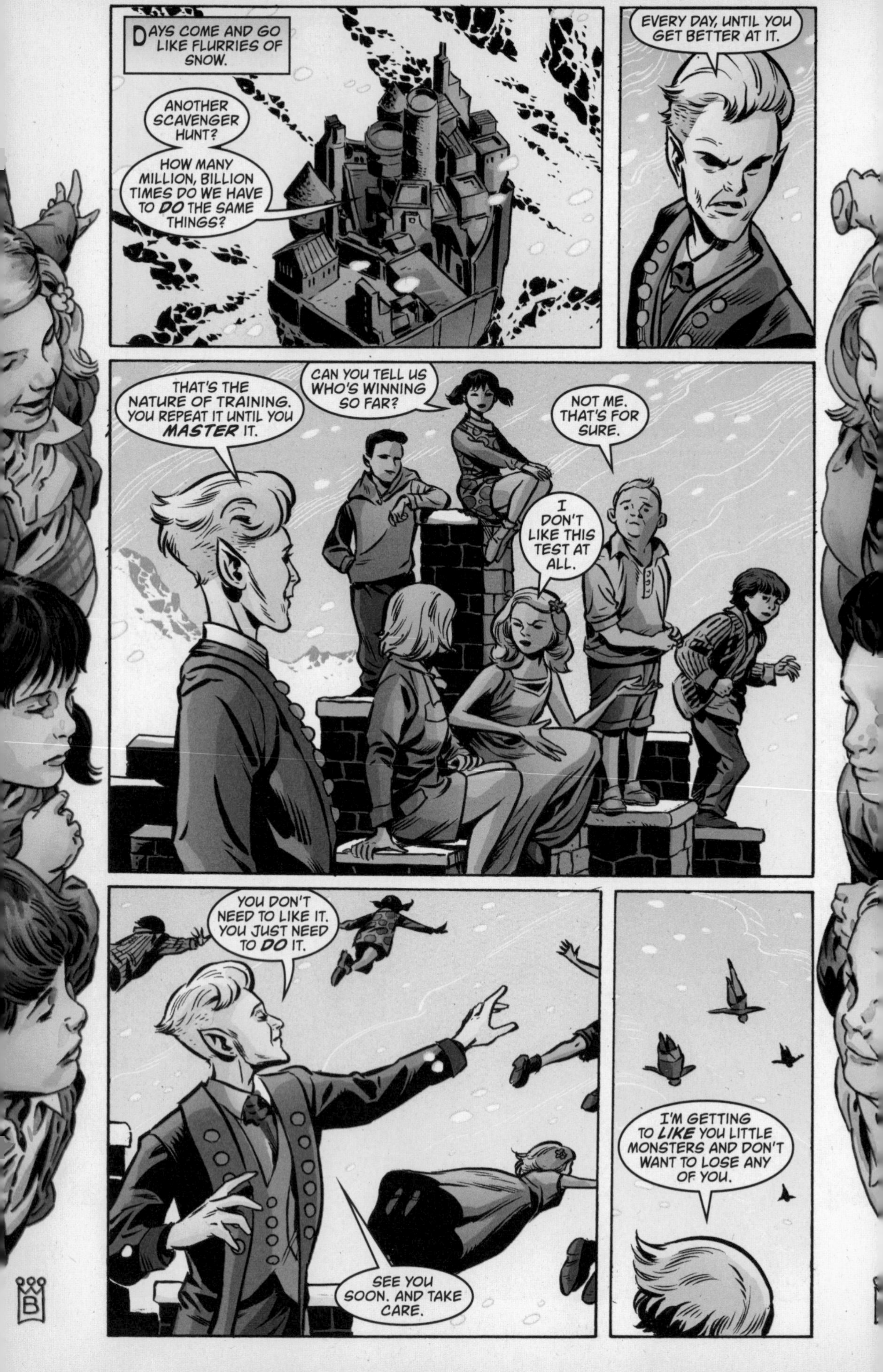
DAYS COME AND GO LIKE FLURRIES OF SNOW.
ANOTHER SCAVENGER HUNT?
HOW MANY MILLION, BILLION TIMES DO WE HAVE TO DO THE SAME THINGS?
EVERY DAY, UNTIL YOU GET BETTER AT IT.
THAT'S THE NATURE OF TRAINING. YOU REPEAT IT UNTIL YOU MASTER IT.
CAN YOU TELL US WHO'S WINNING SO FAR?
NOT ME. THAT'S FOR SURE.
I DON'T LIKE THIS TEST AT ALL.
YOU DON'T NEED TO LIKE IT. YOU JUST NEED TO DO IT.
SEE YOU SOON. AND TAKE CARE.
I'M GETTING TO LIKE YOU LITTLE MONSTERS AND DON'T WANT TO LOSE ANY OF YOU.

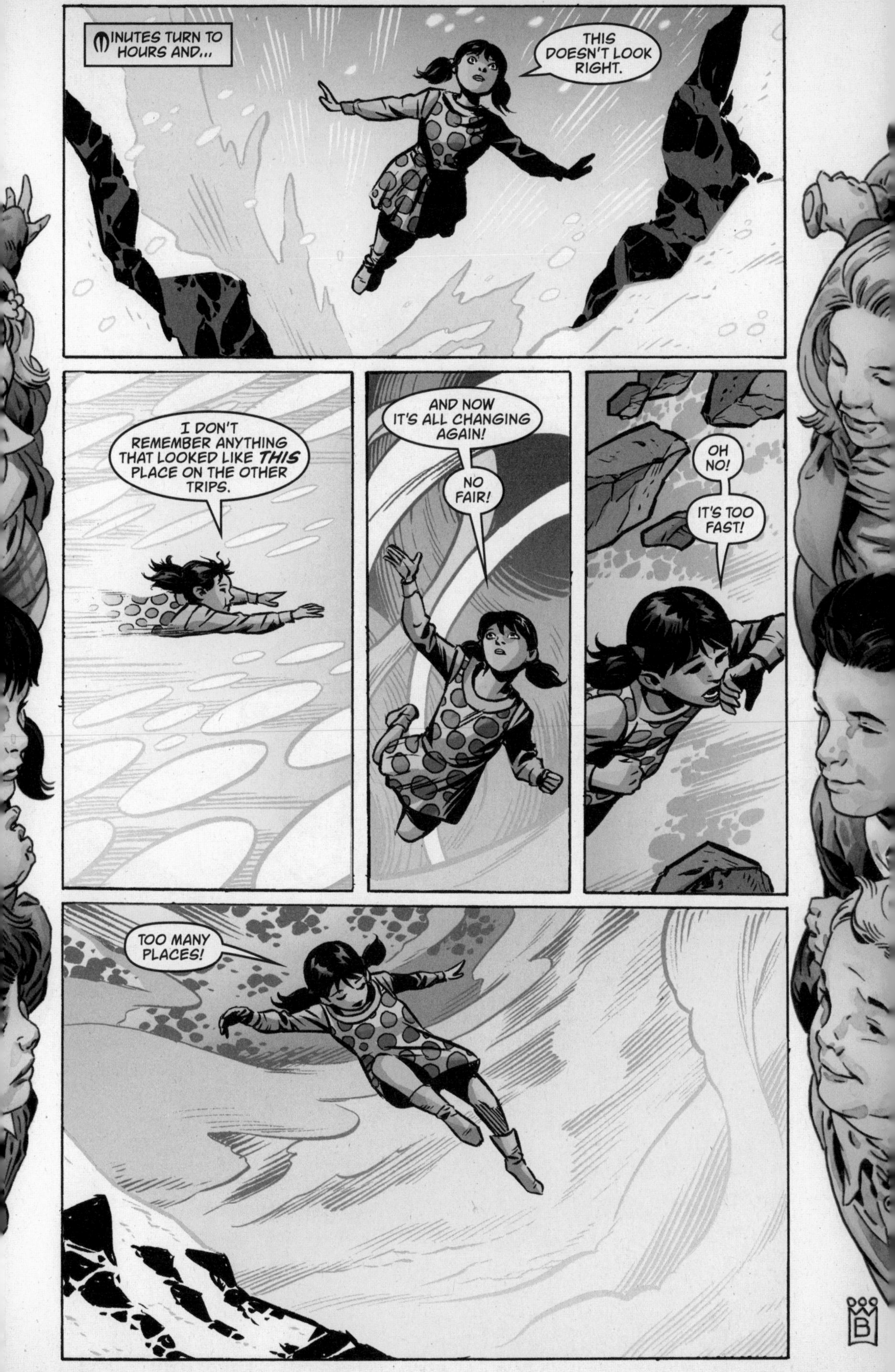
MINUTES TURN TO HOURS AND...
THIS DOESN'T LOOK RIGHT.
I DON'T REMEMBER ANYTHING THAT LOOKED LIKE THIS PLACE ON THE OTHER TRIPS.
AND NOW IT'S ALL CHANGING AGAIN!
NO FAIR!
OH NO!
IT'S TOO FAST!
TOO MANY PLACES!

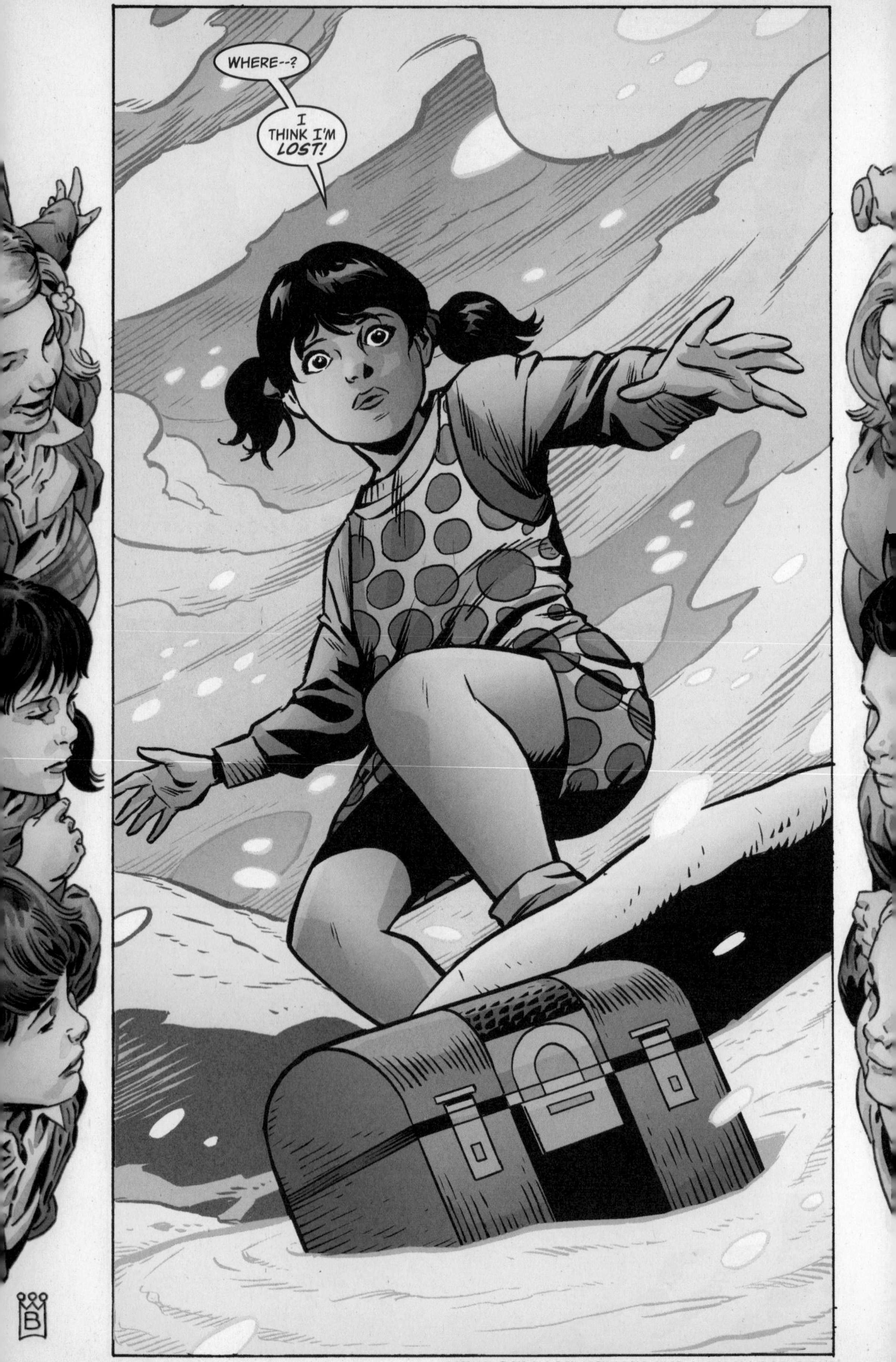
WHERE--?
I THINK I'M *LOST!*

NEXT: DEATH SENTENCES AND LITTLE LOST GIRLS

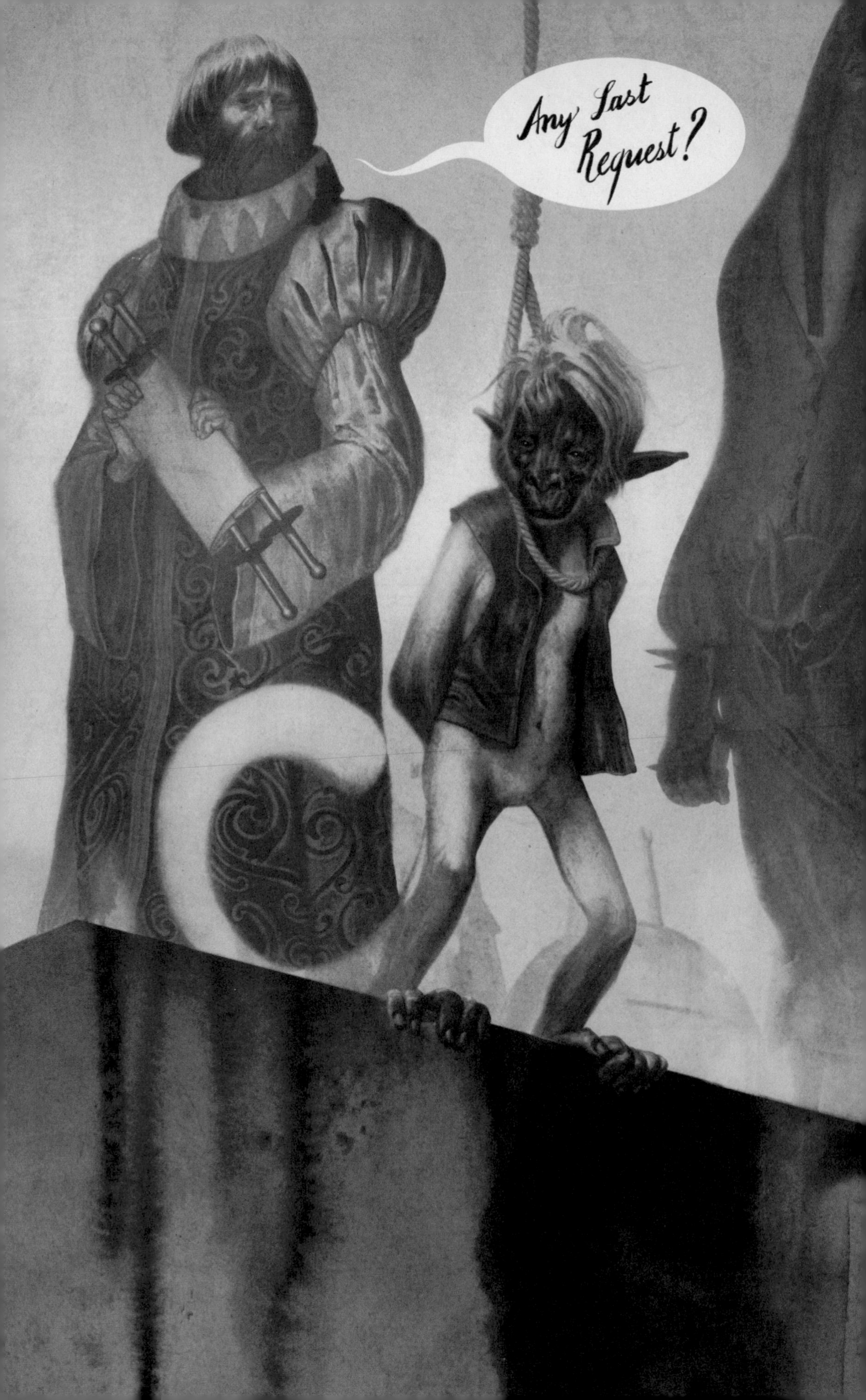
Any Last Request?

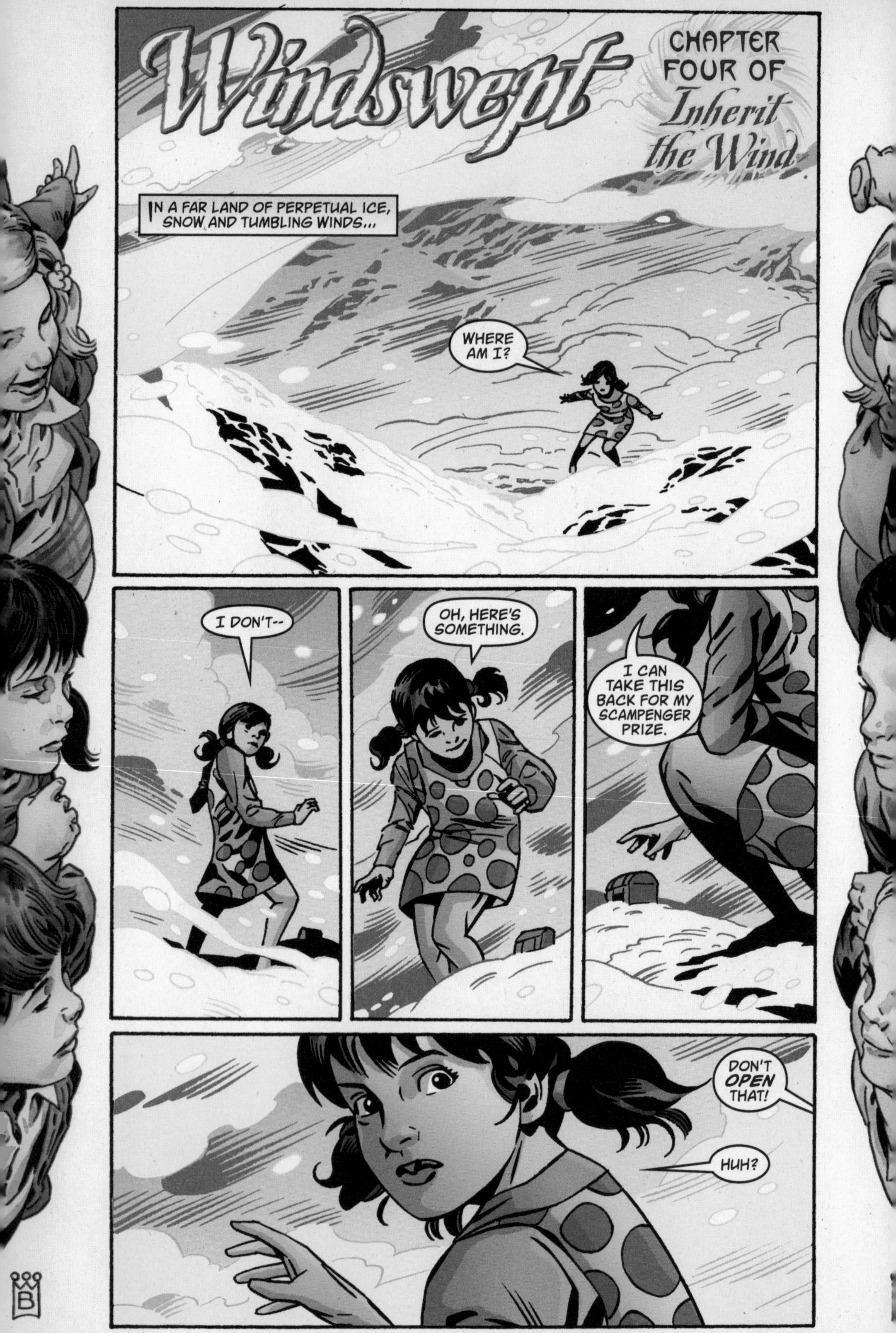
Windswept
CHAPTER FOUR OF Inherit the Wind
IN A FAR LAND OF PERPETUAL ICE, SNOW AND TUMBLING WINDS...
WHERE AM I?
I DON'T--
OH, HERE'S SOMETHING.
I CAN TAKE THIS BACK FOR MY SCAMPENGER PRIZE.
DON'T OPEN THAT!
HUH?

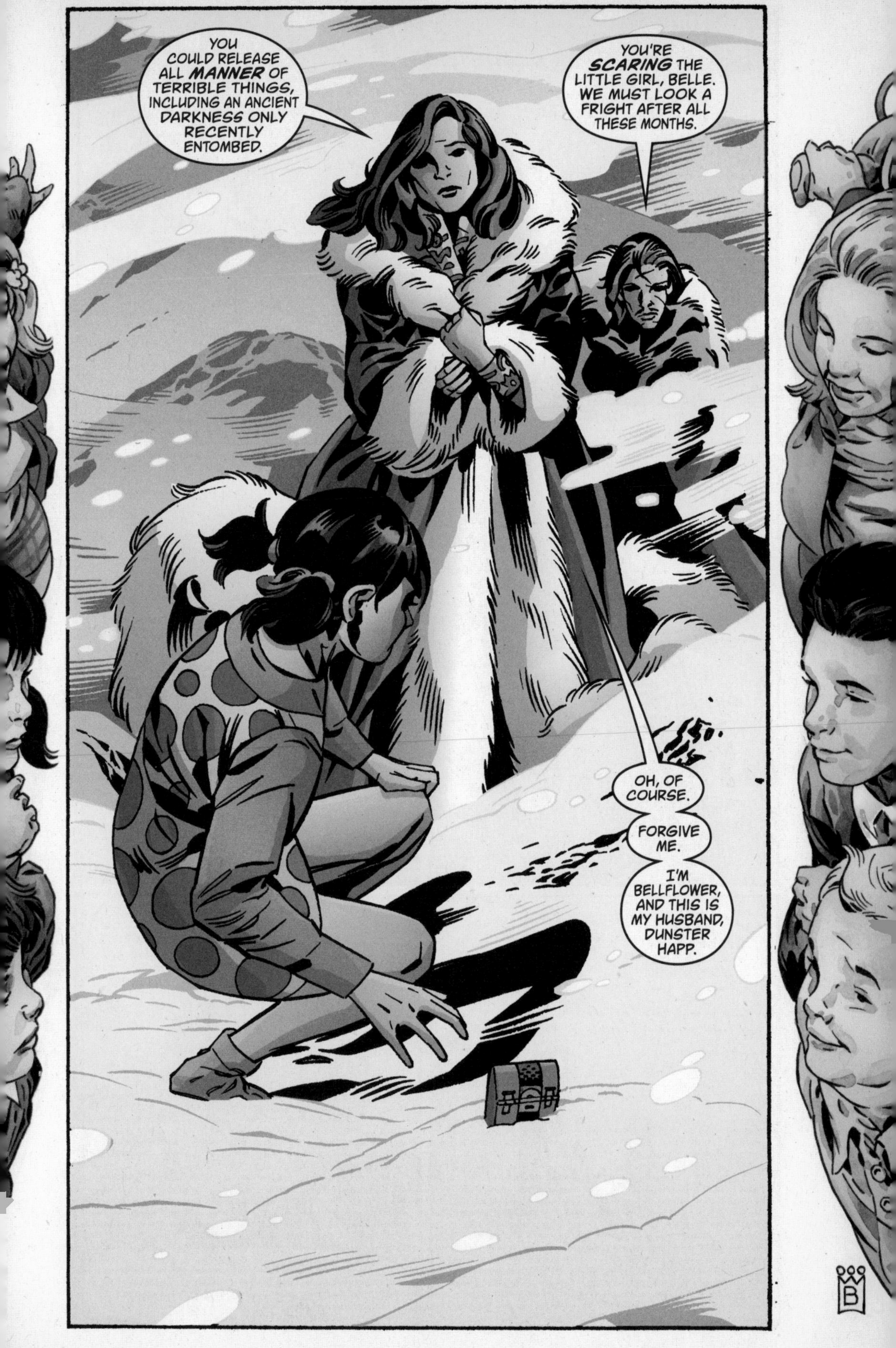
YOU COULD RELEASE ALL MANNER OF TERRIBLE THINGS, INCLUDING AN ANCIENT DARKNESS ONLY RECENTLY ENTOMBED.
YOU'RE SCARING THE LITTLE GIRL, BELLE. WE MUST LOOK A FRIGHT AFTER ALL THESE MONTHS.
OH, OF COURSE.
FORGIVE ME.
I'M BELLFLOWER, AND THIS IS MY HUSBAND, DUNSTER HAPP.

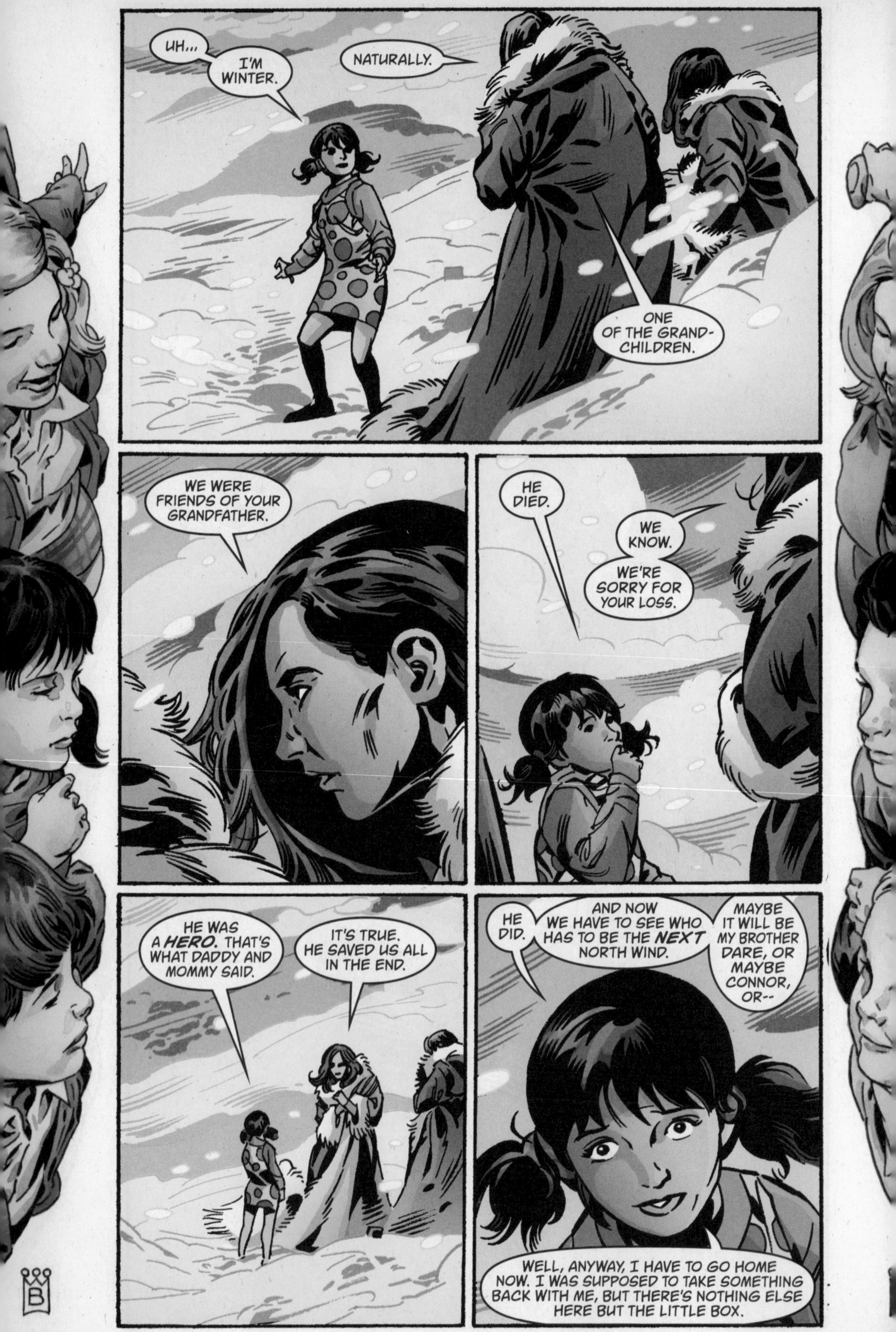
UH...
I'M WINTER.
NATURALLY.
ONE OF THE GRAND-CHILDREN.
WE WERE FRIENDS OF YOUR GRANDFATHER.
HE DIED.
WE KNOW.
WE'RE SORRY FOR YOUR LOSS.
HE WAS A *HERO*. THAT'S WHAT DADDY AND MOMMY SAID.
IT'S TRUE. HE SAVED US ALL IN THE END.
HE DID.
AND NOW WE HAVE TO SEE WHO HAS TO BE THE *NEXT* NORTH WIND.
MAYBE IT WILL BE MY BROTHER DARE, OR MAYBE CONNOR, OR--
WELL, ANYWAY, I HAVE TO GO HOME NOW. I WAS SUPPOSED TO TAKE SOMETHING BACK WITH ME, BUT THERE'S NOTHING ELSE HERE BUT THE LITTLE BOX.

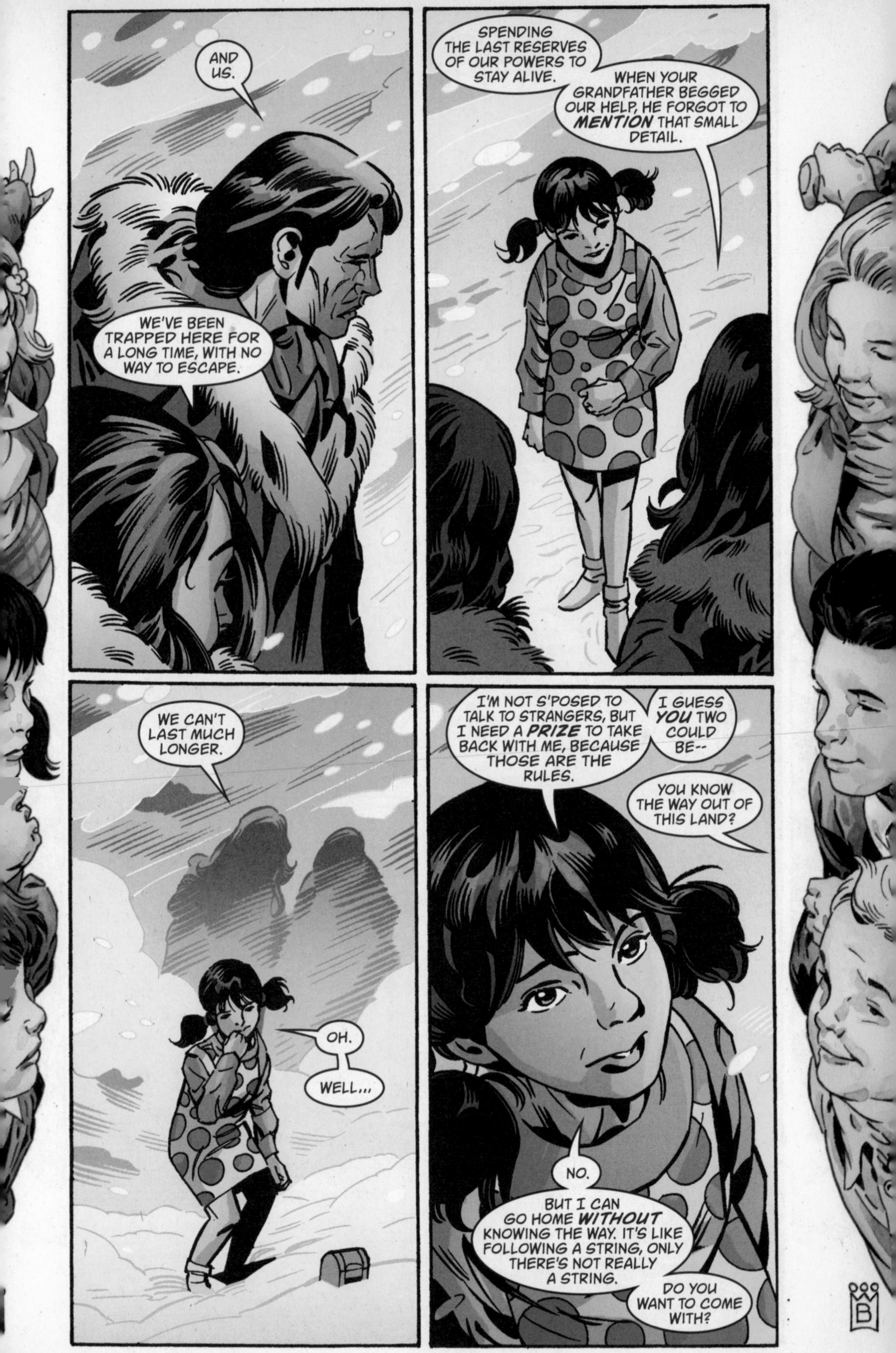
AND US.
WE'VE BEEN TRAPPED HERE FOR A LONG TIME, WITH NO WAY TO ESCAPE.
SPENDING THE LAST RESERVES OF OUR POWERS TO STAY ALIVE.
WHEN YOUR GRANDFATHER BEGGED OUR HELP, HE FORGOT TO MENTION THAT SMALL DETAIL.
WE CAN'T LAST MUCH LONGER.
OH.
WELL...
I'M NOT S'POSED TO TALK TO STRANGERS, BUT I NEED A PRIZE TO TAKE BACK WITH ME, BECAUSE THOSE ARE THE RULES.
I GUESS YOU TWO COULD BE--
YOU KNOW THE WAY OUT OF THIS LAND?
NO.
BUT I CAN GO HOME WITHOUT KNOWING THE WAY. IT'S LIKE FOLLOWING A STRING, ONLY THERE'S NOT REALLY A STRING.
DO YOU WANT TO COME WITH?

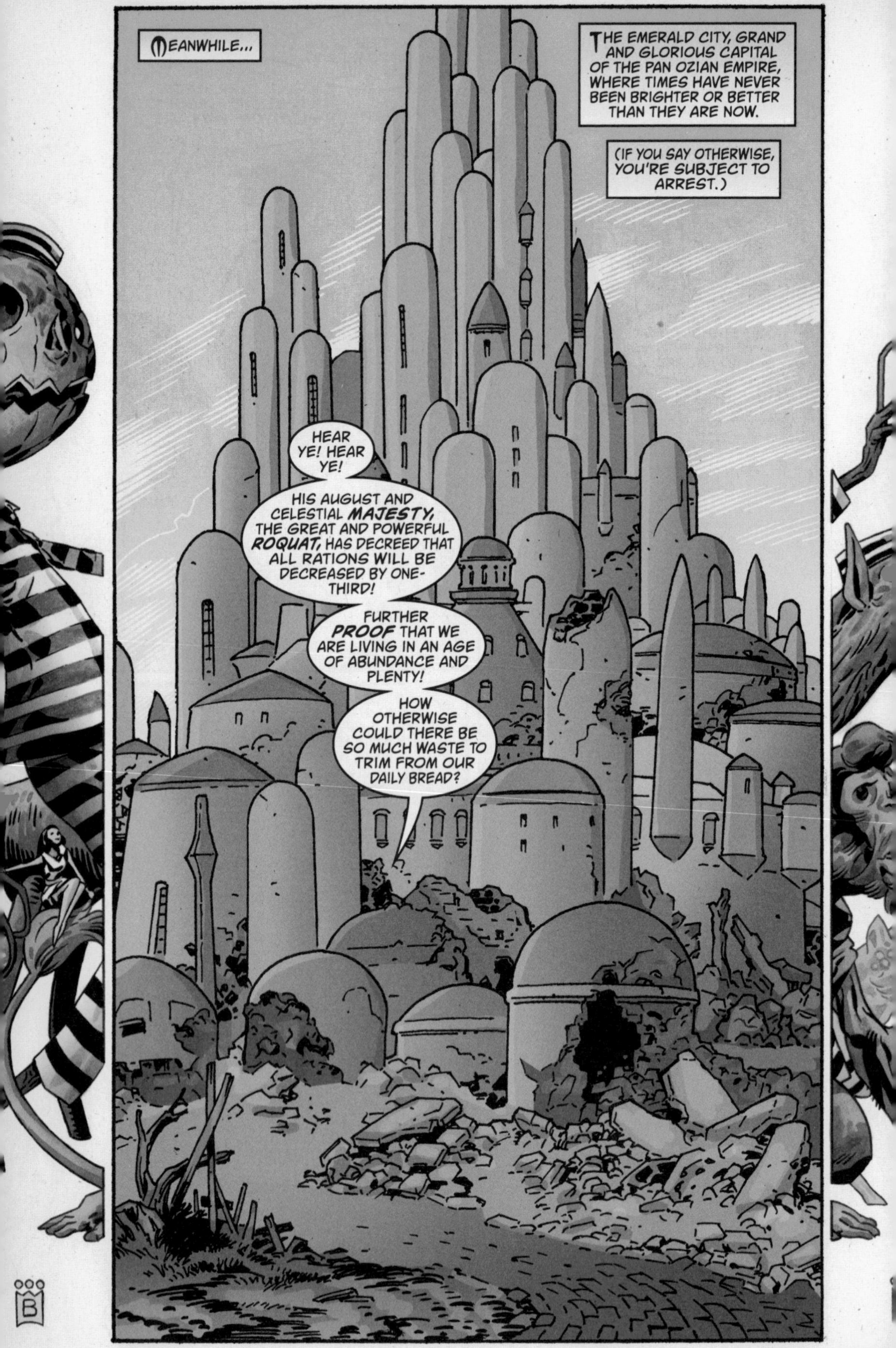

MEANWHILE...
THE EMERALD CITY, GRAND AND GLORIOUS CAPITAL OF THE PAN OZIAN EMPIRE, WHERE TIMES HAVE NEVER BEEN BRIGHTER OR BETTER THAN THEY ARE NOW.
(IF YOU SAY OTHERWISE, YOU'RE SUBJECT TO ARREST.)
HEAR YE! HEAR YE!
HIS AUGUST AND CELESTIAL MAJESTY, THE GREAT AND POWERFUL ROQUAT, HAS DECREED THAT ALL RATIONS WILL BE DECREASED BY ONE-THIRD!
FURTHER PROOF THAT WE ARE LIVING IN AN AGE OF ABUNDANCE AND PLENTY!
HOW OTHERWISE COULD THERE BE SO MUCH WASTE TO TRIM FROM OUR DAILY BREAD?

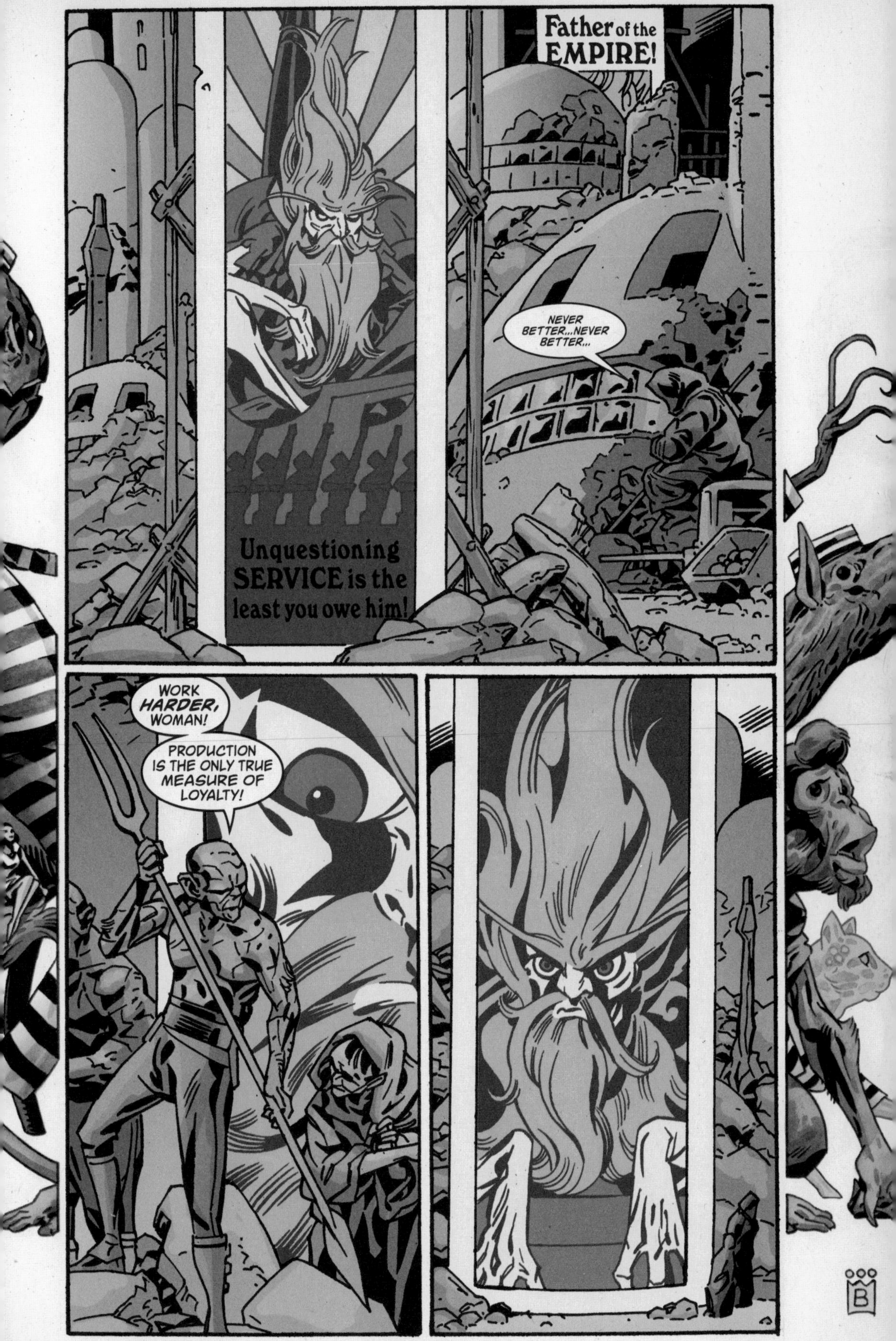
Father of the EMPIRE!
Unquestioning SERVICE is the least you owe him!
NEVER BETTER... NEVER BETTER...
WORK HARDER, WOMAN!
PRODUCTION IS THE ONLY TRUE MEASURE OF LOYALTY!

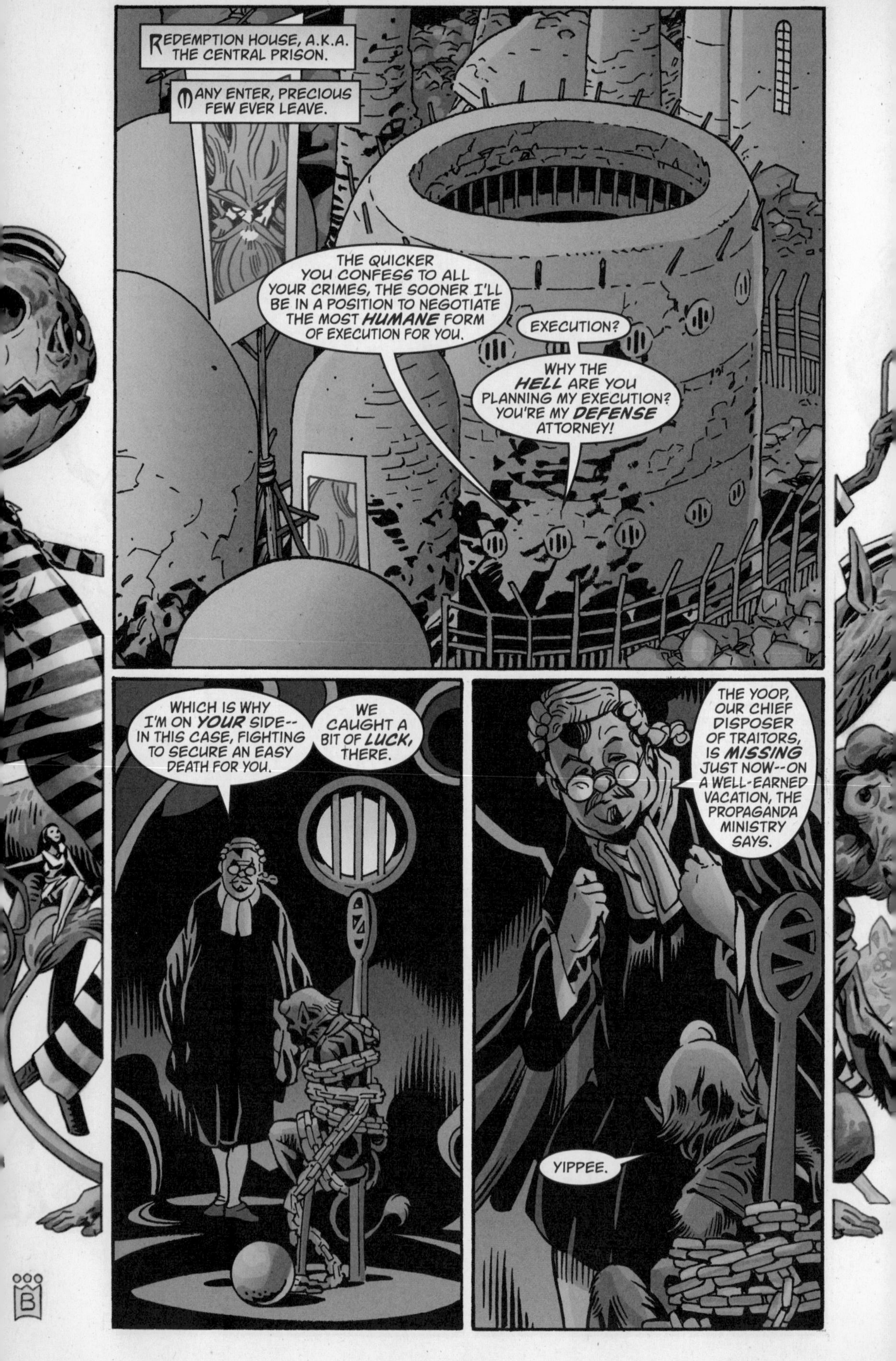
REDEMPTION HOUSE, A.K.A. THE CENTRAL PRISON.
MANY ENTER, PRECIOUS FEW EVER LEAVE.
THE QUICKER YOU CONFESS TO ALL YOUR CRIMES, THE SOONER I'LL BE IN A POSITION TO NEGOTIATE THE MOST HUMANE FORM OF EXECUTION FOR YOU.
EXECUTION?
WHY THE HELL ARE YOU PLANNING MY EXECUTION? YOU'RE MY DEFENSE ATTORNEY!
WHICH IS WHY I'M ON YOUR SIDE-- IN THIS CASE, FIGHTING TO SECURE AN EASY DEATH FOR YOU.
WE CAUGHT A BIT OF LUCK, THERE.
THE YOOP, OUR CHIEF DISPOSER OF TRAITORS, IS MISSING JUST NOW--ON A WELL-EARNED VACATION, THE PROPAGANDA MINISTRY SAYS.
YIPPEE.

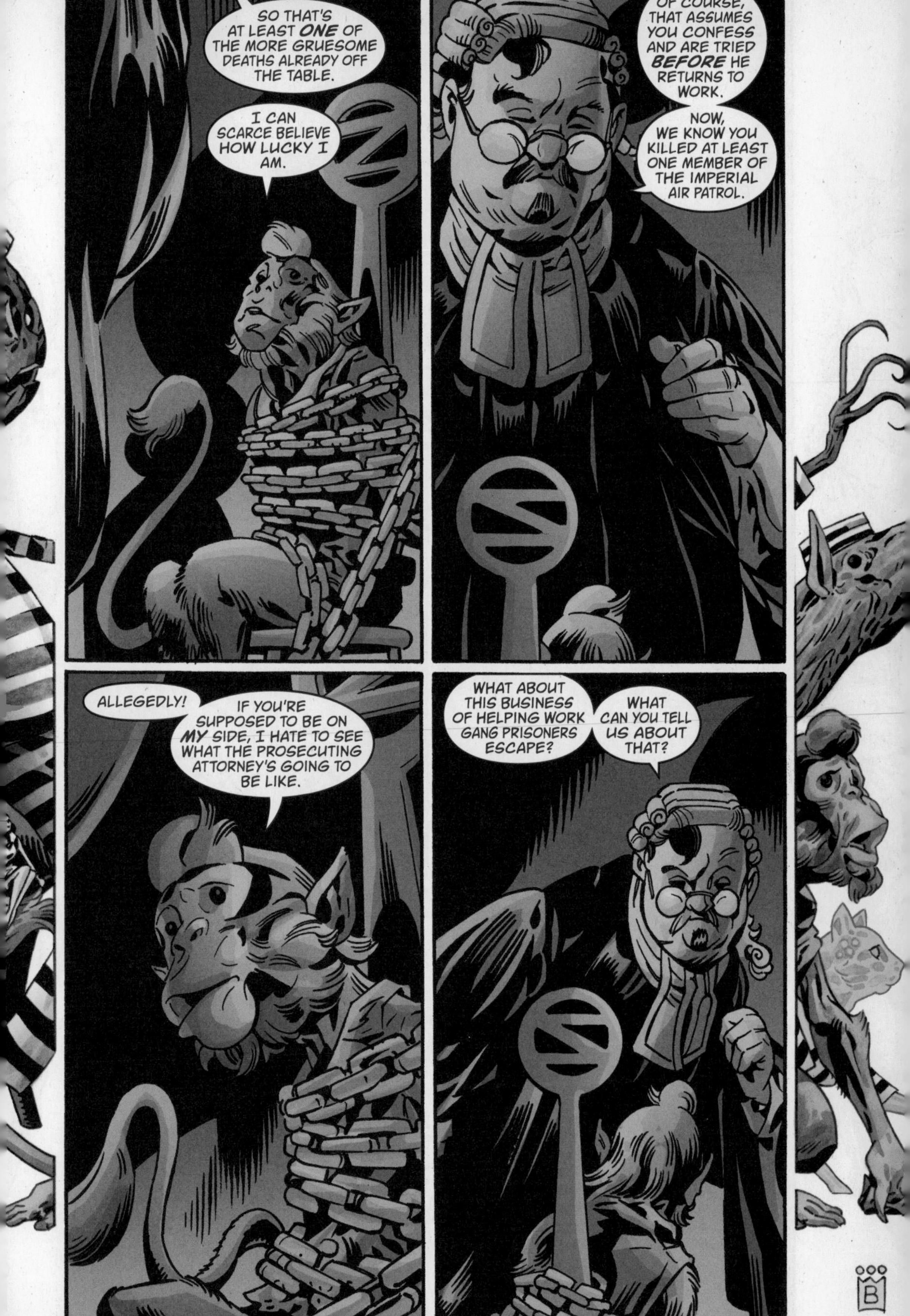
SO THAT'S AT LEAST ONE OF THE MORE GRUESOME DEATHS ALREADY OFF THE TABLE.
I CAN SCARCE BELIEVE HOW LUCKY I AM.
OF COURSE, THAT ASSUMES YOU CONFESS AND ARE TRIED BEFORE HE RETURNS TO WORK.
NOW, WE KNOW YOU KILLED AT LEAST ONE MEMBER OF THE IMPERIAL AIR PATROL.
ALLEGEDLY!
IF YOU'RE SUPPOSED TO BE ON MY SIDE, I HATE TO SEE WHAT THE PROSECUTING ATTORNEY'S GOING TO BE LIKE.
WHAT ABOUT THIS BUSINESS OF HELPING WORK GANG PRISONERS ESCAPE?
WHAT CAN YOU TELL US ABOUT THAT?

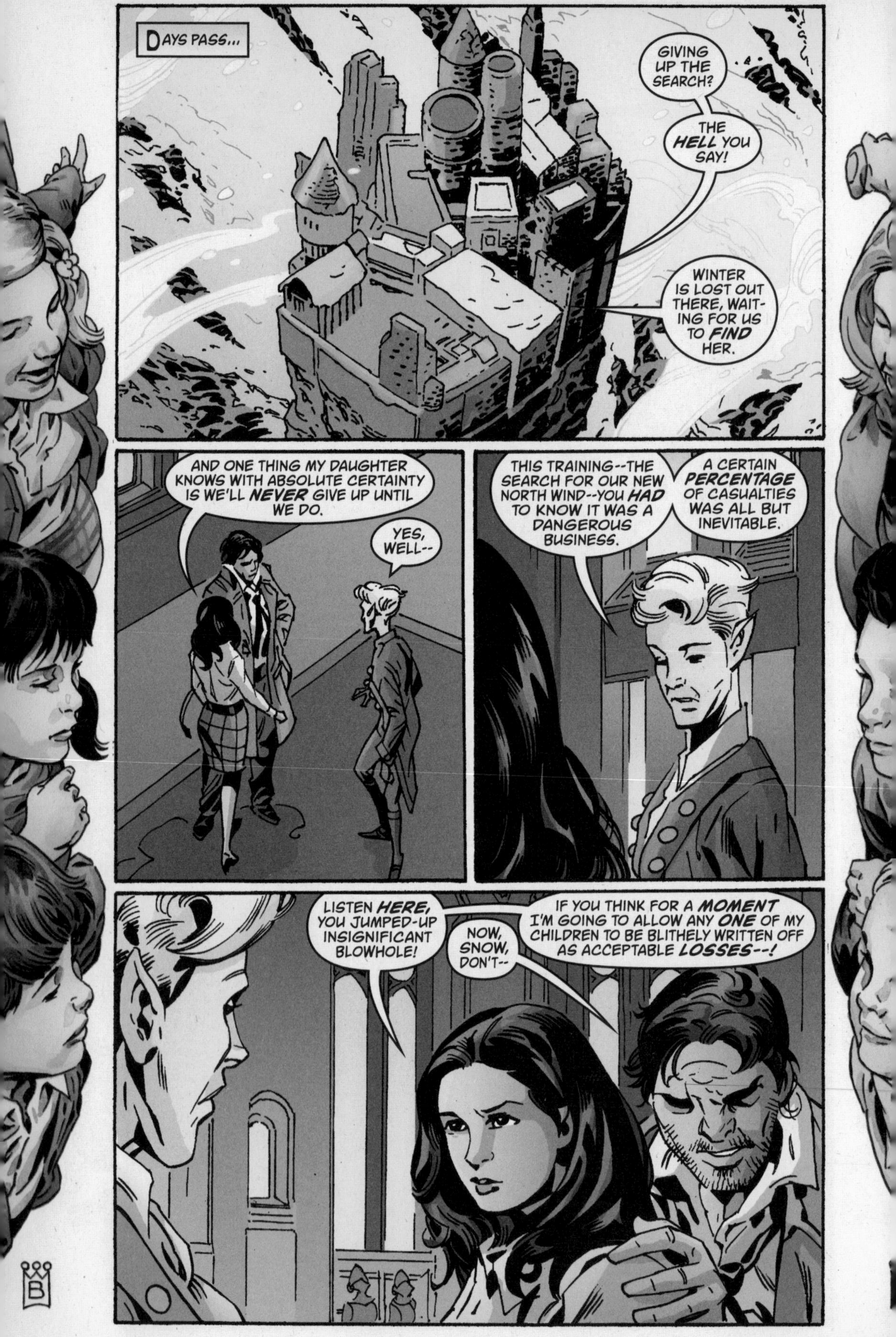
DAYS PASS...
GIVING UP THE SEARCH?
THE HELL YOU SAY!
WINTER IS LOST OUT THERE, WAITING FOR US TO FIND HER.
AND ONE THING MY DAUGHTER KNOWS WITH ABSOLUTE CERTAINTY IS WE'LL NEVER GIVE UP UNTIL WE DO.
YES, WELL--
THIS TRAINING--THE SEARCH FOR OUR NEW NORTH WIND--YOU HAD TO KNOW IT WAS A DANGEROUS BUSINESS.
A CERTAIN PERCENTAGE OF CASUALTIES WAS ALL BUT INEVITABLE.
LISTEN HERE, YOU JUMPED-UP INSIGNIFICANT BLOWHOLE!
NOW, SNOW, DON'T--
IF YOU THINK FOR A MOMENT I'M GOING TO ALLOW ANY ONE OF MY CHILDREN TO BE BLITHELY WRITTEN OFF AS ACCEPTABLE LOSSES--!

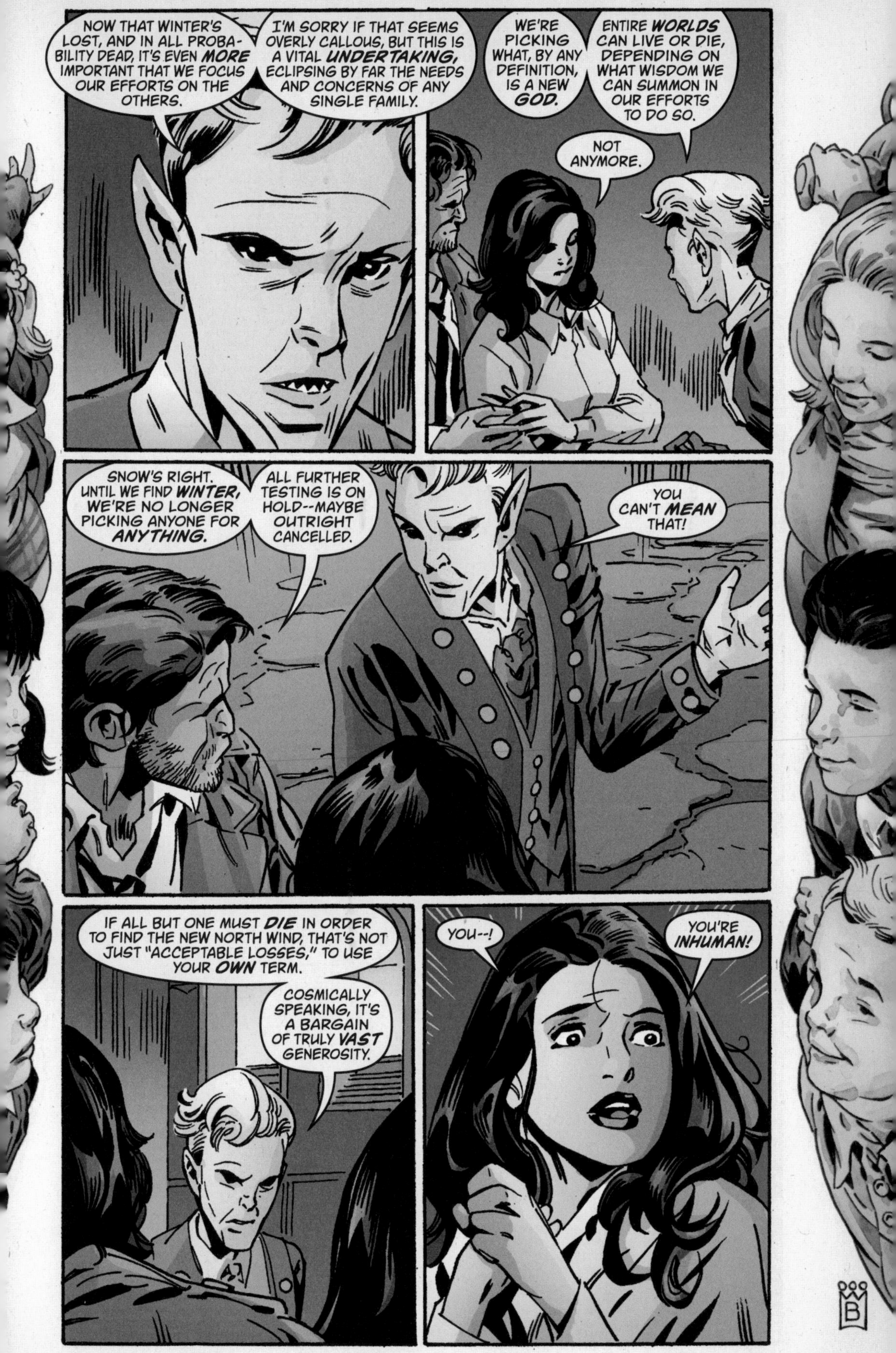
NOW THAT WINTER'S LOST, AND IN ALL PROBABILITY DEAD, IT'S EVEN MORE IMPORTANT THAT WE FOCUS OUR EFFORTS ON THE OTHERS.
I'M SORRY IF THAT SEEMS OVERLY CALLOUS, BUT THIS IS A VITAL UNDERTAKING, ECLIPSING BY FAR THE NEEDS AND CONCERNS OF ANY SINGLE FAMILY.
WE'RE PICKING WHAT, BY ANY DEFINITION, IS A NEW GOD.
ENTIRE WORLDS CAN LIVE OR DIE, DEPENDING ON WHAT WISDOM WE CAN SUMMON IN OUR EFFORTS TO DO SO.
NOT ANYMORE.
SNOW'S RIGHT. UNTIL WE FIND WINTER, WE'RE NO LONGER PICKING ANYONE FOR ANYTHING.
ALL FURTHER TESTING IS ON HOLD--MAYBE OUTRIGHT CANCELLED.
YOU CAN'T MEAN THAT!
IF ALL BUT ONE MUST DIE IN ORDER TO FIND THE NEW NORTH WIND, THAT'S NOT JUST "ACCEPTABLE LOSSES," TO USE YOUR OWN TERM.
COSMICALLY SPEAKING, IT'S A BARGAIN OF TRULY VAST GENEROSITY.
YOU--!
YOU'RE INHUMAN!

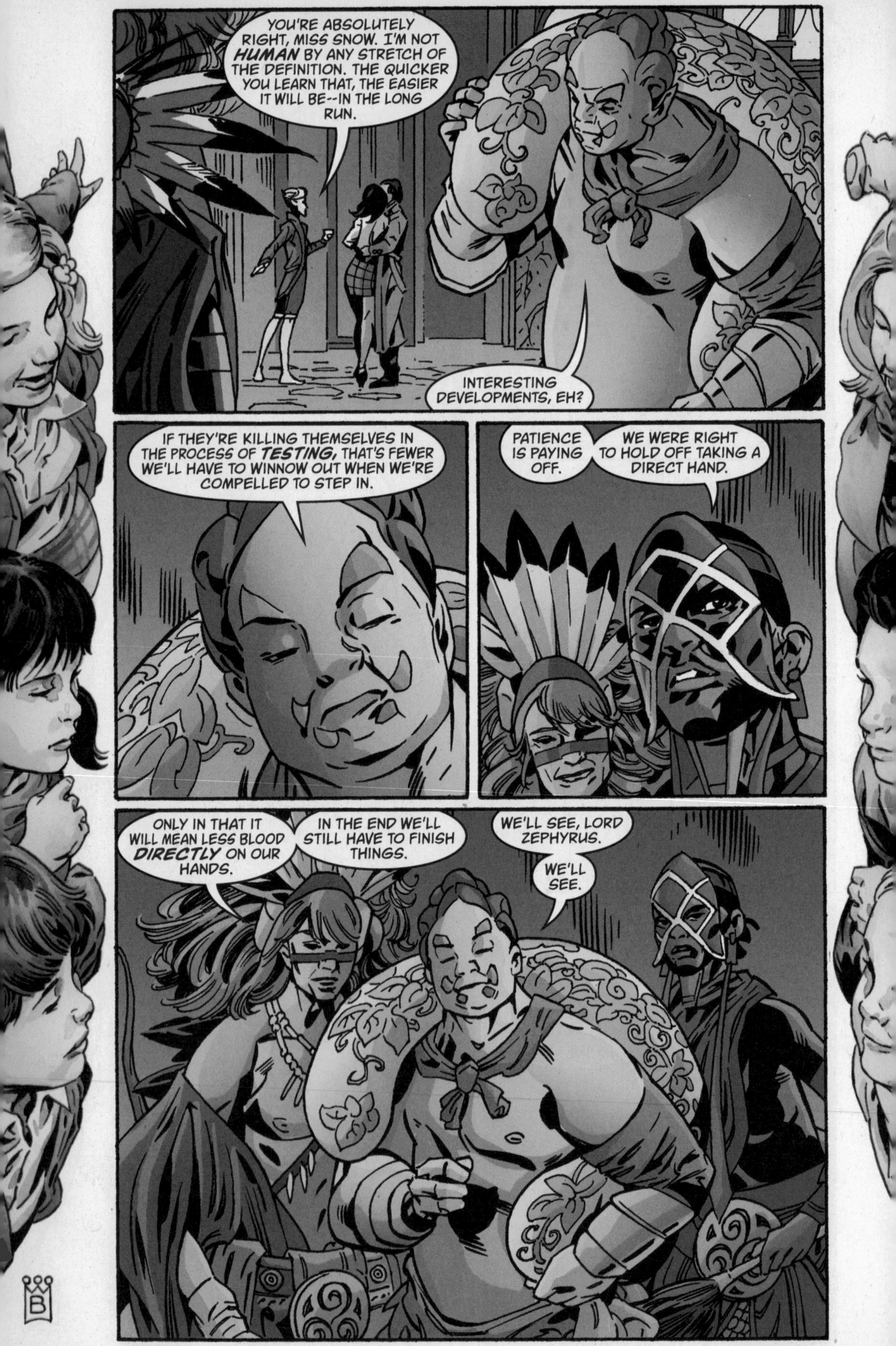
YOU'RE ABSOLUTELY RIGHT, MISS SNOW. I'M NOT HUMAN BY ANY STRETCH OF THE DEFINITION. THE QUICKER YOU LEARN THAT, THE EASIER IT WILL BE--IN THE LONG RUN.
INTERESTING DEVELOPMENTS, EH?
IF THEY'RE KILLING THEMSELVES IN THE PROCESS OF TESTING, THAT'S FEWER WE'LL HAVE TO WINNOW OUT WHEN WE'RE COMPELLED TO STEP IN.
PATIENCE IS PAYING OFF.
WE WERE RIGHT TO HOLD OFF TAKING A DIRECT HAND.
ONLY IN THAT IT WILL MEAN LESS BLOOD DIRECTLY ON OUR HANDS.
IN THE END WE'LL STILL HAVE TO FINISH THINGS.
WE'LL SEE, LORD ZEPHYRUS.
WE'LL SEE.

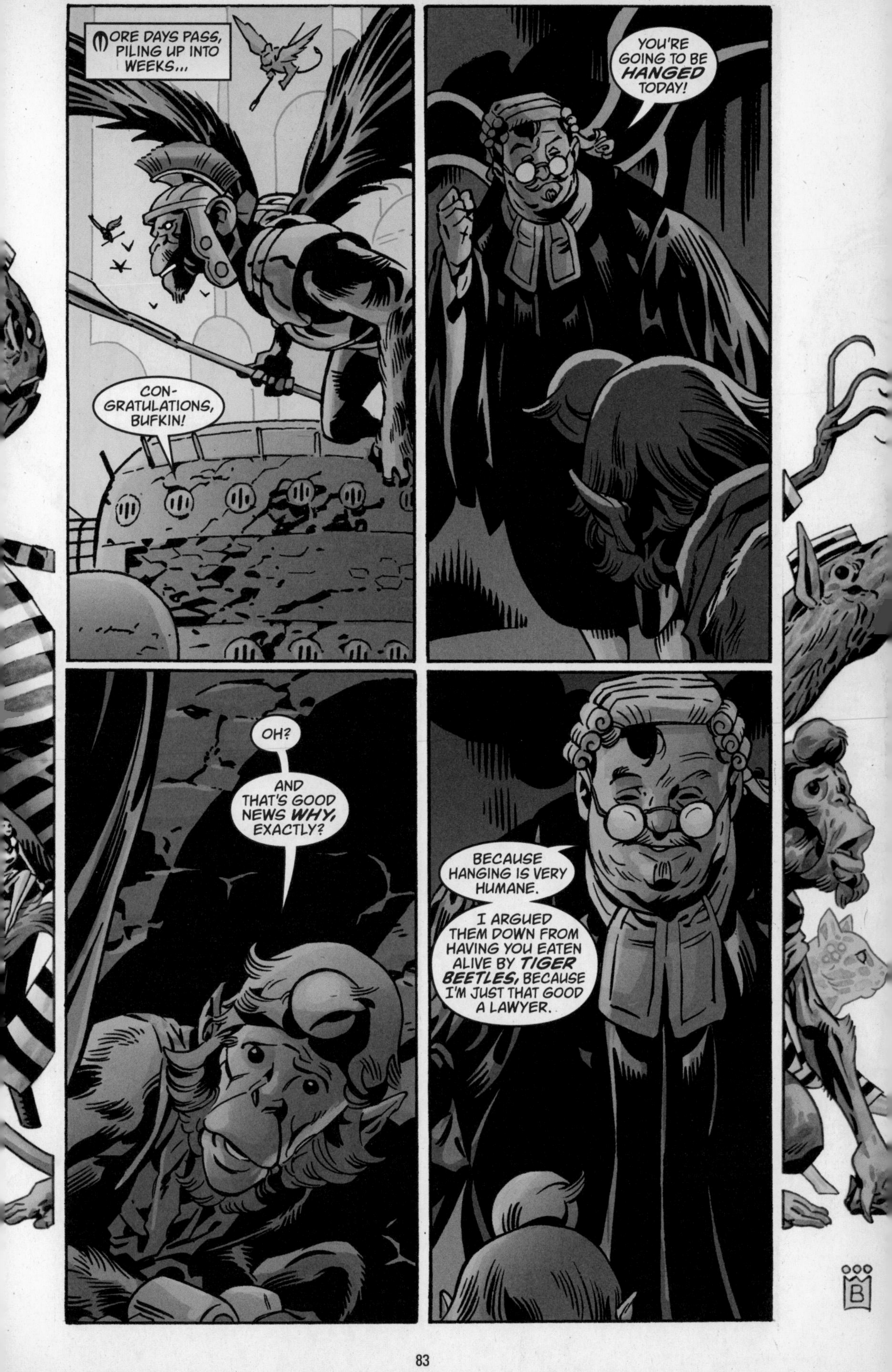
MORE DAYS PASS, PILING UP INTO WEEKS...
CON-GRATULATIONS, BUFKIN!
YOU'RE GOING TO BE HANGED TODAY!
OH?
AND THAT'S GOOD NEWS WHY, EXACTLY?
BECAUSE HANGING IS VERY HUMANE.
I ARGUED THEM DOWN FROM HAVING YOU EATEN ALIVE BY TIGER BEETLES, BECAUSE I'M JUST THAT GOOD A LAWYER.

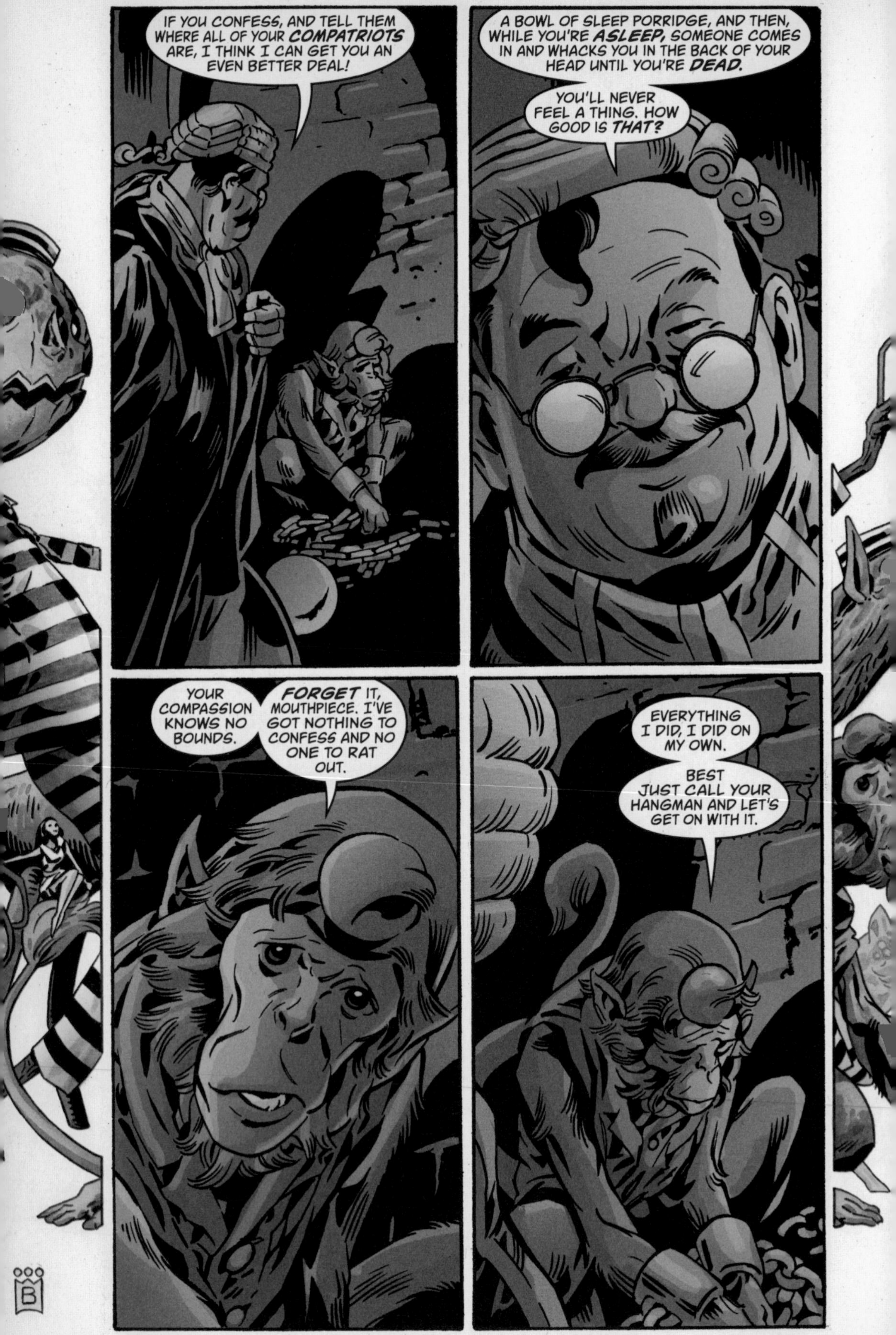
IF YOU CONFESS, AND TELL THEM WHERE ALL OF YOUR COMPATRIOTS ARE, I THINK I CAN GET YOU AN EVEN BETTER DEAL!
A BOWL OF SLEEP PORRIDGE, AND THEN, WHILE YOU'RE ASLEEP, SOMEONE COMES IN AND WHACKS YOU IN THE BACK OF YOUR HEAD UNTIL YOU'RE DEAD.
YOU'LL NEVER FEEL A THING. HOW GOOD IS THAT?
YOUR COMPASSION KNOWS NO BOUNDS.
FORGET IT, MOUTHPIECE. I'VE GOT NOTHING TO CONFESS AND NO ONE TO RAT OUT.
EVERYTHING I DID, I DID ON MY OWN.
BEST JUST CALL YOUR HANGMAN AND LET'S GET ON WITH IT.

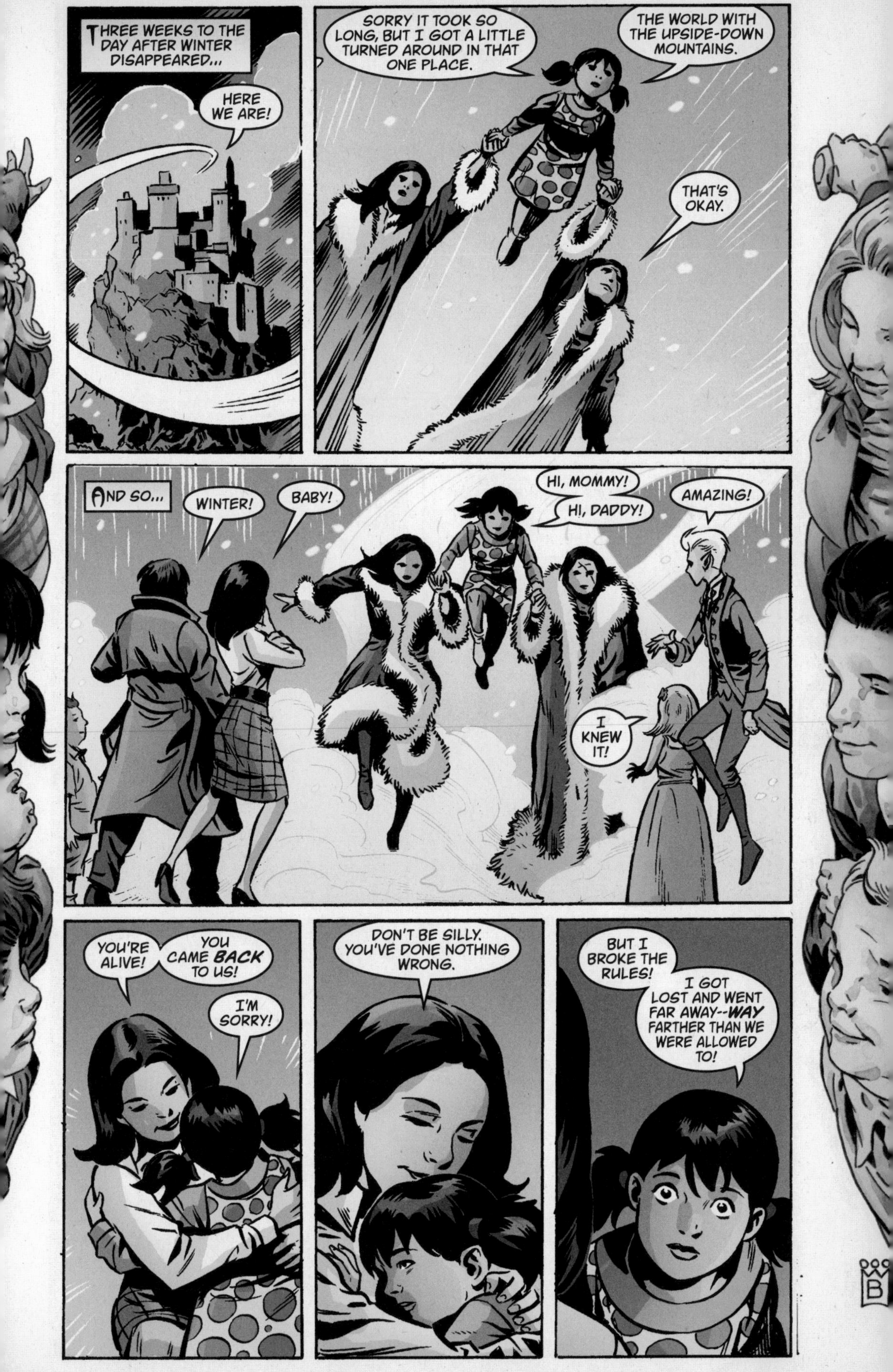

THREE WEEKS TO THE DAY AFTER WINTER DISAPPEARED...
HERE WE ARE!
SORRY IT TOOK SO LONG, BUT I GOT A LITTLE TURNED AROUND IN THAT ONE PLACE.
THE WORLD WITH THE UPSIDE-DOWN MOUNTAINS.
THAT'S OKAY.
AND SO...
WINTER!
BABY!
HI, MOMMY!
HI, DADDY!
AMAZING!
I KNEW IT!
YOU'RE ALIVE!
YOU CAME BACK TO US!
I'M SORRY!
DON'T BE SILLY. YOU'VE DONE NOTHING WRONG.
BUT I BROKE THE RULES!
I GOT LOST AND WENT FAR AWAY--WAY FARTHER THAN WE WERE ALLOWED TO!

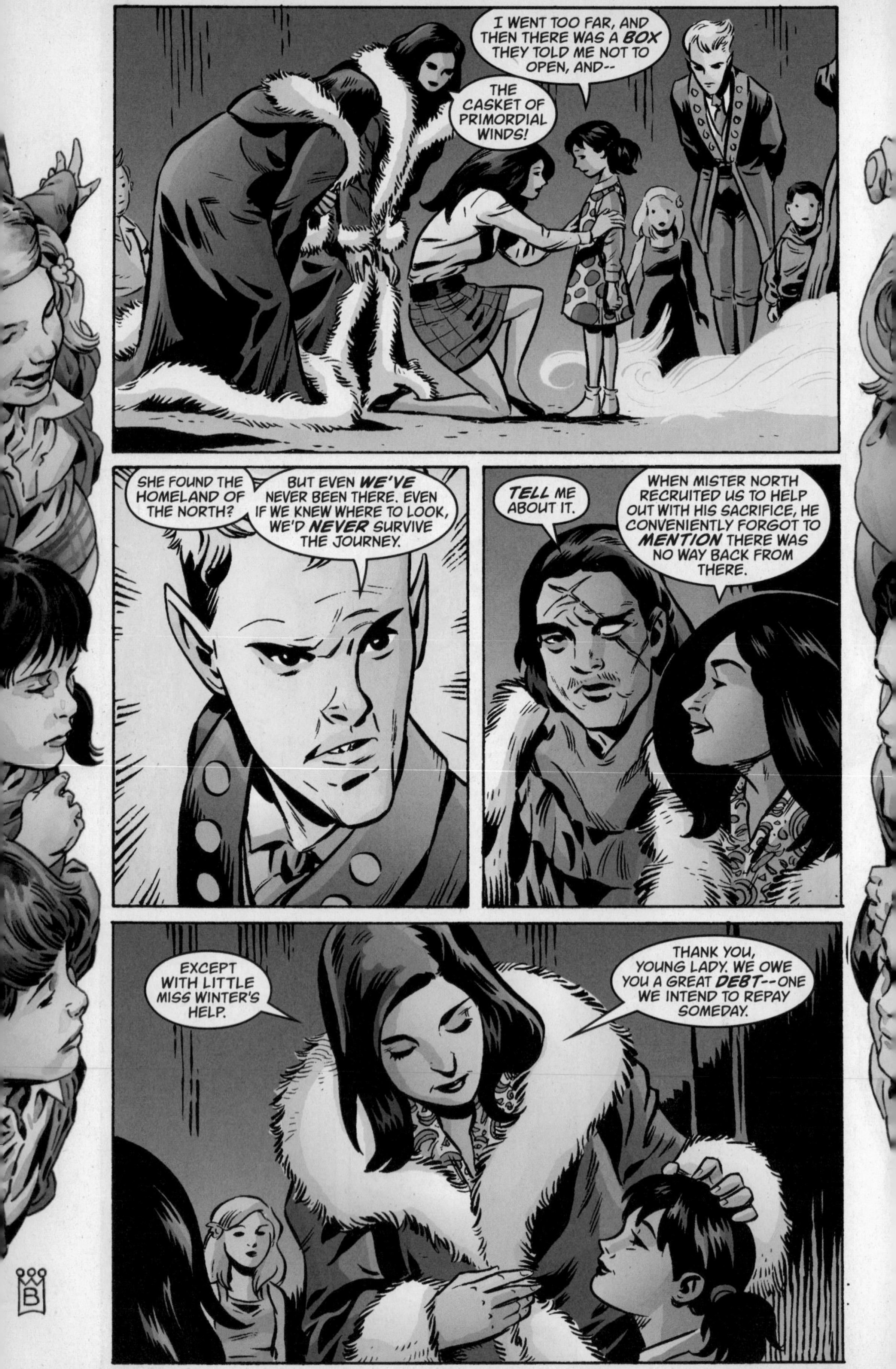

I WENT TOO FAR, AND THEN THERE WAS A BOX THEY TOLD ME NOT TO OPEN, AND--
THE CASKET OF PRIMORDIAL WINDS!
SHE FOUND THE HOMELAND OF THE NORTH?
BUT EVEN WE'VE NEVER BEEN THERE. EVEN IF WE KNEW WHERE TO LOOK, WE'D NEVER SURVIVE THE JOURNEY.
TELL ME ABOUT IT.
WHEN MISTER NORTH RECRUITED US TO HELP OUT WITH HIS SACRIFICE, HE CONVENIENTLY FORGOT TO MENTION THERE WAS NO WAY BACK FROM THERE.
EXCEPT WITH LITTLE MISS WINTER'S HELP.
THANK YOU, YOUNG LADY. WE OWE YOU A GREAT DEBT--ONE WE INTEND TO REPAY SOMEDAY.

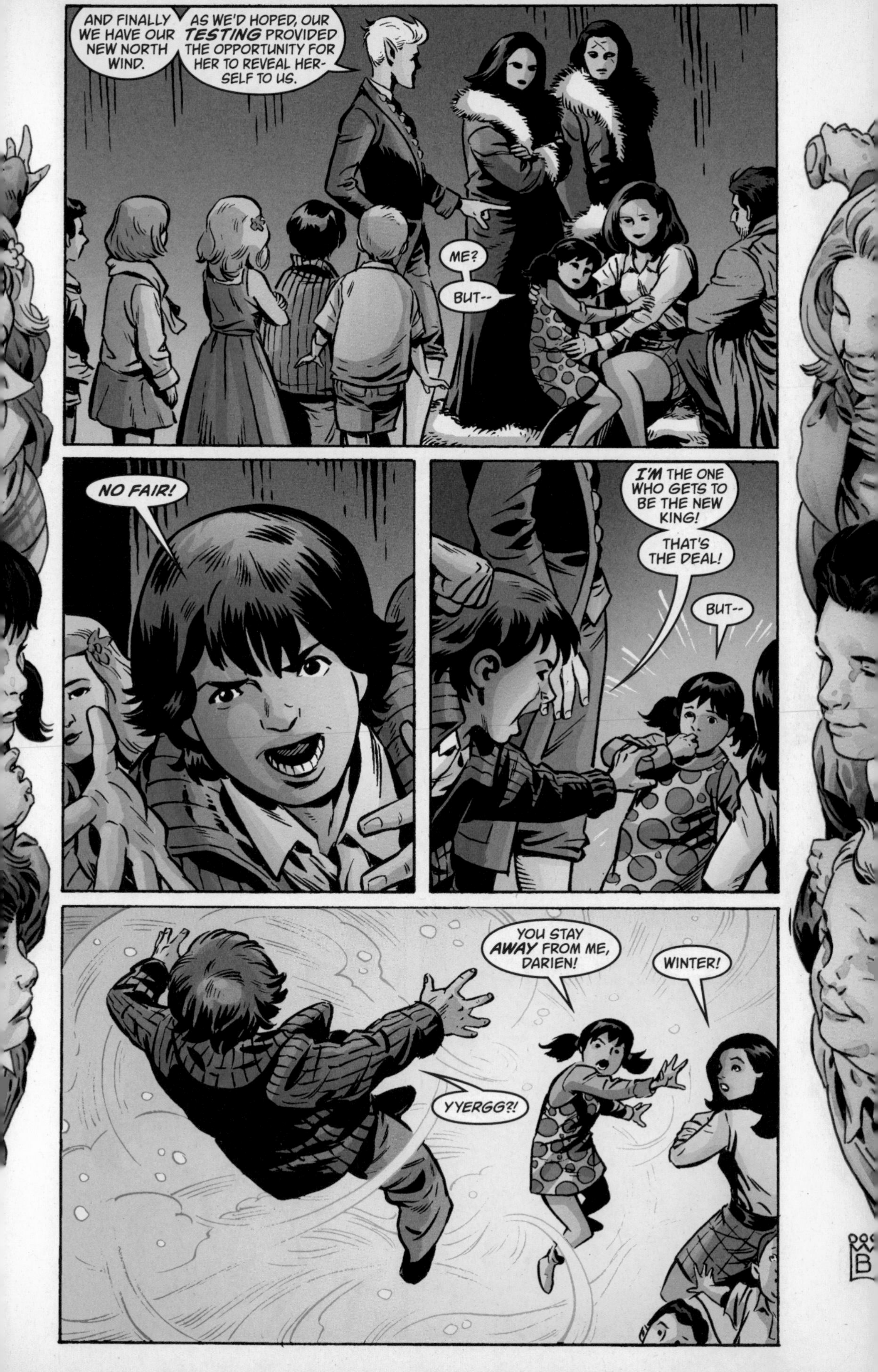
AND FINALLY WE HAVE OUR NEW NORTH WIND.
AS WE'D HOPED, OUR TESTING PROVIDED THE OPPORTUNITY FOR HER TO REVEAL HERSELF TO US.
ME?
BUT--
NO FAIR!
I'M THE ONE WHO GETS TO BE THE NEW KING!
THAT'S THE DEAL!
BUT--
YOU STAY AWAY FROM ME, DARIEN!
WINTER!
YYERGG?!

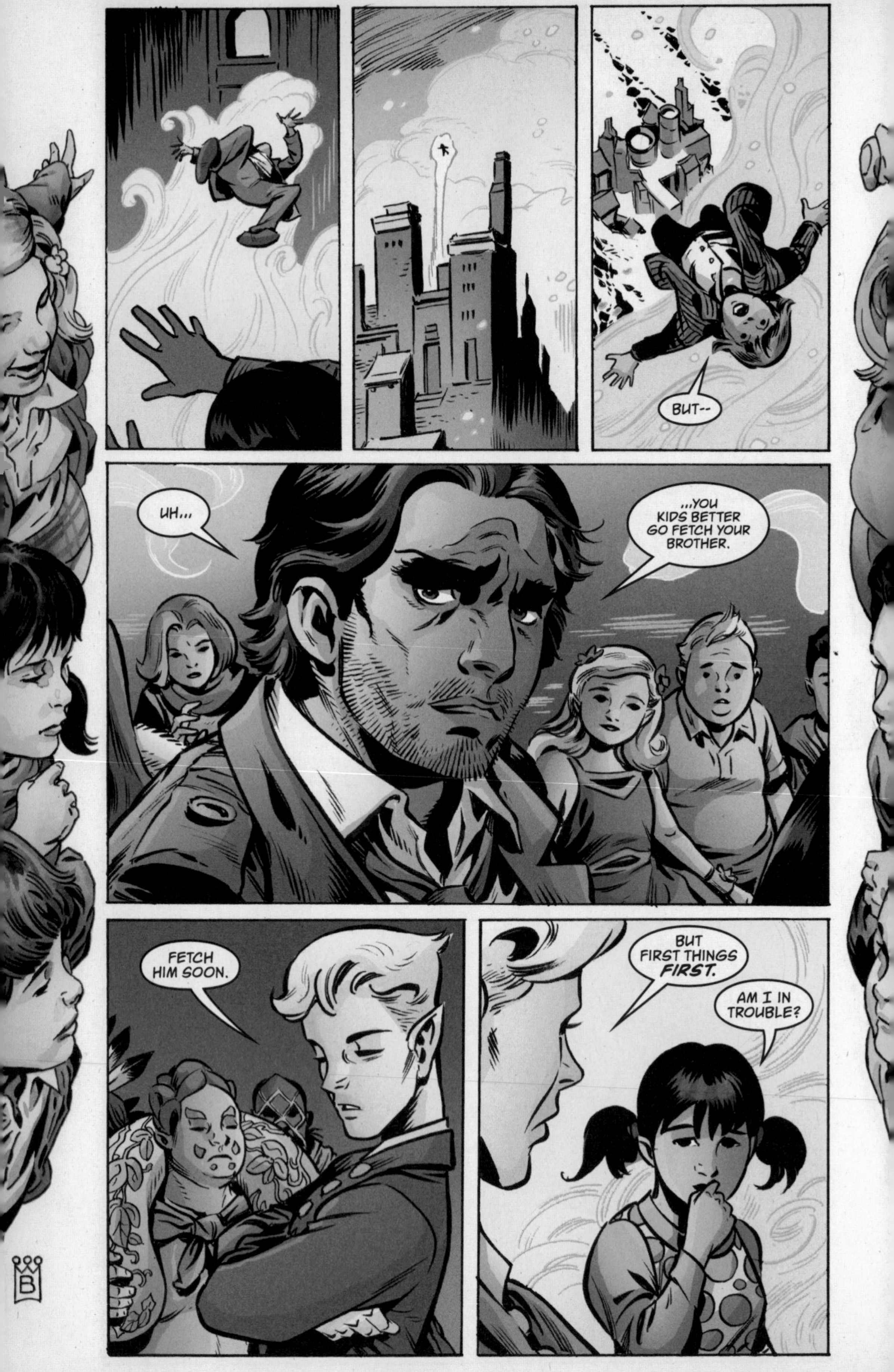
BUT--
UH...
...YOU KIDS BETTER GO FETCH YOUR BROTHER.
FETCH HIM SOON.
BUT FIRST THINGS FIRST.
AM I IN TROUBLE?

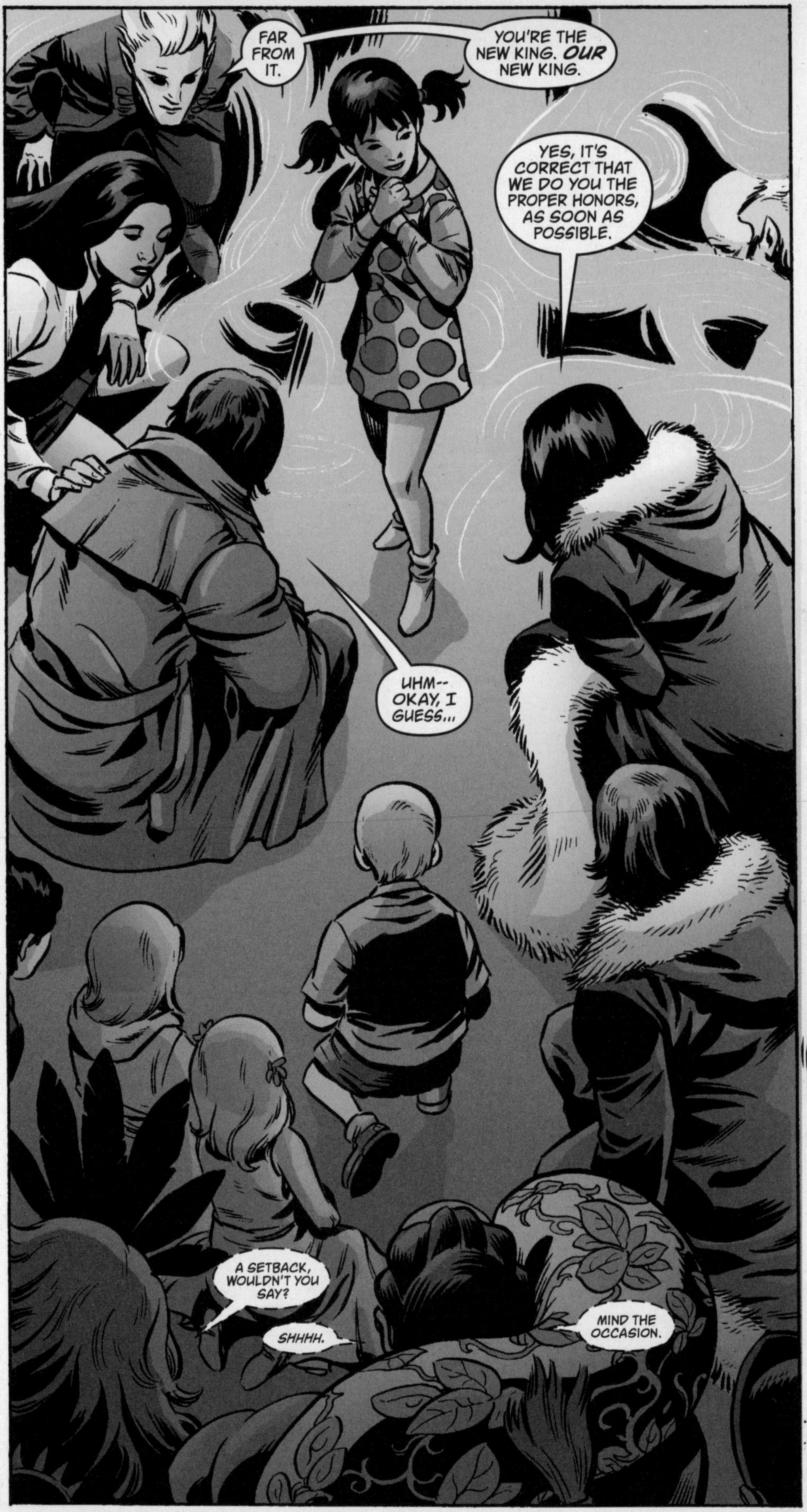
FAR FROM IT.
YOU'RE THE NEW KING. **OUR** NEW KING.
YES, IT'S CORRECT THAT WE DO YOU THE PROPER HONORS, AS SOON AS POSSIBLE.
UHM-- OKAY, I GUESS...
A SETBACK, WOULDN'T YOU SAY?
SHHHH.
MIND THE OCCASION.

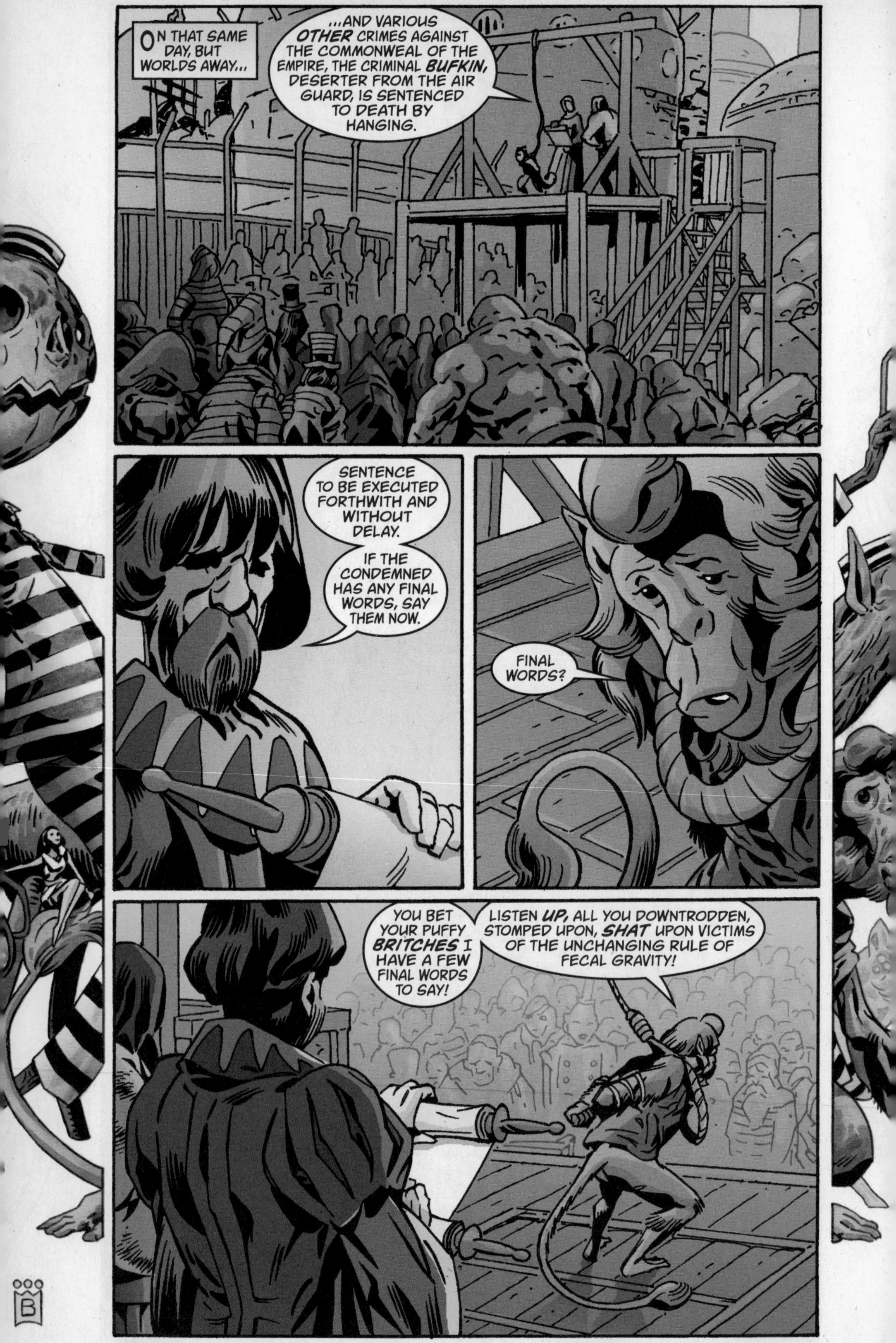
ON THAT SAME DAY, BUT WORLDS AWAY...
...AND VARIOUS OTHER CRIMES AGAINST THE COMMONWEAL OF THE EMPIRE, THE CRIMINAL BUFKIN, DESERTER FROM THE AIR GUARD, IS SENTENCED TO DEATH BY HANGING.
SENTENCE TO BE EXECUTED FORTHWITH AND WITHOUT DELAY.
IF THE CONDEMNED HAS ANY FINAL WORDS, SAY THEM NOW.
FINAL WORDS?
YOU BET YOUR PUFFY BRITCHES I HAVE A FEW FINAL WORDS TO SAY!
LISTEN UP, ALL YOU DOWNTRODDEN, STOMPED UPON, SHAT UPON VICTIMS OF THE UNCHANGING RULE OF FECAL GRAVITY!

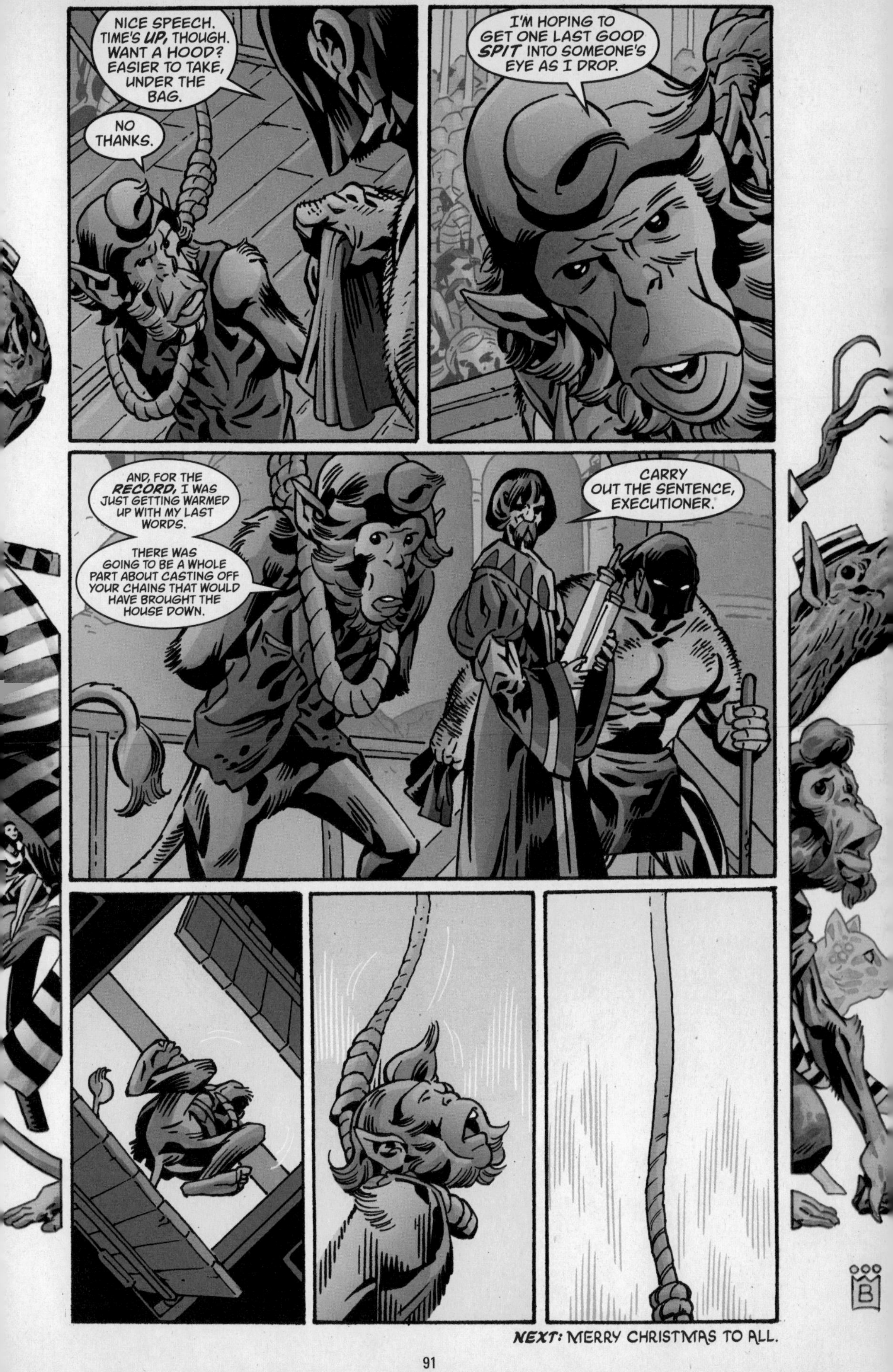
NICE SPEECH. TIME'S UP, THOUGH. WANT A HOOD? EASIER TO TAKE, UNDER THE BAG.
NO THANKS.
I'M HOPING TO GET ONE LAST GOOD SPIT INTO SOMEONE'S EYE AS I DROP.
AND, FOR THE RECORD, I WAS JUST GETTING WARMED UP WITH MY LAST WORDS.
THERE WAS GOING TO BE A WHOLE PART ABOUT CASTING OFF YOUR CHAINS THAT WOULD HAVE BROUGHT THE HOUSE DOWN.
CARRY OUT THE SENTENCE, EXECUTIONER.

NEXT: MERRY CHRISTMAS TO ALL.

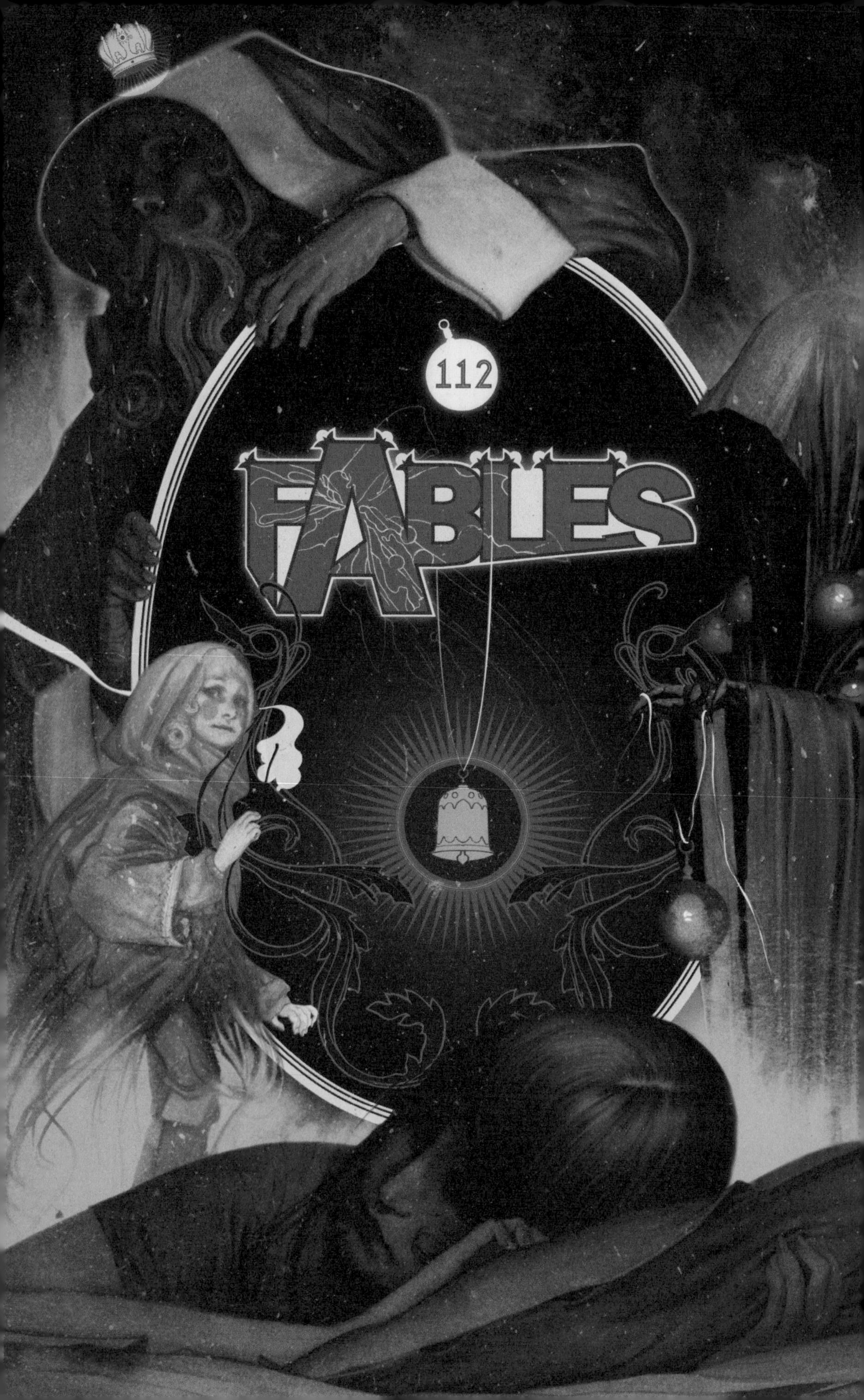
112
FABLES

Chapter One – The Chimes

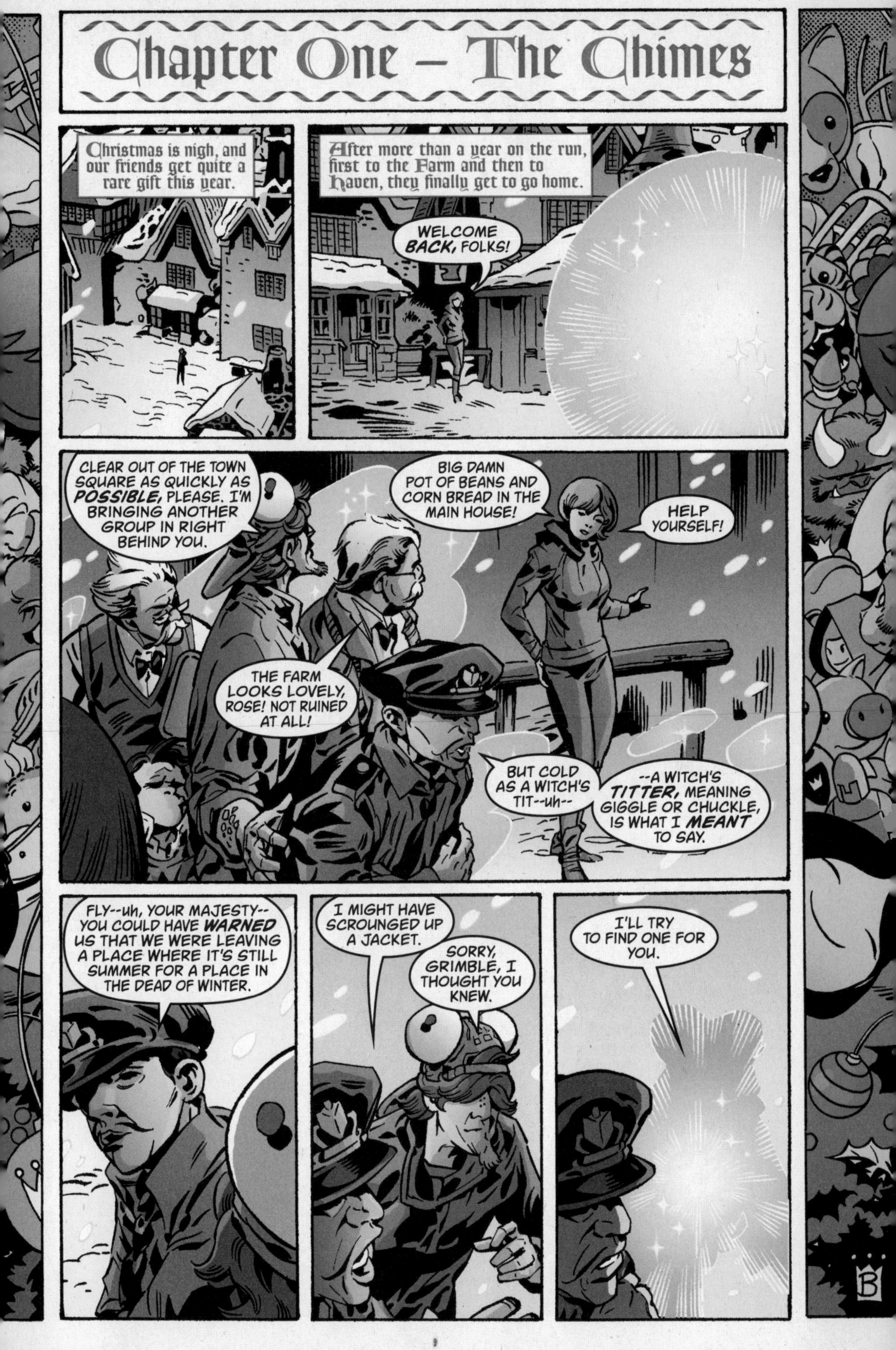

Christmas is nigh, and our friends get quite a rare gift this year.
After more than a year on the run, first to the Farm and then to Haven, they finally get to go home.
WELCOME BACK, FOLKS!
CLEAR OUT OF THE TOWN SQUARE AS QUICKLY AS POSSIBLE, PLEASE. I'M BRINGING ANOTHER GROUP IN RIGHT BEHIND YOU.
BIG DAMN POT OF BEANS AND CORN BREAD IN THE MAIN HOUSE!
HELP YOURSELF!
THE FARM LOOKS LOVELY, ROSE! NOT RUINED AT ALL!
BUT COLD AS A WITCH'S TIT--uh--
--A WITCH'S TITTER, MEANING GIGGLE OR CHUCKLE, IS WHAT I MEANT TO SAY.
FLY--uh, YOUR MAJESTY--YOU COULD HAVE WARNED US THAT WE WERE LEAVING A PLACE WHERE IT'S STILL SUMMER FOR A PLACE IN THE DEAD OF WINTER.
I MIGHT HAVE SCROUNGED UP A JACKET.
SORRY, GRIMBLE, I THOUGHT YOU KNEW.
I'LL TRY TO FIND ONE FOR YOU.

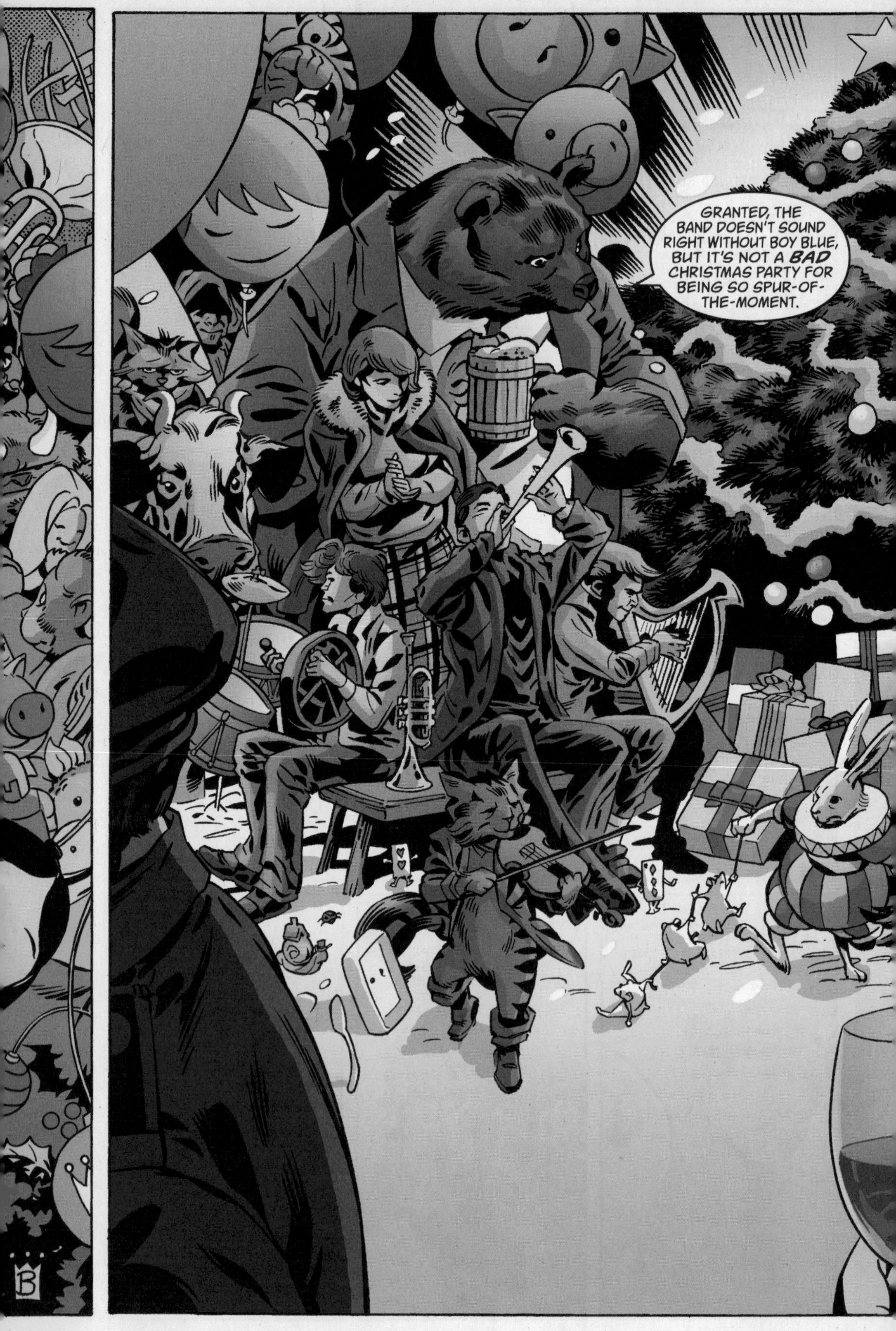
GRANTED, THE BAND DOESN'T SOUND RIGHT WITHOUT BOY BLUE, BUT IT'S NOT A BAD CHRISTMAS PARTY FOR BEING SO SPUR-OF-THE-MOMENT.

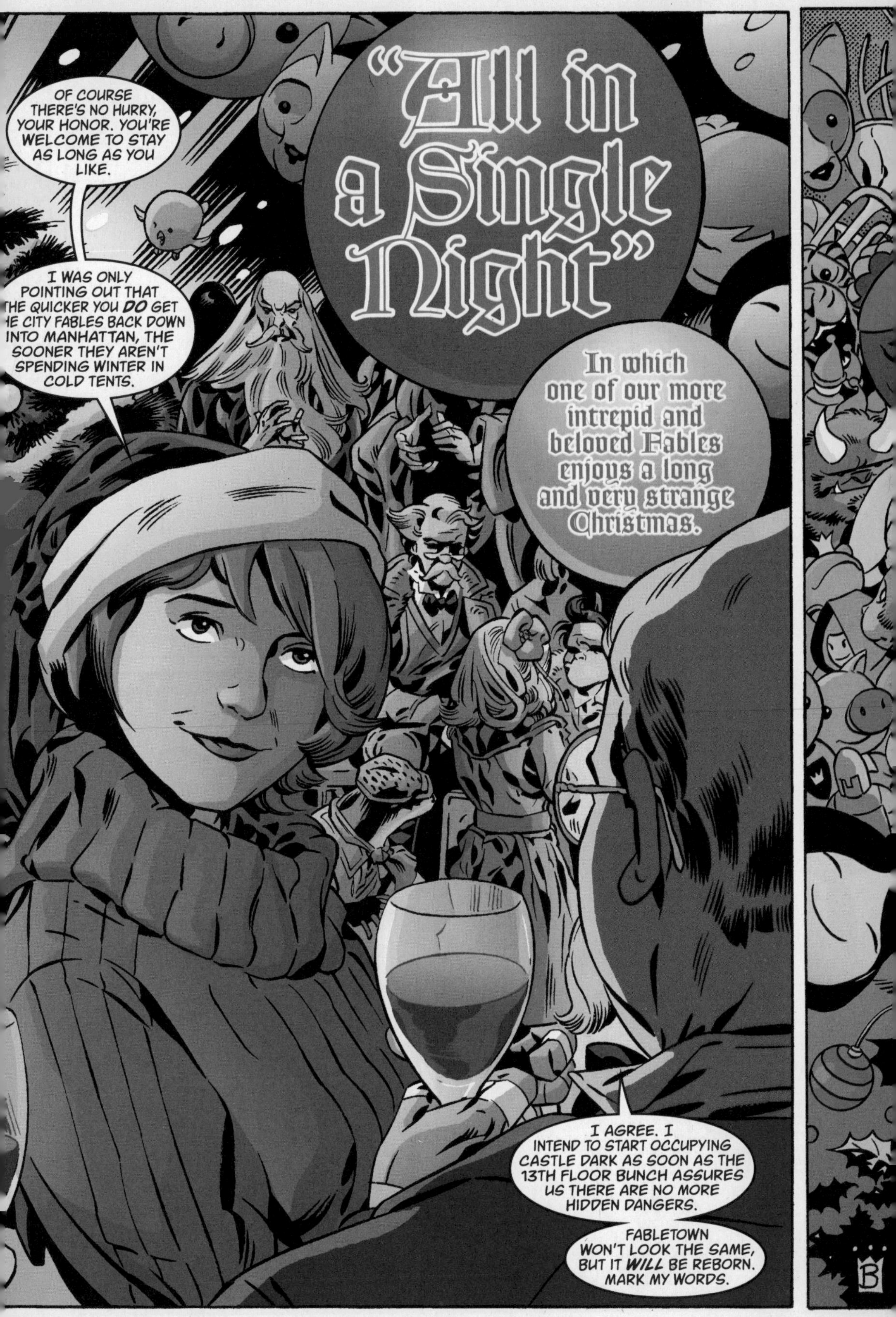
"All in a Single Night"
In which one of our more intrepid and beloved Fables enjoys a long and very strange Christmas.
OF COURSE THERE'S NO HURRY, YOUR HONOR. YOU'RE WELCOME TO STAY AS LONG AS YOU LIKE.
I WAS ONLY POINTING OUT THAT HE QUICKER YOU DO GET IE CITY FABLES BACK DOWN INTO MANHATTAN, THE SOONER THEY AREN'T SPENDING WINTER IN COLD TENTS.
I AGREE. I INTEND TO START OCCUPYING CASTLE DARK AS SOON AS THE 13TH FLOOR BUNCH ASSURES US THERE ARE NO MORE HIDDEN DANGERS.
FABLETOWN WON'T LOOK THE SAME, BUT IT WILL BE REBORN. MARK MY WORDS.

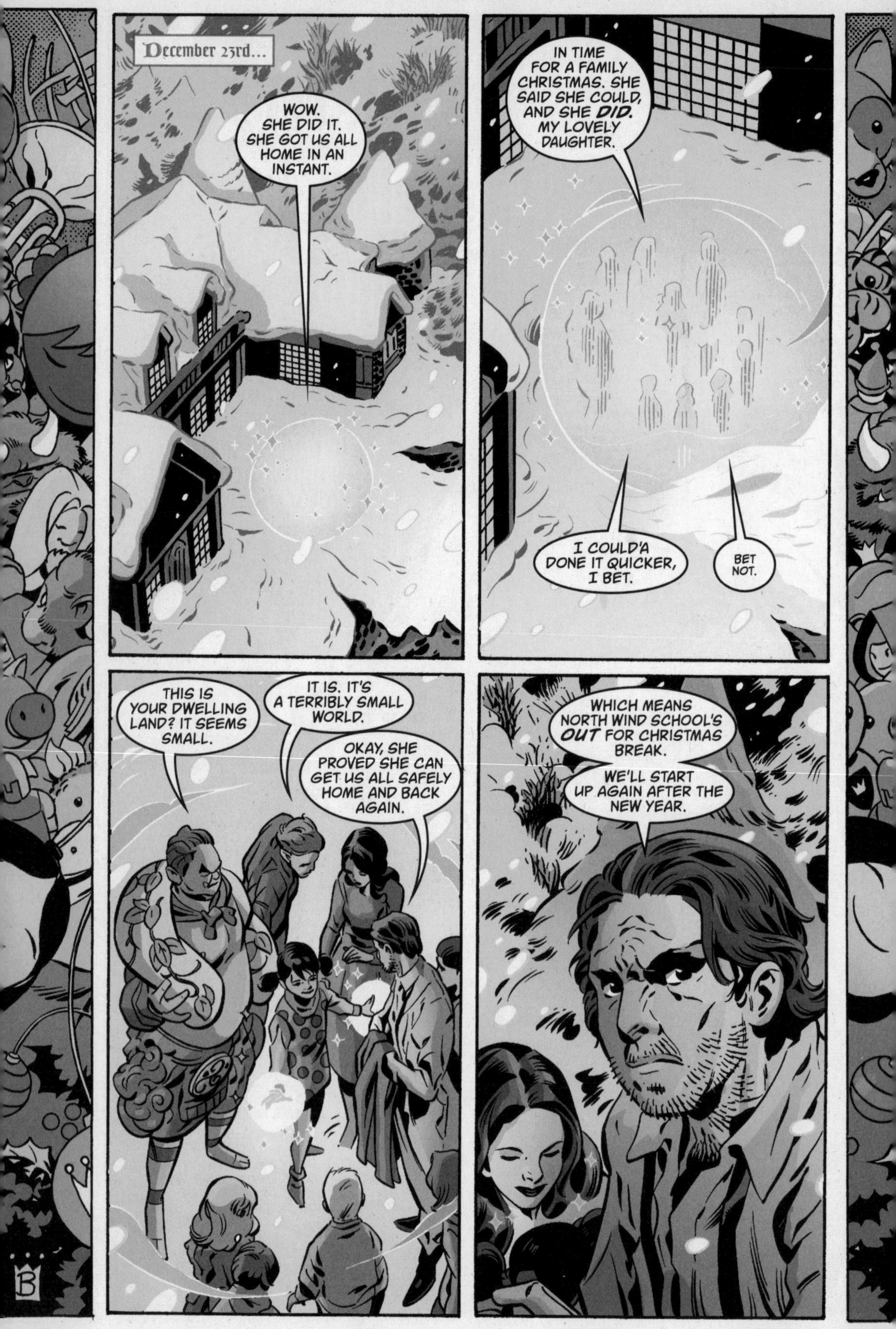
December 23rd...
WOW. SHE DID IT. SHE GOT US ALL HOME IN AN INSTANT.
IN TIME FOR A FAMILY CHRISTMAS. SHE SAID SHE COULD, AND SHE DID. MY LOVELY DAUGHTER.
I COULD'A DONE IT QUICKER, I BET.
BET NOT.
THIS IS YOUR DWELLING LAND? IT SEEMS SMALL.
IT IS. IT'S A TERRIBLY SMALL WORLD.
OKAY, SHE PROVED SHE CAN GET US ALL SAFELY HOME AND BACK AGAIN.
WHICH MEANS NORTH WIND SCHOOL'S OUT FOR CHRISTMAS BREAK.
WE'LL START UP AGAIN AFTER THE NEW YEAR.

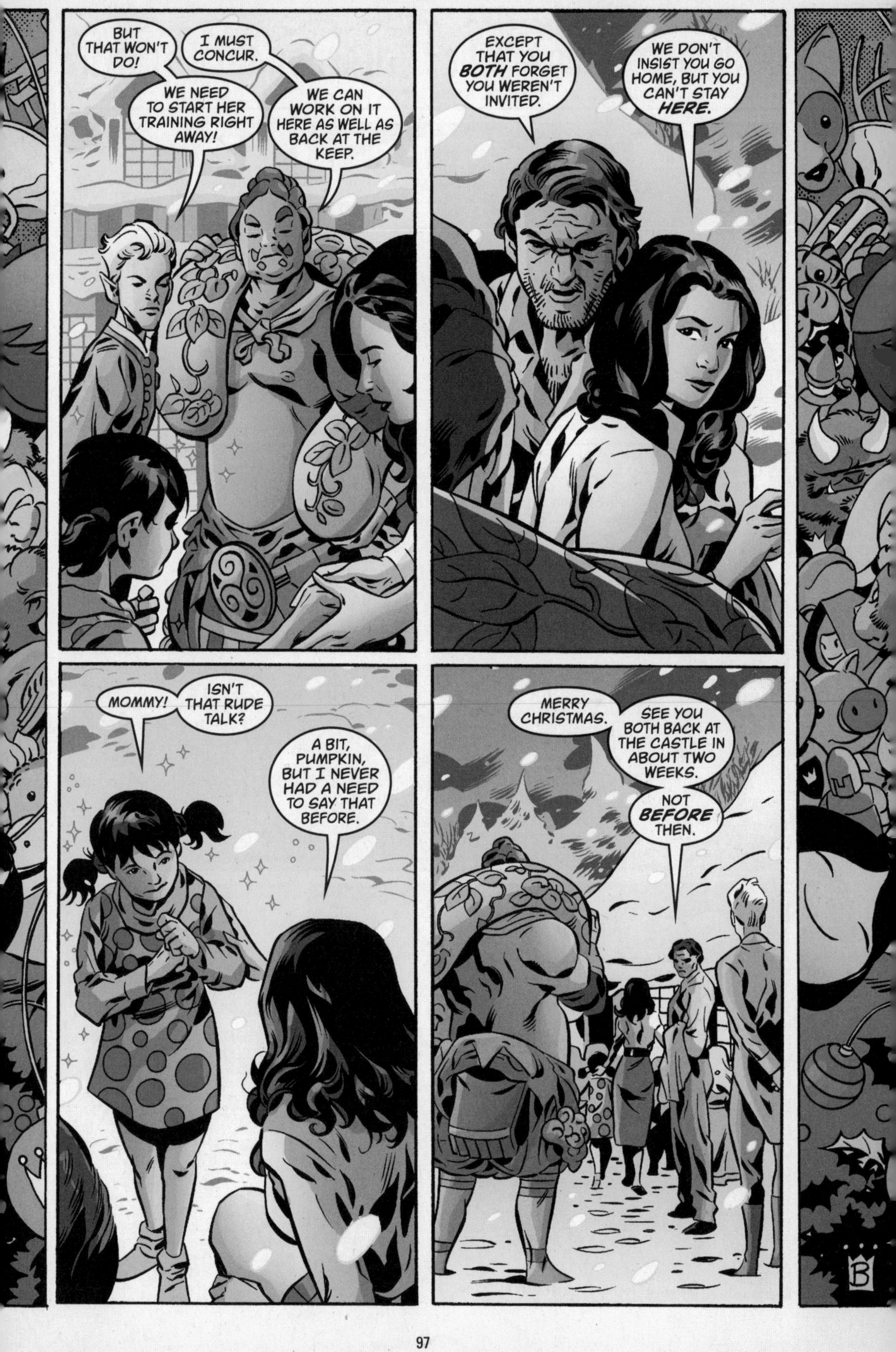

BUT THAT WON'T DO!
WE NEED TO START HER TRAINING RIGHT AWAY!
I MUST CONCUR.
WE CAN WORK ON IT HERE AS WELL AS BACK AT THE KEEP.
EXCEPT THAT YOU BOTH FORGET YOU WEREN'T INVITED.
WE DON'T INSIST YOU GO HOME, BUT YOU CAN'T STAY HERE.
MOMMY!
ISN'T THAT RUDE TALK?
A BIT, PUMPKIN, BUT I NEVER HAD A NEED TO SAY THAT BEFORE.
MERRY CHRISTMAS.
SEE YOU BOTH BACK AT THE CASTLE IN ABOUT TWO WEEKS.
NOT BEFORE THEN.

Chapter Two – The Cricket on the Hearth

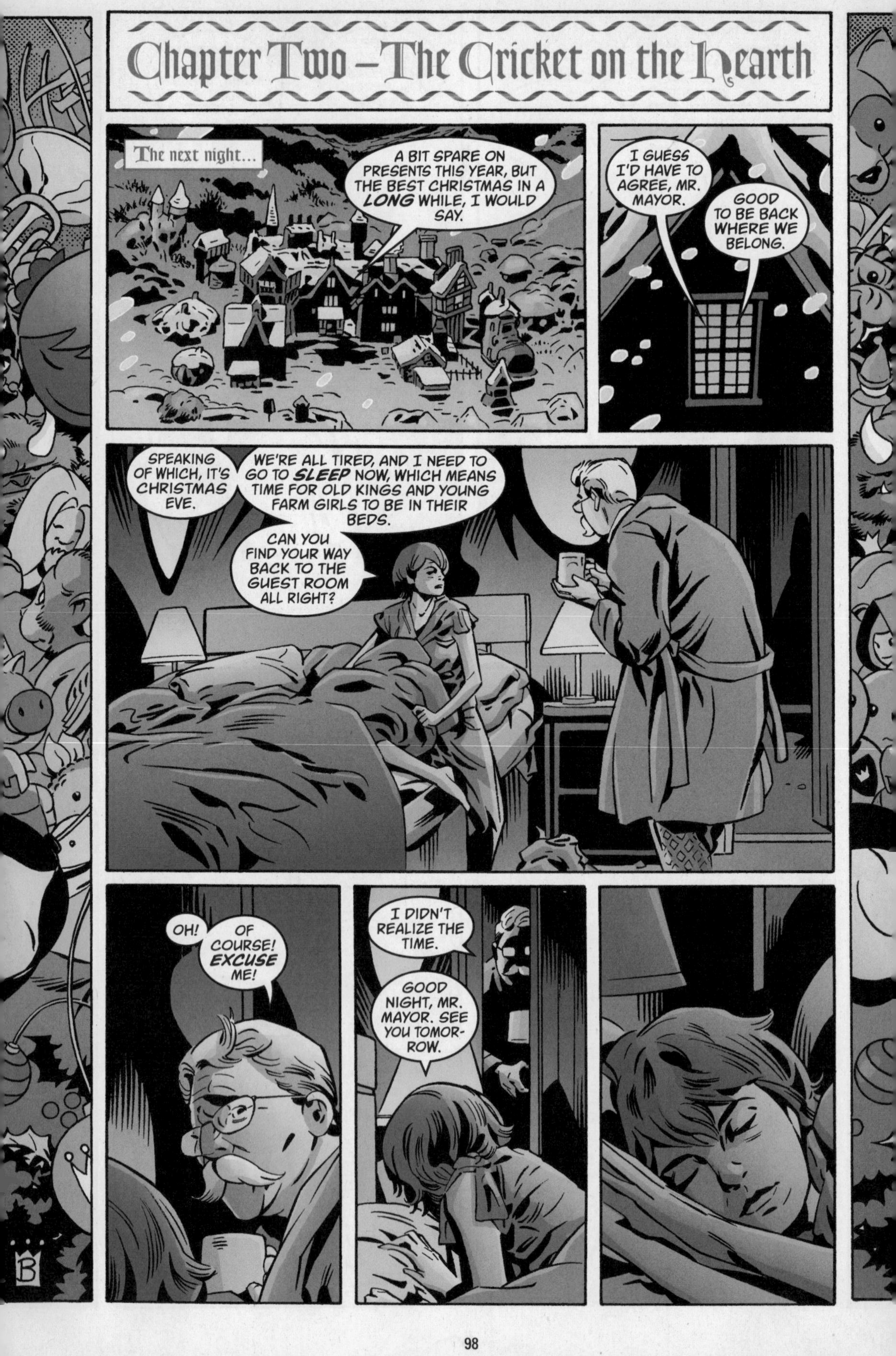

The next night...
A BIT SPARE ON PRESENTS THIS YEAR, BUT THE BEST CHRISTMAS IN A LONG WHILE, I WOULD SAY.
I GUESS I'D HAVE TO AGREE, MR. MAYOR.
GOOD TO BE BACK WHERE WE BELONG.
SPEAKING OF WHICH, IT'S CHRISTMAS EVE.
WE'RE ALL TIRED, AND I NEED TO GO TO SLEEP NOW, WHICH MEANS TIME FOR OLD KINGS AND YOUNG FARM GIRLS TO BE IN THEIR BEDS.
CAN YOU FIND YOUR WAY BACK TO THE GUEST ROOM ALL RIGHT?
OH!
OF COURSE! EXCUSE ME!
I DIDN'T REALIZE THE TIME.
GOOD NIGHT, MR. MAYOR. SEE YOU TOMORROW.

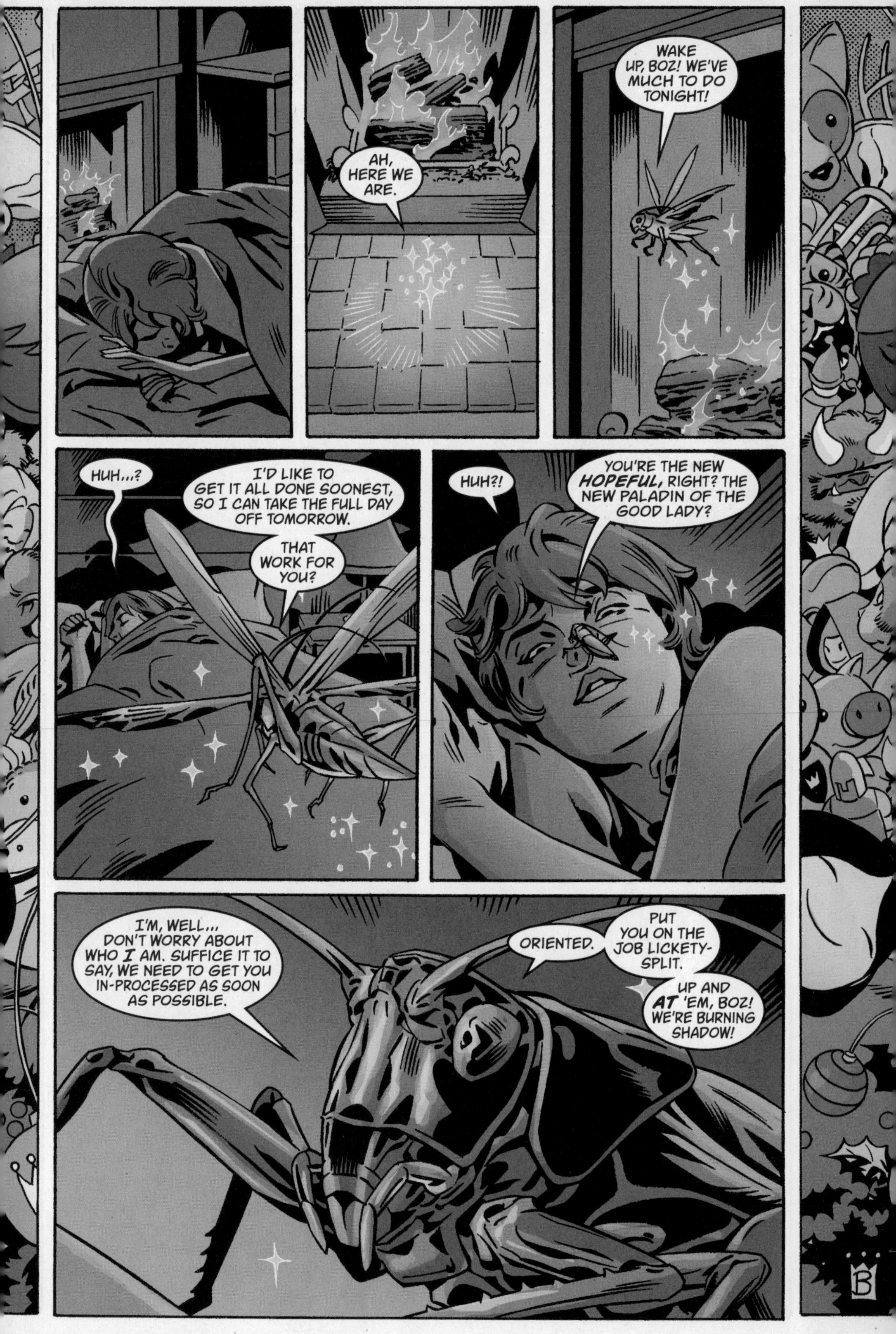
AH, HERE WE ARE.
WAKE UP, BOZ! WE'VE MUCH TO DO TONIGHT!
HUH...?
I'D LIKE TO GET IT ALL DONE SOONEST, SO I CAN TAKE THE FULL DAY OFF TOMORROW.
THAT WORK FOR YOU?
HUH?!
YOU'RE THE NEW HOPEFUL, RIGHT? THE NEW PALADIN OF THE GOOD LADY?
I'M, WELL... DON'T WORRY ABOUT WHO I AM. SUFFICE IT TO SAY, WE NEED TO GET YOU IN-PROCESSED AS SOON AS POSSIBLE.
ORIENTED.
PUT YOU ON THE JOB LICKETY-SPLIT.
UP AND AT 'EM, BOZ! WE'RE BURNING SHADOW!

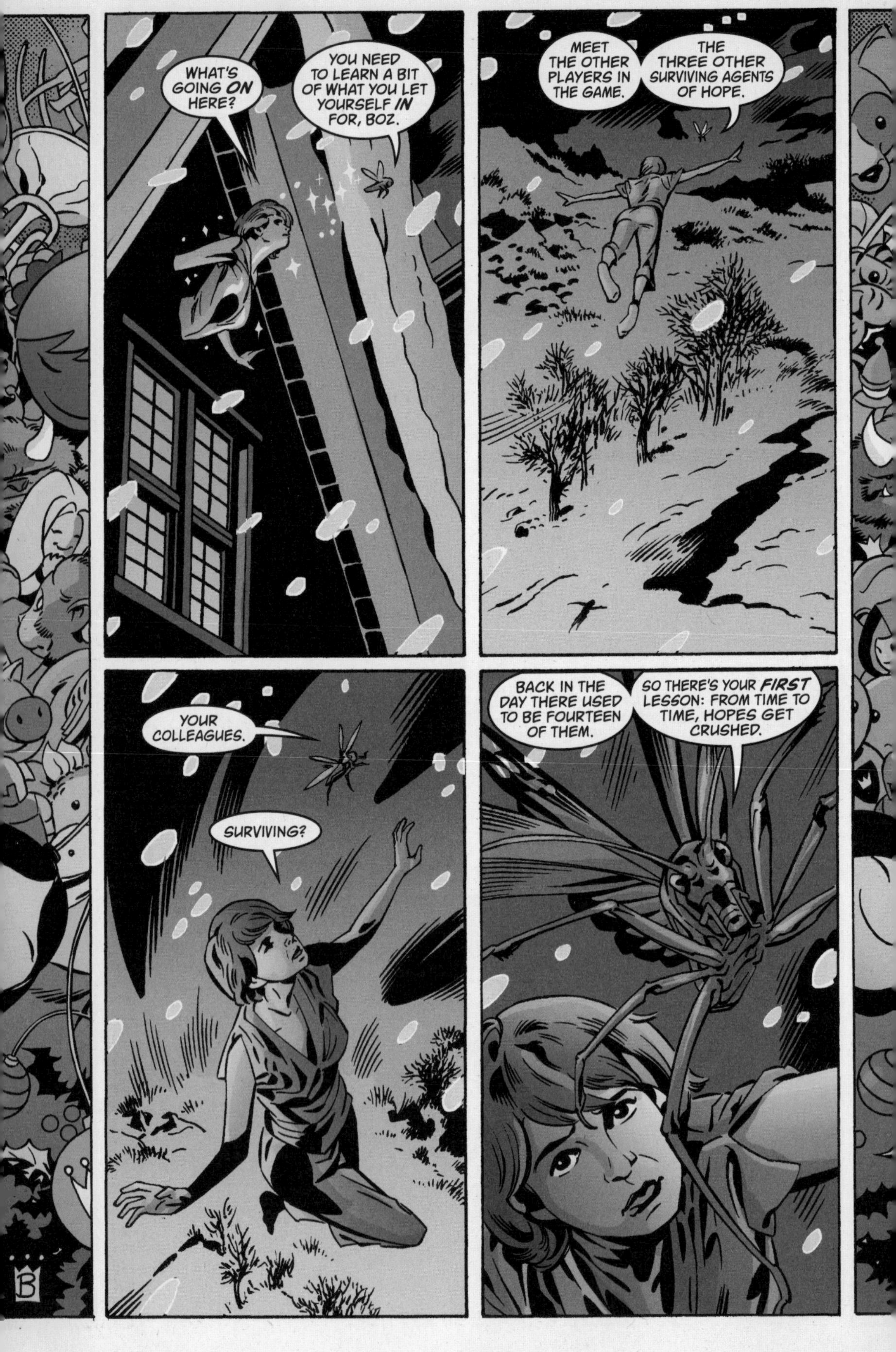
WHAT'S GOING ON HERE?
YOU NEED TO LEARN A BIT OF WHAT YOU LET YOURSELF IN FOR, BOZ.
MEET THE OTHER PLAYERS IN THE GAME.
THE THREE OTHER SURVIVING AGENTS OF HOPE.
YOUR COLLEAGUES.
SURVIVING?
BACK IN THE DAY THERE USED TO BE FOURTEEN OF THEM.
SO THERE'S YOUR FIRST LESSON: FROM TIME TO TIME, HOPES GET CRUSHED.

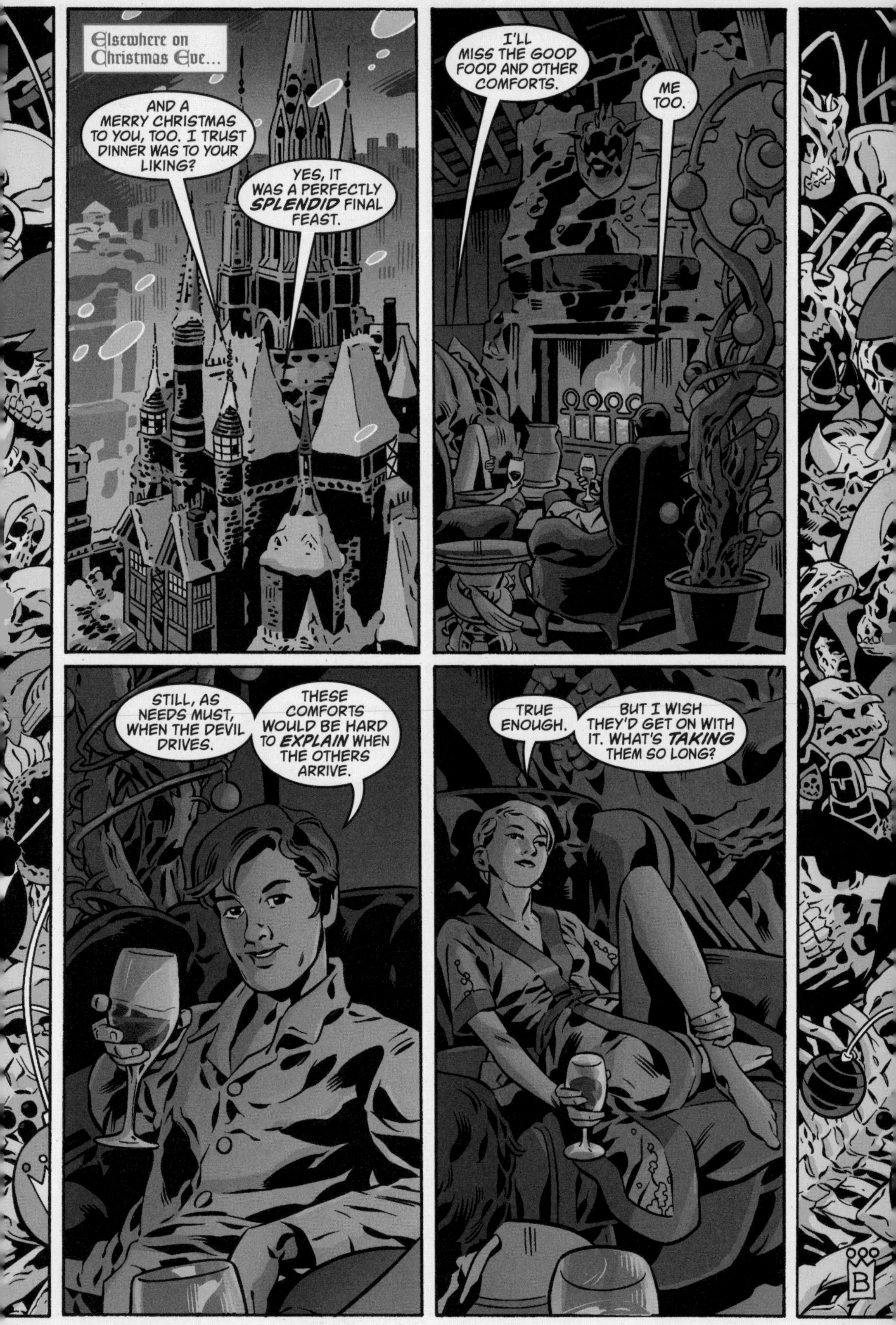
Elsewhere on Christmas Eve...
AND A MERRY CHRISTMAS TO YOU, TOO. I TRUST DINNER WAS TO YOUR LIKING?
YES, IT WAS A PERFECTLY SPLENDID FINAL FEAST.
I'LL MISS THE GOOD FOOD AND OTHER COMFORTS.
ME TOO.
STILL, AS NEEDS MUST, WHEN THE DEVIL DRIVES.
THESE COMFORTS WOULD BE HARD TO EXPLAIN WHEN THE OTHERS ARRIVE.
TRUE ENOUGH.
BUT I WISH THEY'D GET ON WITH IT. WHAT'S TAKING THEM SO LONG?

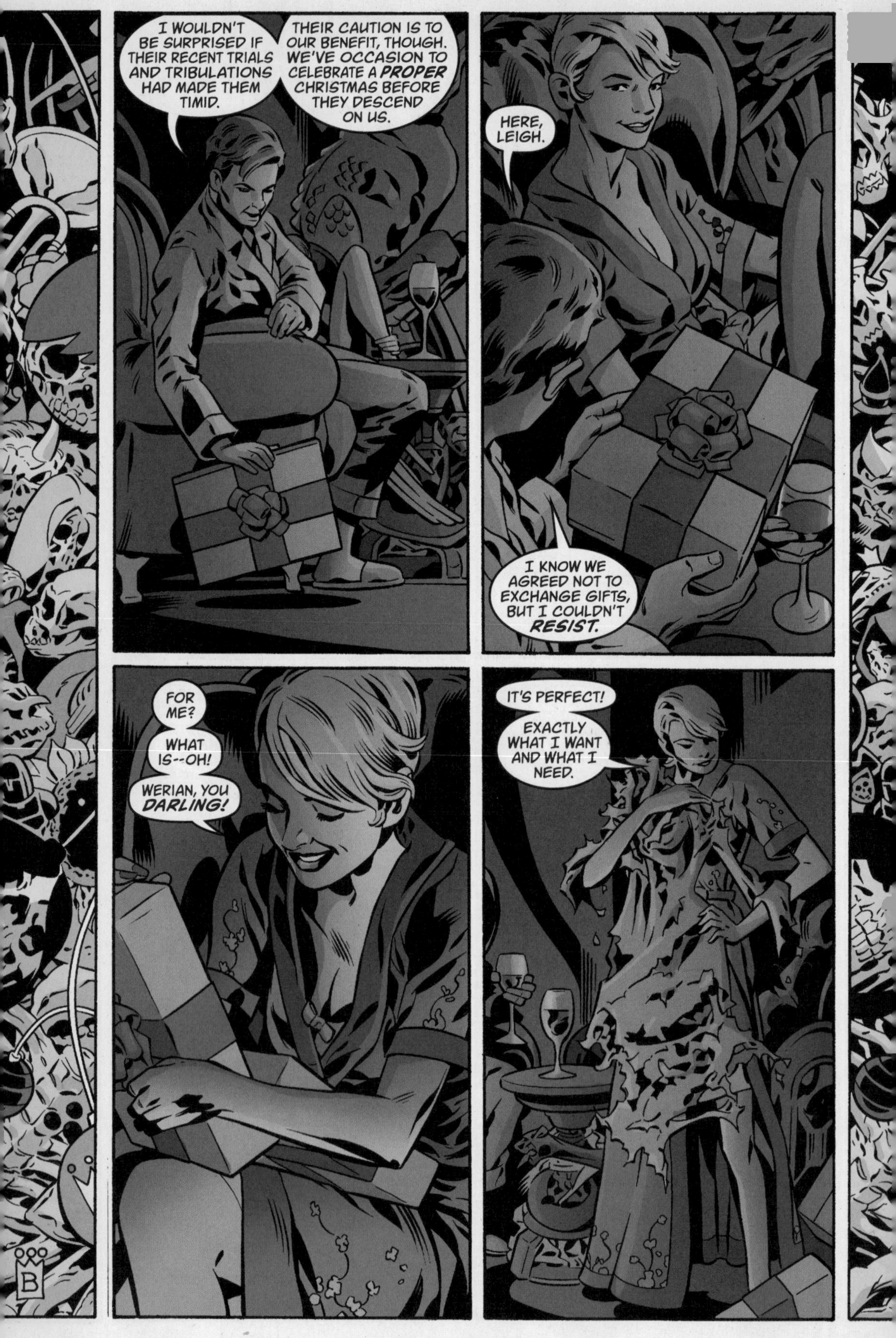
I WOULDN'T BE SURPRISED IF THEIR RECENT TRIALS AND TRIBULATIONS HAD MADE THEM TIMID.
THEIR CAUTION IS TO OUR BENEFIT, THOUGH. WE'VE OCCASION TO CELEBRATE A PROPER CHRISTMAS BEFORE THEY DESCEND ON US.
HERE, LEIGH.
I KNOW WE AGREED NOT TO EXCHANGE GIFTS, BUT I COULDN'T RESIST.
FOR ME?
WHAT IS--OH!
WERIAN, YOU DARLING!
IT'S PERFECT!
EXACTLY WHAT I WANT AND WHAT I NEED.

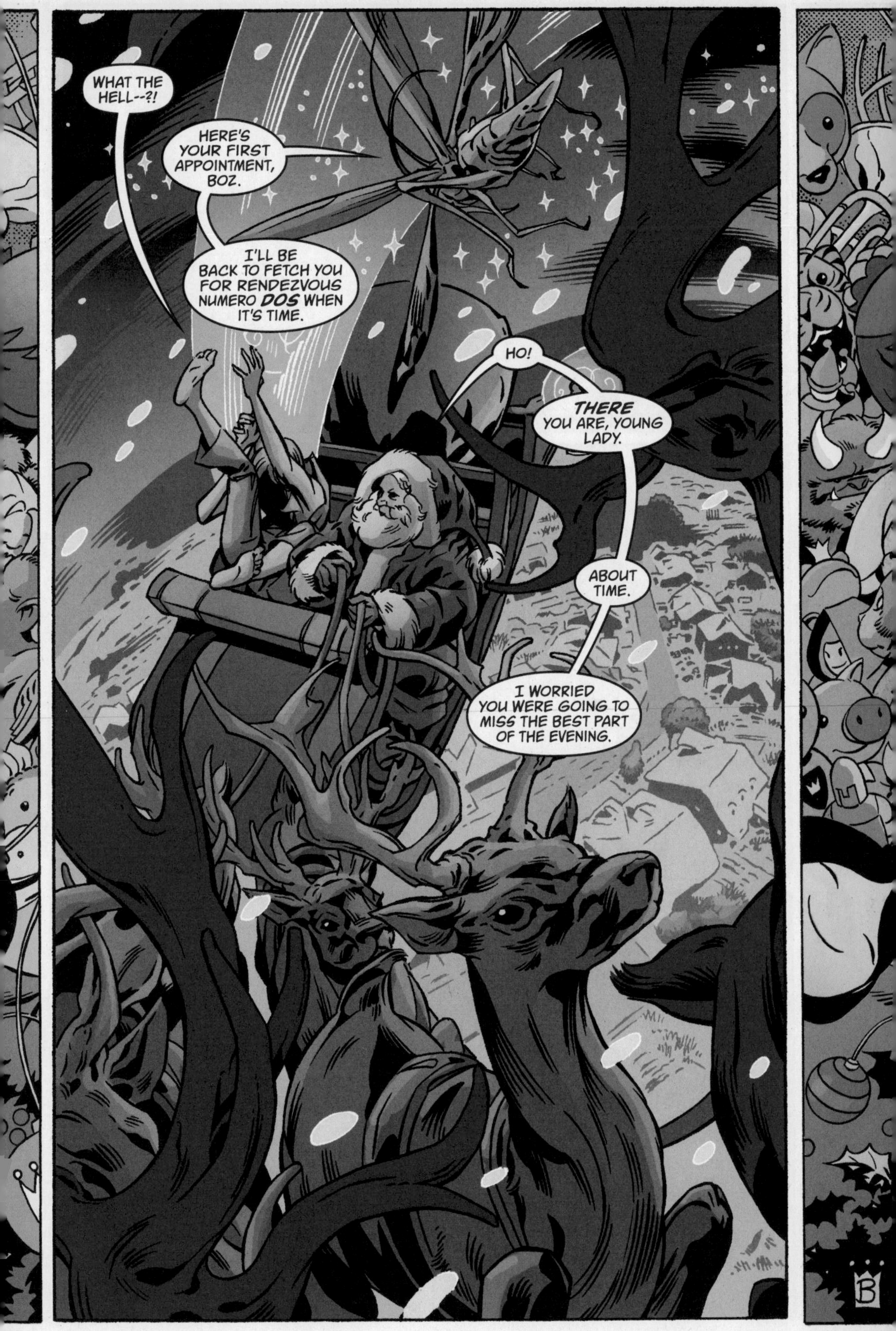

WHAT THE HELL--?!
HERE'S YOUR FIRST APPOINTMENT, BOZ.
I'LL BE BACK TO FETCH YOU FOR RENDEZVOUS NUMERO *DOS* WHEN IT'S TIME.
HO!
THERE YOU ARE, YOUNG LADY.
ABOUT TIME.
I WORRIED YOU WERE GOING TO MISS THE BEST PART OF THE EVENING.

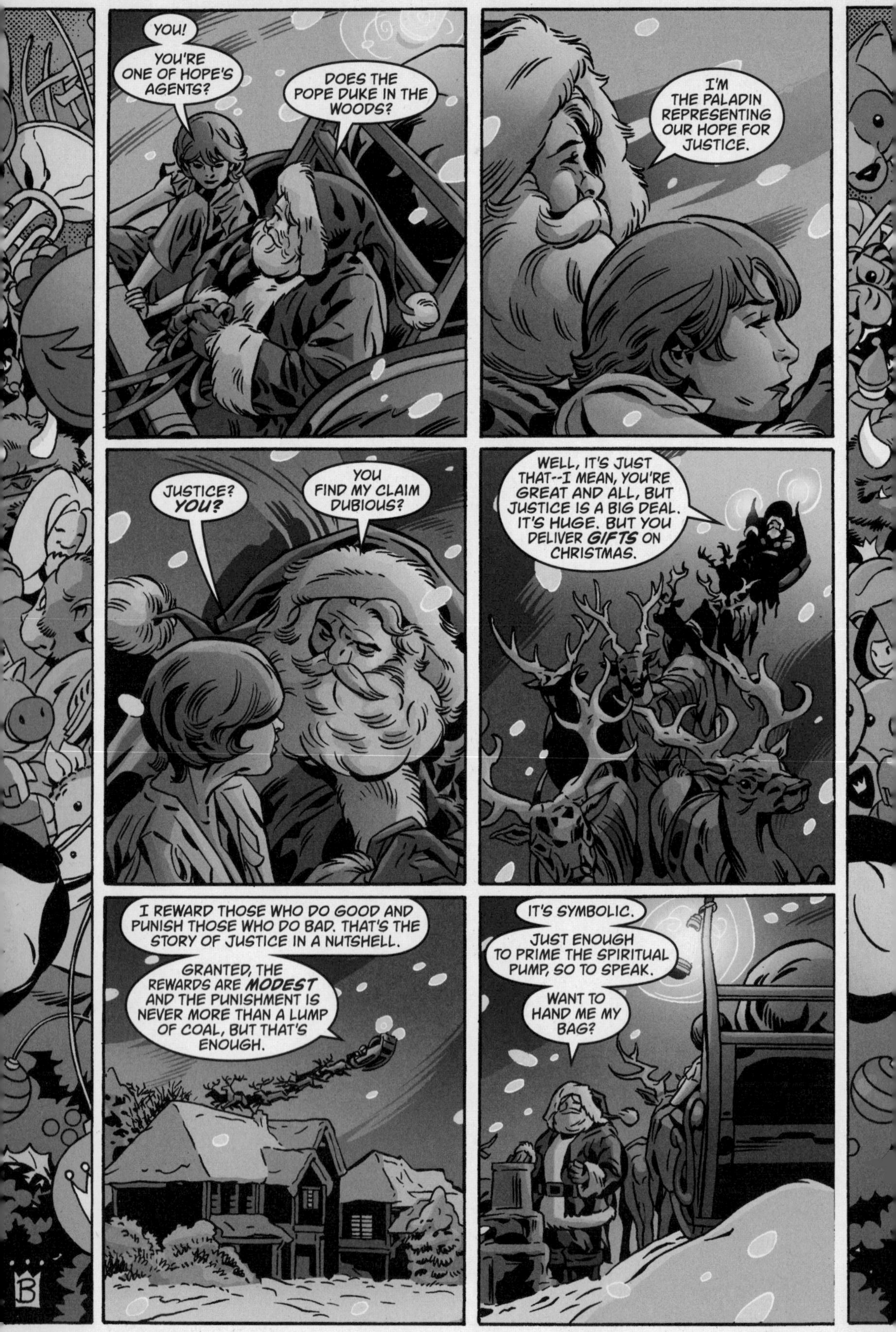
YOU!
YOU'RE ONE OF HOPE'S AGENTS?
DOES THE POPE DUKE IN THE WOODS?
I'M THE PALADIN REPRESENTING OUR HOPE FOR JUSTICE.
JUSTICE? YOU?
YOU FIND MY CLAIM DUBIOUS?
WELL, IT'S JUST THAT--I MEAN, YOU'RE GREAT AND ALL, BUT JUSTICE IS A BIG DEAL. IT'S HUGE. BUT YOU DELIVER GIFTS ON CHRISTMAS.
I REWARD THOSE WHO DO GOOD AND PUNISH THOSE WHO DO BAD. THAT'S THE STORY OF JUSTICE IN A NUTSHELL.
GRANTED, THE REWARDS ARE MODEST AND THE PUNISHMENT IS NEVER MORE THAN A LUMP OF COAL, BUT THAT'S ENOUGH.
IT'S SYMBOLIC.
JUST ENOUGH TO PRIME THE SPIRITUAL PUMP, SO TO SPEAK.
WANT TO HAND ME MY BAG?

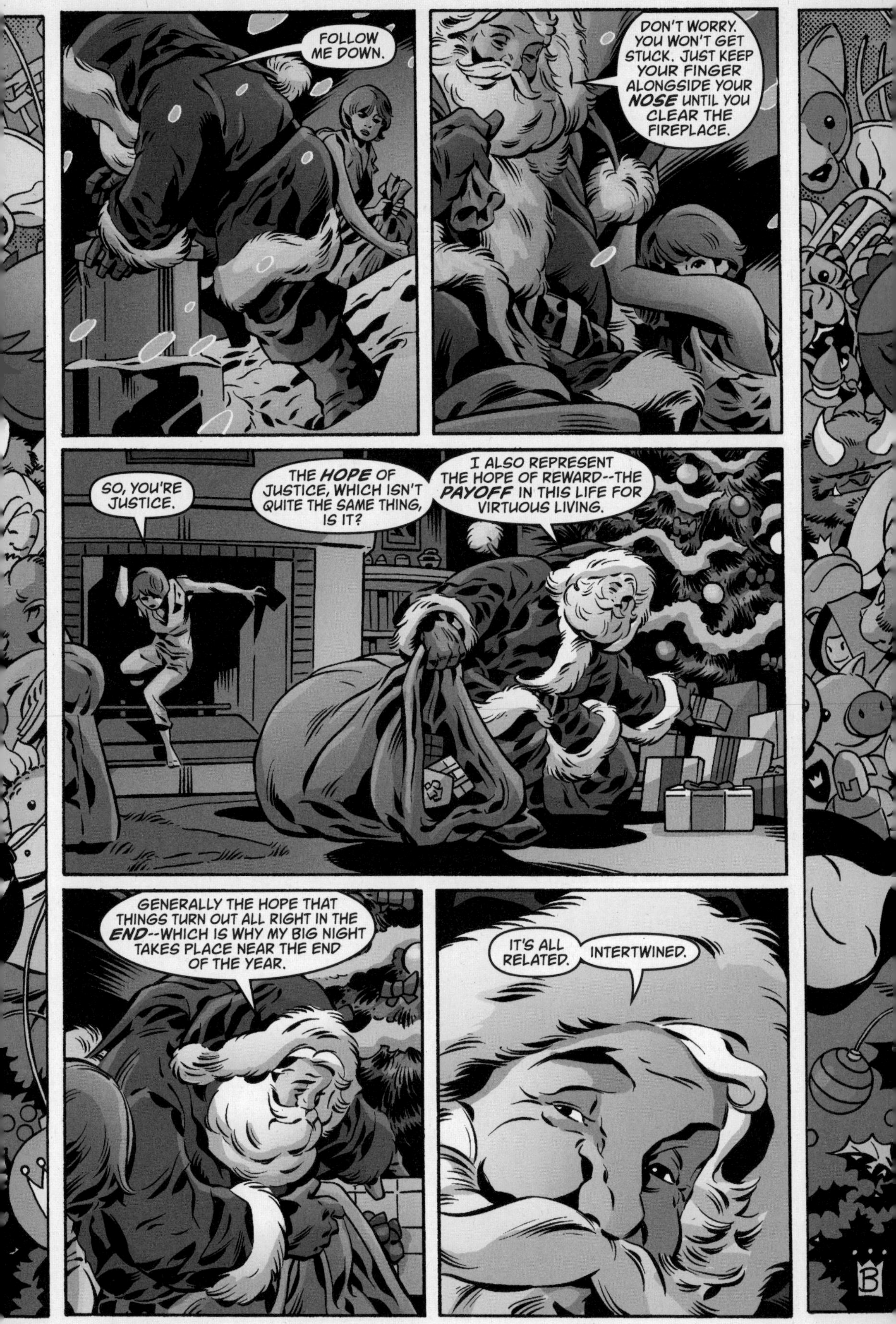
FOLLOW ME DOWN.
DON'T WORRY. YOU WON'T GET STUCK. JUST KEEP YOUR FINGER ALONGSIDE YOUR NOSE UNTIL YOU CLEAR THE FIREPLACE.
SO, YOU'RE JUSTICE.
THE HOPE OF JUSTICE, WHICH ISN'T QUITE THE SAME THING, IS IT?
I ALSO REPRESENT THE HOPE OF REWARD--THE PAYOFF IN THIS LIFE FOR VIRTUOUS LIVING.
GENERALLY THE HOPE THAT THINGS TURN OUT ALL RIGHT IN THE END--WHICH IS WHY MY BIG NIGHT TAKES PLACE NEAR THE END OF THE YEAR.
IT'S ALL RELATED.
INTERTWINED.

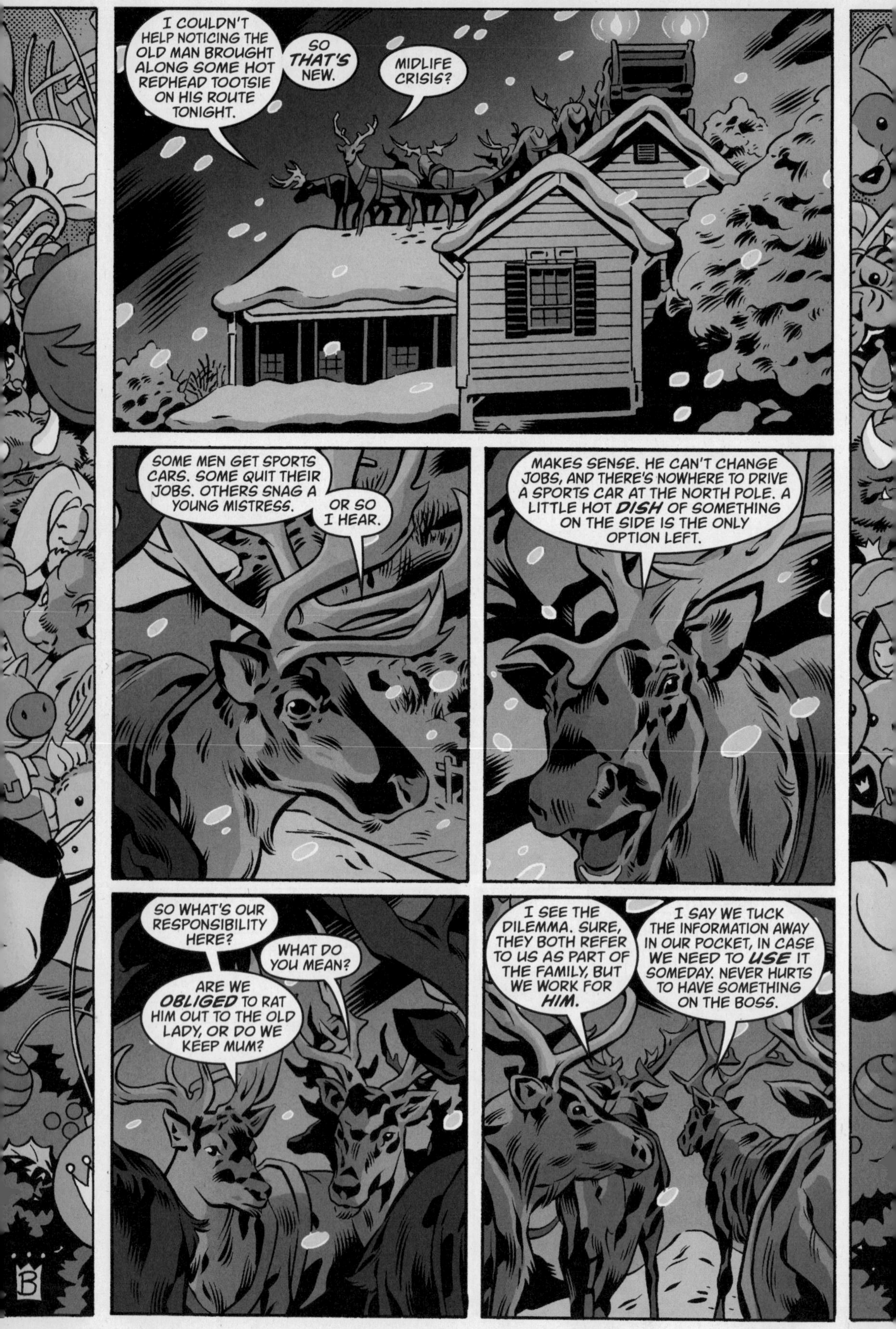
I COULDN'T HELP NOTICING THE OLD MAN BROUGHT ALONG SOME HOT REDHEAD TOOTSIE ON HIS ROUTE TONIGHT.
SO *THAT'S* NEW.
MIDLIFE CRISIS?
SOME MEN GET SPORTS CARS. SOME QUIT THEIR JOBS. OTHERS SNAG A YOUNG MISTRESS.
OR SO I HEAR.
MAKES SENSE. HE CAN'T CHANGE JOBS, AND THERE'S NOWHERE TO DRIVE A SPORTS CAR AT THE NORTH POLE. A LITTLE HOT *DISH* OF SOMETHING ON THE SIDE IS THE ONLY OPTION LEFT.
SO WHAT'S OUR RESPONSIBILITY HERE?
WHAT DO YOU MEAN?
ARE WE *OBLIGED* TO RAT HIM OUT TO THE OLD LADY, OR DO WE KEEP MUM?
I SEE THE DILEMMA. SURE, THEY BOTH REFER TO US AS PART OF THE FAMILY, BUT WE WORK FOR *HIM*.
I SAY WE TUCK THE INFORMATION AWAY IN OUR POCKET, IN CASE WE NEED TO *USE* IT SOMEDAY. NEVER HURTS TO HAVE SOMETHING ON THE BOSS.

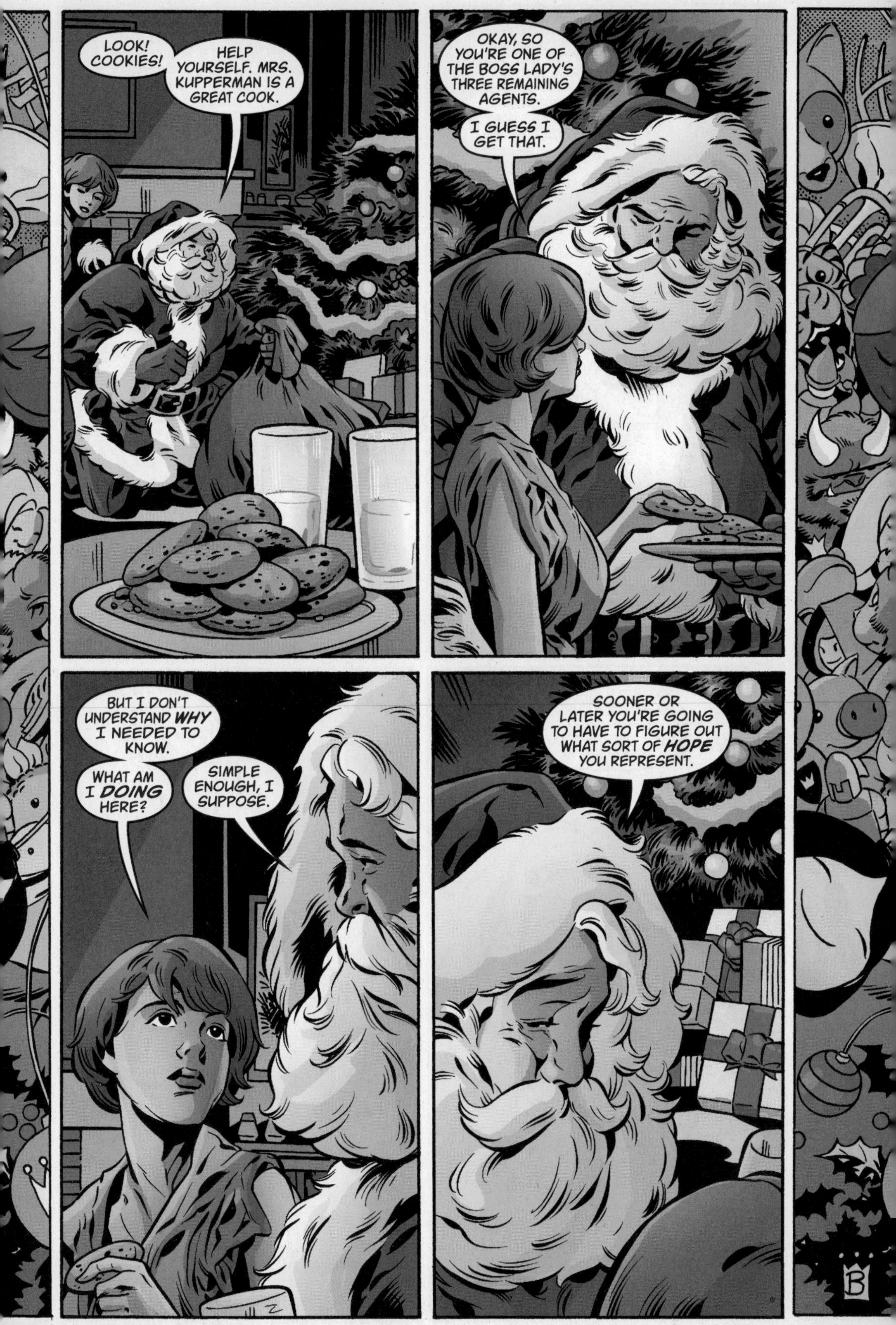
LOOK! COOKIES!
HELP YOURSELF. MRS. KUPPERMAN IS A GREAT COOK.
OKAY, SO YOU'RE ONE OF THE BOSS LADY'S THREE REMAINING AGENTS.
I GUESS I GET THAT.
BUT I DON'T UNDERSTAND WHY I NEEDED TO KNOW.
WHAT AM I DOING HERE?
SIMPLE ENOUGH, I SUPPOSE.
SOONER OR LATER YOU'RE GOING TO HAVE TO FIGURE OUT WHAT SORT OF HOPE YOU REPRESENT.

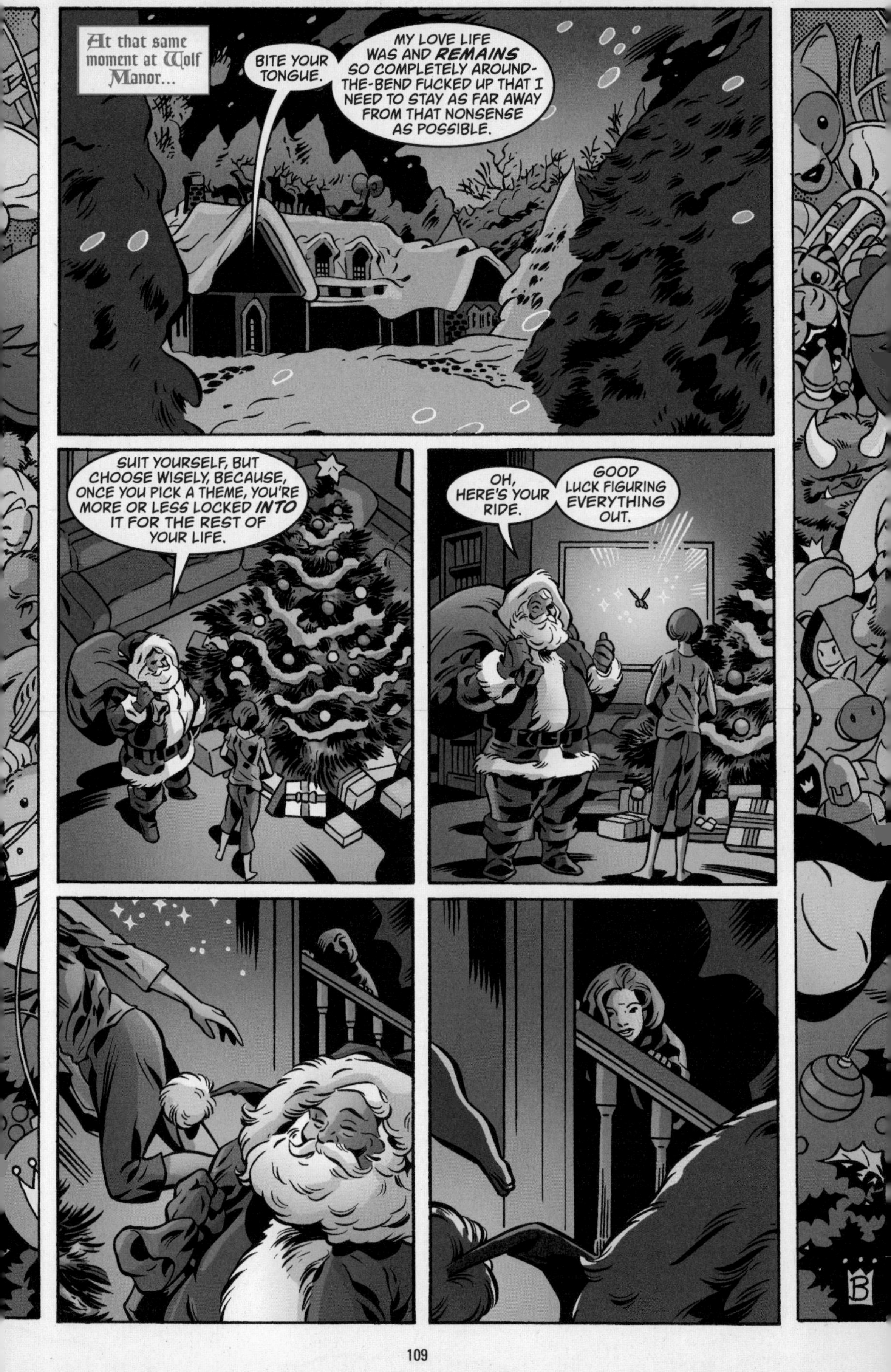
At that same moment at Wolf Manor...
BITE YOUR TONGUE.
MY LOVE LIFE WAS AND REMAINS SO COMPLETELY AROUND-THE-BEND FUCKED UP THAT I NEED TO STAY AS FAR AWAY FROM THAT NONSENSE AS POSSIBLE.
SUIT YOURSELF, BUT CHOOSE WISELY, BECAUSE, ONCE YOU PICK A THEME, YOU'RE MORE OR LESS LOCKED INTO IT FOR THE REST OF YOUR LIFE.
OH, HERE'S YOUR RIDE.
GOOD LUCK FIGURING EVERYTHING OUT.

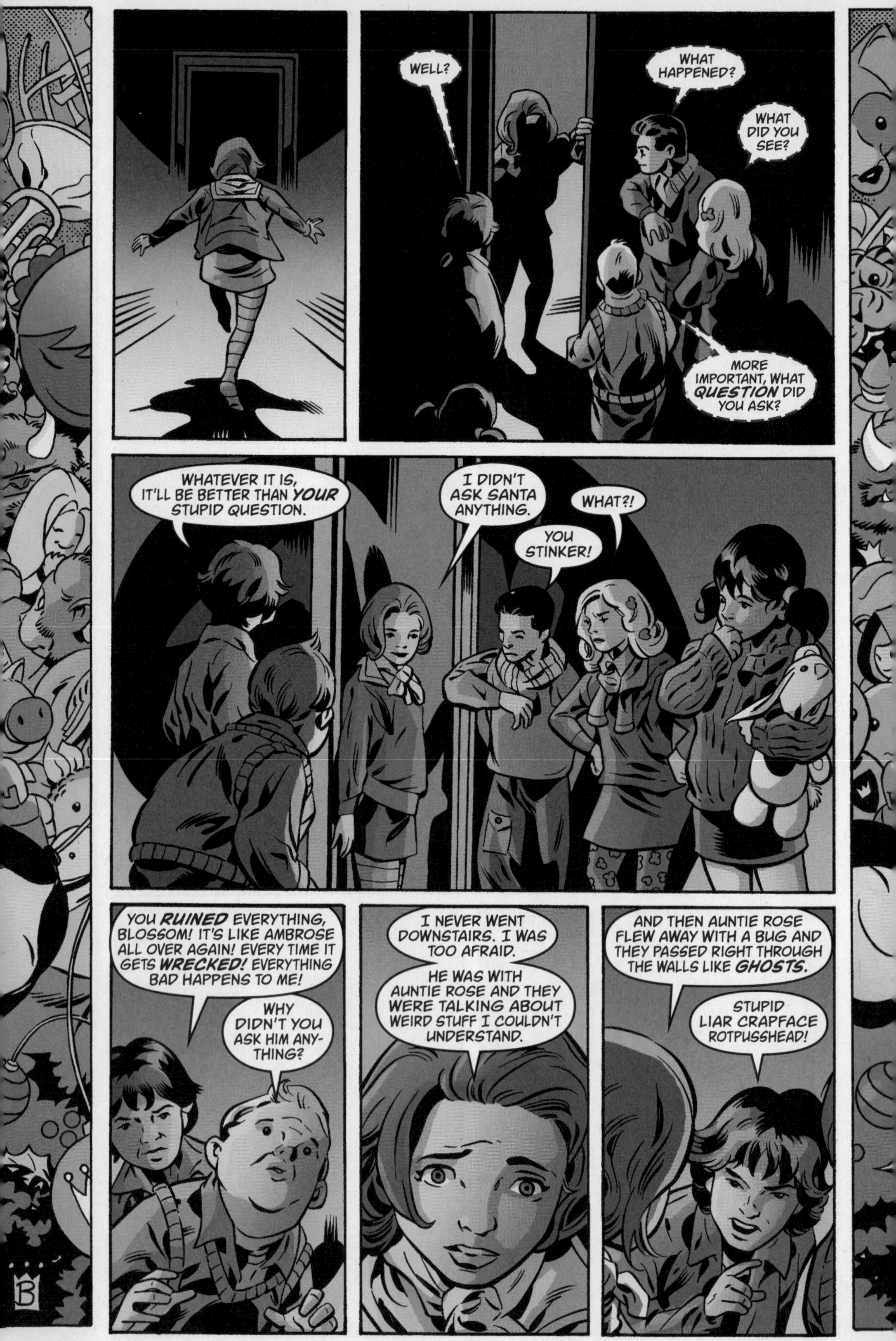
WELL?
WHAT HAPPENED?
WHAT DID YOU SEE?
MORE IMPORTANT, WHAT QUESTION DID YOU ASK?
WHATEVER IT IS, IT'LL BE BETTER THAN YOUR STUPID QUESTION.
I DIDN'T ASK SANTA ANYTHING.
WHAT?!
YOU STINKER!
YOU RUINED EVERYTHING, BLOSSOM! IT'S LIKE AMBROSE ALL OVER AGAIN! EVERY TIME IT GETS WRECKED! EVERYTHING BAD HAPPENS TO ME!
WHY DIDN'T YOU ASK HIM ANYTHING?
I NEVER WENT DOWNSTAIRS. I WAS TOO AFRAID.
HE WAS WITH AUNTIE ROSE AND THEY WERE TALKING ABOUT WEIRD STUFF I COULDN'T UNDERSTAND.
AND THEN AUNTIE ROSE FLEW AWAY WITH A BUG AND THEY PASSED RIGHT THROUGH THE WALLS LIKE GHOSTS.
STUPID LIAR CRAPFACE ROTPUSSHEAD!

Chapter Three – The Battle of Life

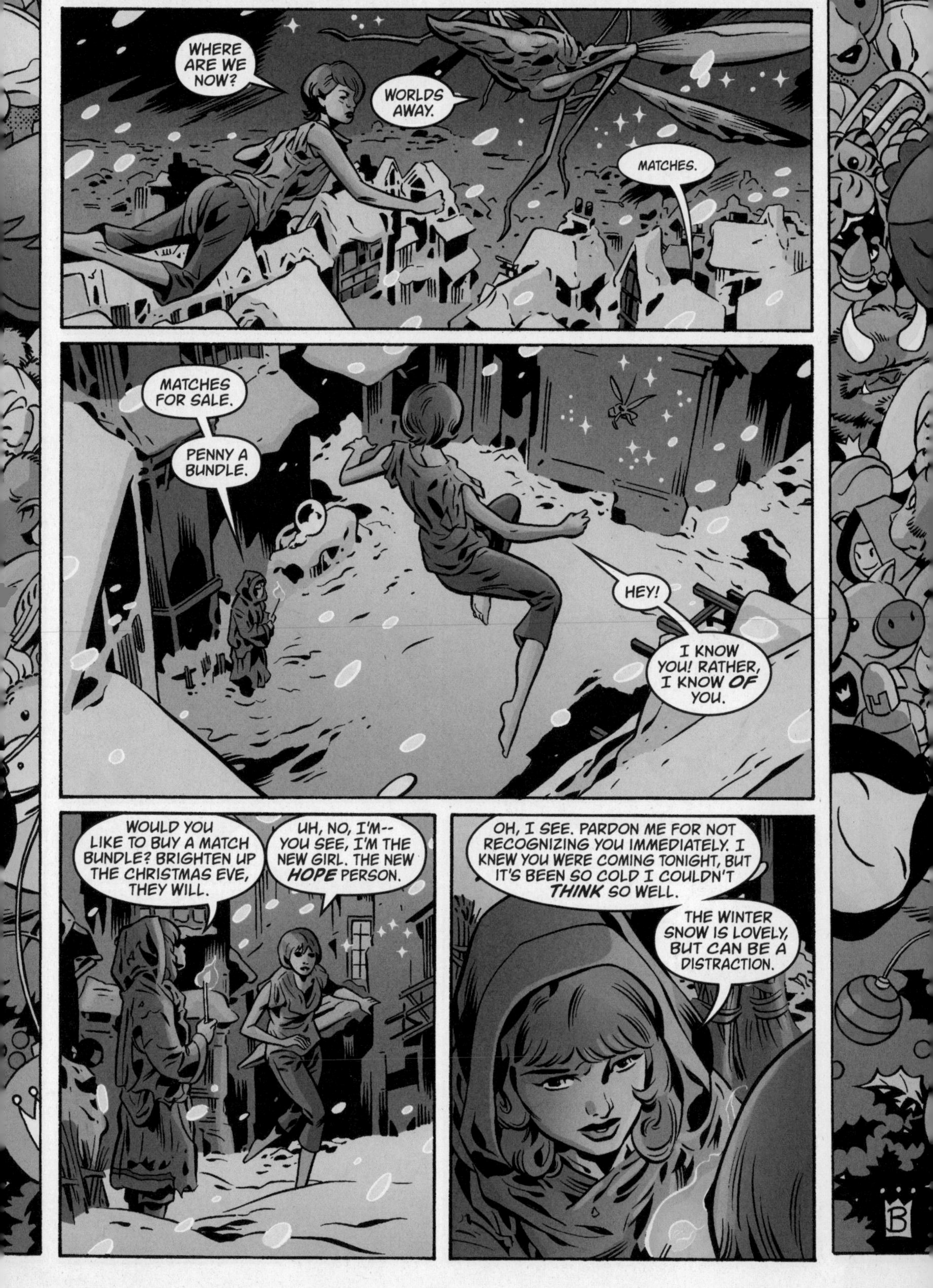

WHERE ARE WE NOW?
WORLDS AWAY.
MATCHES.
MATCHES FOR SALE.
PENNY A BUNDLE.
HEY!
I KNOW YOU! RATHER, I KNOW *OF* YOU.
WOULD YOU LIKE TO BUY A MATCH BUNDLE? BRIGHTEN UP THE CHRISTMAS EVE, THEY WILL.
UH, NO, I'M-- YOU SEE, I'M THE NEW GIRL. THE NEW *HOPE* PERSON.
OH, I SEE. PARDON ME FOR NOT RECOGNIZING YOU IMMEDIATELY. I KNEW YOU WERE COMING TONIGHT, BUT IT'S BEEN SO COLD I COULDN'T *THINK* SO WELL.
THE WINTER SNOW IS LOVELY, BUT CAN BE A DISTRACTION.

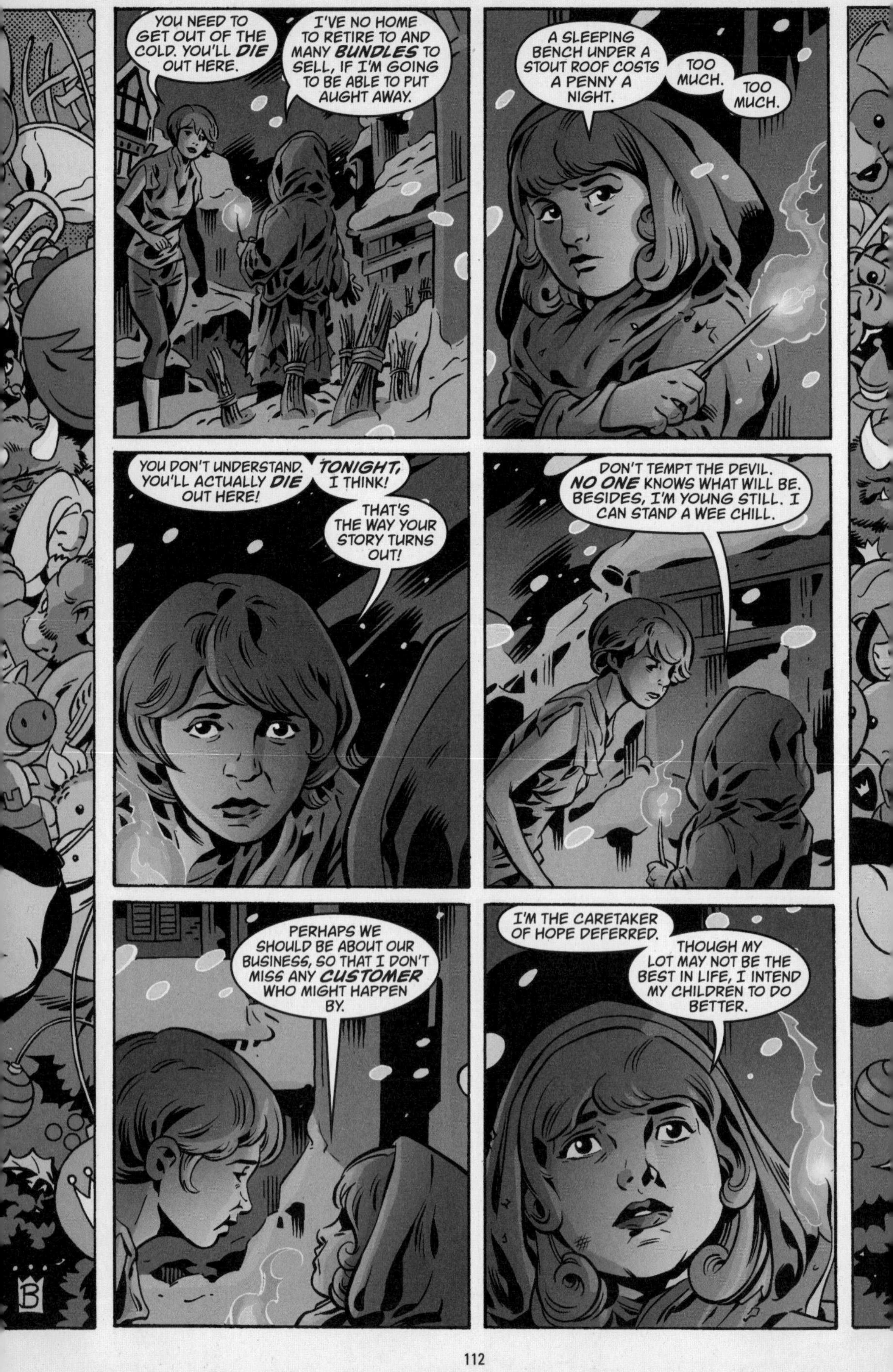
YOU NEED TO GET OUT OF THE COLD. YOU'LL DIE OUT HERE.
I'VE NO HOME TO RETIRE TO AND MANY BUNDLES TO SELL, IF I'M GOING TO BE ABLE TO PUT AUGHT AWAY.
A SLEEPING BENCH UNDER A STOUT ROOF COSTS A PENNY A NIGHT.
TOO MUCH.
TOO MUCH.
YOU DON'T UNDERSTAND. YOU'LL ACTUALLY DIE OUT HERE!
TONIGHT, I THINK!
THAT'S THE WAY YOUR STORY TURNS OUT!
DON'T TEMPT THE DEVIL. NO ONE KNOWS WHAT WILL BE. BESIDES, I'M YOUNG STILL. I CAN STAND A WEE CHILL.
PERHAPS WE SHOULD BE ABOUT OUR BUSINESS, SO THAT I DON'T MISS ANY CUSTOMER WHO MIGHT HAPPEN BY.
I'M THE CARETAKER OF HOPE DEFERRED.
THOUGH MY LOT MAY NOT BE THE BEST IN LIFE, I INTEND MY CHILDREN TO DO BETTER.

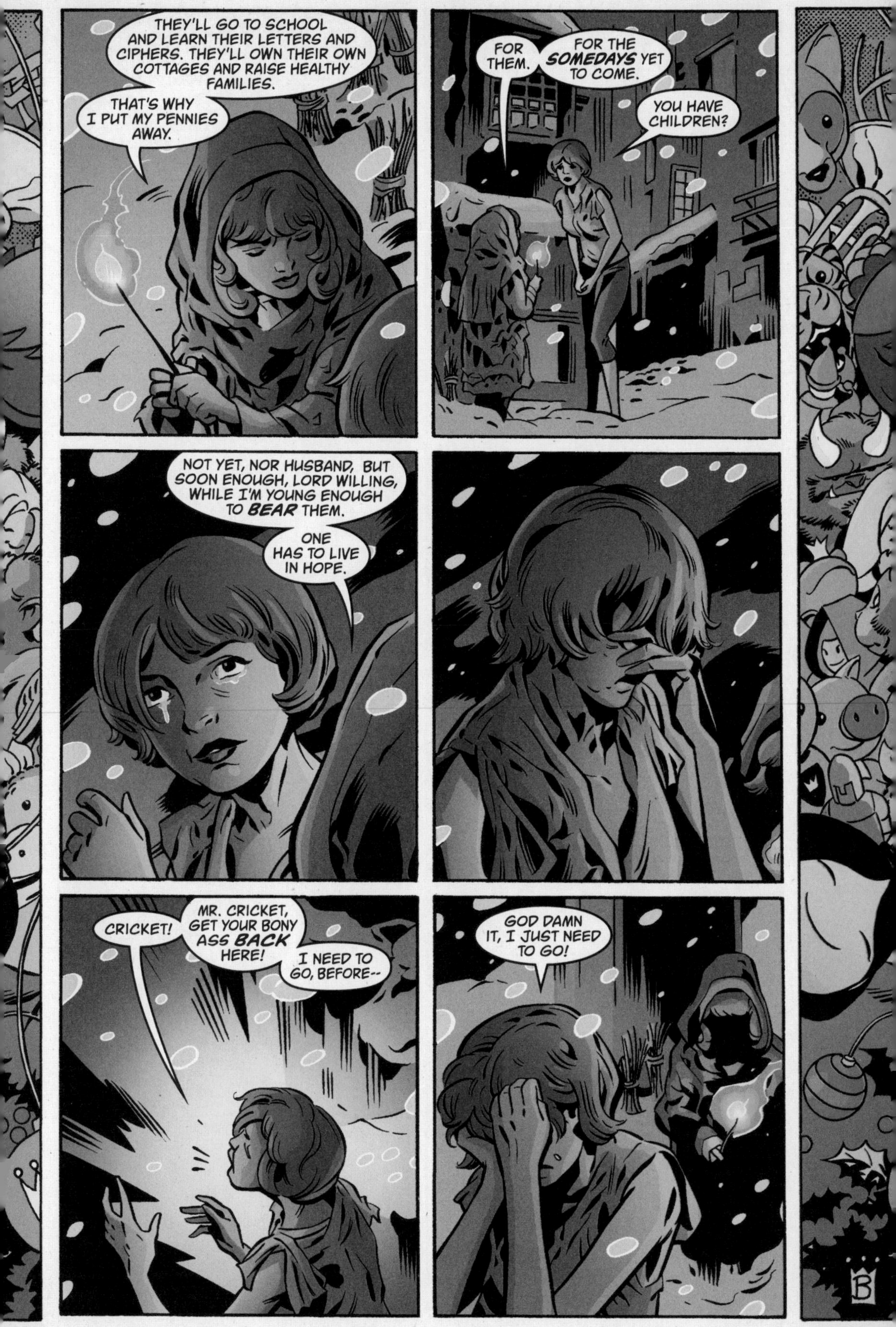
THEY'LL GO TO SCHOOL AND LEARN THEIR LETTERS AND CIPHERS. THEY'LL OWN THEIR OWN COTTAGES AND RAISE HEALTHY FAMILIES.
THAT'S WHY I PUT MY PENNIES AWAY.
FOR THEM.
FOR THE SOMEDAYS YET TO COME.
YOU HAVE CHILDREN?
NOT YET, NOR HUSBAND, BUT SOON ENOUGH, LORD WILLING, WHILE I'M YOUNG ENOUGH TO BEAR THEM.
ONE HAS TO LIVE IN HOPE.
CRICKET!
MR. CRICKET, GET YOUR BONY ASS BACK HERE!
I NEED TO GO, BEFORE--
GOD DAMN IT, I JUST NEED TO GO!

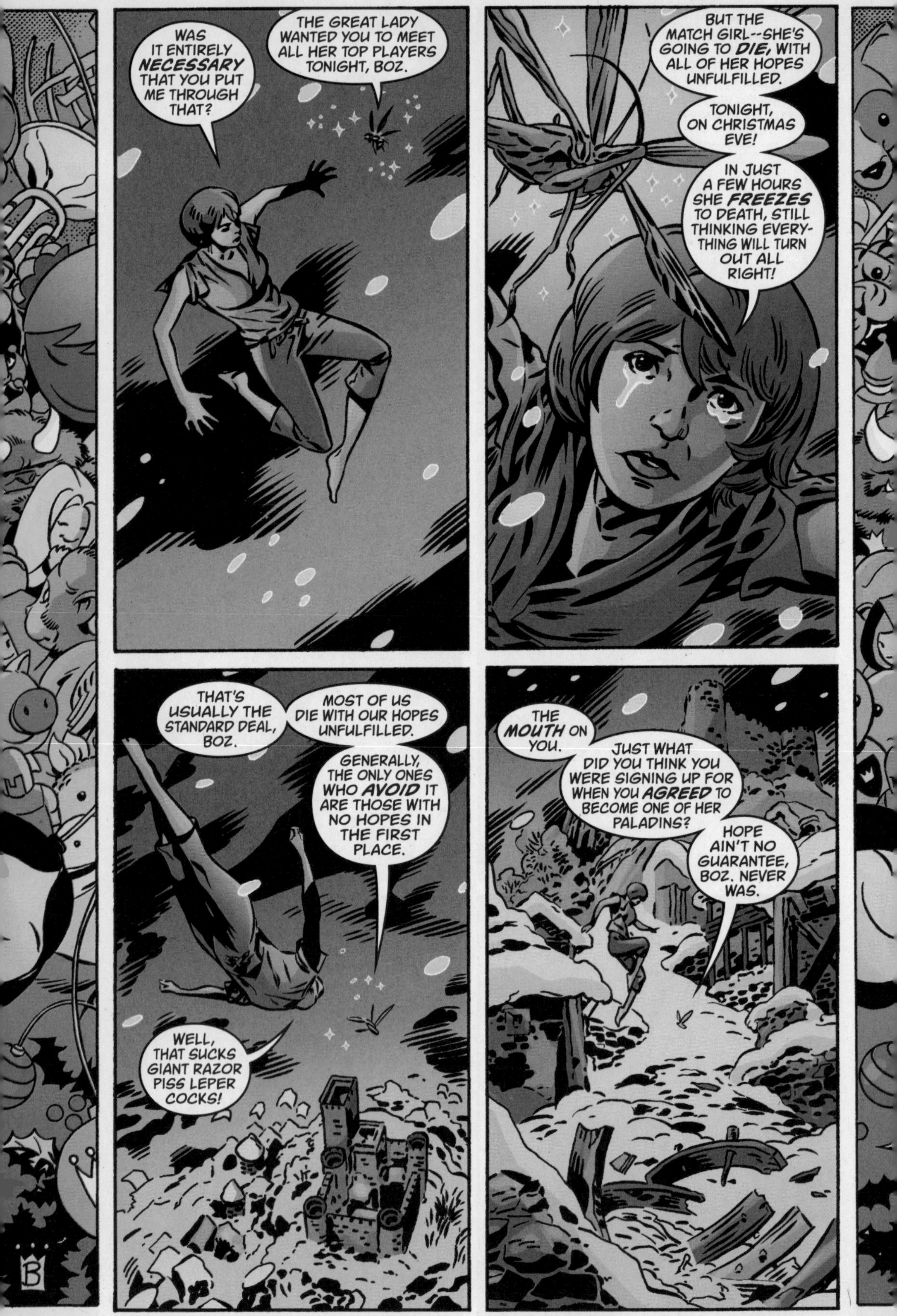
WAS IT ENTIRELY NECESSARY THAT YOU PUT ME THROUGH THAT?
THE GREAT LADY WANTED YOU TO MEET ALL HER TOP PLAYERS TONIGHT, BOZ.
BUT THE MATCH GIRL--SHE'S GOING TO DIE, WITH ALL OF HER HOPES UNFULFILLED.
TONIGHT, ON CHRISTMAS EVE!
IN JUST A FEW HOURS SHE FREEZES TO DEATH, STILL THINKING EVERY-THING WILL TURN OUT ALL RIGHT!
THAT'S USUALLY THE STANDARD DEAL, BOZ.
MOST OF US DIE WITH OUR HOPES UNFULFILLED.
GENERALLY, THE ONLY ONES WHO AVOID IT ARE THOSE WITH NO HOPES IN THE FIRST PLACE.
WELL, THAT SUCKS GIANT RAZOR PISS LEPER COCKS!
THE MOUTH ON YOU.
JUST WHAT DID YOU THINK YOU WERE SIGNING UP FOR WHEN YOU AGREED TO BECOME ONE OF HER PALADINS?
HOPE AIN'T NO GUARANTEE, BOZ. NEVER WAS.

Chapter Four – The Haunted Man and the Ghost's Bargain

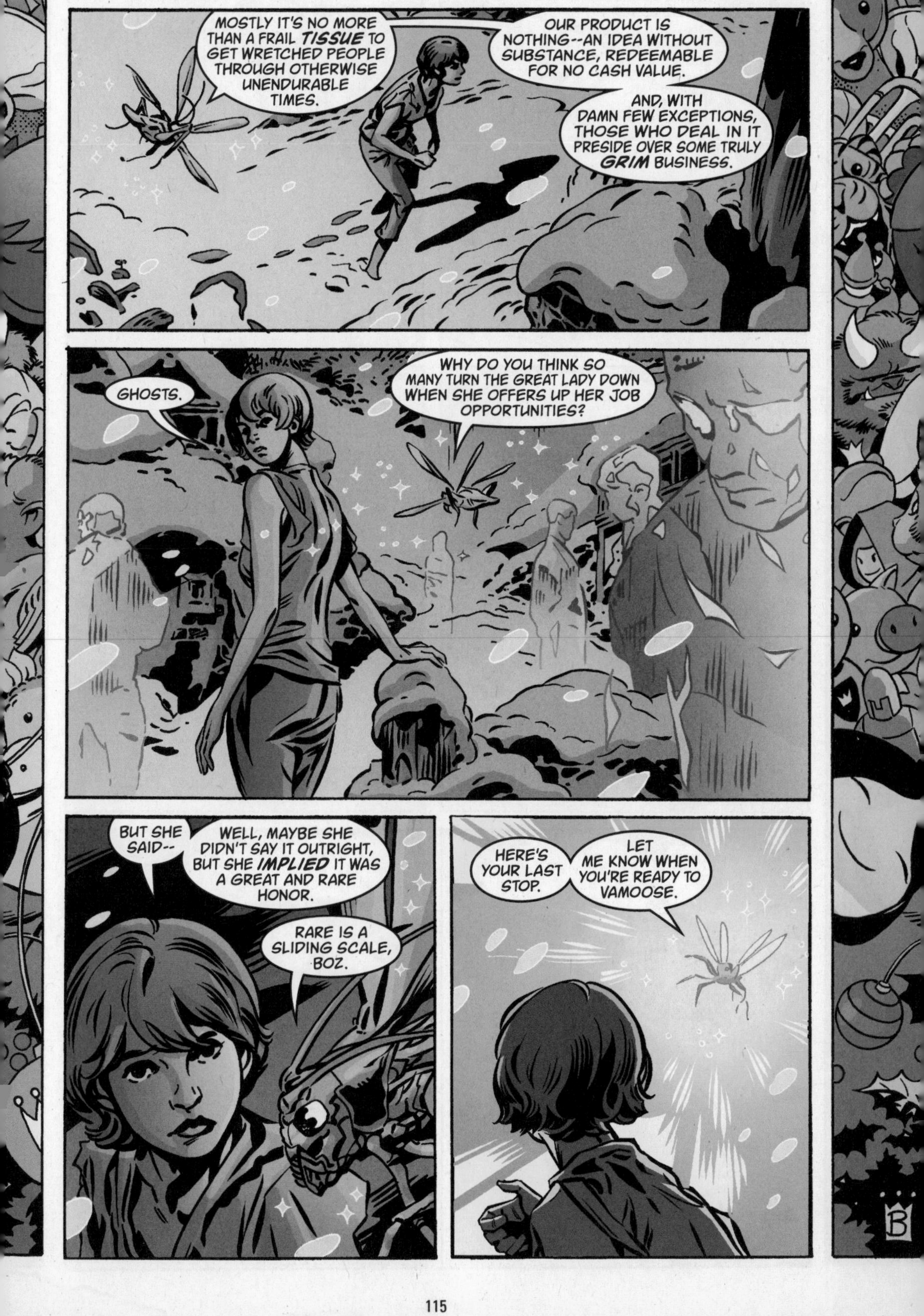
MOSTLY IT'S NO MORE THAN A FRAIL TISSUE TO GET WRETCHED PEOPLE THROUGH OTHERWISE UNENDURABLE TIMES.
OUR PRODUCT IS NOTHING--AN IDEA WITHOUT SUBSTANCE, REDEEMABLE FOR NO CASH VALUE.
AND, WITH DAMN FEW EXCEPTIONS, THOSE WHO DEAL IN IT PRESIDE OVER SOME TRULY GRIM BUSINESS.
GHOSTS.
WHY DO YOU THINK SO MANY TURN THE GREAT LADY DOWN WHEN SHE OFFERS UP HER JOB OPPORTUNITIES?
BUT SHE SAID--
WELL, MAYBE SHE DIDN'T SAY IT OUTRIGHT, BUT SHE IMPLIED IT WAS A GREAT AND RARE HONOR.
RARE IS A SLIDING SCALE, BOZ.
HERE'S YOUR LAST STOP.
LET ME KNOW WHEN YOU'RE READY TO VAMOOSE.

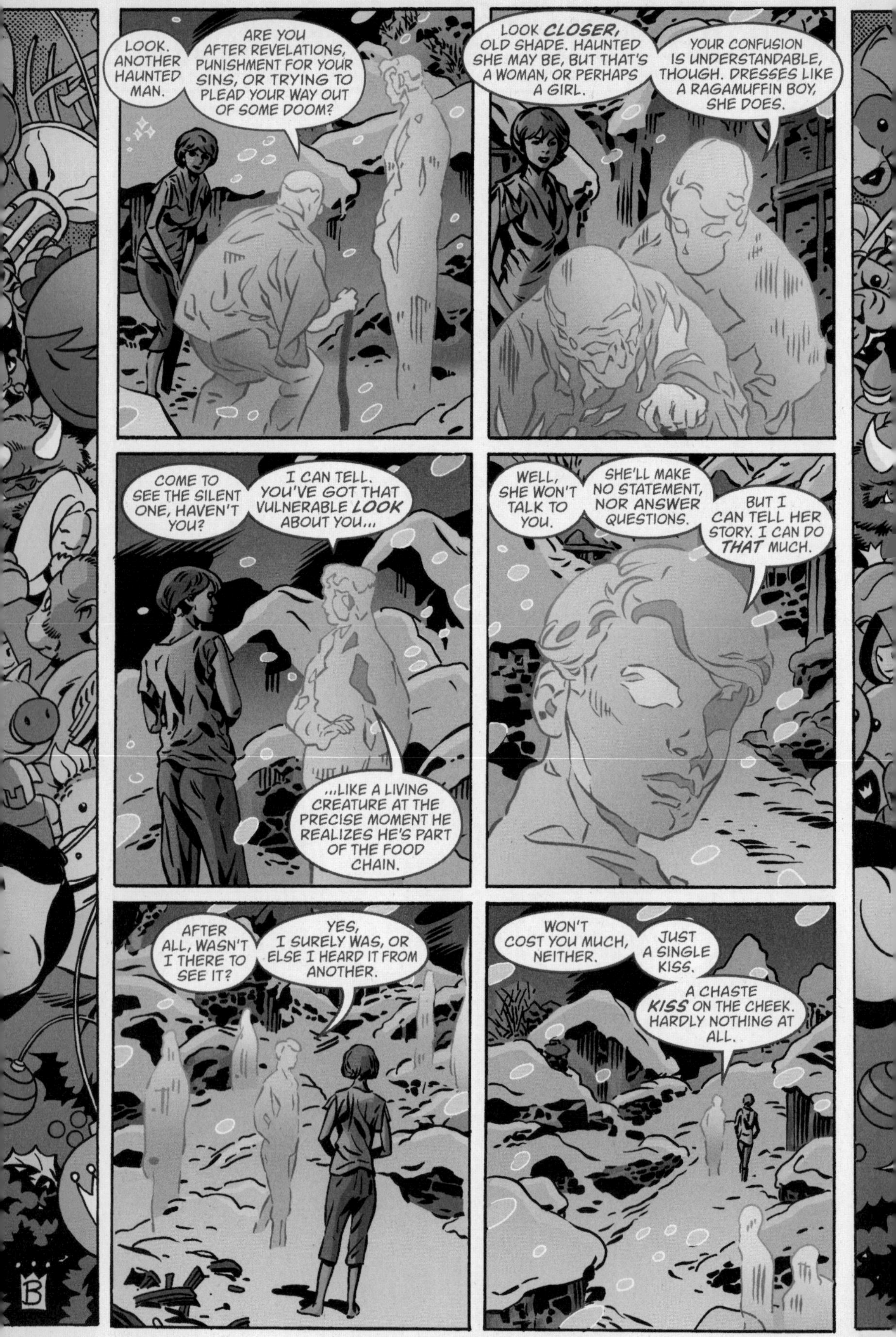
LOOK. ANOTHER HAUNTED MAN.
ARE YOU AFTER REVELATIONS, PUNISHMENT FOR YOUR SINS, OR TRYING TO PLEAD YOUR WAY OUT OF SOME DOOM?
LOOK CLOSER, OLD SHADE. HAUNTED SHE MAY BE, BUT THAT'S A WOMAN, OR PERHAPS A GIRL.
YOUR CONFUSION IS UNDERSTANDABLE, THOUGH. DRESSES LIKE A RAGAMUFFIN BOY, SHE DOES.
COME TO SEE THE SILENT ONE, HAVEN'T YOU?
I CAN TELL. YOU'VE GOT THAT VULNERABLE LOOK ABOUT YOU...
...LIKE A LIVING CREATURE AT THE PRECISE MOMENT HE REALIZES HE'S PART OF THE FOOD CHAIN.
WELL, SHE WON'T TALK TO YOU.
SHE'LL MAKE NO STATEMENT, NOR ANSWER QUESTIONS.
BUT I CAN TELL HER STORY. I CAN DO THAT MUCH.
AFTER ALL, WASN'T I THERE TO SEE IT?
YES, I SURELY WAS, OR ELSE I HEARD IT FROM ANOTHER.
WON'T COST YOU MUCH, NEITHER.
JUST A SINGLE KISS.
A CHASTE KISS ON THE CHEEK. HARDLY NOTHING AT ALL.

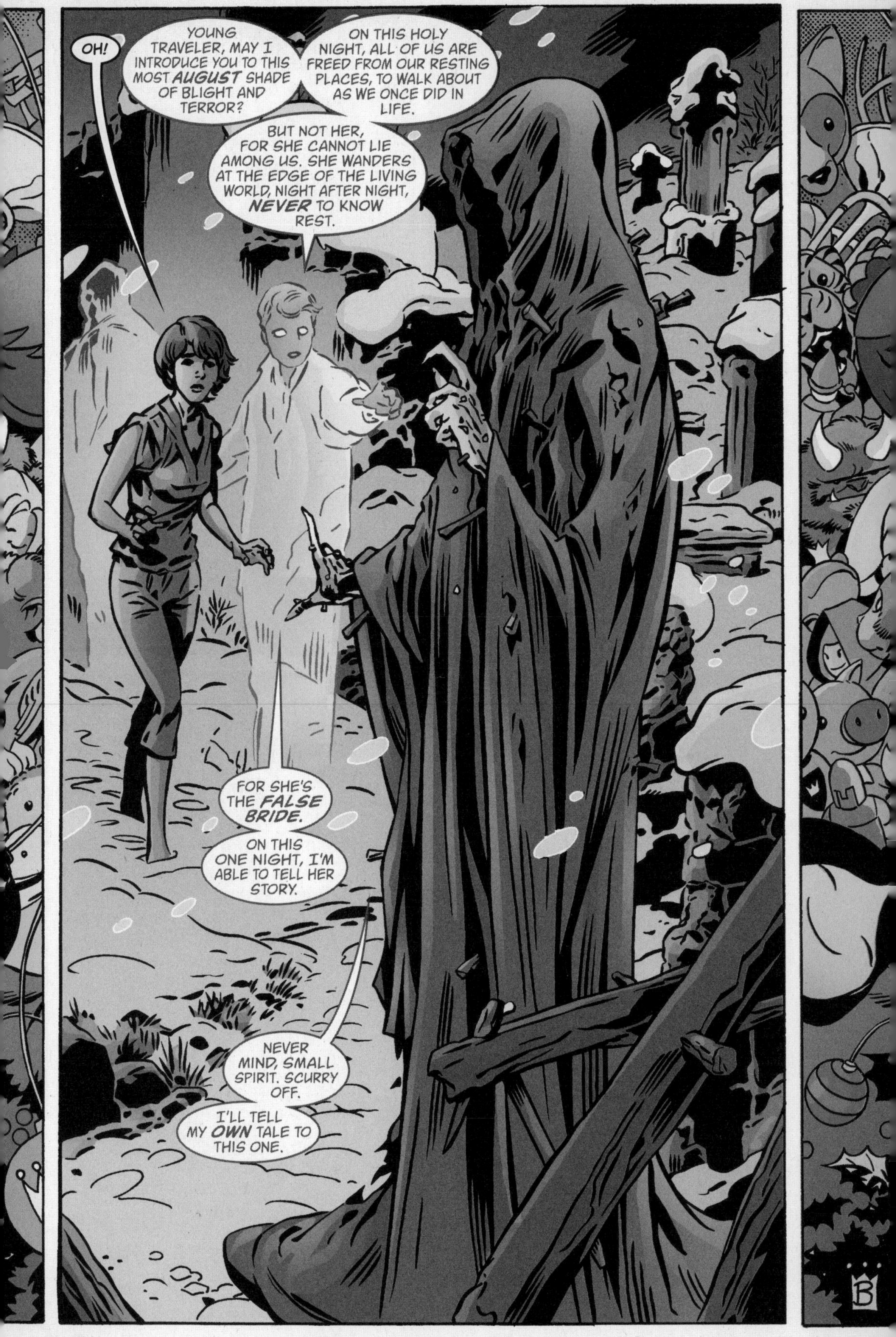
OH!
YOUNG TRAVELER, MAY I INTRODUCE YOU TO THIS MOST AUGUST SHADE OF BLIGHT AND TERROR?
ON THIS HOLY NIGHT, ALL OF US ARE FREED FROM OUR RESTING PLACES, TO WALK ABOUT AS WE ONCE DID IN LIFE.
BUT NOT HER, FOR SHE CANNOT LIE AMONG US. SHE WANDERS AT THE EDGE OF THE LIVING WORLD, NIGHT AFTER NIGHT, NEVER TO KNOW REST.
FOR SHE'S THE FALSE BRIDE.
ON THIS ONE NIGHT, I'M ABLE TO TELL HER STORY.
NEVER MIND, SMALL SPIRIT. SCURRY OFF.
I'LL TELL MY OWN TALE TO THIS ONE.

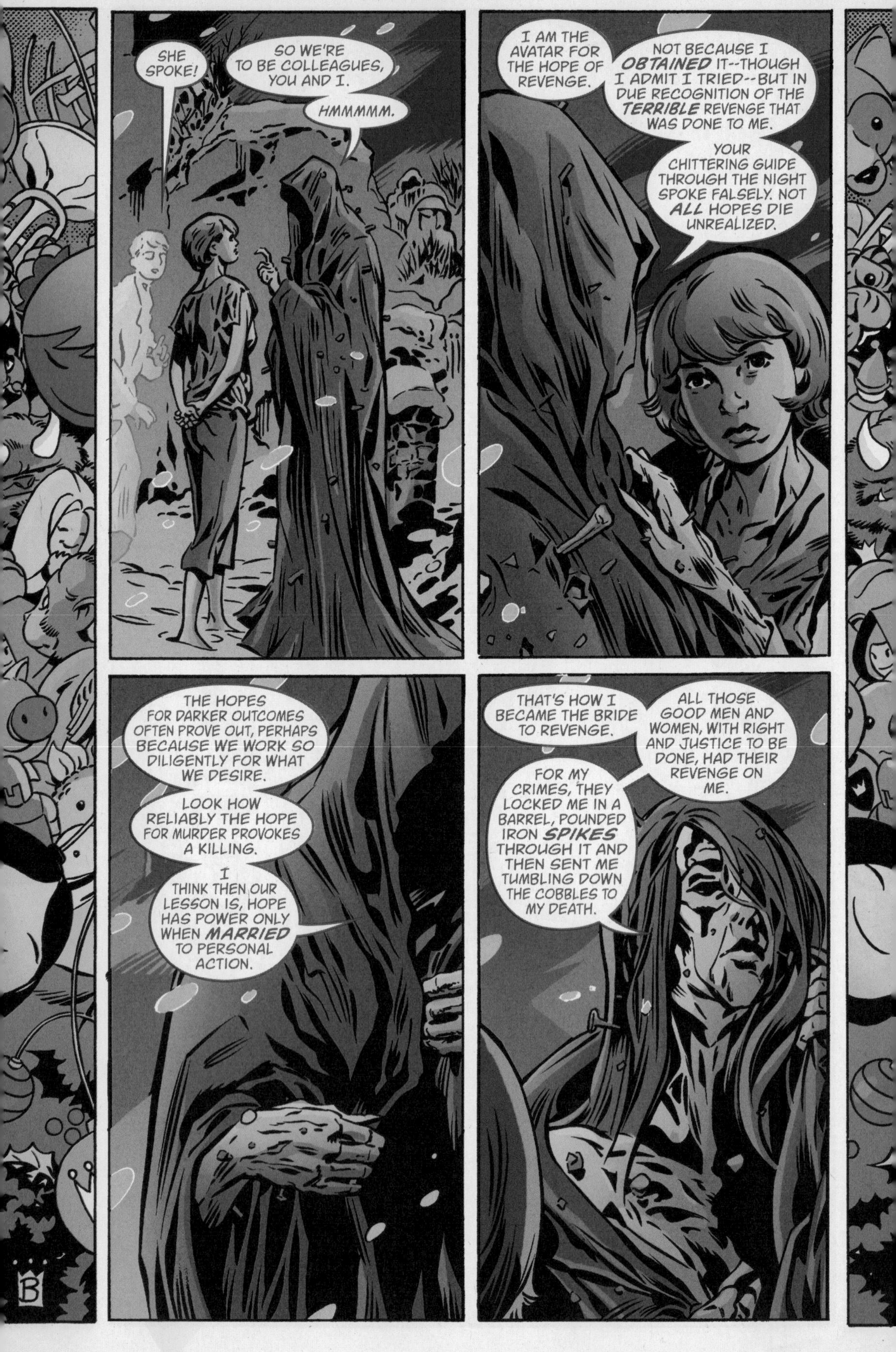
SHE SPOKE!
SO WE'RE TO BE COLLEAGUES, YOU AND I.
HMMMMM.
I AM THE AVATAR FOR THE HOPE OF REVENGE.
NOT BECAUSE I OBTAINED IT--THOUGH I ADMIT I TRIED--BUT IN DUE RECOGNITION OF THE TERRIBLE REVENGE THAT WAS DONE TO ME.
YOUR CHITTERING GUIDE THROUGH THE NIGHT SPOKE FALSELY. NOT ALL HOPES DIE UNREALIZED.
THE HOPES FOR DARKER OUTCOMES OFTEN PROVE OUT, PERHAPS BECAUSE WE WORK SO DILIGENTLY FOR WHAT WE DESIRE.
LOOK HOW RELIABLY THE HOPE FOR MURDER PROVOKES A KILLING.
I THINK THEN OUR LESSON IS, HOPE HAS POWER ONLY WHEN MARRIED TO PERSONAL ACTION.
THAT'S HOW I BECAME THE BRIDE TO REVENGE.
ALL THOSE GOOD MEN AND WOMEN, WITH RIGHT AND JUSTICE TO BE DONE, HAD THEIR REVENGE ON ME.
FOR MY CRIMES, THEY LOCKED ME IN A BARREL, POUNDED IRON SPIKES THROUGH IT AND THEN SENT ME TUMBLING DOWN THE COBBLES TO MY DEATH.

THEY WERE ALL SO FULL OF HOPE.

STILL ARE.

ONLY NOW THEY *EACH* HOPE TO BE RELEASED FROM THEIR CONFINEMENT IN DARK GRAVE AND CRYPT, AND FROM THEIR ANNUAL GHOSTLY PERAMBULATIONS.

THEY HOPE TO PASS ON TO REWARDS LONG DELAYED.

BUT IN THIS THEY HOPE IN *VAIN.* THEY ATTEND *ME* AND I'LL NEVER DISMISS THEM.

SO THEN, MY NEW SISTER.

WHAT SORT OF HOPE WILL *YOU* CHAMPION, I WONDER?

LET US DISCUSS THE POSSIBILITIES.

And so they did, for long, dark hours.

ALL DONE, THEN?

I TRULY HOPE SO.

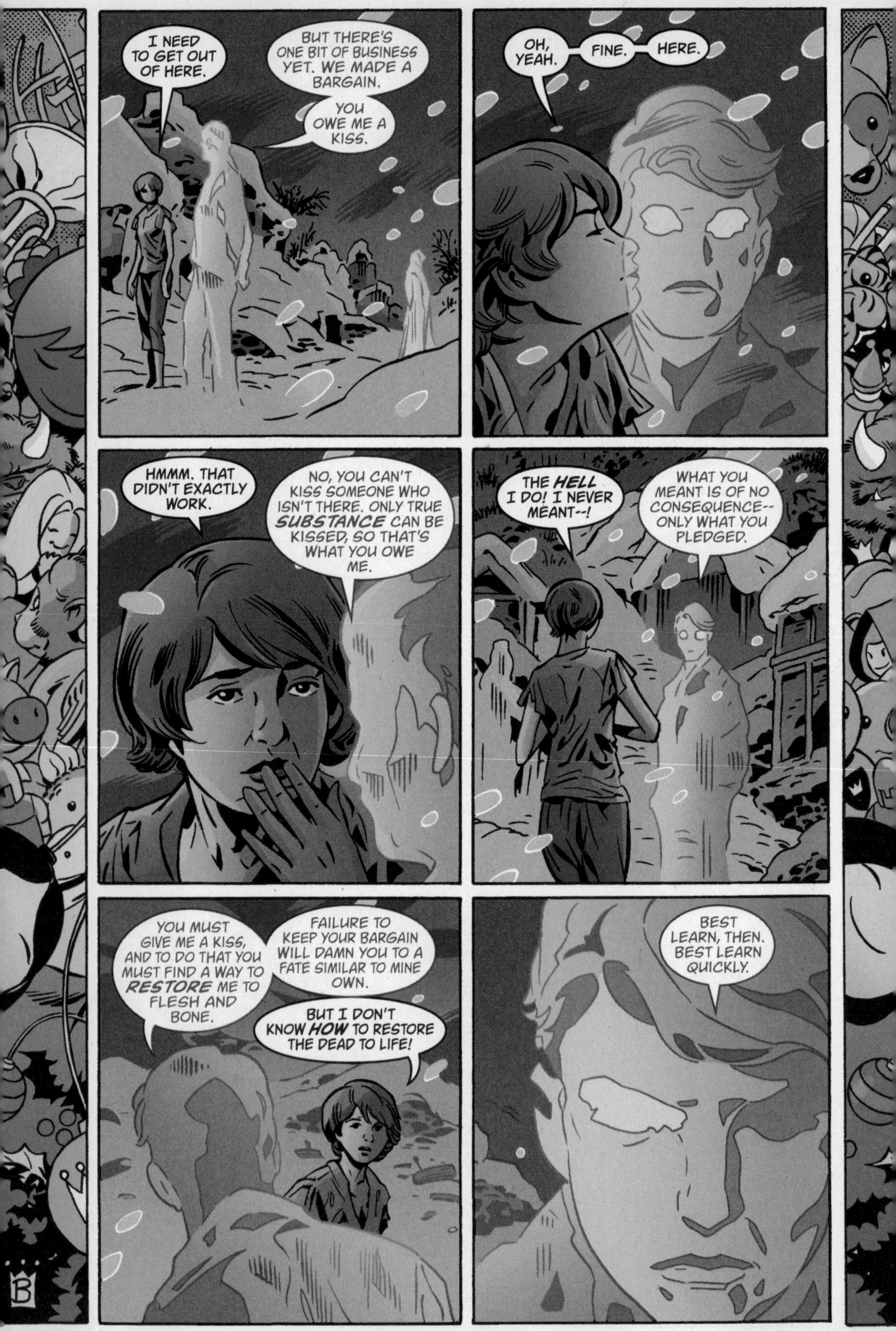
I NEED TO GET OUT OF HERE.
BUT THERE'S ONE BIT OF BUSINESS YET. WE MADE A BARGAIN.
YOU OWE ME A KISS.
OH, YEAH.
FINE.
HERE.
HMMM. THAT DIDN'T EXACTLY WORK.
NO, YOU CAN'T KISS SOMEONE WHO ISN'T THERE. ONLY TRUE SUBSTANCE CAN BE KISSED, SO THAT'S WHAT YOU OWE ME.
THE HELL I DO! I NEVER MEANT--!
WHAT YOU MEANT IS OF NO CONSEQUENCE-- ONLY WHAT YOU PLEDGED.
YOU MUST GIVE ME A KISS, AND TO DO THAT YOU MUST FIND A WAY TO RESTORE ME TO FLESH AND BONE.
FAILURE TO KEEP YOUR BARGAIN WILL DAMN YOU TO A FATE SIMILAR TO MINE OWN.
BUT I DON'T KNOW HOW TO RESTORE THE DEAD TO LIFE!
BEST LEARN, THEN. BEST LEARN QUICKLY.

Chapter Five – A Christmas Carol

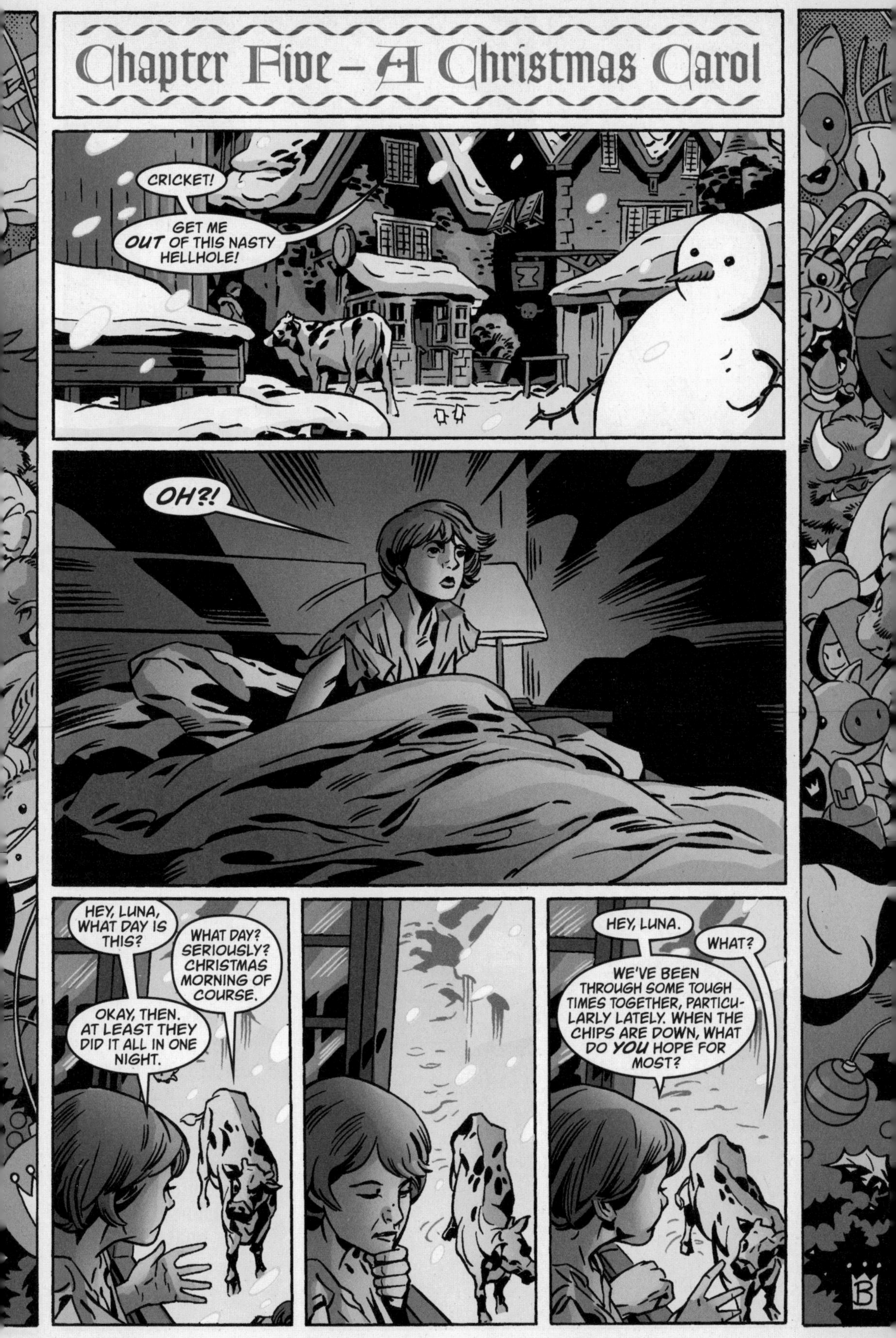
CRICKET!
GET ME OUT OF THIS NASTY HELLHOLE!
OH?!
HEY, LUNA, WHAT DAY IS THIS?
WHAT DAY? SERIOUSLY? CHRISTMAS MORNING OF COURSE.
OKAY, THEN. AT LEAST THEY DID IT ALL IN ONE NIGHT.
HEY, LUNA.
WHAT?
WE'VE BEEN THROUGH SOME TOUGH TIMES TOGETHER, PARTICU-LARLY LATELY. WHEN THE CHIPS ARE DOWN, WHAT DO YOU HOPE FOR MOST?

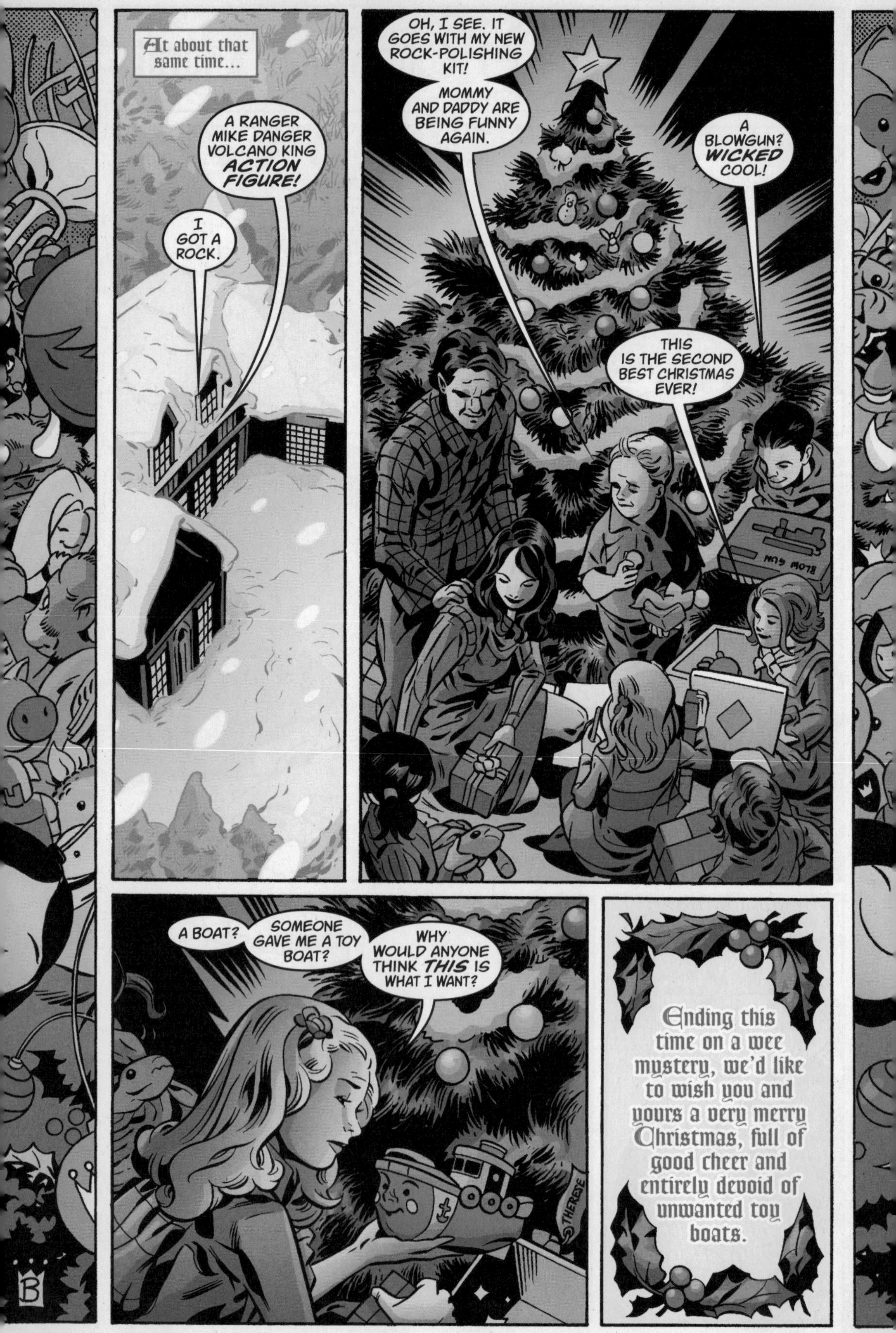
At about that same time...
A RANGER MIKE DANGER VOLCANO KING ACTION FIGURE!
I GOT A ROCK.
OH, I SEE. IT GOES WITH MY NEW ROCK-POLISHING KIT!
MOMMY AND DADDY ARE BEING FUNNY AGAIN.
A BLOWGUN? WICKED COOL!
THIS IS THE SECOND BEST CHRISTMAS EVER!
A BOAT?
SOMEONE GAVE ME A TOY BOAT?
WHY WOULD ANYONE THINK THIS IS WHAT I WANT?
THERESE
Ending this time on a wee mystery, we'd like to wish you and yours a very merry Christmas, full of good cheer and entirely devoid of unwanted toy boats.

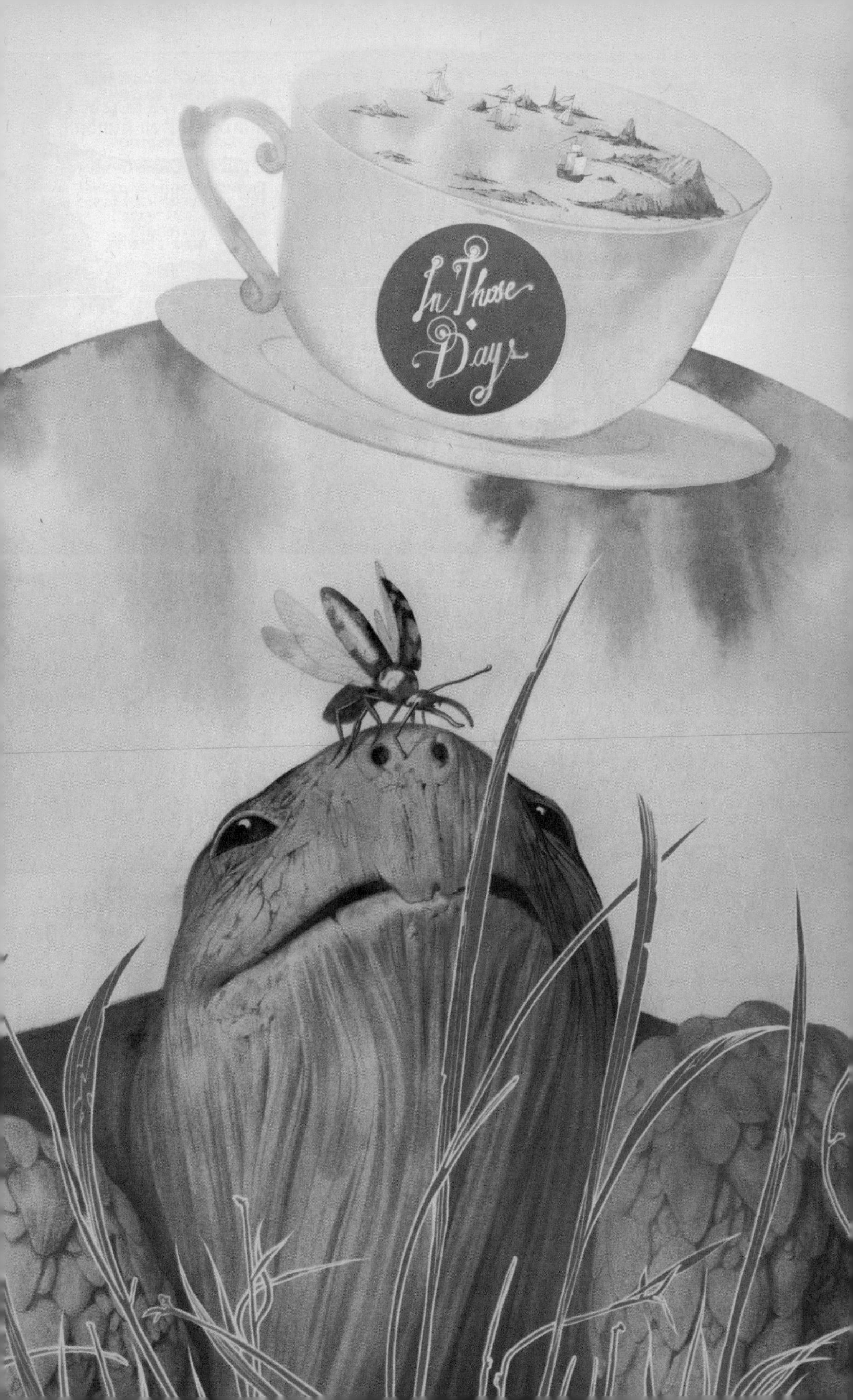
In Those Days

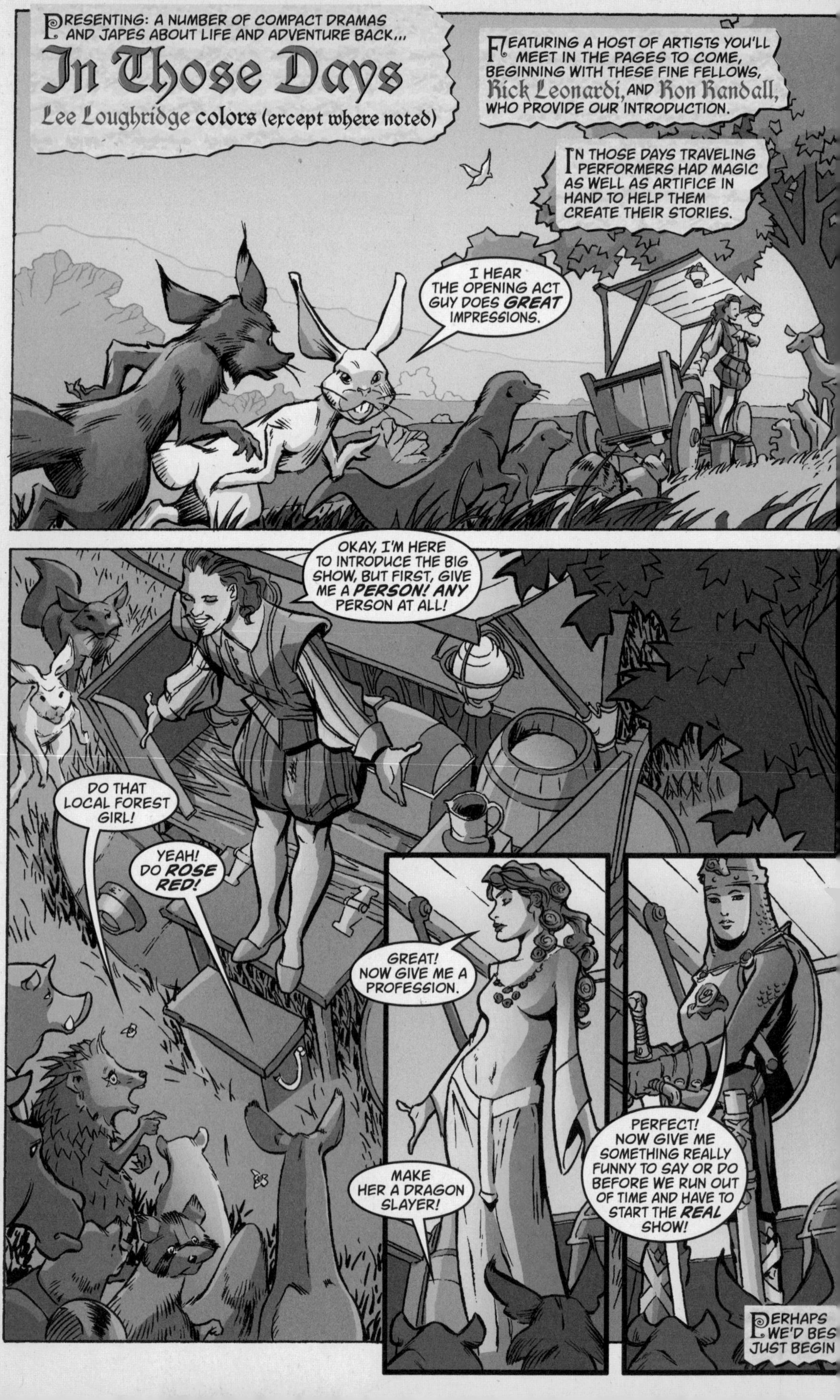
PRESENTING: A NUMBER OF COMPACT DRAMAS AND JAPES ABOUT LIFE AND ADVENTURE BACK...
In Those Days
Lee Loughridge colors (except where noted)
FEATURING A HOST OF ARTISTS YOU'LL MEET IN THE PAGES TO COME, BEGINNING WITH THESE FINE FELLOWS, Rick Leonardi, AND Ron Randall, WHO PROVIDE OUR INTRODUCTION.
IN THOSE DAYS TRAVELING PERFORMERS HAD MAGIC AS WELL AS ARTIFICE IN HAND TO HELP THEM CREATE THEIR STORIES.
I HEAR THE OPENING ACT GUY DOES GREAT IMPRESSIONS.
OKAY, I'M HERE TO INTRODUCE THE BIG SHOW, BUT FIRST, GIVE ME A PERSON! ANY PERSON AT ALL!
DO THAT LOCAL FOREST GIRL!
YEAH! DO ROSE RED!
GREAT! NOW GIVE ME A PROFESSION.
MAKE HER A DRAGON SLAYER!
PERFECT! NOW GIVE ME SOMETHING REALLY FUNNY TO SAY OR DO BEFORE WE RUN OUT OF TIME AND HAVE TO START THE REAL SHOW!
PERHAPS WE'D BES JUST BEGIN

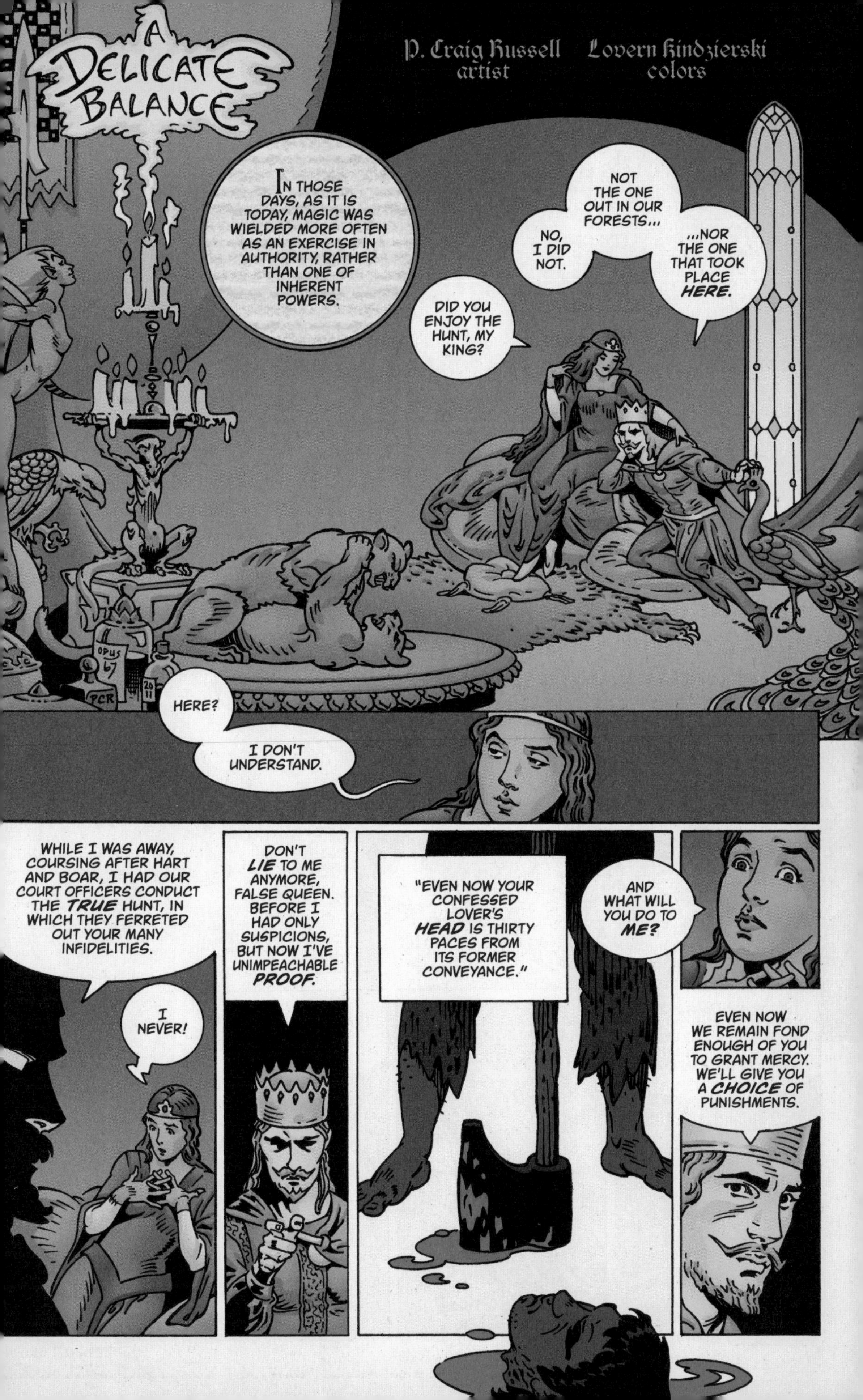
A DELICATE BALANCE
P. Craig Russell artist
Lovern Kindzierski colors
IN THOSE DAYS, AS IT IS TODAY, MAGIC WAS WIELDED MORE OFTEN AS AN EXERCISE IN AUTHORITY, RATHER THAN ONE OF INHERENT POWERS.
DID YOU ENJOY THE HUNT, MY KING?
NO, I DID NOT.
NOT THE ONE OUT IN OUR FORESTS...
...NOR THE ONE THAT TOOK PLACE HERE.
OPUS 67
PCR
2011
HERE?
I DON'T UNDERSTAND.
WHILE I WAS AWAY, COURSING AFTER HART AND BOAR, I HAD OUR COURT OFFICERS CONDUCT THE TRUE HUNT, IN WHICH THEY FERRETED OUT YOUR MANY INFIDELITIES.
I NEVER!
DON'T LIE TO ME ANYMORE, FALSE QUEEN. BEFORE I HAD ONLY SUSPICIONS, BUT NOW I'VE UNIMPEACHABLE PROOF.
"EVEN NOW YOUR CONFESSED LOVER'S HEAD IS THIRTY PACES FROM ITS FORMER CONVEYANCE."
AND WHAT WILL YOU DO TO ME?
EVEN NOW WE REMAIN FOND ENOUGH OF YOU TO GRANT MERCY. WE'LL GIVE YOU A CHOICE OF PUNISHMENTS.

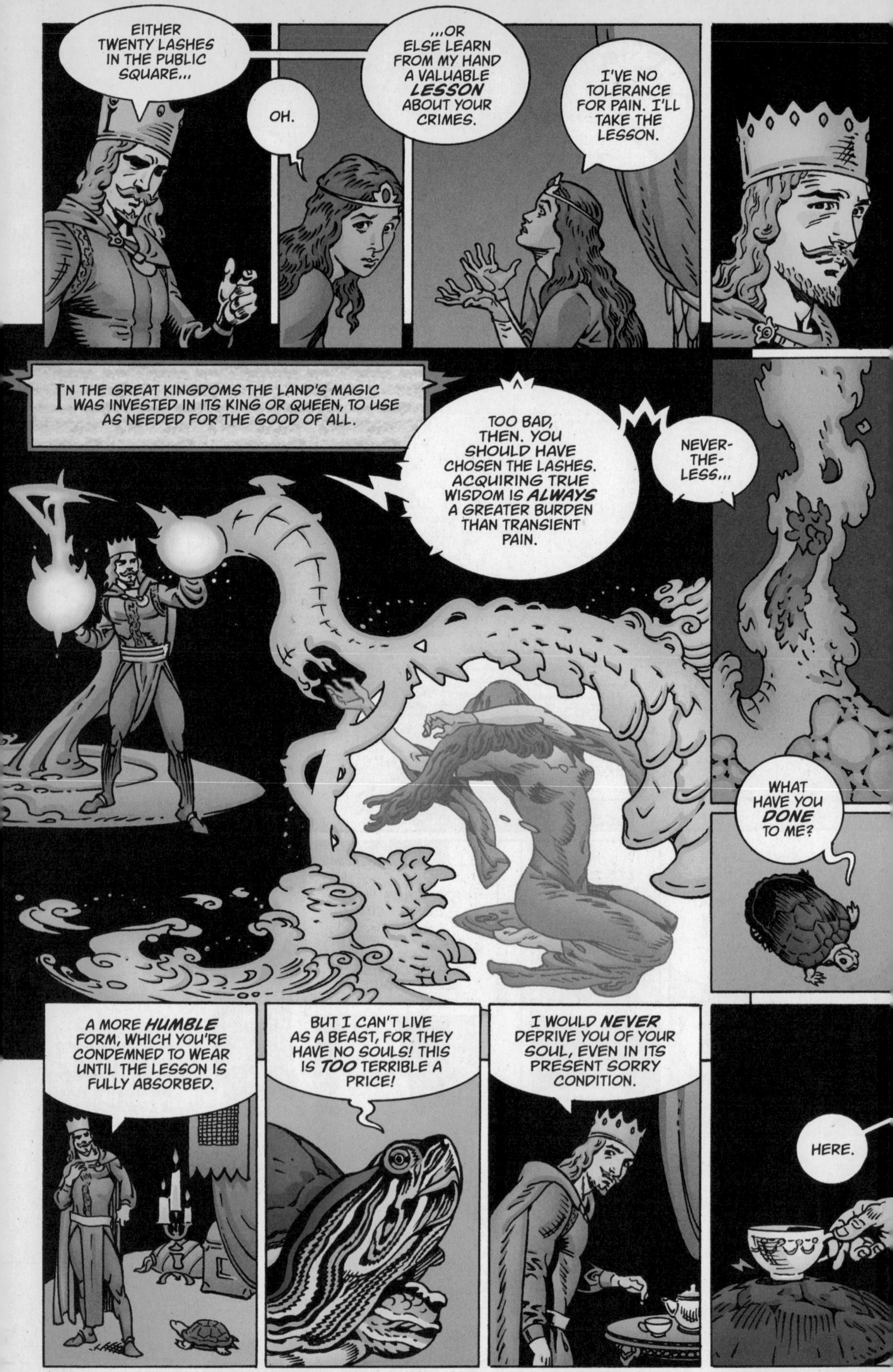
EITHER TWENTY LASHES IN THE PUBLIC SQUARE...
OH.
...OR ELSE LEARN FROM MY HAND A VALUABLE LESSON ABOUT YOUR CRIMES.
I'VE NO TOLERANCE FOR PAIN. I'LL TAKE THE LESSON.
IN THE GREAT KINGDOMS THE LAND'S MAGIC WAS INVESTED IN ITS KING OR QUEEN, TO USE AS NEEDED FOR THE GOOD OF ALL.
TOO BAD, THEN. YOU SHOULD HAVE CHOSEN THE LASHES. ACQUIRING TRUE WISDOM IS ALWAYS A GREATER BURDEN THAN TRANSIENT PAIN.
NEVER-THE-LESS...
WHAT HAVE YOU DONE TO ME?
A MORE HUMBLE FORM, WHICH YOU'RE CONDEMNED TO WEAR UNTIL THE LESSON IS FULLY ABSORBED.
BUT I CAN'T LIVE AS A BEAST, FOR THEY HAVE NO SOULS! THIS IS TOO TERRIBLE A PRICE!
I WOULD NEVER DEPRIVE YOU OF YOUR SOUL, EVEN IN ITS PRESENT SORRY CONDITION.
HERE.

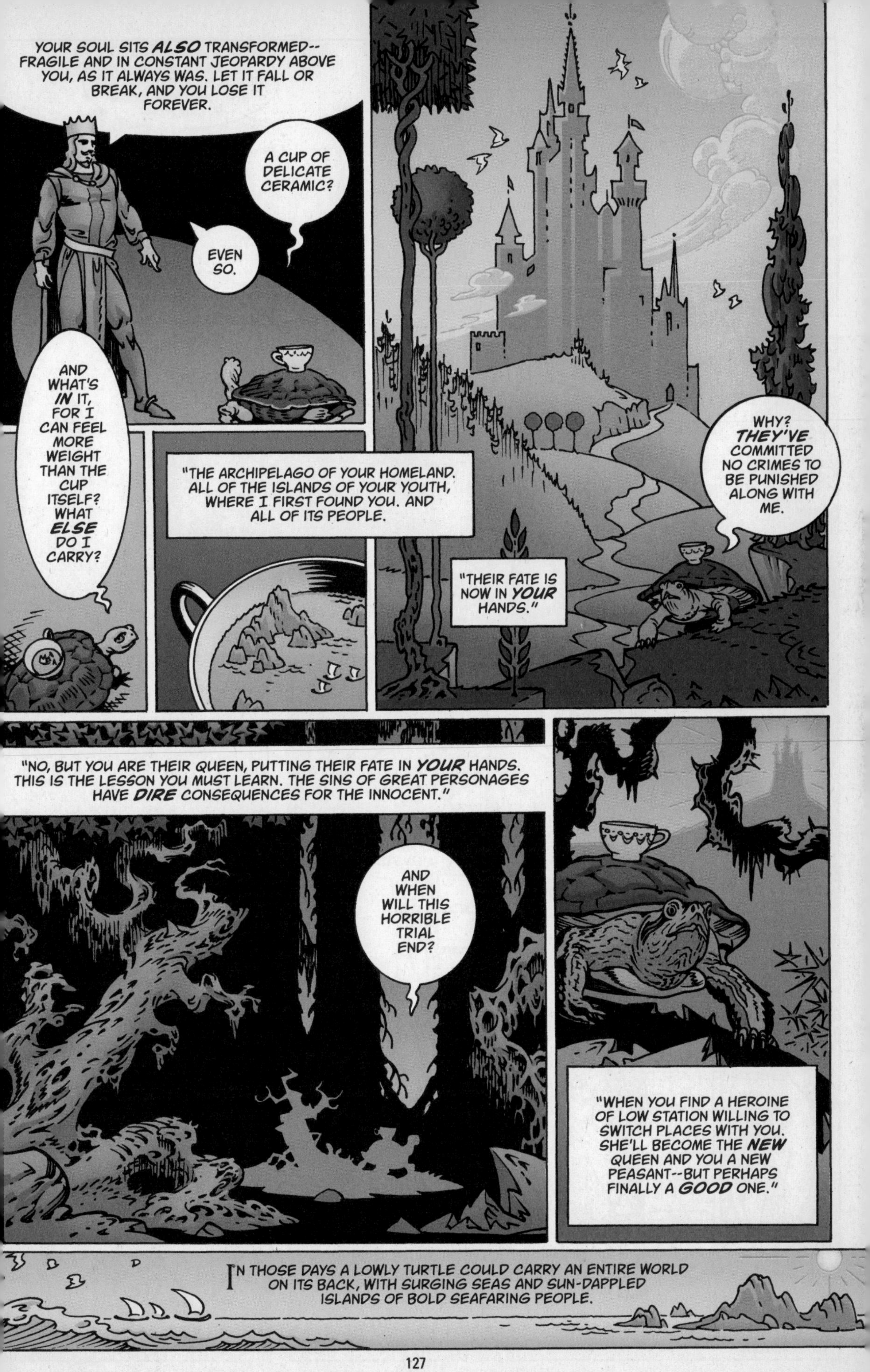
YOUR SOUL SITS ALSO TRANSFORMED-- FRAGILE AND IN CONSTANT JEOPARDY ABOVE YOU, AS IT ALWAYS WAS. LET IT FALL OR BREAK, AND YOU LOSE IT FOREVER.
A CUP OF DELICATE CERAMIC?
EVEN SO.
AND WHAT'S IN IT, FOR I CAN FEEL MORE WEIGHT THAN THE CUP ITSELF? WHAT ELSE DO I CARRY?
"THE ARCHIPELAGO OF YOUR HOMELAND. ALL OF THE ISLANDS OF YOUR YOUTH, WHERE I FIRST FOUND YOU. AND ALL OF ITS PEOPLE.
"THEIR FATE IS NOW IN YOUR HANDS."
WHY? THEY'VE COMMITTED NO CRIMES TO BE PUNISHED ALONG WITH ME.
"NO, BUT YOU ARE THEIR QUEEN, PUTTING THEIR FATE IN YOUR HANDS. THIS IS THE LESSON YOU MUST LEARN. THE SINS OF GREAT PERSONAGES HAVE DIRE CONSEQUENCES FOR THE INNOCENT."
AND WHEN WILL THIS HORRIBLE TRIAL END?
"WHEN YOU FIND A HEROINE OF LOW STATION WILLING TO SWITCH PLACES WITH YOU. SHE'LL BECOME THE NEW QUEEN AND YOU A NEW PEASANT--BUT PERHAPS FINALLY A GOOD ONE."
IN THOSE DAYS A LOWLY TURTLE COULD CARRY AN ENTIRE WORLD ON ITS BACK, WITH SURGING SEAS AND SUN-DAPPLED ISLANDS OF BOLD SEAFARING PEOPLE.

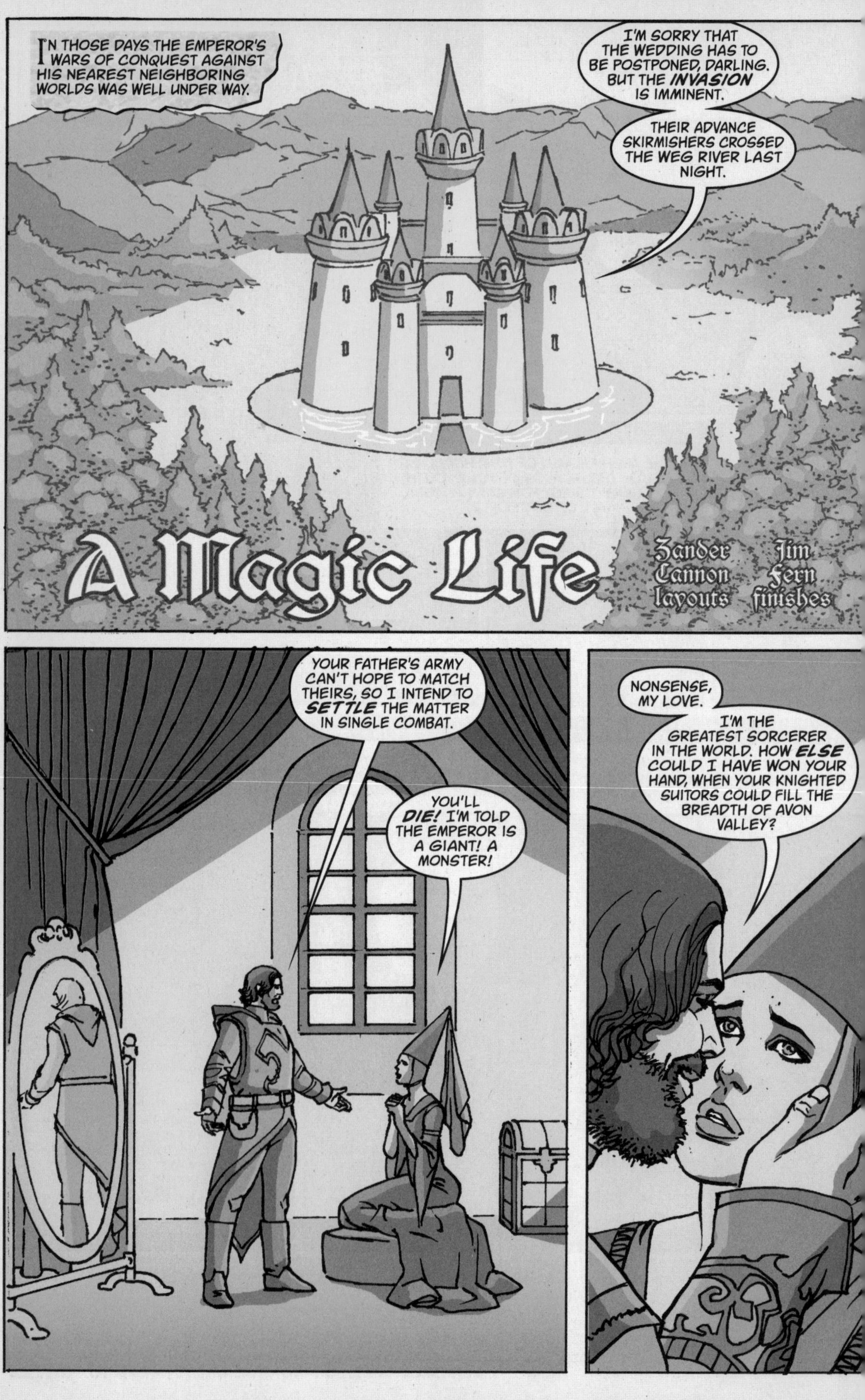
IN THOSE DAYS THE EMPEROR'S WARS OF CONQUEST AGAINST HIS NEAREST NEIGHBORING WORLDS WAS WELL UNDER WAY.
I'M SORRY THAT THE WEDDING HAS TO BE POSTPONED, DARLING. BUT THE INVASION IS IMMINENT.
THEIR ADVANCE SKIRMISHERS CROSSED THE WEG RIVER LAST NIGHT.
A Magic Life
Zander Cannon layouts
Jim Fern finishes
YOUR FATHER'S ARMY CAN'T HOPE TO MATCH THEIRS, SO I INTEND TO SETTLE THE MATTER IN SINGLE COMBAT.
YOU'LL DIE! I'M TOLD THE EMPEROR IS A GIANT! A MONSTER!
NONSENSE, MY LOVE.
I'M THE GREATEST SORCERER IN THE WORLD. HOW ELSE COULD I HAVE WON YOUR HAND, WHEN YOUR KNIGHTED SUITORS COULD FILL THE BREADTH OF AVON VALLEY?

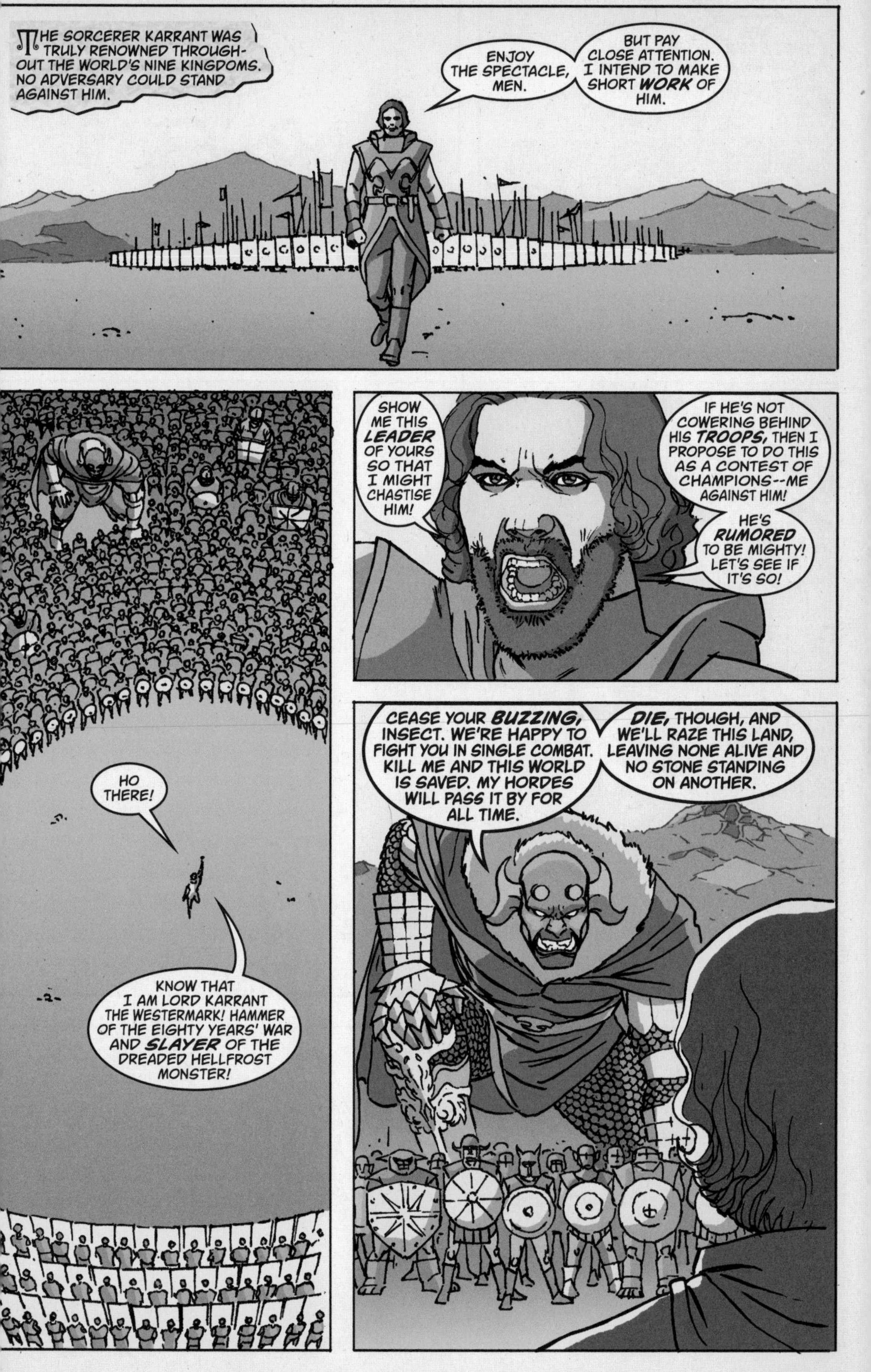
THE SORCERER KARRANT WAS TRULY RENOWNED THROUGH-OUT THE WORLD'S NINE KINGDOMS. NO ADVERSARY COULD STAND AGAINST HIM.
ENJOY THE SPECTACLE, MEN.
BUT PAY CLOSE ATTENTION. I INTEND TO MAKE SHORT WORK OF HIM.
HO THERE!
KNOW THAT I AM LORD KARRANT THE WESTERMARK! HAMMER OF THE EIGHTY YEARS' WAR AND SLAYER OF THE DREADED HELLFROST MONSTER!
SHOW ME THIS LEADER OF YOURS SO THAT I MIGHT CHASTISE HIM!
IF HE'S NOT COWERING BEHIND HIS TROOPS, THEN I PROPOSE TO DO THIS AS A CONTEST OF CHAMPIONS--ME AGAINST HIM!
HE'S RUMORED TO BE MIGHTY! LET'S SEE IF IT'S SO!
CEASE YOUR BUZZING, INSECT. WE'RE HAPPY TO FIGHT YOU IN SINGLE COMBAT. KILL ME AND THIS WORLD IS SAVED. MY HORDES WILL PASS IT BY FOR ALL TIME.
DIE, THOUGH, AND WE'LL RAZE THIS LAND, LEAVING NONE ALIVE AND NO STONE STANDING ON ANOTHER.

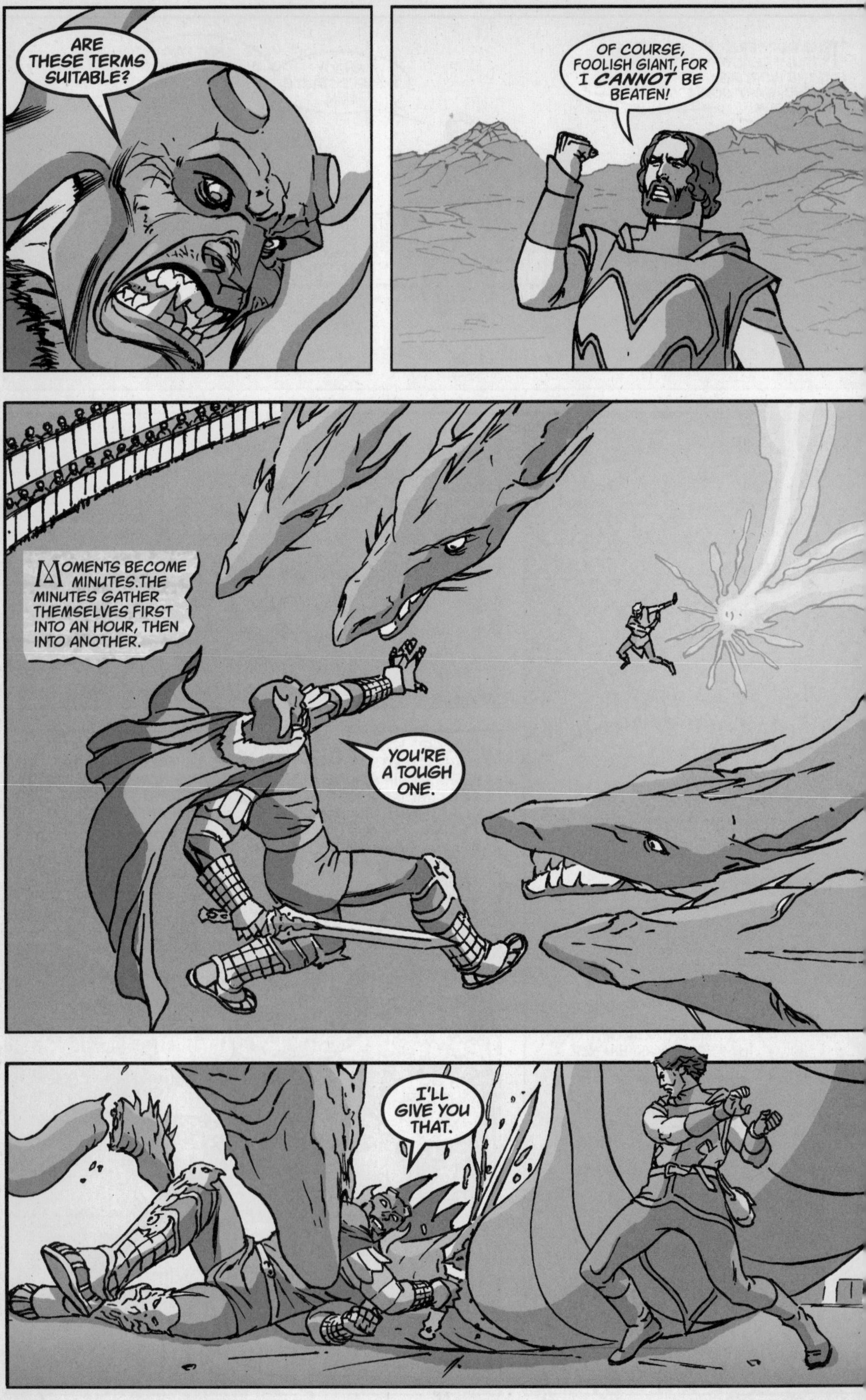
ARE THESE TERMS SUITABLE?
OF COURSE, FOOLISH GIANT, FOR I CANNOT BE BEATEN!
MOMENTS BECOME MINUTES. THE MINUTES GATHER THEMSELVES FIRST INTO AN HOUR, THEN INTO ANOTHER.
YOU'RE A TOUGH ONE.
I'LL GIVE YOU THAT.

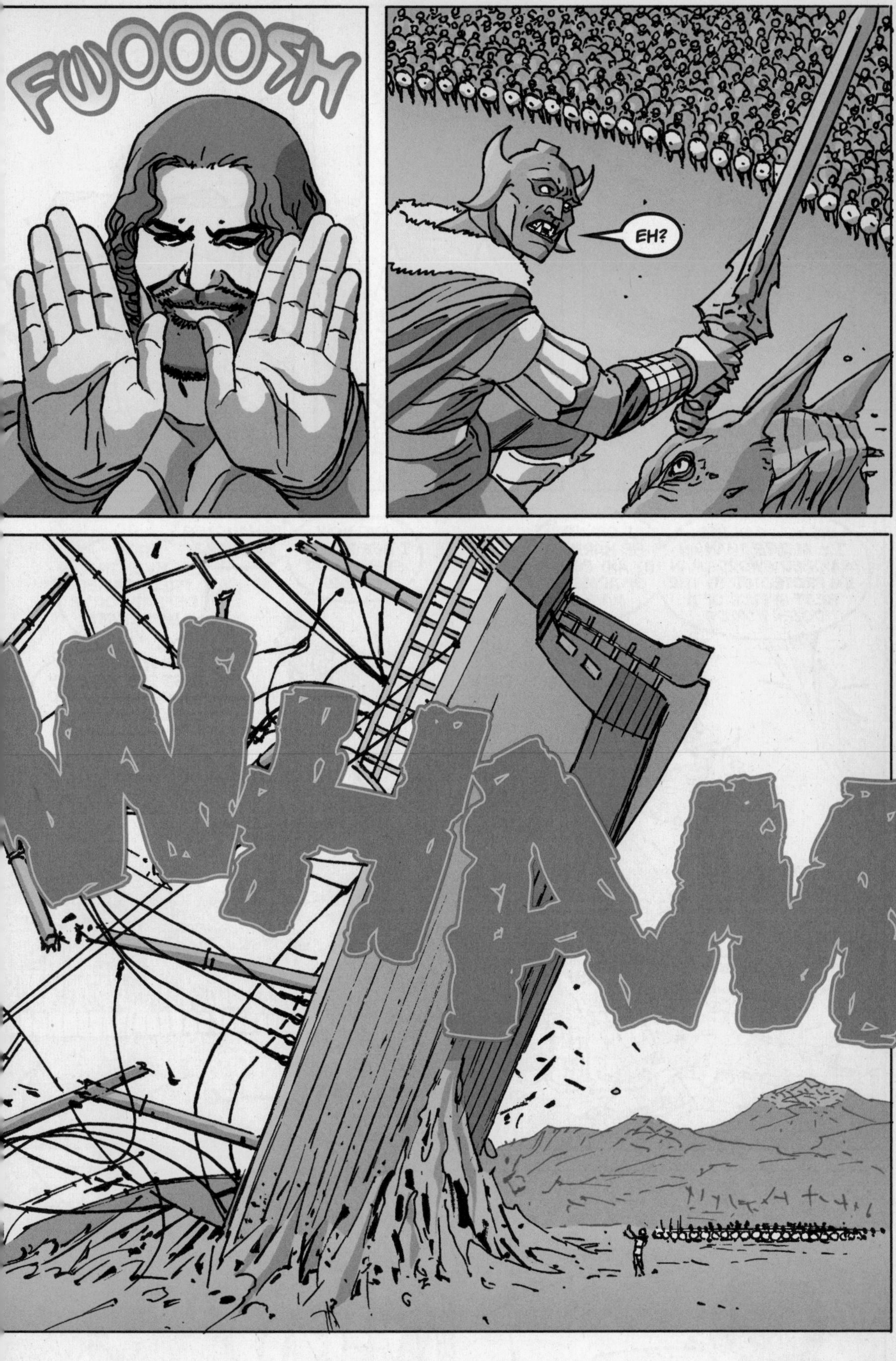
FWOOOSH
EH?
WHAM

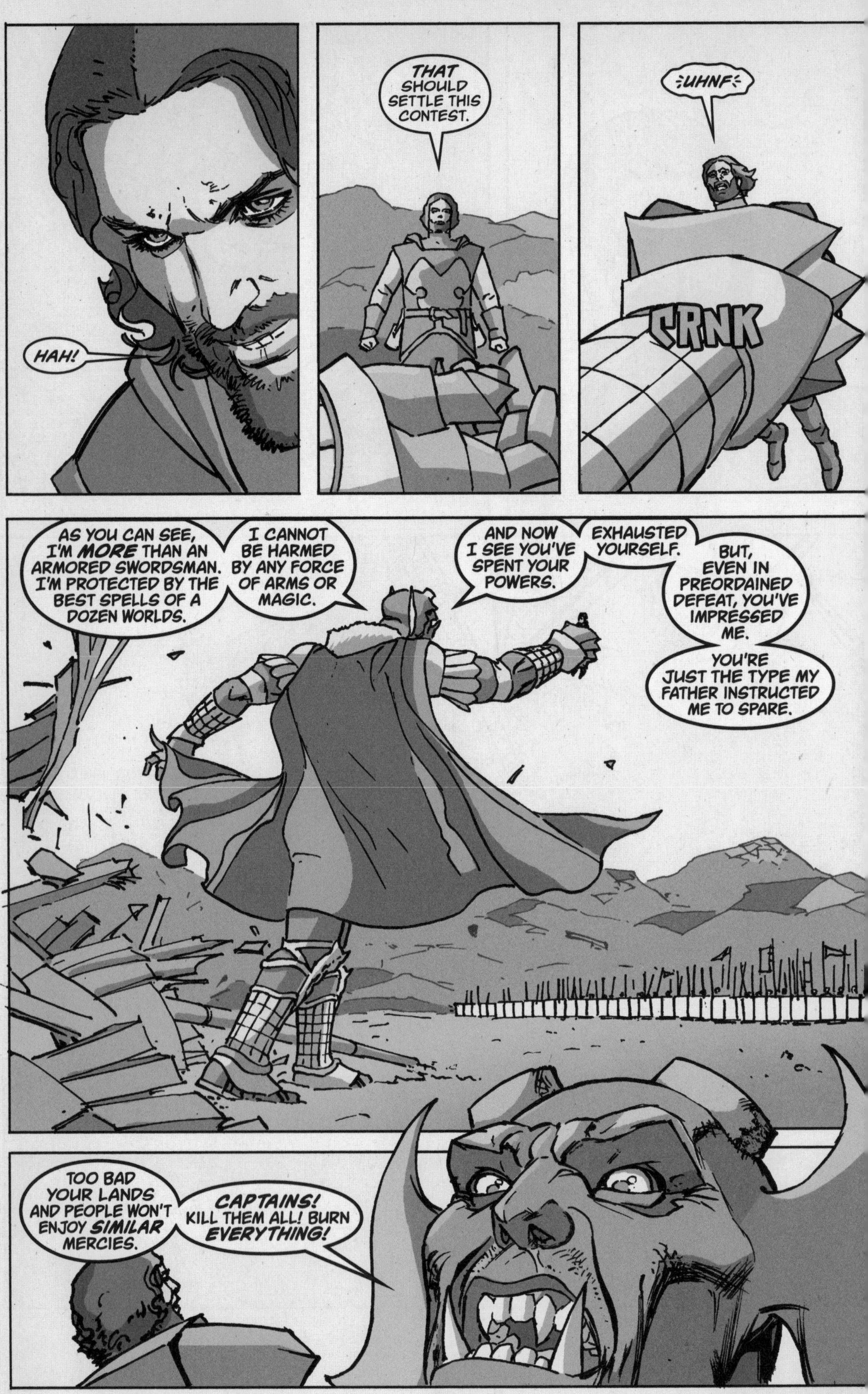
HAH!
THAT SHOULD SETTLE THIS CONTEST.
UHNF
CRNK
AS YOU CAN SEE, I'M MORE THAN AN ARMORED SWORDSMAN. I'M PROTECTED BY THE BEST SPELLS OF A DOZEN WORLDS.
I CANNOT BE HARMED BY ANY FORCE OF ARMS OR MAGIC.
AND NOW I SEE YOU'VE SPENT YOUR POWERS.
EXHAUSTED YOURSELF.
BUT, EVEN IN PREORDAINED DEFEAT, YOU'VE IMPRESSED ME.
YOU'RE JUST THE TYPE MY FATHER INSTRUCTED ME TO SPARE.
TOO BAD YOUR LANDS AND PEOPLE WON'T ENJOY SIMILAR MERCIES.
CAPTAINS! KILL THEM ALL! BURN EVERYTHING!

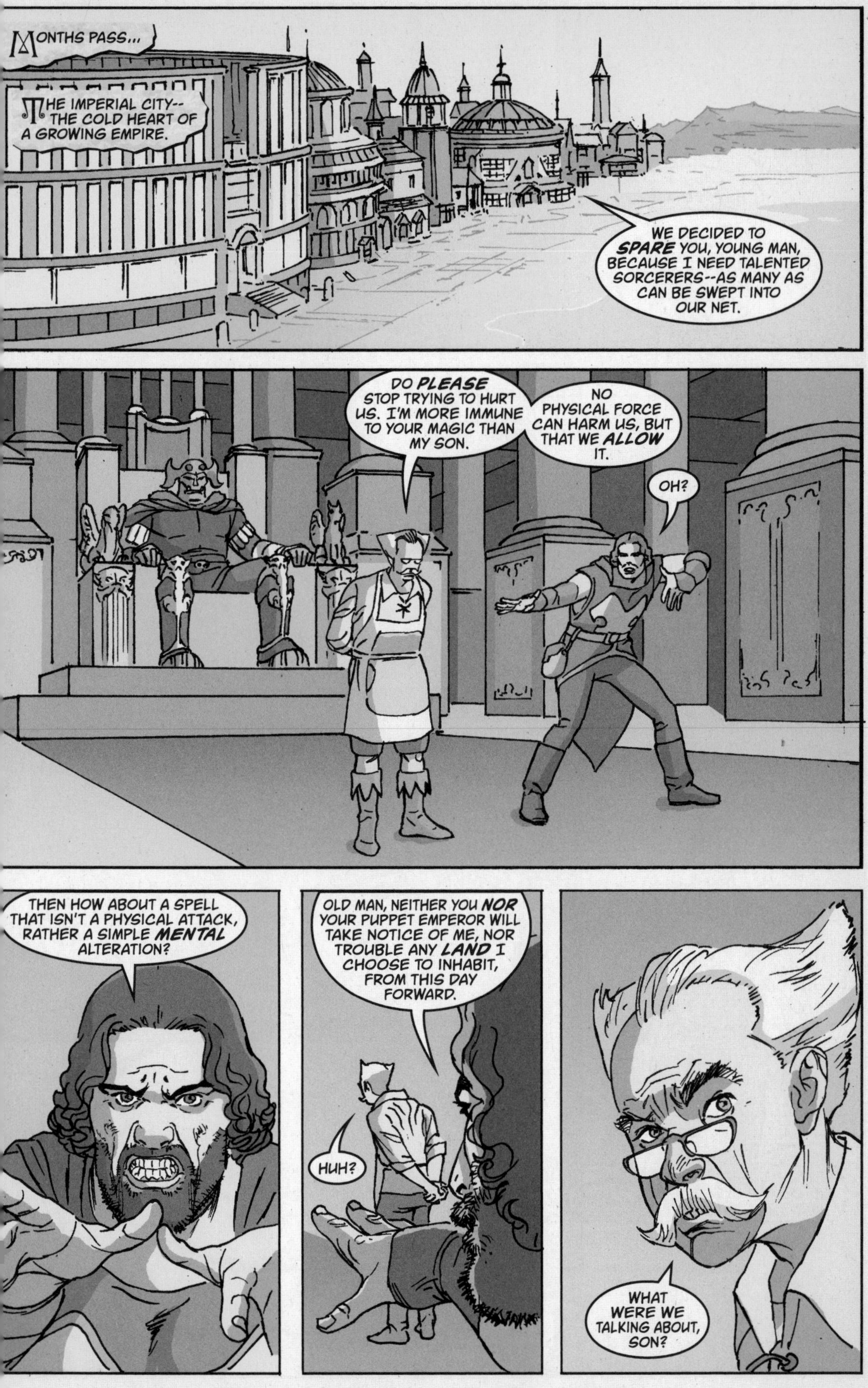
MONTHS PASS...
THE IMPERIAL CITY-- THE COLD HEART OF A GROWING EMPIRE.
WE DECIDED TO SPARE YOU, YOUNG MAN, BECAUSE I NEED TALENTED SORCERERS--AS MANY AS CAN BE SWEPT INTO OUR NET.
DO PLEASE STOP TRYING TO HURT US. I'M MORE IMMUNE TO YOUR MAGIC THAN MY SON.
NO PHYSICAL FORCE CAN HARM US, BUT THAT WE ALLOW IT.
OH?
THEN HOW ABOUT A SPELL THAT ISN'T A PHYSICAL ATTACK, RATHER A SIMPLE MENTAL ALTERATION?
OLD MAN, NEITHER YOU NOR YOUR PUPPET EMPEROR WILL TAKE NOTICE OF ME, NOR TROUBLE ANY LAND I CHOOSE TO INHABIT, FROM THIS DAY FORWARD.
HUH?
WHAT WERE WE TALKING ABOUT, SON?

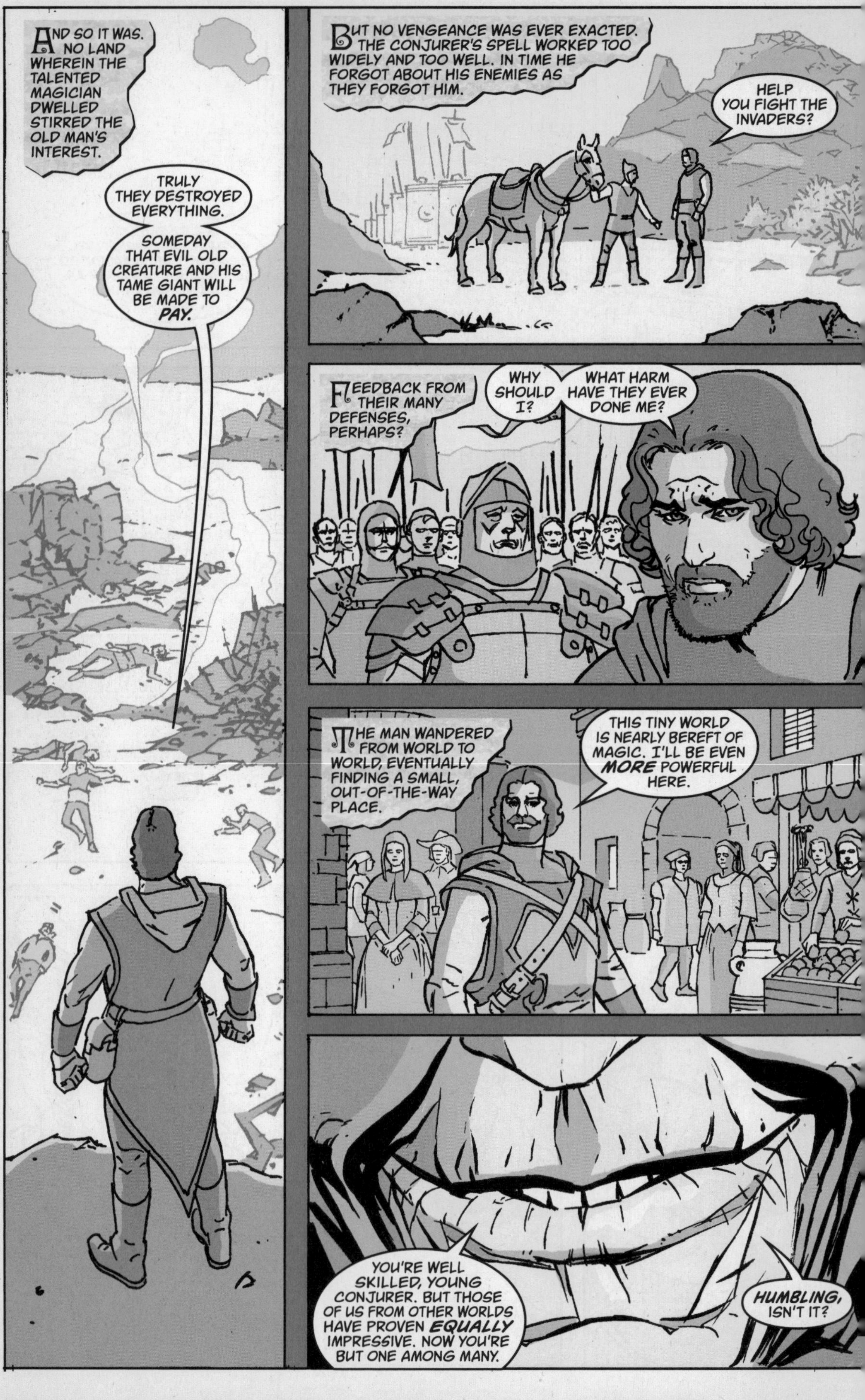

AND SO IT WAS. NO LAND WHEREIN THE TALENTED MAGICIAN DWELLED STIRRED THE OLD MAN'S INTEREST.
TRULY THEY DESTROYED EVERYTHING.
SOMEDAY THAT EVIL OLD CREATURE AND HIS TAME GIANT WILL BE MADE TO *PAY.*
BUT NO VENGEANCE WAS EVER EXACTED. THE CONJURER'S SPELL WORKED TOO WIDELY AND TOO WELL. IN TIME HE FORGOT ABOUT HIS ENEMIES AS THEY FORGOT HIM.
HELP YOU FIGHT THE INVADERS?
FEEDBACK FROM THEIR MANY DEFENSES, PERHAPS?
WHY SHOULD I?
WHAT HARM HAVE THEY EVER DONE ME?
THE MAN WANDERED FROM WORLD TO WORLD, EVENTUALLY FINDING A SMALL, OUT-OF-THE-WAY PLACE.
THIS TINY WORLD IS NEARLY BEREFT OF MAGIC. I'LL BE EVEN *MORE* POWERFUL HERE.
YOU'RE WELL SKILLED, YOUNG CONJURER. BUT THOSE OF US FROM OTHER WORLDS HAVE PROVEN *EQUALLY* IMPRESSIVE. NOW YOU'RE BUT ONE AMONG MANY.
HUMBLING, ISN'T IT?

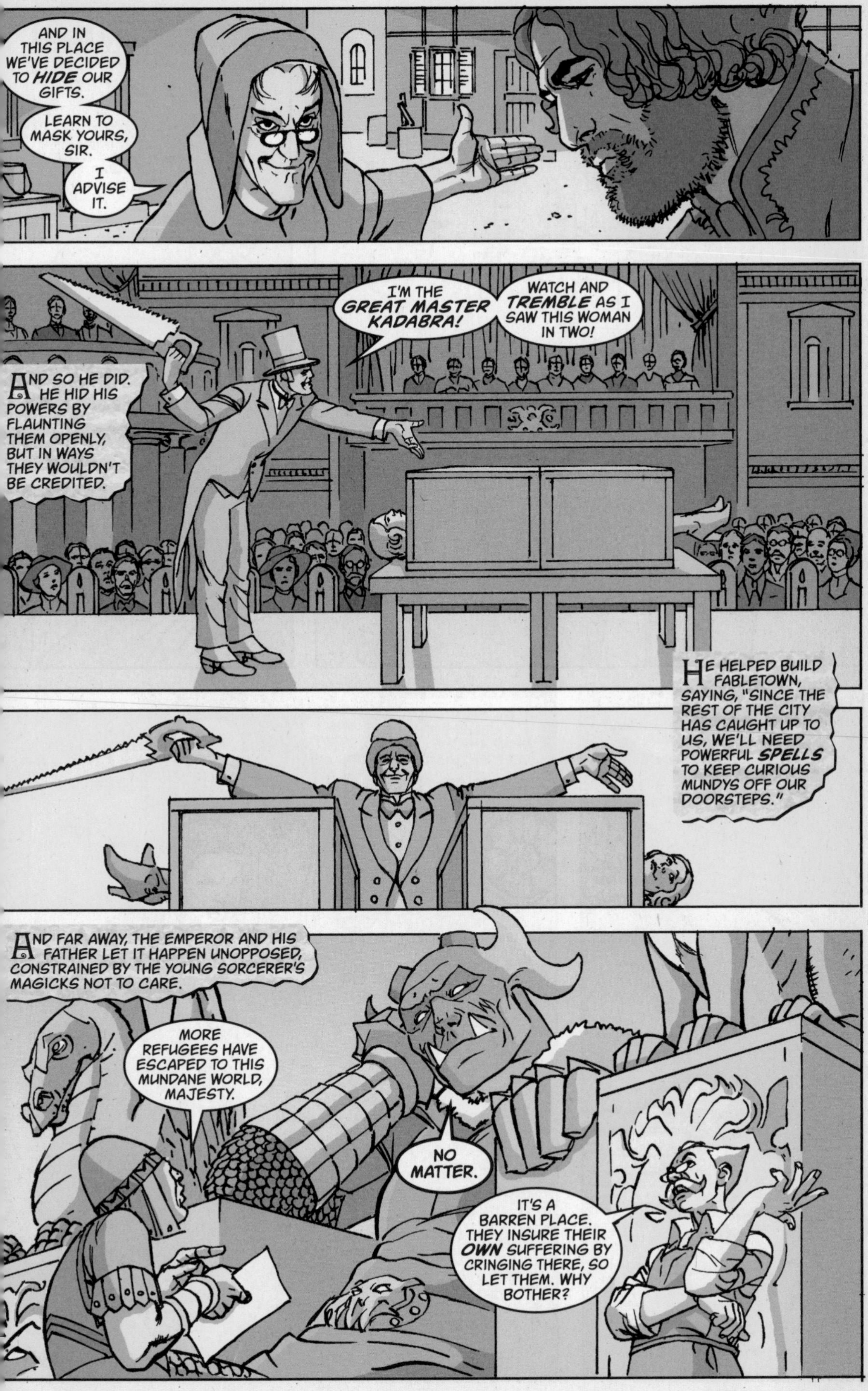
AND IN THIS PLACE WE'VE DECIDED TO HIDE OUR GIFTS.
LEARN TO MASK YOURS, SIR.
I ADVISE IT.
AND SO HE DID. HE HID HIS POWERS BY FLAUNTING THEM OPENLY, BUT IN WAYS THEY WOULDN'T BE CREDITED.
I'M THE GREAT MASTER KADABRA!
WATCH AND TREMBLE AS I SAW THIS WOMAN IN TWO!
HE HELPED BUILD FABLETOWN, SAYING, "SINCE THE REST OF THE CITY HAS CAUGHT UP TO US, WE'LL NEED POWERFUL SPELLS TO KEEP CURIOUS MUNDYS OFF OUR DOORSTEPS."
AND FAR AWAY, THE EMPEROR AND HIS FATHER LET IT HAPPEN UNOPPOSED, CONSTRAINED BY THE YOUNG SORCERER'S MAGICKS NOT TO CARE.
MORE REFUGEES HAVE ESCAPED TO THIS MUNDANE WORLD, MAJESTY.
NO MATTER.
IT'S A BARREN PLACE. THEY INSURE THEIR OWN SUFFERING BY CRINGING THERE, SO LET THEM. WHY BOTHER?

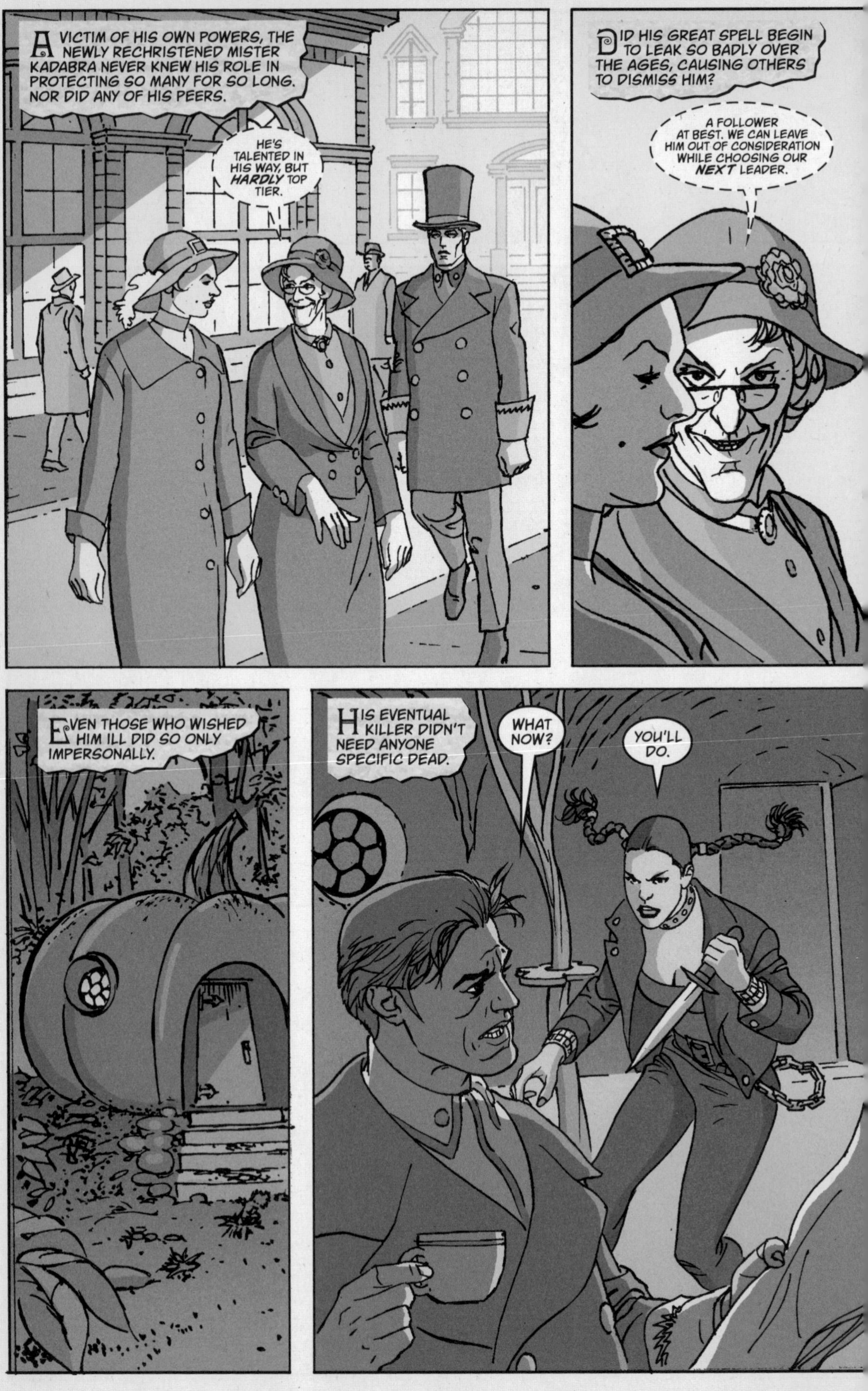
A VICTIM OF HIS OWN POWERS, THE NEWLY RECHRISTENED MISTER KADABRA NEVER KNEW HIS ROLE IN PROTECTING SO MANY FOR SO LONG. NOR DID ANY OF HIS PEERS.
HE'S TALENTED IN HIS WAY, BUT HARDLY TOP TIER.
DID HIS GREAT SPELL BEGIN TO LEAK SO BADLY OVER THE AGES, CAUSING OTHERS TO DISMISS HIM?
A FOLLOWER AT BEST. WE CAN LEAVE HIM OUT OF CONSIDERATION WHILE CHOOSING OUR NEXT LEADER.
EVEN THOSE WHO WISHED HIM ILL DID SO ONLY IMPERSONALLY.
HIS EVENTUAL KILLER DIDN'T NEED ANYONE SPECIFIC DEAD.
WHAT NOW?
YOU'LL DO.

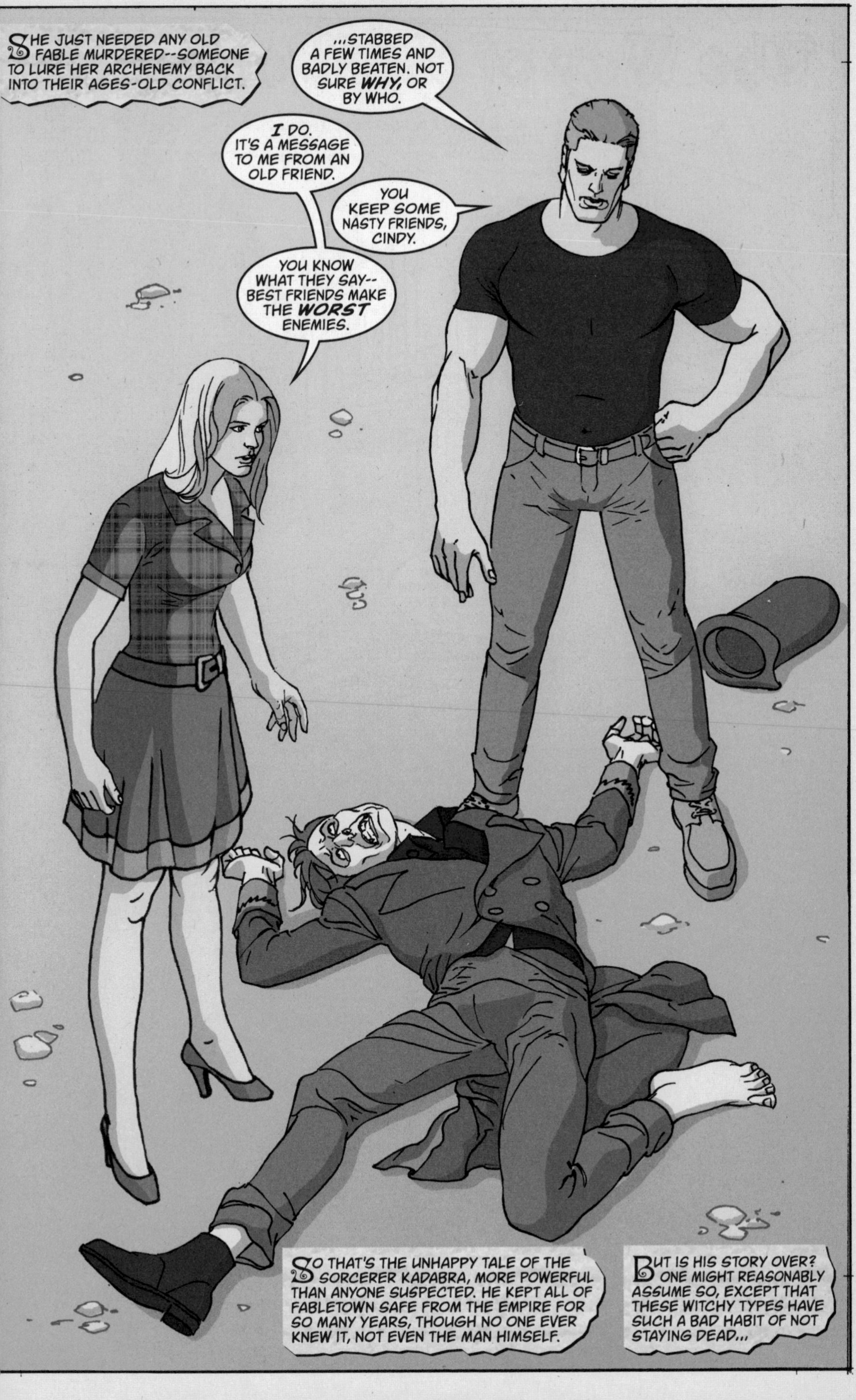
SHE JUST NEEDED ANY OLD FABLE MURDERED--SOMEONE TO LURE HER ARCHENEMY BACK INTO THEIR AGES-OLD CONFLICT.
...STABBED A FEW TIMES AND BADLY BEATEN. NOT SURE WHY, OR BY WHO.
I DO. IT'S A MESSAGE TO ME FROM AN OLD FRIEND.
YOU KEEP SOME NASTY FRIENDS, CINDY.
YOU KNOW WHAT THEY SAY-- BEST FRIENDS MAKE THE WORST ENEMIES.
SO THAT'S THE UNHAPPY TALE OF THE SORCERER KADABRA, MORE POWERFUL THAN ANYONE SUSPECTED. HE KEPT ALL OF FABLETOWN SAFE FROM THE EMPIRE FOR SO MANY YEARS, THOUGH NO ONE EVER KNEW IT, NOT EVEN THE MAN HIMSELF.
BUT IS HIS STORY OVER? ONE MIGHT REASONABLY ASSUME SO, EXCEPT THAT THESE WITCHY TYPES HAVE SUCH A BAD HABIT OF NOT STAYING DEAD...

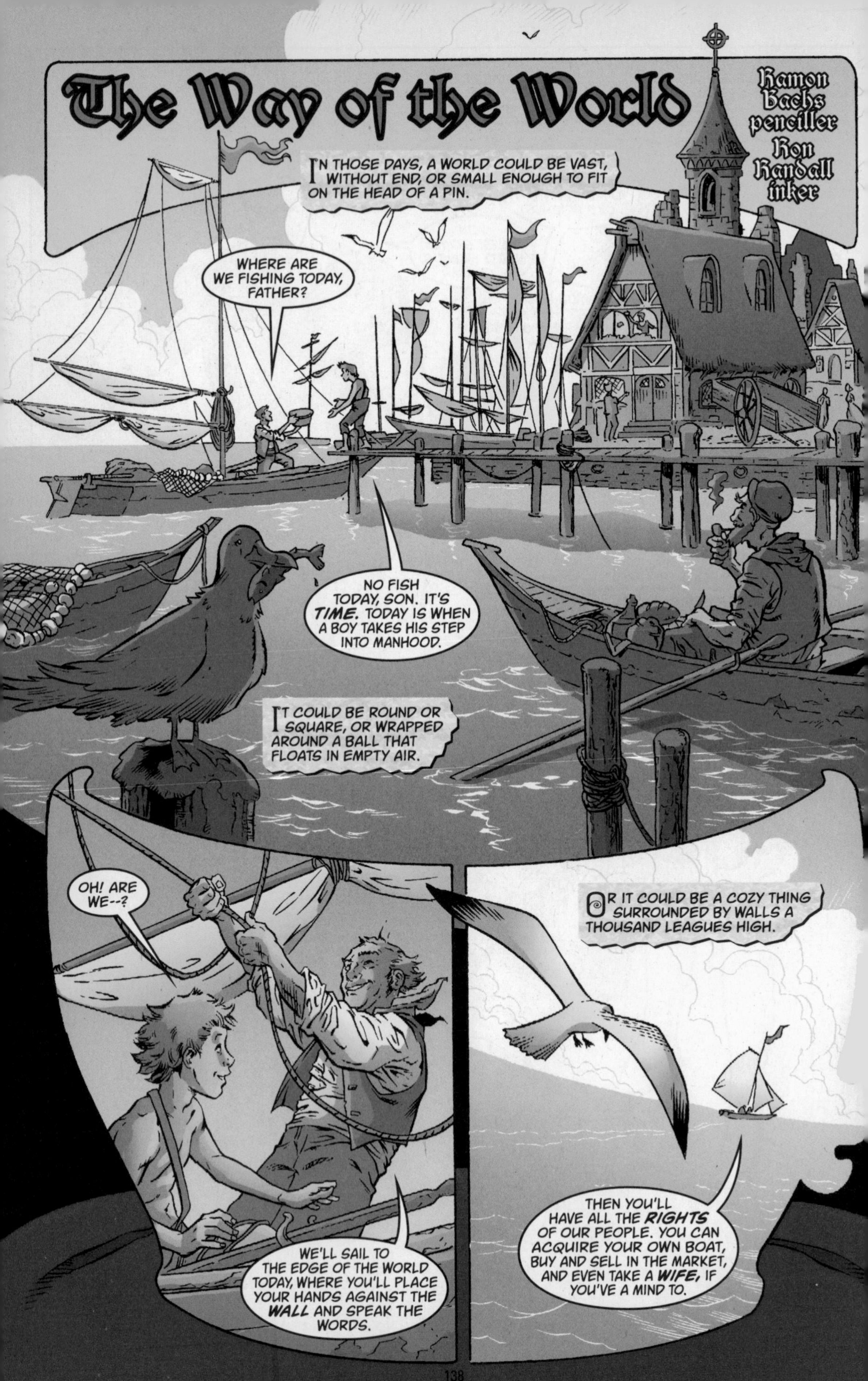

The Way of the World
Ramon Bachs penciller
Ron Randall inker
IN THOSE DAYS, A WORLD COULD BE VAST, WITHOUT END, OR SMALL ENOUGH TO FIT ON THE HEAD OF A PIN.
WHERE ARE WE FISHING TODAY, FATHER?
NO FISH TODAY, SON. IT'S TIME. TODAY IS WHEN A BOY TAKES HIS STEP INTO MANHOOD.
IT COULD BE ROUND OR SQUARE, OR WRAPPED AROUND A BALL THAT FLOATS IN EMPTY AIR.
OH! ARE WE--?
WE'LL SAIL TO THE EDGE OF THE WORLD TODAY, WHERE YOU'LL PLACE YOUR HANDS AGAINST THE WALL AND SPEAK THE WORDS.
OR IT COULD BE A COZY THING SURROUNDED BY WALLS A THOUSAND LEAGUES HIGH.
THEN YOU'LL HAVE ALL THE RIGHTS OF OUR PEOPLE. YOU CAN ACQUIRE YOUR OWN BOAT, BUY AND SELL IN THE MARKET, AND EVEN TAKE A WIFE, IF YOU'VE A MIND TO.

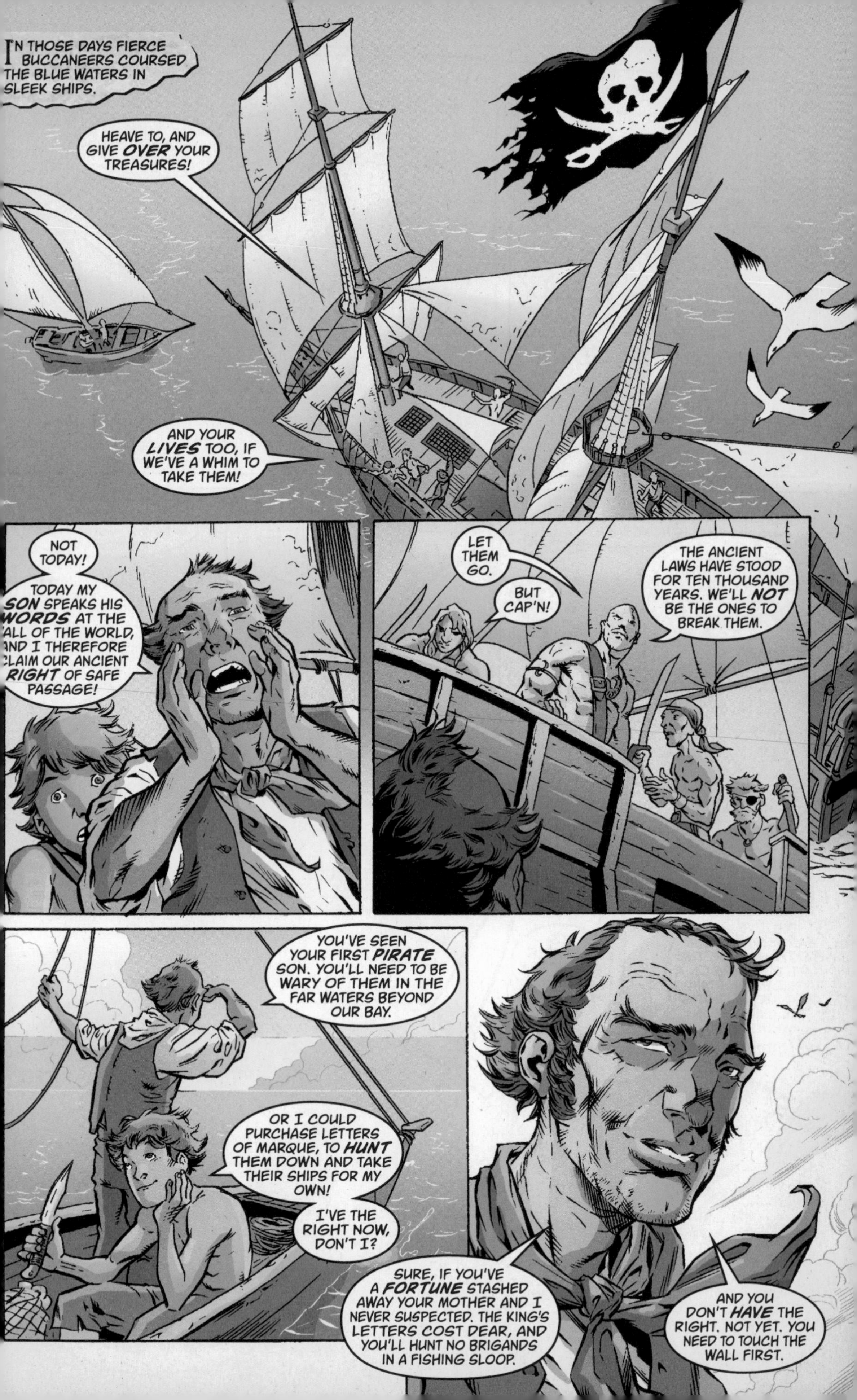
IN THOSE DAYS FIERCE BUCCANEERS COURSED THE BLUE WATERS IN SLEEK SHIPS.
HEAVE TO, AND GIVE OVER YOUR TREASURES!
AND YOUR LIVES TOO, IF WE'VE A WHIM TO TAKE THEM!
NOT TODAY!
TODAY MY SON SPEAKS HIS WORDS AT THE WALL OF THE WORLD, AND I THEREFORE CLAIM OUR ANCIENT RIGHT OF SAFE PASSAGE!
LET THEM GO.
BUT CAP'N!
THE ANCIENT LAWS HAVE STOOD FOR TEN THOUSAND YEARS. WE'LL NOT BE THE ONES TO BREAK THEM.
YOU'VE SEEN YOUR FIRST PIRATE SON. YOU'LL NEED TO BE WARY OF THEM IN THE FAR WATERS BEYOND OUR BAY.
OR I COULD PURCHASE LETTERS OF MARQUE, TO HUNT THEM DOWN AND TAKE THEIR SHIPS FOR MY OWN!
I'VE THE RIGHT NOW, DON'T I?
SURE, IF YOU'VE A FORTUNE STASHED AWAY YOUR MOTHER AND I NEVER SUSPECTED. THE KING'S LETTERS COST DEAR, AND YOU'LL HUNT NO BRIGANDS IN A FISHING SLOOP.
AND YOU DON'T HAVE THE RIGHT. NOT YET. YOU NEED TO TOUCH THE WALL FIRST.

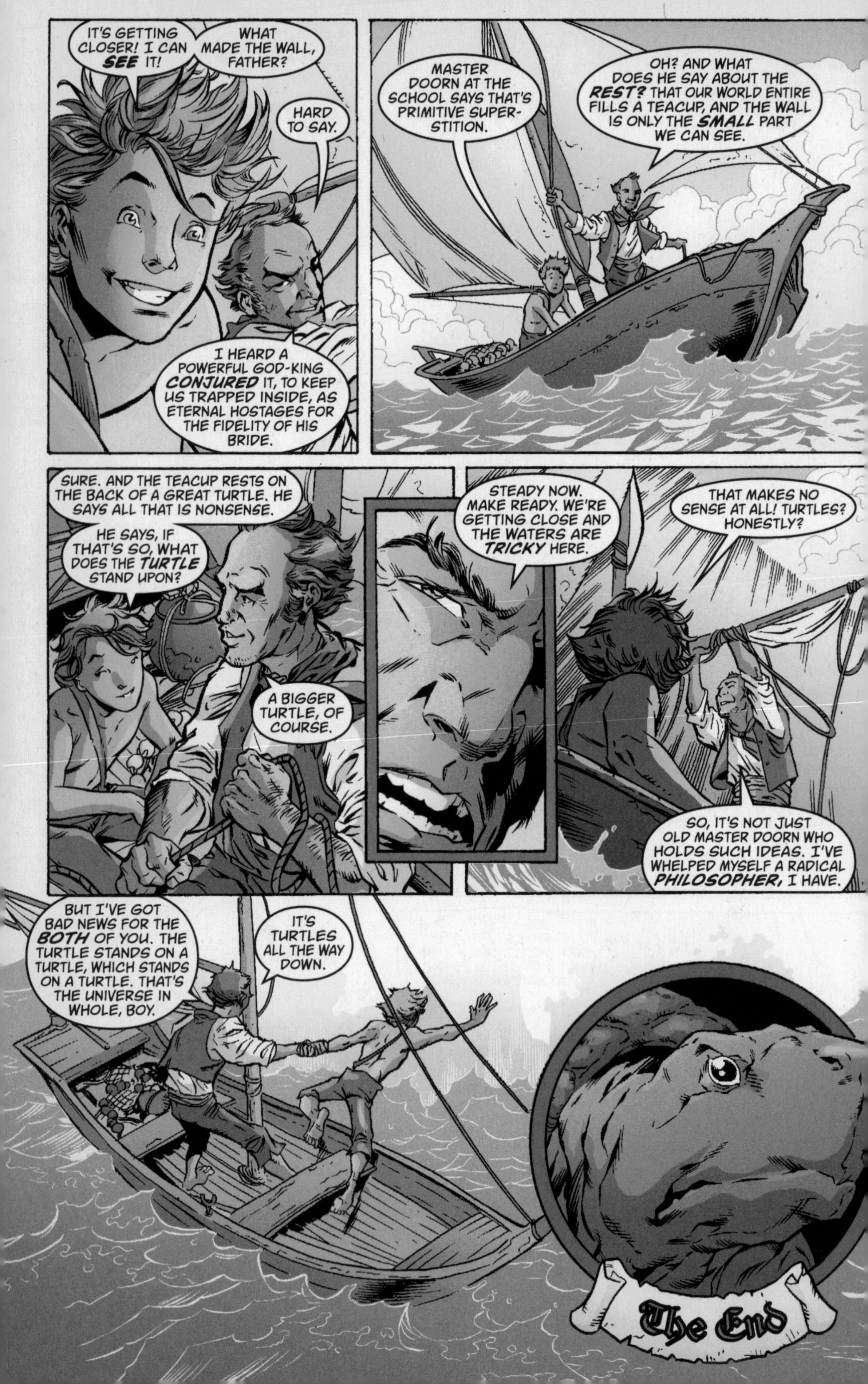
IT'S GETTING CLOSER! I CAN SEE IT!
WHAT MADE THE WALL, FATHER?
HARD TO SAY.
I HEARD A POWERFUL GOD-KING CONJURED IT, TO KEEP US TRAPPED INSIDE, AS ETERNAL HOSTAGES FOR THE FIDELITY OF HIS BRIDE.
MASTER DOORN AT THE SCHOOL SAYS THAT'S PRIMITIVE SUPER-STITION.
OH? AND WHAT DOES HE SAY ABOUT THE REST? THAT OUR WORLD ENTIRE FILLS A TEACUP, AND THE WALL IS ONLY THE SMALL PART WE CAN SEE.
SURE. AND THE TEACUP RESTS ON THE BACK OF A GREAT TURTLE. HE SAYS ALL THAT IS NONSENSE.
HE SAYS, IF THAT'S SO, WHAT DOES THE TURTLE STAND UPON?
A BIGGER TURTLE, OF COURSE.
STEADY NOW. MAKE READY. WE'RE GETTING CLOSE AND THE WATERS ARE TRICKY HERE.
THAT MAKES NO SENSE AT ALL! TURTLES? HONESTLY?
SO, IT'S NOT JUST OLD MASTER DOORN WHO HOLDS SUCH IDEAS. I'VE WHELPED MYSELF A RADICAL PHILOSOPHER, I HAVE.
BUT I'VE GOT BAD NEWS FOR THE BOTH OF YOU. THE TURTLE STANDS ON A TURTLE, WHICH STANDS ON A TURTLE. THAT'S THE UNIVERSE IN WHOLE, BOY.
IT'S TURTLES ALL THE WAY DOWN.
The End

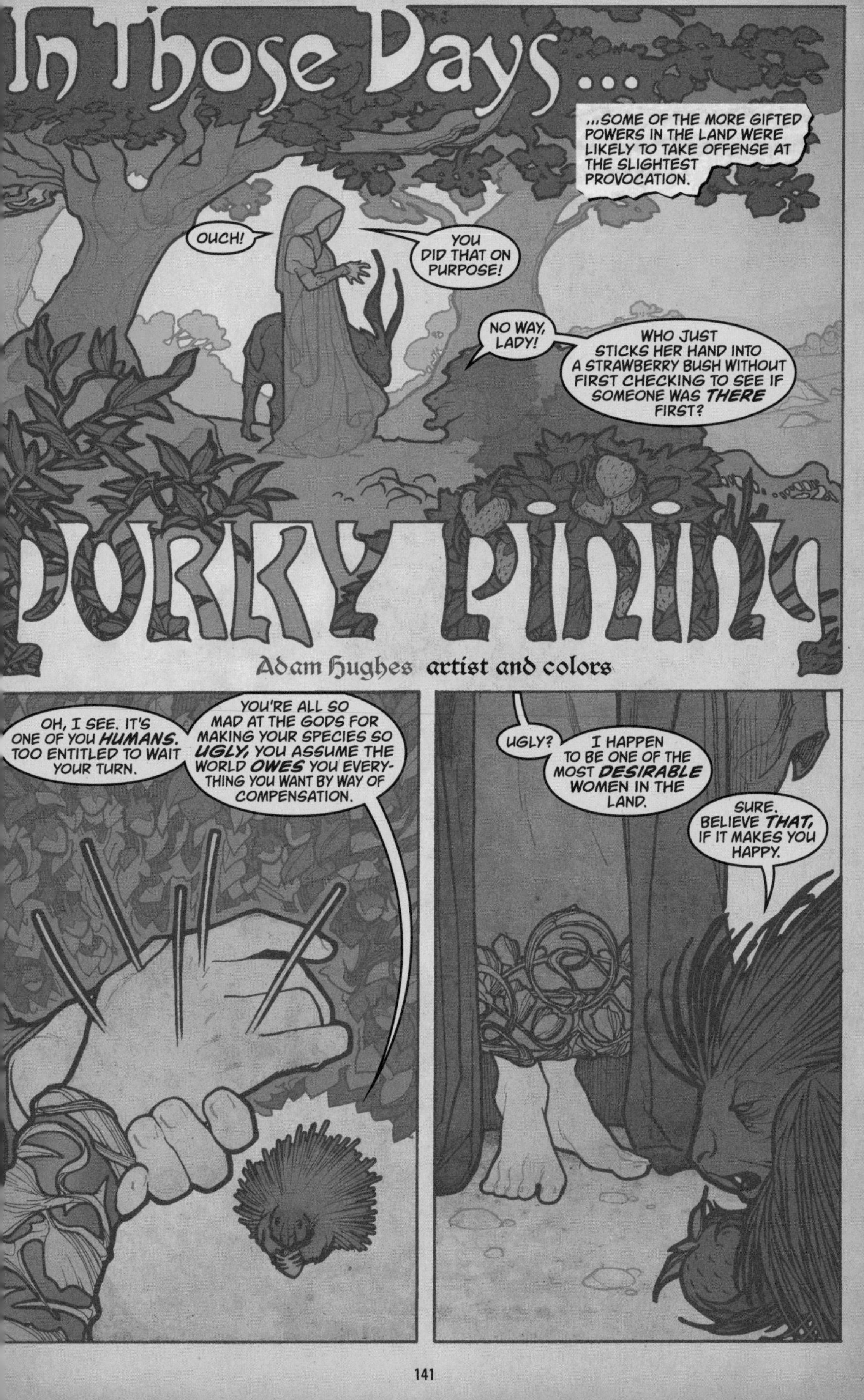

In Those Days...
...SOME OF THE MORE GIFTED POWERS IN THE LAND WERE LIKELY TO TAKE OFFENSE AT THE SLIGHTEST PROVOCATION.
OUCH!
YOU DID THAT ON PURPOSE!
NO WAY, LADY!
WHO JUST STICKS HER HAND INTO A STRAWBERRY BUSH WITHOUT FIRST CHECKING TO SEE IF SOMEONE WAS *THERE* FIRST?
PORKY PINING
Adam Hughes artist and colors
OH, I SEE. IT'S ONE OF YOU *HUMANS*. TOO ENTITLED TO WAIT YOUR TURN.
YOU'RE ALL SO MAD AT THE GODS FOR MAKING YOUR SPECIES SO *UGLY,* YOU ASSUME THE WORLD *OWES* YOU EVERYTHING YOU WANT BY WAY OF COMPENSATION.
UGLY?
I HAPPEN TO BE ONE OF THE MOST *DESIRABLE* WOMEN IN THE LAND.
SURE. BELIEVE *THAT,* IF IT MAKES YOU HAPPY.

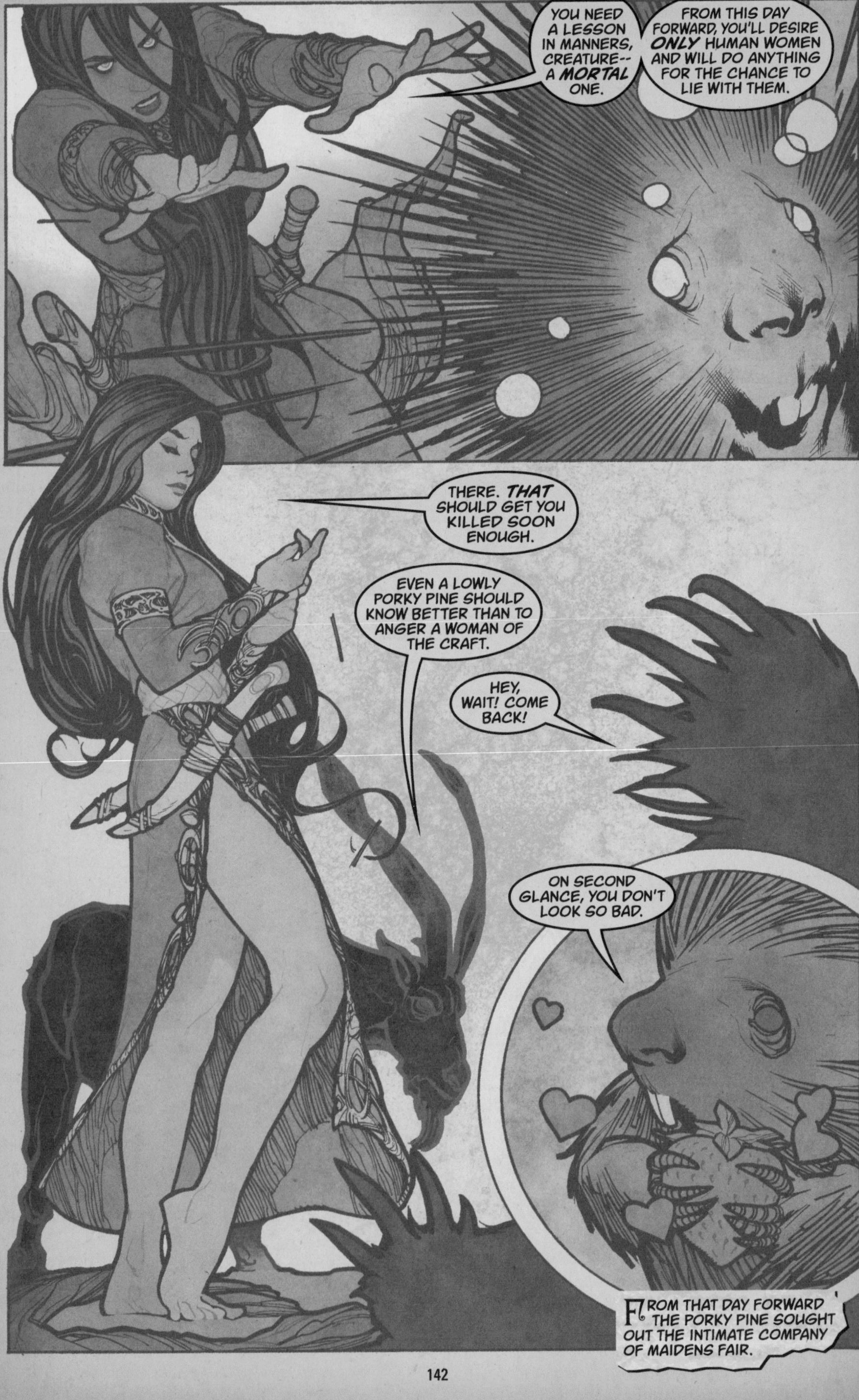

YOU NEED A LESSON IN MANNERS, CREATURE-- A MORTAL ONE.
FROM THIS DAY FORWARD, YOU'LL DESIRE ONLY HUMAN WOMEN AND WILL DO ANYTHING FOR THE CHANCE TO LIE WITH THEM.
THERE. THAT SHOULD GET YOU KILLED SOON ENOUGH.
EVEN A LOWLY PORKY PINE SHOULD KNOW BETTER THAN TO ANGER A WOMAN OF THE CRAFT.
HEY, WAIT! COME BACK!
ON SECOND GLANCE, YOU DON'T LOOK SO BAD.
FROM THAT DAY FORWARD THE PORKY PINE SOUGHT OUT THE INTIMATE COMPANY OF MAIDENS FAIR.

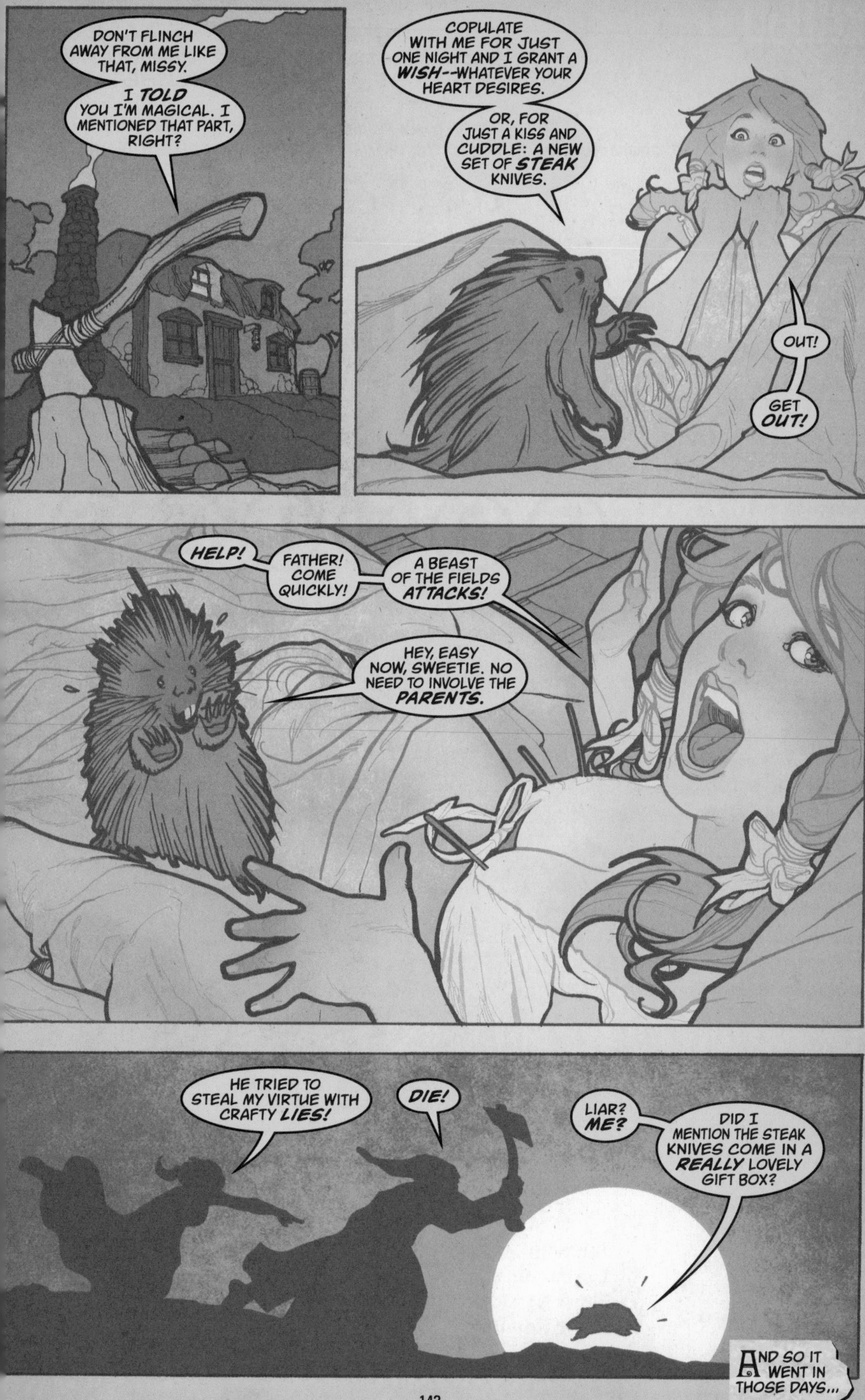
DON'T FLINCH AWAY FROM ME LIKE THAT, MISSY.
I TOLD YOU I'M MAGICAL. I MENTIONED THAT PART, RIGHT?
COPULATE WITH ME FOR JUST ONE NIGHT AND I GRANT A WISH--WHATEVER YOUR HEART DESIRES.
OR, FOR JUST A KISS AND CUDDLE: A NEW SET OF STEAK KNIVES.
OUT!
GET OUT!
HELP!
FATHER! COME QUICKLY!
A BEAST OF THE FIELDS ATTACKS!
HEY, EASY NOW, SWEETIE. NO NEED TO INVOLVE THE PARENTS.
HE TRIED TO STEAL MY VIRTUE WITH CRAFTY LIES!
DIE!
LIAR? ME?
DID I MENTION THE STEAK KNIVES COME IN A REALLY LOVELY GIFT BOX?
AND SO IT WENT IN THOSE DAYS...

"Fables is an excellent series in the tradition of Sandman, one that rewards careful attention and loyalty."
—PUBLISHERS WEEKLY

"[A] wonderfully twisted concept..." "features fairy tale characters banished to the noirish world of present-day New York." —WASHINGTON POST

"Great fun." —BOOKLIST

BILL WILLINGHAM
FABLES VOL. 1: LEGENDS IN EXILE

THE #1 NEW YORK TIMES BEST-SELLING SERIES

FABLES
Legends in Exile

"A top-notch fantasy comic that is on a par with SANDMAN."
— *Variety*

DIRECTOR

BULLFINCH STREET

Bill Willingham
Lan Medina
Steve Leialoha
Craig Hamilton